Law and the Economy in a Young Democracy

Markets and Governments in Economic History

A series edited by Price Fishback

Also in the series:

FROM OLD REGIME TO INDUSTRIAL STATE: A HISTORY OF GERMAN INDUSTRIALIZATION FROM THE EIGHTEENTH CENTURY TO WORLD WAR I
by Richard H. Tilly and Michael Kopsidis

BANKRUPT IN AMERICA: A HISTORY OF DEBTORS, THEIR CREDITORS, AND THE LAWS IN THE TWENTIETH CENTURY
by Mary Eschelbach Hansen and Bradley A. Hansen

HAWAI'I: EIGHT HUNDRED YEARS OF POLITICAL AND ECONOMIC CHANGE
by Sumner La Croix

A LAND OF MILK AND BUTTER: HOW ELITES CREATED THE MODERN DANISH DAIRY INDUSTRY
by Markus Lampe and Paul Sharp

DECONSTRUCTING THE MONOLITH: THE MICROECONOMICS OF THE NATIONAL INDUSTRIAL RECOVERY ACT
by Jason E. Taylor

THE PUBLIC GOOD AND THE BRAZILIAN STATE: MUNICIPAL FINANCE AND PUBLIC SERVICES IN SÃO PAULO, 1822–1930
by Anne G. Hanley

SELLING POWER: ECONOMICS, POLICY, AND ELECTRIC UTILITIES BEFORE 1940
by John L. Neufeld

LAW AND THE ECONOMY IN COLONIAL INDIA
by Tirthankar Roy and Anand V. Swamy

GOLDEN RULES: THE ORIGINS OF CALIFORNIA WATER LAW IN THE GOLD RUSH
by Mark Kanazawa

THE POX OF LIBERTY: HOW THE CONSTITUTION LEFT AMERICANS RICH, FREE, AND PRONE TO INFECTION
by Werner Troesken

WELL WORTH SAVING: HOW THE NEW DEAL SAFEGUARDED HOME OWNERSHIP
by Price Fishback, Jonathan Rose, and Kenneth Snowden

THE CHARLESTON ORPHAN HOUSE: CHILDREN'S LIVES IN THE FIRST PUBLIC ORPHANAGE IN AMERICA
by John Murray

THE INSTITUTIONAL REVOLUTION: MEASUREMENT AND THE ECONOMIC EMERGENCE OF THE MODERN WORLD
by Douglas W. Allen

Law and the Economy in a Young Democracy

India 1947 and Beyond

TIRTHANKAR ROY
AND ANAND V. SWAMY

THE UNIVERSITY OF CHICAGO PRESS   CHICAGO AND LONDON

The University of Chicago Press, Chicago 60637
The University of Chicago Press, Ltd., London

Published 2021
Printed in the United States of America

30 29 28 27 26 25 24 23 22 21   1 2 3 4 5

ISBN-13: 978-0-226-79900-1 (cloth)
ISBN-13: 978-0-226-79914-8 (e-book)
DOI: https://doi.org/10.7208/chicago/9780226799148.001.0001

Library of Congress Cataloging-in-Publication Data

Names: Roy, Tirthankar, author. | Swamy, Anand V., author.
Title: Law and the economy in a young democracy : India 1947 and beyond / Tirthankar Roy and Anand V. Swamy.
Other titles: Markets and governments in economic history.
Description: Chicago : The University of Chicago Press, 2021. | Series: Markets and governments in economic history | Includes bibliographical references and index.
Identifiers: LCCN 2021027304 | ISBN 9780226799001 (cloth) | ISBN 9780226799148 (e-book)
Subjects: LCSH: India—Economic conditions—1947– | India—Politics and government—1947–
Classification: LCC HC435.2.R673 2021 | DDC 330.954—dc23
LC record available at https://lccn.loc.gov/2021027304

♾ This paper meets the requirements of ANSI/NISO Z39.48-1992 (Permanence of Paper).

TO GITA ROY AND VASANTHA VENKASWAMY

Contents

Illustrations

TABLES

FIGURES

CHAPTER ONE

Introduction

Economic and social democracy cannot be in India merely the end products of industrial revolution; they must accompany it, keep pace with it and, what is more important, by releasing the initiative and energies of the people, be the very instruments that bring them about. — India, Planning Commission[1]

The Questions

It is widely agreed that it is difficult to "do business" in India. Buying a piece of land can be time consuming and complicated. A dispute with a buyer or creditor may take a long time to resolve. A permit required from a pollution control board may be slow in coming.[2] These transactions can also potentially involve bribery. How has the situation come to this? In our previous book, *Law and the Economy in Colonial India*, we explored the colonial roots of this problem and told the story up to 1947. This book extends our analysis to roughly 2015. We begin below with some background before asking five specific questions, the answers to which constitute this book.

British colonial rule in India began with a series of alliances and conquests that the East India Company organized between 1757 and 1856. The Mutiny in the following year almost ended the rule. The Crown took over in 1858 and continued to govern India until 1947. The Company had effectively ceased to be a commercial body and became a partner of the parliament in running the empire from around 1800. The Indian empire emerged from a series of events, some of them unplanned, and in its final shape contained a little over half of the land area. Still, it was enormous in both geographical scale and population size. A tiny administration ruled over this vast empire.[3]

A central goal of colonial law, therefore, was to stabilize an insecure regime. Especially in rural India, the British colonial rule in India, or the Raj for short, was reluctant to undermine a very unequal status quo.[4] At the same time, the law had to serve the Raj's goals of facilitating trade and, so long as it did not hurt British interests, modestly facilitate Indian economic development. All this had to be done with limited resources.[5] There was too much legislation in some areas, too little in others, and underinvestment in the legal infrastructure. Courts became slow and intimidating for the ordinary citizen. In some areas, such as eminent domain and control over forested areas, the colonial state assumed extraordinary power.[6]

The institutions of colonialism have continued to matter a great deal in independent India, as have the profound social inequalities of the late colonial period. However, postindependence there was a new trajectory. India became a democracy with universal adult franchise. The government was committed to promoting economic development and had the moral authority to act in ways British India would never have dared—for instance, it attempted to redistribute land to reduce inequality.[7] In contrast with the Raj—which purported to favor free markets, open trade, and small government—the government of independent India was far more willing to intervene in markets and even to own and operate the "means of production." It was also highly skeptical of the potential benefits of international trade and foreign investment.[8] It eventually came to call itself socialist via a constitutional amendment in 1976.

This new trajectory itself, as well as the colonial legacy, later changed in two fundamental ways. First, from about 1980, Indian democracy became more substantive as the less privileged sections of society became more assertive and courts were more willing to challenge the government. Human rights lawyer Upendra Baxi wrote in 1985, "The Supreme Court of India is at long last becoming, after thirty-two years of the Republic, the Supreme Court for Indians."[9] Second, there was a fundamental change in economic policy after 1991. Frustrated by a long period of slow economic development, after 1991, India's policy makers decided to "liberalize," that is, reduce the role of government, allow freer markets and international trade, and welcome foreign investment.[10]

In each phase, existing law has been "sticky"—there is plenty of inertia—and legal change has often been contentious. The efforts to redistribute land from rich to poor in the first three decades after independence faced fierce resistance. These land reforms also added new restrictions on land sale and lease to an already opaque set of land rights. From the 1980s onward, protest movements challenged the state's eminent domain rights, still largely based on a law passed in 1894. This led to conflict, a weakening of the eminent domain power via new legislation in 2013, and criticism of the law on the grounds that it swung the pendulum too far in the other direction.[11] While the economic policy fundamentally changed after 1991, legal changes have lagged. For instance, it has been difficult to put in place a bankruptcy law that allows a firm to exit in an orderly way without too much loss of economic value. Some observers are optimistic that a 2016 legislation may finally address the problem.[12] There is also still ambivalence regarding foreign investment, with foreign control viewed as a threat in some sectors of the economy. Even when laws have been aligned with international norms, the practice can remain at odds with them.[13]

Given this history, we organize the book around five questions. First, how have existing laws emerged? Are their roots in the colonial past, in developmental goals, in response to populist pressures, or in other factors? Second, laws were often framed with egalitarian objectives: did they meet them? Our third question requires some explanation. It seems self-evident that the legal environment must affect economic development. For instance, a farmer who does not have a secure title to his or her land may be unwilling to dig a well on it. But when there are many potential constraints, it is not always clear which one matters. For example, if the groundwater gets exhausted and no canal irrigation is available, there may be few investment opportunities available to the farmer. His insecure property right is not the binding constraint. In this spirit, *Which* laws constrained growth and *when*?[14] The fourth question is perhaps the most relevant to policy. When a law constrains economic development, why isn't it changed? What accounts for inertia? Our final question is, How much did case law and precedence, as opposed to legislation, matter to the evolution of law in postindependence India? Did case law act as a positive agent of change? Was it a constraint on needed reform? Was it relevant at all?

The Answers

Our answers to these questions will, we hope, be more meaningful to readers after we have discussed the relevant history and institutional detail. For now, we offer the following brief observations.

Regarding the origins of law, our answers are sector specific. Broadly speaking, the colonial inheritance has been "thick" and hard to let go in relation to land and natural resources. Developmental goals with an allegedly "socialist" tinge have played a large role in labor law and credit-related legislation. Company law has proved the most malleable in the liberalization era. Policy makers' intuitions align with international practice, and they are explicitly targeting international recognition.[15] We will, of course, have to nuance each of these claims as our discussion becomes more detailed.

On the question of equity, the law has rarely been effective unless backed by social movements of the poor. Where there is potential for mobilization, the passing of law can provide a focal point for social movements.[16] We will discuss several examples of this, for instance, in the context of land redistribution and the rights of forest dwellers.

Has the law been a binding constraint on growth? We sense that until the 1990s, when Indian economic policy more broadly was not conducive to growth, the shortcomings of the law and the legal system were not hugely consequential. After economic policy became more market and private-sector friendly, economic growth has accelerated. More complex contracts need to be written and enforced. Natural resources have to change hands, going from (say) farmer to the industrialist. Now the legal constraint is more likely to bind. There is one partial exception. India *has* made considerable progress in clarifying company law and the rights of investors. This has been particularly relevant for facilitating the inflow of foreign funds into the stock market and also foreign direct investment.

When a legal constraint is binding, why is it difficult to change? This requires a longer discussion even in this introductory chapter. In enacting a body of law on (say) corporate governance, there isn't a large body of potential losers from reform, and it will not cost the government too many votes. Therefore, once policy makers' ideas change, legal change follows relatively easily (which does not mean it is easy). However, if the law pertains to (say) the terms on which an industrialist can acquire farmers' lands, this is now a politically far more potent question. A wealthy corporation will have various resources at its disposal, including the ability to lobby or bribe, but the farmers are more numerous, and each one of them votes. In principle, the government can be a good-faith intermediary and work out satisfactory legislation that balances the interests of the parties. In practice, the weaker party in the transaction rarely trusts the implementing government agency, so it is difficult to design appropriate legislation. As we write, there are numerous and intractable conflicts over, for instance, land, forests, and the regulation of industrial relations.

Electoral politics also creates other perverse incentives. Governments tend to be highly sensitive to short-run growth, which has immediate electoral implications. Economic development in the long run is a lesser priority. Therefore, while rural credit markets might work better if farmers were (usually) held legally liable for their debts, large-scale debt waivers can be electorally beneficial.[17] The short-term thinking of elected governments also probably explains why some of the most important environmental laws in India have not come from the legislatures but from the courts. Supreme Court judges are not up for election and can afford to think about notions like sustainable development or intergenerational equity. These are unaffordable luxuries for the politician seeking votes next year.

The short time horizon of elected governments may also explain the extraordinary persistence of a problem that has been acknowledged since independence: understaffing and inadequate expenditure on legal infrastructure. A simple measure of the underinvestment is the number of judges as a ratio of the population. This, the top Indian judiciary thinks, should be fifty per million. In fact it is a little over one per million, one of the smallest proportions among common law countries. Measured by the average duration of cases or the number of outstanding cases at any time, the Indian legal system is a monstrously inefficient institution. In June 2018, eight million civil cases were pending in Indian courts. On average, each case had been pending for about five to six years. In about 9% of the total pending, cases were waiting for a conclusion for more than ten years.[18] Between 1968 and 2018, pending civil cases as a proportion of the population increased from 177 to 1,298 per million. There is now a substantial literature using econometric methods that demonstrates the adverse effect of court congestion.[19]

There is a consensus that India needs more investment in its legal infrastructure. However, the benefit of investment in legal infrastructure will probably be seen long after the next election, and even then, voters may not be able to identify the cause. The expansion of the number of courts is not a catchy campaign slogan! It is no surprise that it gets low priority.

We should note, in fairness, that the pressures of democratic politics have also led to legal changes that have *removed* constraints on economic development. For instance, until 2006, a forest dweller in possession of a small patch of land most probably did not have title to it. The Forest Rights Act of 2006, pushed by protest movements and NGOs, gave him or her title and the motivation to increase productivity.[20]

To understand why growth-constraining law remains law in place, it is important to recognize that even after 1991, there are three dimensions in which even India's policy-making elites remain skeptical of markets. The first has to do with the fear that if the poor are permitted to sell or lease their assets, they will be cheated. This anxiety goes back to the late nineteenth century when laws were passed preventing tribals from transferring their land to nontribals.[21] Laws like this have not merely been retained, they have been expanded in independent India. The Forest Rights Act of 2006 acknowledged the property rights of a small owner but forbade him or her to sell the right. A historic 2014 legislation that recognizes the rights of an urban street vendor to operate in a particular location also prohibits him or her to sell that right. Economic theory tells us that restrictions like this lead to misallocation of resources. However, the intuition that the poor will be exploited if the assets become transferable runs deep. The corruption and delay in India's legal system make this intuition plausible.

A second and related reason why Indians tolerate market restrictions is that income growth is not the only goal, and income stability matters a great deal. As we will see, India has in place laws that make it hard for firms above a certain size to retrench workers, potentially discouraging hiring. Despite decades of consensus among policy makers on the need for reform, it has not occurred. One of the reasons for this is that in India's "dualistic" economy, a factory worker's earnings are much larger than his or her alternative in the informal sector. A worker who is fired will experience a dramatic fall in living standards. This is distress that even tough-minded policy makers are reluctant to impose, and at least to date, reform of labor law has been half-hearted (but see the postscript to chap. 6).[22]

Finally, there is a fear of foreign ownership, especially in areas like the media and intellectual property. This is partly the legacy of antipathy toward colonial rule, but it also follows from the sense that powerful international players don't always play fair. The Bhopal gas disaster of 1984, which killed over fifteen hundred people and harmed many more, is Exhibit A for this argument. There are also some notorious instances where multinational corporations have tried to patent medicines or rice varieties indigenous to India.[23] In the media industry, incumbents gain from politicians' anxiety over foreign ownership of news production. Therefore, even as Indian law becomes more open to the global players, in practice they can face obstacles.

What role, if any, did case law play in the dynamics outlined? Did it play an independent role in shaping laws? Was that role positive or constructive? We do refer to a few specific cases as "landmark" or "historic," but only a few of them. It is safe to say that overall, the judges followed the political trend that legislation ruled, and the courts played a broadly passive role. But there are important exceptions to this rule. One exception is the Supreme Court in the last thirty-odd years when, in cases concerning fundamental rights, constitutional law, and public interest, the decisions did set precedence. In specific types of disputes, again, case law did matter. Three come to mind. First, in the case of land law, courts often sided with the landowners. Second, on environmental law, the state abdicated its responsibility, and the Supreme Court stepped in. A third and quite recent example is street vendors' rights, where legislation was passed in 2014, but the story really began with case law from the late 1980s. While the Supreme Court set precedents, at the same time, it empowered social movements for rights, justice, and equality. These movements traditionally had two weapons: mass protests and electoral campaigns. The Supreme Court gave them a third one: public interest litigation. Even when the court ruled against the activists (e.g., in a movement against a river valley project on the river Narmada and its tributaries in the 1980s), it still gave both parties a platform to conduct disputes.

These are the central arguments of this book. We will now flesh them out as we describe the remaining chapters.

The Chapters

As we have mentioned above, rural land was distributed very unequally in colonial India. This was not a concern for the Raj—indeed, they regarded a category of landlords known as zamindars as their allies. For precisely this reason, the Indian nationalist movement, which had fought British rule, was not sympathetic to the zamindars. After independence, one of the first orders of business for the new government was to take on the zamindars, rentier-landlords who owned enormous tracts of land in some parts of the country. The ambition was to transfer ownership to the tiller of the land. But this had to be done within the framework of the Indian Constitution, adopted in 1950, which had built in two contradictory features. On the one hand, in the section on fundamental rights, which were justiciable, the Constitution recognized the right to property and compensation if the state seized it. On the other hand, the section on directive principles, the Constitution's moral vision, hoped for a more egalitarian India. Something had to give, and after bitter battles on the ground and in courts and legislatures, zamindars were dispossessed of their land.[24] Eventually, the right to property was removed from the list of fundamental rights in 1978. Chapter 2 tells the story of zamindari abolition as well as of various other efforts to reduce inequality via ceilings on land ownership and protection of tenants. These efforts did dent extreme inequality but were, on the whole, only modestly successful in promoting equity. For instance, landlords who were able to anticipate legislation that gave their tenants legal rights often preemptively evicted them.[25] Tenancy also went underground.[26] Efforts toward land redistribution and tenant protection made rights even more complex and opaque than before. In a rapidly growing economy, often land has to change hands, and this is difficult if ownership and tenancy rights cannot be identified. Insecure tenancy rights also discourage effective land use. Clarification of land rights remains one of India's most challenging problems.[27]

The rural poor needed more than land. They also needed credit and insurance. The British Raj had viewed the peasant as vulnerable to exploitation by the moneylender and had, in the interest of preserving the status quo, imposed interest-rate ceilings and other contractual restrictions. By the late colonial period, Indians had acquired a measure of self-governance, and provincial governments doubled down on such laws. As we discuss in chapter 3, the government in independent India picked up where they left off and drove the moneylender out of business or, more likely, underground. But the influence of the moneylender was the symptom, not the problem, which was low and precarious agricultural productivity. The government tried credit cooperatives, then subsidized bank lending, then microfinance, and now various digital initiatives to provide access to credit. But none of these policies or legal suppression has undercut the moneylender because the moneylender provides more than credit. The lender also, de facto, provides insurance, which the state has struggled to do. Chapter 3 is titled "Overreliance on Law" because the

Indian State has taken unnecessary and even harmful legal steps against moneylenders when the core problems are in the low and variable profitability of agriculture. When it comes to lending by formal institutions (banks and credit cooperatives), repeated loan waivers, for electoral advantage, have created what some have called a culture of default.[28]

Our discussion thus far has positioned the state as a benefactor of the poor. In contrast, chapter 4 considers the state as potentially oppressive and needing to be constrained. The Government of India freely used the strong eminent domain powers it had inherited from the British Raj to acquire privately owned land for infrastructure projects such as large dams. As economic growth accelerated after 1991, the private sector also increasingly sought the assistance of the government for land acquisition, and the government often obliged. The amount of compensation provided was often low, and eminent domain law did not provide for rehabilitation. Starting in the 1980s and supported by middle-class activists and NGOs, peasants and tribals who were losing their land protested vigorously. The conflict intensified in the early 2000s, when violence erupted in West Bengal and industrial projects were stopped and relocated. Eminent domain law emerged as an electoral issue, and in 2013 a new law was passed seeking to empower the landowner vis-à-vis the state and the industrialist.[29] Particularly because of a clause requiring that 70% of the land needed for a project be acquired via private negotiation before the government invokes its eminent domain power, industrialists complain that land acquisition has now become very difficult. Another rule requiring that a rural owner be paid up to four times the market price has also been controversial. The central government's efforts to modify this legislation have failed thus far, though some state governments have amended the law. A key problem is that farmers who stand to lose their land do not trust the state to treat them fairly in matters of compensation or rehabilitation. Farmers are numerous, and they vote, so changing the law is a politically sensitive matter.[30]

Chapter 4 also tells a broadly similar story about the industry's use of forested land for mining, timber, or other produce. The British Raj assumed that it owned most forested areas and undercut the rights of local users. The state in independent India embraced this perspective, viewing forests as a national resource rather than one over which local users had rights. Again, this led to protests, and in 2006 new legislation, usually called the Forest Rights Act, empowered local forest users (in principle). This new legislation has been criticized for going too far in the other direction and hurting the needs of industrialization.[31] Changing the law may alienate tribal communities that are heavily dependent on forests and are an important voting bloc. Thus, this chapter highlights the point the Planning Commission made in 1958—unlike the West, "in India political democracy has come first," preceding rapid economic growth and industrialization. There can be no Indian equivalent to Britain's notorious Enclosure Acts.[32]

Industrialization can lead to environmental problems like pollution and deforestation, but it also creates jobs, which voters want. Also, industrialists can have insider access in policy circles. For both these reasons, Indian governments at the center and the states have been passive on issues of environmental degradation. The Supreme Court has stepped in, often in response to public interest litigation filed by activists. It has laid down principles (e.g., polluter pays) and even participated extensively in the implementation of its decisions. This led to the formation of a National Green Tribunal in 2010, which in principle can take speedy decisions informed by technical expertise on environmental questions. Despite this, industrialists complain that the process of obtaining "environmental clearance" and "forest clearance" is slow and provides government officials and politicians the opportunity to demand bribes. For their part, environmentalists complain that law is commonly evaded and environmental degradation continues. Some major Indian cities are the most polluted in the world. Indian law has struggled to balance the needs of growth, sustainability, and environmental justice. This is the subject of chapter 5.

Some of the Indian industrialists' biggest complaints are about labor law, the subject of chapter 6. By far the most contentious issue has been legislation passed in 1976 and strengthened in 1982 requiring firms larger than a certain size to seek the government's permission before retrenching workers. These laws were passed when India's so-called socialism was at its peak under Prime Minister Indira Gandhi. Economists and businessmen have argued for decades that these laws inhibit hiring and prevent firms from reaping economies of scale. But since the colonial period, labor unions have had close relations with political parties, and it is not easy to change these laws. Their influence is being diluted by permitting workers to be hired for fixed-term contracts and other devices that have been called reform by "stealth." Indeed reform by stealth is a fixture of Indian economic policy now as governments seek to promote growth or placate industrial interests even as they position themselves as populist, or at least proworker.[33] In addition to the specific law we have just discussed, Indian enterprises are also subject to a huge number of intrusive inspections and regulations, which raise their costs.

While the majority of policy discussion on labor law has been on the rights of workers in the formally registered private enterprise, most workers—in agriculture, construction, or street vending (say)—have received little protection from the state and the law, and indeed in some instances they have been vulnerable to abuse by government functionaries. This is beginning to change, as these groups have mobilized politically. The government at the center and the states (provinces) has, via a process that some have called "competitive populism," begun to extend them welfare benefits.[34] That said, the expression "legal dualism" still applies to Indian labor law. There is a stark difference between the status of (some) workers in the organized sector and those in the informal sector.[35] India also has a significant number of bonded laborers (in servitude because of debt) despite a 1976 legislation banning it.

We have discussed the needs of private enterprises, especially industrial, and how legislation on the farmer/worker/citizen impinges on them. Chapters 7 and 8 focus on companies and corporate governance. They cover topics ranging from antimonopoly legislation to regulation of stock markets to intellectual property and bankruptcy. As we have mentioned earlier, these are the domains in which the Indian State has had a relatively free hand, at least in comparison to (say) land law, where electoral politics and mass movements have affected legislation. Chapter 7 focuses on changes that we might call endogenous, that is, generated by Indian policy makers. Chapter 8 discusses what we might call exogenous changes, which are driven by the need to conform to international standards in an era of globalization.

During India's developmental-socialist phase (roughly 1950–1985), policy makers appear to have had extraordinary confidence in the government's capacity to manage the economy. One prominent antitrust legislation, the Monopolies and Restrictive Trade Practices Act (MRTP), aimed to restrict and regulate economic concentration, and another, the Sick Industrial Companies Act (SICA), allowed the government to take over "sick" firms and bring them back to life, keeping their workers employed.[36] Unfortunately, the MRTP focused on firm size rather than behavior. From the 1980s onward, the emphasis changed toward regulating firm behavior via court decisions, amendments to the MRTP, and eventually fresh legislation in 2002 and 2013. SICA failed because the task was too challenging—the government could not effectively play supermanager. It also created a moral hazard. The firm's owners could benefit from the firm in its healthy years and leave the government to deal with the sickness. An act repealing SICA was passed in 2003, but it has taken fifteen years to pass a comprehensive Insolvency and Bankruptcy Code (2016). Still, crony capitalism is not easily eliminated. This is especially true because, again in its "socialist" phase, the government had nationalized major commercial banks. Loans could be obtained by the politically connected, who could also get away with default. As we write, the sheer volume of nonperforming assets on the books of Indian banks is a significant drag on growth.

Other areas, like corporate governance and the regulation of stock markets, also needed attention. To ensure that law is enforced, special tribunals have been created so that disputes can sidestep India's creaky judicial system. Thus, we now have another kind of legal dualism—the old, slow, and cumbersome courts for some types of economic activity and relatively speedy tribunals for others.

As India globalized after 1991, it was under pressure to create or adopt global norms for mergers and acquisitions and relating to intellectual property. The latter was included in the World Trade Organization (WTO) agreement in 1995 and is generally known by its acronym, TRIPS (Trade-Related Aspects of Intellectual Property Rights). While India has adapted to international standards and foreign investment has responded, substantive change has lagged behind the legal change. There are persistent (and sometimes convenient) anxieties about foreign ownership of assets viewed as critical to the national interest. As we write, there is controversy about foreign firms like Google or Mastercard having information about Indian citizens on servers located abroad. Mukesh Ambani, the largest shareholder of Reliance Industries Limited, a major Indian conglomerate, recently complained about "data colonization." Ambani argued that "India's data must be controlled and owned by Indian people and not by corporates, especially global corporations." The Reserve Bank has recently passed data localization rules.[37]

Our final thematic chapter (chapter 9) turns to the role of religion in shaping economic life. Many of the laws we have discussed, from land reforms to corporate governance to labor law, usually do not have their origins in religious text or practice. However, from colonial times, religion was central to shaping the law on succession and inheritance of private property. The reference to religion related to the rights of women as opposed to those of the men and the rights of castes. India's two major religions, Hinduism and Islam, both built in a lower status for women, especially in matters of property. There is also sanction for discrimination based on caste in some Hindu texts. The Constitution of India took a very clear position on caste; the main distinction it permitted favored the underprivileged Scheduled Castes and Tribes. Gender was a much more complicated question because there was a tension between respecting religious freedom and guaranteeing equality, both of which the Indian Constitution wanted to do. There was also the legacy, from the colonial period, of allowing a religion-specific "Personal Law," however hard that was to define. Chapter 9 describes the process through which equality has won the day, in court and legislation, more quickly and with less controversy among Hindus than Muslims. Caste and gender inequity today are largely rooted in social norms, not in laws.

Conclusion

We can now restate the argument of this book. Colonial rule left India a highly unequal society with a complicated structure of land rights, a slow and dysfunctional legal system, and a state that was all powerful in some areas. In the first three decades after independence, the law created in the service of "socialism" achieved modest success in restoring equity but also distorted markets and created opportunities for rent-seeking. In this period, there were many other, perhaps more important, policy distortions, such as trade restrictions and extreme overregulation, often called the "license-permit Raj." The weaknesses of the legal framework were probably not the binding constraint on growth. After the 1980s there was a major change in economic policy aimed at a much smaller role for the state. After the economy was liberalized, various policy distortions were eliminated, especially on trade and licensing. Growth has accelerated, and the shortcomings of the legal system have now come to bite. Legal reform and investment in legal infrastructure are necessary, but this has to occur in the context of India's vigorous democracy—the political engagement of citizens, a sometimes-activist Supreme Court, and short-term electoral compulsions. The task is complicated by distrust of government, which limits its capacity to reassure potential losers from reforms that they will be compensated. Moreover, in a country where there are many poor people, there is still a reluctance to expose those who have obtained some security to the vicissitudes of markets. There is also continuing ambivalence toward globalization, especially foreign investment in some areas. All this suggests that at least in the short-term, the Indian economy will have to develop *in spite* of its legal system.

CHAPTER TWO

Land Rights

Equity versus Transferability?

The Committee feels that there cannot be any lasting improvement in agricultural production and efficiency without comprehensive reforms in the country's land system. — Indian National Congress, Agrarian Reforms Committee[1]

The cultivator will have permanent, transferable, and heritable right of cultivation, subject to the following conditions: (1) that he does not sub-let his holding; (2) that he transfers his holding according to well-defined priorities laid down by the appropriate authority. — Indian National Congress, Agrarian Reforms Committee[2]

Introduction

In 1947, when India became independent, ownership of land was highly unequal. This was not only unjust, it was widely believed that this contributed to low agricultural productivity. Many large landowners were absentee and neglected their properties. Landowners could evict tenants at any time or increase their rents arbitrarily. They had neither the means nor the incentive to invest in increasing productivity. Therefore, it was argued, reforms were necessary to ensure the tiller owned the land. In much of this thinking, the ruling Congress party was in sync with many present-day economists. The idea that insecure tenancy can be inefficient and agrarian inequality is harmful has many takers even today. However, in contrast with mainstream economic theory today, the Congress was ambivalent about land transfers: it wanted to ban temporary transfers (land lease) and restrict permanent transfers (sales). In the first few decades after independence, land reforms performed unevenly in terms of reducing inequality, with some important successes and many failures. The skepticism regarding transferability did not matter too much because the economy was growing slowly, and land did not often need to be repurposed. However, as growth has picked up in the last three decades, the inability to easily transfer land has become an important constraint.

Roughly speaking, in Indian land reforms, the wealthiest lost, the poorest gained only a little, and an intermediate class benefited substantially. After land reforms, landed magnates were not nearly as important in India as they have been in parts of Latin America or even in Pakistan.[3] Instead, Indian land reforms strengthened, in terms of numbers as well as political clout, a "middle class" among India's farmers. This middle class has been very active in electoral politics. They are now an important political constituency with a huge influence on economic policy. Land reforms usually failed to significantly improve the fortunes of the poorest sections of Indian agrarian society, the landless, who are often low caste. This has contributed to political tensions, including Maoist movements. Women have benefited only modestly, reinforcing India's long-standing problems with gender equity.

As an economy grows, land has to change hands from traditional farmers to more productive farmers, to industrialists, to real estate developers, or to road construction. If land is transferable, it can also be used as collateral: a person can borrow from a bank, which can seize the land in the event of default. However, for the architects of Indian land reform, transferability was not a priority. For reasons we will explain below, they often viewed land transfer as potentially exploitative rather than productivity enhancing. Indian land-reform legislation often explicitly prevented, or at least discouraged, an owner from mortgaging, selling, or leasing land.

One of the reasons it was difficult to implement land reforms was that land rights had not been adequately recorded in the colonial period.[4] There was little transparency. If there is not a reliable record of ownership, how can land be confiscated from one person and given to another? However, the causation also ran in the other direction—from land reforms to lack of transparency. As we will describe below, potential losers from land reforms took various evasive measures, such as transferring title to a family member and sometimes even a fictitious person, while retaining control of the land. Therefore, the response to land reforms widened the gulf between facts on the ground and the record of rights on paper. In the absence of a clear record of rights, more than one person may claim, opportunistically or otherwise, to own a particular piece of land. A widely quoted study in 2001 claimed that the rights to 90%of India's land parcels are disputed.[5]

This chapter evaluates land law primarily from three perspectives: equity of land ownership, transferability of land, and transparency of land rights. Most of our discussion pertains to rural India, but we also briefly discuss land ceilings in urban India. As mentioned above, we argue that Indian land reforms met their equity objective partially and in the process made land less transferable and land rights less transparent. We begin in the next section by describing the nature of land relations, which varied across regions, at the point of Indian independence. Once the reader has this background, we will describe the three most important types of land reforms—abolition of intermediaries between the cultivator and the state, protection of tenants, and ceilings on the amount of land that a person can own. For each of these policies, we provide examples of success and failure. As the reader will see, the judiciary was often able to delay the implementation of the law, allowing the landed to take defensive action. The bureaucracy was also an obstacle. Bihar is perhaps the most notorious example of these processes. At the other end of the spectrum, Kerala carried out perhaps India's most successful land reforms. After discussing land reforms in terms of their own objectives (especially equity), we will turn to the issues of transparency and transferability. As we mentioned above, these have become a compelling concern (a "binding constraint") after India has become a more market-oriented economy. We conclude by commenting on the current policy trajectory: the land market is slowly opening up, but there is still ambivalence.

The Colonial Period[6]

Britain conquered India over a period of one hundred years (1757–1857) and then ruled for another ninety years, until 1947. Each time it conquered a new region, one of its first tasks was to decide how it would collect land taxes, which were its most important source of revenue. In each case, the Raj gave a set of people de facto ownership rights along with the obligation to pay taxes.[7] Failure to pay the taxes would lead to the confiscation of ownership rights. India's precolonial agrarian structure was highly complex and varied across regions and sometimes even across very small distances. Many people could have rights to a piece of land. One person might have the right to collect taxes, give a portion to the ruler, and retain the rest. Another might have the right to occupy and use the land so long as he or she paid rent. This rent might be variable or fixed in perpetuity. The right to sell or mortgage the land might be restricted. For instance, the owner might have to first offer the land to residents of the village before selling to an outsider (the right of first refusal).

Inevitably, British-Indian land law also varied across time and space. It depended on the preexisting facts on the ground, the extent to which the colonial regime understood them, the size and capacity of its bureaucracy, its need for funds, resistance from local landed classes, and previous experience from other regions, among other things. Therefore, in 1947 the new Indian state inherited a complex array of land-related laws. For our purposes, four sets of questions are relevant. First, who had ownership rights, the cultivator, or a landlord-rentier? Second, were tenants given protection? Could they be easily evicted or subjected to arbitrary rent increases? Third, could owners or tenants sell, lease, or mortgage their rights? Fourth, was there an adequate record of rights? Did the government know who all had claims on a particular piece of land?

On the matter of ownership and taxation, the authorities chose variants of two systems, zamindari and raiyatwari. We will now provide a thumbnail sketch of each, beginning with the former. When the East India Company became Diwan (roughly, finance minister) of Bengal in 1765, it had very little administrative capacity and local knowledge. At the same time, it needed tax revenues urgently for both military and commercial endeavors. It took the easy way out by giving ownership rights to a group of tax collectors, zamindars; hence, this came to be called the zamindari system. Further, the Company fixed the amount of tax it would collect from a given zamindar's land in perpetuity (the "Permanent Settlement"). The tax would never change because of inflation, investment, or anything else that would increase or decrease the zamindars' earnings from the land. The tax was high for the moment, but over time inflation whittled it away. Thus, the Company addressed its short-term financial needs at the expense of long-term tax collection.

Some of the larger zamindars came to own enormous tracts of land. The Raja (literally King) of Darbhanga was one. According to Stephen Henningham, his estate, the Darbhanga Raj, covered 2,400 square miles

(1.5 million acres) spread across six districts.[8] The senior ranks of his administration had three thousand employees. Other zamindars might have as little as ten acres. The zamindari system with a permanently fixed tax was later extended to parts of the Madras Presidency as well. In some other parts of India, such as the Central Provinces and Awadh, a similar arrangement appeared except that the tax was not fixed in perpetuity.

A zamindar in possession of a large tract of land would need to have it cultivated by tenants. Could they be evicted or have rents enhanced at will? Initially, in Bengal, customary protections available to tenants were ignored. However, on the ground, tenants could be quite powerful. After a long period of resistance from them, the Bengal Tenancy Act of 1885 created a category of "occupancy tenants" who could not be evicted so long as they paid a rent fixed by the government (note that in 1885 Bihar was part of Bengal Presidency). A similar category of tenants was also later created in the other zamindari regions. By the end of the colonial period, occupancy tenants were powerful in many areas and had de facto control of the land. Many had tenants of their own. A significant fraction of the land was under tenants-at-will, who had no legal protections. We will focus on four players: zamindar, occupancy tenant, tenant-at-will, and landless laborer.

Could an occupancy tenant sell or mortgage his right? The answer varied. This was permitted in the zamindari areas of Madras Presidency, but the law was ambiguous in Bengal. In some regions, especially the tribal areas, transfer of land was restricted because of the fear that moneylenders who understood the legal system better would cheat unsophisticated peasants and expropriate land. This intuition was later written into the Constitution of India. In a set of areas identified in Schedule V, state governments could pass regulations banning the transfer of land owned by a member of a so-called Scheduled Tribe to another person who was not from a Scheduled Tribe.

By 1820 the zamindari system had many critics. They believed that the zamindars had become lazy rentiers, farming out their responsibilities for tax collection and often creating a chain of intermediaries between the state and the cultivator ("subinfeudation"). A new arrangement came up in large parts of the Bombay Presidency and the Madras Presidency around 1820. In principle, the government sought to confer ownership rights and the obligation to pay tax on the cultivator (raiyat) himself, hence the name *raiyatwari*. In practice, the raiyat might own a large piece of land that was leased out. This was often true in the southern region of Malabar, in present-day Kerala. These tenants got no legal protections until the late colonial period. Raiyatwari land could usually be freely transferred except in the case of Scheduled Tribes, as we have discussed above.

In large parts of North India, including the Punjab and the Northwest Provinces (in modern-day Uttar Pradesh), the colonial regime put in place a third tax-and-ownership arrangement (Mahalwari), acknowledging the importance of an allegedly cohesive village community. In principle the payment of land tax was a collective responsibility. In practice, depending on facts on the ground, Mahalwari approximated either raiyatwari (if the tax-owing collective was large) or zamindari (if the tax-owing collective was small). However, the idea of a village brotherhood that needed to be preserved had a long-lasting effect. In Punjab, an Act was passed in 1900 prohibiting the transfer of land from "agriculturists" to professional (noncultivating) moneylenders. Some other regions followed suit. The demonization of the moneylender became official policy and remained so after independence as well. We will return to this issue in chapter 3.

Whatever the arrangement, rights were poorly documented by the state. The Raj was primarily interested in recovering the land tax. In raiyatwari regions and some zamindari regions, the land tax was revised only every few decades, at which point a survey would be conducted. In the zamindari regions, the rights of occupancy tenants were rerecorded after long intervals. Tenants-at-will often had oral contracts, and the state had no information regarding them.

Another complication was that the registration department, which recorded sales and mortgages, did not coordinate with the revenue department, which recorded who owed the land tax. Person A could point to a sale deed and claim he owned a piece of land, whereas person B could point out that she owed the property tax and was the owner. British-Indian law also allowed a practice known as *benami* (without name), where person A's property could be in the name of person B. The use of this device was legitimate when, for instance, person A was a minor. However, benami could also be misused to protect property from creditors or to defeat the intent of land-reform legislation. In either case, it created a discrepancy between official records and facts on the ground.

To sum up, the new Indian state inherited a system of land rights that was unequal and opaque and that included restrictions on the transferability of land. What legislation would it introduce? A key fact to remember is that in the Indian Constitution, land is under the purview of the state (province) rather than the central (federal) government. Each state would introduce its own legislation. Anyone could challenge it in the state's high court, and a final appeal would be with the Supreme Court in Delhi.

The Proposed Reforms

Figure 2.1 shows, in a highly simplified form, the status quo at the end of the colonial period. In the interest of simplicity, we limit ourselves to four categories of people: the zamindar, the zamindar's secure occupancy tenant, the raiyatwari owner, and the insecure tenant-at-will (whose landlord could be the zamindar, the occupancy tenant, or the raiyatwari owner). The first proposed reform was to eliminate the zamindar, who was an intermediary between the tenant and the state. The occupancy tenant would become the owner, and instead of paying rent to the zamindar, the occupancy tenant would pay a land tax to the state. Legislations to abolish zamindari were passed in the late 1940s and early 1950s. Efforts to protect the tenant-at-will began at more or less the same time. They usually involved protection from eviction and arbitrary rent increases, and sometimes they gave ownership rights to the

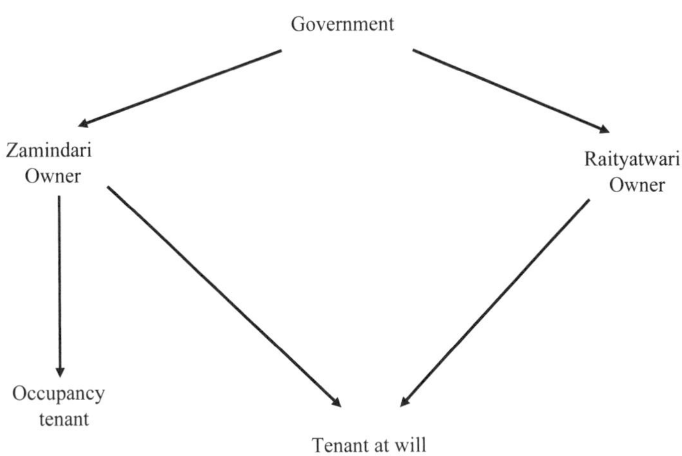

FIGURE 2.1. Colonial-era agrarian structure

tenant. They could be stand-alone legislation, or they could be a part of a larger land-reform package. In some raiyatwari areas, laws to protect the tenant-at-will had appeared during the late colonial period itself, the Bombay Tenancy Act of 1938 being a prominent example. However, protecting the tenant-at-will was a very challenging task and became a protracted affair. The last policy success in this domain came in the late 1970s in West Bengal.

A third type of reform was land-ceiling legislation. If a person (or family) owned more than a certain amount of land, it would be confiscated and redistributed to the landless. The Congress Economic Reform Committee headed by Jawaharlal Nehru proposed land-ceiling legislation in 1947–1948, but the proposal was controversial. After some debate, it was introduced in the later years of the second five-year plan (1956–1961). It largely failed. In the early 1970s land-ceiling laws were amended, and there was a fresh push to implement them, which was slightly more successful.

Who designed land reforms? Typically, it was the Congress party, which had spearheaded the anticolonial movement in India. The Congress party was a big tent. It had representation from various sections of agrarian society, including landowners, large and small, as well as occupancy tenants. Even the poorest sections of Indian rural society, the landless or those with tiny plots of land, needed to be paid at least lip service. Agrarian structure varied across states as did the class composition of the party. Therefore, the politics of land reform varied. That said, on the whole, a party in which large landowners were well represented was in charge of designing a policy to redistribute their property. Therefore, legislation often had loopholes. The instrument for implementing the law, the bureaucracy, was also sympathetic to the landed. But there was an earlier question, even before implementation—Was land-reform legislation consistent with the Indian Constitution?

Land Reforms versus the Right to Property

India adopted the parliamentary system of government along the lines of Britain, with an upper and lower house. However, unlike Britain, there is a written constitution, drafted between 1946 and 1949 by a Constituent Assembly consisting largely of Congress party members. The Constituent Assembly decided that policies on land would be decided at the state (province) level. This was a consequential choice because the government at the center included figures like the first Indian prime minister, Jawaharlal Nehru, who was, in some loose sense, "socialist." Politicians at the state level were often more conservative, willing to maintain the status quo. Therefore, the tale of Indian land reforms is a diverse collection of state-level stories often with the state government and the central government at odds.

The Indian Constitution includes a list of fundamental rights along American lines. The fundamental rights are justiciable; a citizen can approach the court to have them enforced. One of these fundamental rights was the right to property. The Constitution also includes a set of Directive Principles of State Policy, which represent the egalitarian values of the postcolonial state. The Directive Principles are not justiciable but are very influential and frequently invoked in public debates as well as judicial decisions. Land-reform policies were in the spirit of the Directive Principles but were in tension with the fundamental rights.

Three articles in the Constitution were especially relevant to land reforms. Article 14 gave the right to "equal protection before the law"; Article 19(f) gave the right to "acquire, hold, and dispose of property," and Article 31 protected against arbitrary seizure of property. Initially, the model for Article 31 was the Fifth Amendment to the American Constitution, which includes the phrase "nor shall private property be taken for public use without just compensation." Several members of the Constituent Assembly worried that if the word *just* was used, every case would end up in court.[9] This was a reasonable worry, because the government could not afford to give every expropriated owner fair market value. After extensive discussion, the Indian Constitution included this tortured formulation: property could not be seized even for public purposes "unless the law provides compensation for the property taken possession of or acquired and either fixes the amount of compensation, or specifies the principles on which, and the manner in which, the compensation is to be determined and given."[10] Article 31 also included a temporary expedient to protect zamindari abolition legislation that had already been passed by state legislatures before the Indian Constitution became operational. No such law could be questioned on the grounds of insufficient compensation to zamindars. These precautions notwithstanding, the real challenges were still to come in the form of landlords questioning the constitutionality of land-reform legislation.

In 1950 the Bihar Land Reforms Act was passed, abolishing zamindari. The big zamindars of Bihar were accomplished litigators. They had fought their tenants in court for generations. They were not about to simply accept the act as passed. They successfully challenged the compensation provision in Patna High Court. As mentioned above, compensation had to be financially viable for the impoverished Indian state. It also had to protect the smaller zamindars and not push them into poverty. Therefore, as a proportion of lost assets, smaller zamindars had to be compensated more than larger zamindars (we might call this "progressive expropriation"). The act chose to pay multiples of annual earnings from land confiscated. They varied from twenty times for annual income less than Rs. 500 to three times for more than Rs. 100,000. The differential compensation was successfully challenged by the Raja of Darbhanga (see above) in *Kameshwar Singh and Others v. State of Bihar.*[11] Justice Reuben argued that he could see "no reasonable basis on which this application of different multiples to net incomes of different amounts can be justified."[12] The Bihar attorney general tried to appeal to the notion of progressive taxation, but Judge Shearer was not convinced; compensation was not the same as taxation, he argued. He concluded that the act violated Article 14, the equality clause of the Constitution. The other two judges agreed, and the act was struck down.

The government had been blindsided. It had anticipated legal challenges to land-reform legislation based on the compensation provision, and the Constituent Assembly had written in language to protect it. The Patna High Court had surprised the government by finding that the Bihar Land Reform Act contravened a different fundamental right, the equality clause. An angry Prime Minister Jawaharlal Nehru commented that "this business of the equality of the law may very well mean, as it has come to mean often enough, making rigid the existing inequities before the law."[13] In response to the Patna high court's decision, the parliament then passed the First Amendment to the Indian Constitution. No one could challenge legislation on "estates" (zamindaris) on the ground that they violated *any* fundamental right. Further, the amendment created an extraordinary shelter, the Ninth Schedule. A law placed in this schedule could not become void because it violated a fundamental right. The Bihar Act was placed in the Ninth Schedule, as were several legislations by other states.

The zamindars then challenged the First Amendment itself (*Shankari Prasad Deo v. Union of India*) based on Article 13(2) of the Constitution, which asserted that the "state shall not make any law which takes away or abridges the rights conferred by this Part [the fundamental rights]." The challenge failed. Judge Patanjali Shastri was quite explicit: "No doubt our constitution makers, following the American model, have incorporated certain fundamental rights in Part III and made them immune from interference by laws made by the state. We find it, however, difficult, in the absence of a clear indication to the contrary, to suppose that they also intended to make those rights immune from constitutional amendment."[14] After endorsing the First Amendment, the Supreme Court declared the Bihar Land Reforms Act constitutional, though it took issue with some provisions.

This became a pattern. A state would pass a land-reform legislation; it would be challenged in a high court as violating a fundamental right; the challenge would be upheld, and the law declared unconstitutional; there would then be an amendment to the Constitution to protect the legislation. This process was jolted in 1967 when petitioners who had lost property under land-reform legislation in Punjab and Mysore approached the Supreme Court in *Golaknath v. State of Punjab*. The Supreme Court reopened the issue that had emerged when the First Amendment faced a challenge: Could a constitutional amendment contravene a fundamental right? The court concluded that it could not and that the Supreme Court had made a mistake when it had upheld the First Amendment in *Shankari Prasad Deo v. Union of India*. The court decided to let the existing amendments stay in place but ruled that "fundamental rights are outside the amendatory process and parliament will have no power in future to amend provisions of Part III to abridge or amend fundamental rights therein."[15]

There was a difficult problem at hand. On the one hand, it was meaningless to call something a fundamental right if the parliament could pass an amendment and take it away. On the other hand, if the fundamental right to property were to be defended in all earnestness, with market value compensation for the expropriated owner, land reforms would not be possible. The solution was to remove the right to property from the fundamental rights but to protect the remaining fundamental rights from future amendments by the parliament. This happened via an extended tug-of-war between executive and judiciary over a tumultuous period, 1967–1980. This story has been told many times by people more expert than us, so we will not repeat it here.[16] Suffice to say that in 1978 the Forty-Fourth Amendment to the Constitution removed the right to property from the fundamental rights. Along the way, in arguably the single most important case in modern Indian history, *Kesavanada Bharathi v. State of Kerala* (1973), the Supreme Court placed limits on the parliament's right to amend the Constitution: its "basic structure" could not be changed. The issue was not quite settled, because judges did not spell out the elements of this basic structure.

Even if land reforms were constitutional, they could be frustrated by writing loopholes into the legislation and by the unwillingness and incapacity of the bureaucracy to implement them. The extent to which this happened depended on local political configurations, the attitudes of the government in power, and the extent to which potential beneficiaries were mobilized. We now turn to the issues of design and implementation for each of the three main types of reform: abolition of zamindari, protection of tenants-at-will, and land-ceiling legislation.

Abolition of Intermediaries

Among the three main types of reform, the abolition of zamindari was the most successful. Bihar is perhaps the state where implementation was worst, and Jammu and Kashmir was the best. We will discuss these sequentially with brief comments on some other zamindari regions.

As we have seen above, the Bihar zamindars lost their battle in the Supreme Court. They could still use their influence within the Congress party to introduce loopholes in the legislation aimed at them, to take preemptive steps to evade the legislation, and to use illegal methods after it was passed.

The first issue had to do with the extent to which the zamindar would be expropriated. They had to be left with some land to cultivate ("personal cultivation") and to live on ("homestead"). "Personal cultivation" was defined as including cultivation with hired workers. How would a court of law know the distinction between a tenant and a hired worker? The tenant needed documentary proof. Many of them did not have it. So zamindars evicted tenants and claimed the land was under personal cultivation. The "homestead" provision was also defined to favor the zamindar. It defined a "dwelling house used by the intermediary for the purposes of his own residence or for the purpose of letting out on rent together with any courtyard, compound . . . and includes any outbuildings used for purposes connected with agriculture or horticulture and any tank, library, and place of worship appertaining to such dwelling house."[17] The provision allowing "homestead" land to be rented out in particular stands out as odd.

The eviction of tenants was also facilitated by the fact that the state had not updated occupancy rights. The last preindependence record of occupancy rights appeared in 1922. This had to be revised, and this happened slowly. The Planning Commission reported in 1966, "For the implementation of land-reform laws, the entire revenue administrative agency had to be built up as it was previously practically non-existent."[18]

The prozamindar attitude of the Patna High Court reinforced the loopholes in the law. In 1958 the court considered a case, *Mahanth Sukhdeo Das v. Kashi Prasad Tiwari*, in which the zamindar had mortgaged some of his lands to a lender who had taken possession of it. The loan had been repaid, but the land had remained in the possession of the lender for many years. Was the lender an occupancy tenant? If so, under the Bihar Act, the lender would now be the owner. The spirit of the act was that zamindars could retain land only if they were personally cultivating it. Despite this, the Patna High Court ruled in favor of the zamindars, arguing that they had had "constructive possession" of the land even if they did not physically control it. In another decision, the Patna High Court ruled in favor of the zamindars on the grounds that they had "juridical possession." Eventually, the Supreme Court ruled against these zamindar-friendly interpretations of the law, stressing the criterion of personal cultivation as grounds for retention of the property by the zamindar.[19]

Bihari zamindars used loopholes in the law, their social power, and even violence to retain thousands of acres of land. They were not unique in this. Daniel Thorner argued that the landed gentry of Rajasthan had offered "savage resistance to land reform," and "a number of leases were shortened by the termination of the lives of the tenants."[20] According to a 1978 article, the biggest landowner in Bihar retained more than twenty thousand acres.[21] That said, even in Bihar, zamindari abolition had a huge effect. Ninety percent of the area of the state—38.7 million acres—had been under zamindari.[22] After zamindari abolition, 22 million acres had come into "direct contact with the state" as 7.1 million tenants got ownership rights. Zamindars had received ownership of their "personally cultivated" land to the tune of 1.65 million acres. The state had also taken possession of 7.4 million acres of private forests.[23]

Zamindari abolition proceeded smoothly when the politics of the times put the government squarely behind the reform. During the Partition of British India, India and Pakistan went to war over Kashmir. Sheikh Abdullah, the chief minister of Jammu and Kashmir, needed the support of the peasantry against the external threat posed by Pakistan, and land reform was a way to ensure this. The Jammu and Kashmir Big Landed Estates Abolition Act of 1950 was toughly worded and relatively effectively implemented. According to the act, "tiller means a person who tills land with his own hand."[24] The landlord would be left with 22.75 acres of cultivated land plus grazing land and orchards. This was in effect a hybrid legislation—abolition of the intermediary plus a land ceiling. The zamindar was given no compensation. The government confiscated and distributed 450,000 acres of land, which was 17.77% of the operated area. Of this, 230,000 acres went to tenants who were cultivating the land.[25]

Daniel Thorner summarized the effect of these reforms:

> Whatever the defects of implementation, the fact of agrarian change cannot be denied. Many tillers have become landowners and some land has even gone to the landless. The peasantry of the valley . . . were not so long ago as fearful and submissive as the Jat tenantry of Rajasthan. No one who has spent time with the Kashmiri villagers since 1947 will say the same today.[26]

Zamindari abolition was also effective in Saurashtra, a region in peninsular Gujarat that had been formed by the amalgamation of princely states, which had been ruled indirectly by the British. The zamindars, often of the Rajput caste, were closely identified with the British Raj, whereas their insecure tenants were, by caste, kanbi-patidars, closely allied with the ruling Congress party. Zamindars' holdings reduced to modest levels, and their tenants gained ownership rights.[27] Ghanshyam Shah notes that "to ensure that no intermediate interests between the government and the cultivators were created in the future, the government passed the Saurashtra Prohibition of Leases of Agricultural Lands 1953. Accordingly, the occupants of land were enjoined to cultivate their lands personally and not to lease out their land in the future."[28] In other words, the ownership right explicitly excluded the right to temporary transfer. We will return to this issue below.

The authoritative overview of land reforms in India is by P. S. Appu. He estimates that the abolition of intermediaries brought approximately twenty-five million tenants into direct contact with the state as owners.[29]

This is an impressive number even for a country the size of India, but there are two caveats. First, many of these tenants had already obtained secure occupancy rights via tenant protection legislation passed in the colonial period. It is not clear how much extra benefit they obtained by paying their dues to the state rather than to the zamindar. Second, as we have seen above, during the reforms zamindars evicted many tenants. Still, it is widely agreed that zamindari abolition reduced the social and political power of the old landed magnates and empowered castes that had been resident in the village and in physical possession of land.[30] Wolf Ladejinsky, an expert on Indian land reforms, neatly summarized the outcome of zamindari abolition: though "not every 't' was crossed and not every 'i' was dotted . . . the job was done."[31]

The former occupancy tenant of the zamindar was now an owner. The owner might have leased out some of the lands. Similarly, even in the raiyatwari areas, the owner could have a tenant. What were the rights of these tenants? How could they be protected?

Protecting the Undocumented Tenant

Measures to protect tenants-at-will were partially successful. We will go through the spectrum, beginning again with Bihar, which performed poorly, to Gujarat and Maharashtra, which did better, and then Kerala and West Bengal, where tenant protection was most effective.

The Bengal Tenancy Act of 1885 (which applied to Bihar as well) had paid lip service to the tenant of the occupancy tenant (now owner after zamindari abolition), and now the land reforms in Bihar did the same. But these tenants-at-will had to be identified before they could be protected. In July 1964 the Bihar government issued instructions for recording the tenants, but this was not just a routine administrative matter. In September the government sent another letter:

> Reports have been received about the eviction of under-raiyats [tenants] and other agrarian disturbances. Government desires that every effort should be made to maintain peaceful relations between the raiyat [owner] and the under-raiyat and requisite steps should be taken to avoid any action which may give rise to disorder. In order to achieve the same, the collection of details to that extent should be kept in abeyance.[32]

In plain English, Bihari landlords had physically prevented the recording of the existence of their tenants.

Tenant protection was more successful in the raiyatwari regions of Gujarat and Maharashtra under the aegis of the Bombay Tenancy Act, first passed in 1938 and strengthened in 1948. The Bombay Tenancy Act protected tenants from eviction and fixed a maximum rent. However, the act allowed the landowner to take back his or her land if he or she needed it for personal use, subject to a ceiling of fifty acres or two hundred acres for a family. There was a significant loophole. If the tenant decided to surrender land voluntarily, the ceiling did not apply. In their classic study of the sixteen Maharashtra and Karnatak districts in Bombay State, Dandekar and Khudanpur wrote, "There thus existed a real possibility of the landlord using unfair means to induce the tenant into surrendering his land particularly when the resumption would result in raising the landlord's holding above the ceiling." They argued that "this single loophole made all the provisions for protection ineffective in practice."[33] The Bombay Tenancy Act was then amended in 1956 so that on Tiller's Day, April 1, 1957, all tenants were "deemed to have purchased the land."[34] The purchase price was determined by an Agricultural Land Tribunal and had to be paid in twelve installments. Again, even as the ownership right was conferred, the right to transfer was restricted. The new owner could not transfer the land in any way without the permission of the government. Further, a nonagriculturist could not buy agricultural land.[35]

The Bombay Tenancy Act succeeded to a fair extent in Maharashtra. Ownership rights went to 1.5 million tenants, who got 1.6 million hectares of land. Another million could not obtain ownership rights because they returned the land to the landlord allegedly voluntarily or simply did not show up at the Land Tribunal or could not pay the installments.[36] According to Henry Hart and Ronald Herring, the tenants whose landlords were absentee were able to get ownership rights, whereas those whose landlords were residents were "induced to give up their purchase rights."[37]

The story in Gujarat, also under the Bombay Tenancy Act, was broadly similar. Approximately half of the area under tenancy came to be owned by the tenants. Caste seems to have played an important role. The losers from the reform, Patidar and Brahmin-Bania landholders, were influential in the Congress and the administration, so implementation was weak. As Nikita Sud has put it, "local and provincial politicians and bureaucrats did not see it fit to disempower their caste fellows and often themselves by allocating land to their former tenant employees."[38]

As our discussion has shown, for tenants with oral contracts to be protected, the political and physical power of the landlord had to be neutralized at the village level. Also, the legal procedure had to be changed to give the poor and often illiterate tenant a chance. Perhaps the two most successful instances of this occurred, unsurprisingly, when communist parties won elections. This happened in Kerala and West Bengal. In Kerala the policy was more radical—tenants, including sharecroppers, were given ownership rights.[39] In West Bengal, sharecroppers were protected from eviction and rent increases and given heritable rights. But this was a long time coming. In both states land reforms to protect insecure tenants were effectively implemented only in the 1970s.

In a typical legal proceeding, the burden of proof is on the plaintiff. It follows that in the context of land reform, a person claiming tenant status will have to prove it. As we have seen, this was often difficult. An alternative was to reverse the procedure and put the onus on the landlord to prove that the person in question was *not* a tenant. This strategy had been articulated at least as early as 1948 in the Bombay Tenancy Act but had been implemented poorly.[40] The strongest protenant legal formulation was in Kerala: "Any person in occupation at the commencement of the Kerala Land Reforms (Amendment) Act, 1969 . . . shall be deemed to be a tenant if he or his predecessor-in-interest was continuously in occupation of such land honestly believing himself to be a tenant for not less than two years within a period of twelve years immediately preceding the 11th day of April, 1967." How would it be determined what this person "honestly believed"? The legislation explained: "Where a person has been continuously in occupation of any such land for two years within the said period of 12 years, it shall be presumed until the contrary is proved that he has been in such occupation honestly believing himself to be a tenant." In other words, occupation implied "honest belief" until proven otherwise.

After the inevitable legal challenge, the "deemed tenant" provision was struck down by the Kerala high court in *Chami Chettiar v. Thirumandham Kunnu Bhagavathi Devaswom* in a two-to-one decision.[41] The majority's argument was reasonable. The judges worried that as the law was framed, even a trespasser or land grabber would have to be deemed a tenant and potentially become an owner. But there was no perfect law. With a weaker provision, legitimate tenants might have been evicted. For instance, one way of concealing a tenancy was to disguise it as a mortgage: the tenant was the lender, the landlord was a borrower, and the land was collateral.[42] The choice was between two types of errors: rejecting the genuine tenant or affirming the fraudulent tenant. The legislature was willing to take the latter risk in the interests of the poor.[43] Ultimately the "deemed tenant" provision was saved because the Communist Party's mobilization had radicalized a large section of the rural population. Even the youth wing of the Congress party had been influenced. Eventually, the Congress party at the center agreed to give the Kerala Land Reform Act the shelter of the Ninth Schedule (see above), so it was protected.

While this warfare was in sophisticated legalese, in the high court, the Kerala government also worried about the nitty-gritty at the lower levels of the judiciary. To expedite the work, the government set up 150 land tribunals. The Revenue Minister K. T. Jacob explained that "their territorial jurisdiction being rather small, their workload will be comparatively little."[44] This was common sense; the staffing increased to deal with the extra workload, and the judiciary came closer to the village. More striking was the fact that the Kerala government preferred to staff its tribunals with officials who were *not* judicial officers. K. T. Jacob explained why in a pamphlet written just six months after the "deemed tenant" amendment was passed.

> The act provided that the Land Tribunals may be constituted either with judicial officers or other officers. The government preferred other officers because the past experience revealed that the proceedings in Land Tribunals presided over by judicial officers entailed great delay and resulted in cumbersome and lengthy procedure with all the niceties and legal subtleties. The present band of officers in the land tribunals are [*sic*] drawn from the executive services. Most of them are not law graduates. . . . They are quite competent to bring about effective implementation consistent with the principles of natural justice.[45]

Clearly, Kerala communists viewed the judiciary, at all levels, as an obstruction to land reforms.

The Kerala land reforms were successful. As many as 1.3 million tenants, representing 43.3% of agricultural households in 1971, benefited. They acquired ownership rights over two million acres, 36.5% of the net sown area.[46] Tenancy was prohibited.

When the Left Front government came to power in West Bengal in 1977, it, too, believed that ordinary judicial procedure would not be adequate. It launched a program known as Operation Barga (a sharecropper was known as a *bargadar*). Again, Operation Barga shifted the burden of proof from tenant to landlord: "a person lawfully cultivating any land belonging to another person shall be presumed to be a *bargadar* [sharecropper] . . . and the burden of proving that such person is not a *bargadar* or that the land is in his personal cultivation shall . . . lie on the person who alleges that the person cultivating the land is not a *bargadar* in respect of such land."[47] This provision was challenged in *Biswanath Ghosh v. State of West Bengal* but was upheld by the Calcutta High Court, which commented that "it only provides a special mode of proving the claim of a bargadar where a dispute arises under certain circumstances."

The government of West Bengal believed that the support and encouragement of peers and government officials would be necessary for sharecroppers to dare to claim their rights. It organized "reorientation camps" at which officials were present and sharecroppers could have their names registered. Owners could also present their objections. Suhas Chattopadhyay describes a camp organized in May 1978 in an area where sharecroppers needed reassurance to come forward. The camp was given "wide publicity" via "the beat of drums, distribution of leaflets, and personal contact." Two hundred sharecroppers came to the camp, landowners raised thirty-five objections, and the names of 191 sharecroppers were recorded.[48] The government had adopted a rough-and-ready procedure designed to favor sharecroppers. Predictably, this was challenged in court. The legal story involves some bureaucratic minutia, for which we beg the reader's indulgence.

The West Bengal government formalized its implementation strategy for Operation Barga in a circular sent to its officials in July 1978.[49] Key elements were the formation of "squads" of officials who would meet with sharecroppers to "bring home to them the benefits that will be thrown open to them once they are brought into the settlement record thereby to enable them to overcome the fear psychosis." The instructions were that in the process of verifying rights, the presumption should be in favor of the sharecropper. The circular also warned that some "affluent" people might have leased in land as sharecroppers, but they should not be recorded as such. There might also be cases where the relatives of some landowners might present themselves as sharecroppers of owners to keep the land within the family. Officials received instruction to "discreetly" look into "relationships between landowners and claimants." In *Biswanath Ghosh v. State of West Bengal*, landowners complained to the Calcutta High Court that in effect, officials were being told to collect information behind the backs of interested parties. They also argued that the instruction to ignore "affluent" claimants was contrary to the statute. The judge agreed and ruled that the official should ignore the circular. Left-wing critics of Operation Barga believe that this judgment weakened it significantly and turned it into a conventional reform. Ratan Khasnabis noted that in the year following the issuance of the circular, 730,000 sharecroppers had been registered. However, in the two and a half years after the high court judgment, only 250,000 were registered.[50] We don't know the counterfactual, that is, what would have happened had the Calcutta High Court ruled differently, but even Operation Barga's staunch supporters described the judgment as a "severe test."[51] That said, estimates of the percentage of tenants protected vary between 48% and 80%.[52] This contributed to the electoral success of the Communist Party of India (Marxist) for the next few decades.

Finally, it is worth remembering that tenancy reforms led to preemptive evictions of tenants. Jonathan Conning and James Robinson found, using data from fifteen Indian states over the period 1961–1992, that the anticipation of tenancy reform reduced the extent of tenancy.[53] This finding is subject to the caveat that the tenancy data may be unreliable because it was driven underground. We will return to this issue below.

As we have noted, land-ceiling legislation first came in the Second Plan period, 1956–1961, and was given a fresh impetus in the early 1970s. It was usually ineffectual. Why?

Land Ceilings

Land-ceiling legislation specified the maximum amount of land a person or a family could own. The state would confiscate the "surplus" beyond that. The most obvious way to avoid land ceilings was to claim to have given the surplus land away to someone else. In Bihar, a person who had more than the ceiling was permitted to "gift" it to anyone who might have received this property had the person died intestate. Moreover, the intention to pass land-ceiling legislation was declared long before actual legislation, giving landowners enough time to take defensive measures. A land-ceiling bill was debated in 1955 but could not pass. But it gave fair warning. The Bihar Civil Justice Report of 1960 noted "the filing of partition suits [to distribute the ownership among family members] to circumvent the proposed legislation in fixing ceiling of lands."[54] When the legislation became operational in 1961, it allowed yet another year for partition. The Planning Commission candidly noted that "with these provisions on the statute book, little surplus land is expected."[55] A 1973 publication of the Planning Commission provided figures for the amount of land that had been declared surplus or taken possession of under land-ceiling legislation. For several states, including Bihar, the figure was "Nil."[56] By June 1975 only 11,000 acres of land had been acquired in Bihar.[57]

By the end of the 1960s, there had been little success with land-ceiling legislation. Two factors led to a renewed emphasis. One was the rise of Maoist movements. The other was Prime Minister Indira Gandhi's turn toward populism. In 1972 the central government introduced new guidelines for amendments to land-ceiling legislation. Various states lowered the ceilings. More land could potentially be seized.

Land-ceiling legislation continued to be fought in various ways. Another way to evade the land ceiling was to engage in fictitious transfers. A. K. Singh, who had served as district magistrate in Gaya, Bihar, has provided a detailed and entertaining account of the extraordinary effort required to prove that a transfer was bogus.[58] One of the biggest landowners in South Bihar was a monastery known as the Bodh Gaya Math. The story begins with the additional collector (revenue official) doubting the existence of eighty disciples of the Bodh Gaya Math to whom it had allegedly transferred land. The head of the monastery hired a group of people, made them shave their heads, and "on the appointed date all these saffron-clad persons were paraded before the court of the Additional Collector as Chelas [disciples] of the math." The skeptical officials went to the villages where the lands were. Nobody had heard of the alleged purchasers. After decades of legal dispute, the Bodh Gaya Math finally gave up its surplus land in 1987 after a Supreme Court decision. The reader can follow the rest of this bizarre story, which includes the allegation that the henchmen of the monastery threw homemade grenades at workers who had occupied its land, in the work of A. K. Singh and David Geary.[59]

P. S. Appu has commented that "the imposition of the ceiling on agricultural holdings in India is a case of inchoate policy, imperfect legislation, and inefficient implementation."[60] The land redistributed, as a

TABLE 2.1 **Distribution of surplus area on imposition of land ceilings (ca. 1992)**

State	Percentage of operated area distributed
Andhra Pradesh	1.44
Assam	5.92
Bihar	1.03
Gujarat	0.54
Haryana	1.23
Himachal Pradesh	0
Jammu and Kashmir	17.77
Karnataka	0.40
Kerala	1.47
Madhya Pradesh	0.33
Maharashtra	1.00
Orissa	1.15
Punjab	1.01
Rajasthan	0.86
Tamil Nadu	0.76
Uttar Pradesh	0.84
West Bengal	6.72
Total	1.24

Source: P. S. Appu, *Land Reforms in India: A Survey of Policy, Legislation, and Implementation* (New Delhi: Vikas, 1996), 312.

proportion of operated area, rarely crossed 1%. There were only three states where it exceeded 5%: West Bengal, Assam, and Jammu and Kashmir (see table 2.1).

The land-ceiling laws for rural areas led to demands from rural elites for urban land ceilings. There was also the concern that the rural rich, limited in the amount of land they could own in the rural areas, would buy up too much urban land.[61] The 1976 Urban Land (Ceiling and Regulation) Act (ULCRA)placed a ceiling on the amount of land that could be owned in an urban area. Of course, there were loopholes and exemptions in ULCRA. For instance, above-ceiling surplus land did not have to be surrendered to the government if the land would be used for a public purpose, in particular, housing for the poor.

Urban land is and was unequally owned. In Mumbai, ninety-one individuals owned 55%of vacant urban land.[62] There was a case for redistribution. However, in practice, ULCRA led to corruption as developers bribed officials to retain or acquire land. They also bought up land in the fringes of the city, where the ceiling law did not apply, driving up prices. By 2005 in Mumbai alone, 1,000 acres of land had been exempted from land-ceiling law, whereas the Maharashtra government had acquired only 82.5 acres of land. Even this was encroached on. In September 2005, the Mumbai government shut down 757 housing projects because they violated ULCRA.[63] ULCRA served neither equity nor efficiency. It was repealed by the central government in 1999, and most states followed suit.[64] Maharashtra waited until 2007 to repeal ULCRA and retained ("saved") some clauses. Some knotty problems persisted more than a decade later. For instance, were Mumbai-region developers still required to honor the conditions under which they had received exemptions? A large number were in violation.[65]

Our discussion thus far has focused on landowners and their tenants. How did the landless agricultural laborers, often Dalits (Scheduled Castes), fare? And did women gain from land reforms?

Excluded Groups

While agricultural laborers were not going to gain directly from either tenancy reform or abolition of intermediaries, there were a few other ways for them to benefit. One was if the state allocated them land it had seized under land-ceiling legislation. Another was if the state gave them its own land. A third way was by giving them security in or ownership of homes built on rented property and the small areas around them ("homestead"). This last option shows the most promise.

As early as 1948, Bihar passed legislation to ensure security to landless people who lived on very small pieces of rented land. This was the Bihar Privileged Persons Homestead Tenancy Act (BPPHT). It was poorly implemented. The Planning Commission noted in 1966 that in one of the villages it visited, there were twenty such households, but their occupancy had been recorded in pencil. The officer recommended dryly that after verification, records should be written in ink! Still, according to government figures, more than 580,000 households have received land grants under the BPPHT Act, though we cannot be sure they have actual possession.[66] The Bihar government is continuing schemes to provide small plots of land to the most disadvantaged Dalit communities. These are promising initiatives, but the jury is still out on their effectiveness.[67]

Kerala successfully implemented reforms along these lines in the 1970s. A laborer with a hut on a landlord's property only had to establish occupation between August 1968 and January 1970, without necessarily producing any documentation. The laborer then received protection against eviction and could be charged a maximum rent of Rs. 24 for an area of one-tenth of an acre. The laborer could also buy the homestead for 12.5% of the market value, payable in 12 annual installments.[68] More than 265,000 laborers, 77%of those estimated to be eligible, purchased their plots.[69] This modest but important step in land reforms can still be implemented across the country. Even as we write, legislation to provide homestead to agricultural laborers has been passed in Karnataka and awaits the president's approval.[70]

The Bodh Gaya Monastery case, which we discussed above, is the first instance (of which we are aware) where surplus land above the ceiling was given to women. Land-reform programs have really started to target women only in the twenty-first century. Even in West Bengal, when distributing above-ceiling land, the Left Front government started giving joint titles to men and women only in 1994–1995. By then most of the available land had been redistributed. By 1999, of the 2.16 million beneficiaries, 90% were men.[71] In Bihar, recent figures indicate that only 12.8% of land parcels are titled in women's names. In 2009 the Land Ceiling Act in Bihar was amended, requiring that 50% of land seized under land-ceiling legislation should go to women. Titles are now in the name of both husband and wife. This has had an impact: 47% of women beneficiaries since independence received land in the period 2010–2014.[72] Efforts like these are taking on what seems to be a deep-rooted preference for males to inherit land. Sonia Bhalotra and coauthors find that receiving land through Operation Barga intensified son preference for households; if a family's first child was a girl, getting land rights under Operation Barga increased the survival probability of a later boy relative to a later girl.[73] We will return to the connection between son preference and landownership in chapter 9, when we discuss inheritance-law reform that gives land rights to women.

Our discussion thus far has focused on equity in land ownership. However, as we have discussed, land often needs to be transferred, either temporarily or permanently. This could be, for instance, from a less productive farmer to a more productive farmer, by a family whose sons go off to the city, or from farmer to industrialist. At least three things are necessary. First, the law should allow sale or lease. Second, it is easier and safer to buy land if there is transparency, that is, a clear record of who owns the land and of encumbrances such as mortgages. Third, if a person leases out land, he or she should be confident of getting it back. Even by the end of the colonial period, these three conditions were not easy to satisfy. Land reforms aggravated the problem. Moreover, as the

Indian economy has begun to grow rapidly, the share of agriculture in output has fallen, the share of the urban population has increased, and there is a greater need for rural land to be repurposed. The difficulties in transferring it are now of greater consequence.

Transparency and Transferability

Transparency and transferability are closely linked. On the one hand, it is difficult to buy or lease a plot of land if you don't know who has what rights in relation to it. On the other hand, if the law places restrictions on transfer, people will adopt subterfuges when they sell or lease it; this will reduce transparency. We will begin below with a description of unclear ownership rights and then discuss restrictions on transfer and their consequences.

Even during the colonial period, it was not easy to establish the ownership of a piece of land. The revenue department identified who owed the land tax as one part of a record of rights. However, a sale or a mortgage was recorded by the registration department. The two were not automatically reconciled. Moreover, it was legal for one person to be nominally identified as the owner when the real interest in the property was with someone else. These problems have persisted, and in some ways they have been aggravated in independent India.

The problem of murky land ownership led D. C. Wadhwa, a distinguished scholar of Indian land law, to launch a one-man crusade to persuade the Government of India to adopt the Torrens System of land titling. Under this system, the government would create a unified record of title and encumbrances (such as mortgages) and guarantee their validity. Under the Torrens system a third party can challenge the title but cannot obtain it; at best, he or she can receive compensation from the government. Wadhwa made the case systematically, drawing on the experience of many other countries, in an article published in *Economic and Political Weekly* in 1989. After more than a decade of nonresponse from the government, he wrote a lament in 2002, beginning with a letter to Arun Shourie, a journalist-economist-politician who had become the minister of communication and information technology.[74] Wadhwa quoted an article Shourie had written in the *Indian Express*, noting that of the eight hotels in Delhi owned by the Indian Tourism Development Corporation (ITDC), a government-owned undertaking, not even one had title deeds or lease in order. Indeed, there was illegal construction in Delhi's iconic Ashoka Hotel, a few hundred yards from the prime minister's residence. In Varanasi, a famous Hindu religious city in Uttar Pradesh, the ITDC had purchased roughly 9 acres of land from the department of tourism, but there was no record that the department of tourism had ever owned it.

Eventually, the Government of India was persuaded and has decided to move to a system of conclusive titling via an initiative begun in 2008 and subsequently renamed the Digital India Land Records Modernization Programme. Computerization is the easier part of the task—obtaining accurate information to digitize is the challenge. Progress is uneven across states.[75] There is some evidence that digitization is facilitating access to credit.[76] The problem with land titles, however, is still so severe that buyers are approaching the government to use its eminent domain powers to acquire land for them because only this makes them secure. K. P. Krishnan of the ministry of skill development and entrepreneurship said recently, "The private sector's interest in government land acquisition is mainly because there is no other way to get a secure land title."[77] This is a heavy price to pay because, as we will see in chapter 4, the use of eminent domain is itself highly controversial.

There are three major types of legal restrictions on transfer. First, there are bans on certain types of permanent or potentially permanent transfer such as sale or mortgage. Second, there are bans on land lease, or accrual of occupancy rights if a tenant can prove continuous possession for a specified period. And third, there is the requirement of the government's permission to transfer agricultural land to a nonagriculturist or from agricultural use to nonagricultural use. We will briefly discuss each.

The Raj had concluded that tribal communities were too naive and unsophisticated to engage in land-market transactions mediated by the formal legal system. It resorted to the crude but straightforward device of banning transfers from a tribal person to a nontribal, especially in the context of moneylending. In the same spirit, the Constitution of India designated a set of areas in Schedule V within which state governments could pass laws restricting land transfer by tribals. Many states passed legislation driven by the intuition that tribals are vulnerable to fraud. However, this has not eliminated land transfer from tribals to others; rather, it has spawned illegal workarounds. Here is a list of methods from a 2014 report submitted to the Ministry of Tribal Affairs: "(i) sale,

(ii) mortgage, (iii) benami transfer [to a tribal proxy], (iv) forcible occupation, (v) oral transfer of possession, (vi) marital alliance, (vii) in the name of concubines, and (viii) other fraudulent means."[78] The report provides examples. An energy company has purchased the land of an entire village in the name of three tribals. One of them allegedly paid Rs. 2.84 crores (more than US$400,000), an enormous sum obviously beyond his reach, and disappeared. A famous multinational telecom purchased tribal land worth Rs. 3.36 crore (more than US$500,000) in the name of one tribal person.[79] In cases like these, transparency was lost because the nominal owner was not the real owner.

If land cannot be sold, the buyer may be willing to settle for a secure long-term lease. However, as we have seen, land-reform legislation often took a dim view of tenancy, banning or restricting it. For instance, in Kerala, there is an outright ban on tenancy. Still, the 2003 National Sample Survey found that 5%–6%of cultivating households leased in land. Microstudies in the early 2000s found much higher figures: between 27% and 62%of holdings included land that was leased in.[80] In other states, tenancy is kept informal and oral because of laws that give tenants occupancy rights after continuous residence for a specified period. A recent study in Assam found that 49% of cultivating households leased in land, but virtually all were oral contracts, often for less than three years. This is because three years of continuous occupation gives the tenant occupancy rights.[81] In a creative paper in 1991, S. D. Sawant was able to estimate the extent of concealed tenancy by comparing the area reported as leased out by landlords to the area reported as leased in by tenants. He interpreted the difference as concealed tenancy. By this metric, 37% of the leased area was concealed.[82] Again, the restrictions on transfer had undercut transparency.

As we write there is a push in policy circles to ease restrictions on leasing land. A recent paper has argued, using state-level data, that restrictions on land lease are not serving equity and are undermining productivity.[83] In 2016, the Niti Aayog, which recently replaced the Planning Commission as an advisory body to the Government of India, produced a model land-leasing bill. However, it has met with some skepticism. As of March 2019, only four states had adopted it fully or in part.[84]

As we have seen, land-reform legislation in India placed restrictions on converting land from agricultural to nonagricultural use. For instance, the Maharashtra Land Revenue Code of 1966 required the government's permission to use agricultural land for a nonagricultural purpose and indeed to alter the use from one nonagricultural purpose to another.[85] This rule and similar restrictions in other states were in the paternalistic spirit of protecting farmers from being duped by urban buyers. A recent newspaper article recommending repeal of these rules argued that the process of getting a certificate creates an opportunity for bribery. This is not a surprise, because land that has such a certificate sells at a considerable premium over land that does not.[86] The rules were eased in Maharashtra in 2017 and earlier in Gujarat, but they remain in place in many states.[87] As we revise this chapter for the last time (June 2020), the government of Karnataka has decided to allow nonagriculturists to buy agricultural land. It also plans to lift restrictions that prevented even agriculturists whose nonagricultural income exceeded Rs. 2.5 million from buying agricultural land. It also intends to raise the land ownership ceilings.[88]

Our discussion of land transfer would be incomplete without a mention of organized crime, involving the use of forgery and violence, to capture land. The "land mafia" is widespread in both rural and urban India. Mafias have the manpower and resources to bribe the appropriate officials to manipulate records as well as to forcibly take possession of the land or house. The Uttar Pradesh government recently opened an "anti-bhu [land] Mafia portal" at which citizens can lodge complaints.[89] In March 2019 it listed a member of parliament for allegedly having coerced twenty-six farmers to surrender their land for a university.[90]

Conclusion

Two intuitions drove land reforms in India. The first, that extreme inequality in landownership is both unjust and inimical to growth, is plausible even today. The second, ambivalence regarding transfers of land, both temporary (e.g., lease) and permanent (e.g., sale), was consistent with an economic model in which the state, rather than private market players, would drive economic growth. Now that the model has changed and growth has picked up, transferability has become more important. The policy circles have recognized this. However, there is still the fear that the poor will be cheated in land-market transactions. In 2013 the Government of India released for discussion a draft land-reform policy that attempted to address all three of the issues we have discussed in this chapter: equity, transparency, and transferability. The policy recommended steps to provide land to the landless and to women as well as to change laws that ban land lease or discourage it and to improve the quality of land records. However, the concern that Scheduled Tribes will be cheated in land transactions remained. The draft policy recommended that with a few exceptions, "any transfer of immovable property in a Scheduled Area by any person, whether or not such a person is a member of a Scheduled Tribe, shall be absolutely null and void."[91] The roots of this fear may be partly ideological, but they also come from the concern that the legal system, through which land is transferred, is corrupt and manipulated by the better off. Land law is liberalizing slowly and cautiously, though the trajectory is clear.

Did land reforms facilitate growth, as the reformers had hoped? This is a difficult question to answer because, while we can document legislation, implementation is difficult to measure reliably because of the various subterfuges we have discussed. Also, other policies affect growth as well, such as agricultural prices, the availability of irrigation, the costs of inputs, and the availability of credit. In pioneering work, Timothy Besley and Robin Burgess examined the effect of land-reform legislation, setting aside the extent of implementation, in sixteen major states over the period 1958–1992. They found that of the three types of reforms we have discussed, only tenancy reform affected agricultural income per capita or acre, but the effect was *negative*. Maitreesh Ghatak and Sanchari Roy revisited this evidence using output per acre for six major crops as their measure of productivity. They, too, found that land reforms reduced productivity, but they identified the primary culprit as land-ceiling legislation, which had led to fragmentation. The clearest evidence that tenancy reform promoted growth has come from West Bengal, where Banerjee, Gertler, and Ghatak used variation in the extent of implementation of Operation Barga across districts to identify its positive effect on rice yields.[92] However, even in this case, recent evidence suggests that for increasing the value of output per acre, government provision of seed and fertilizer mattered more than the protection of tenants.[93] In sum, based on the available statistical evidence, it is difficult to make the case that land reforms increased agricultural productivity.

Did land reforms reduce poverty and inequality? Besley and Burgess find that land reforms reduced the poverty gap by one percentage point, which is a modest amount for such a large endeavor.[94] The evidence regarding inequality is mixed; it depends on what metric we use. Besley and Burgess did not find any change in rural consumption inequality as a result of land reforms. However, the measure of inequality they use, the Gini coefficient, is an aggregate measure and can conceal considerable change.[95] We can get a more nuanced picture by looking at the fortunes of different social groups. It is clear from our earlier discussion that zamindari abolition did hurt the big landlord. The zamindars' stronger tenants gained by getting property rights, but their weaker tenants may have been evicted and therefore lost out. Ghatak and Roy find that if the state of West Bengal is excluded, tenancy reforms increased inequality in the size distribution of operated holdings but not owned holdings. This is consistent with Conning and Robinson's finding, which we discussed above, that tenancy reform led to the eviction of tenants. In a paper focusing on the four states in South India, Besley et al. found that tenancy reform increased access to land for middle-caste households but made Scheduled Caste and Scheduled Tribe households more dependent on agricultural labor.[96] Overall, land reforms seem to have dented the very top of the rural hierarchy and helped the rural middle class more than the poor. The empowerment of the rural middle class is now a central fact of Indian politics; this, more than any effect on productivity, is the enduring legacy of land reforms.

Early Indian policy makers believed that in addition to skewed land ownership, social inequality manifested itself in the market power of lenders and high borrowing costs for the poor, hurting growth and increasing poverty. The state had to intervene to break the monopoly power of lenders and make credit more accessible. This would go hand in hand with land reforms. This is the subject of our next chapter.

CHAPTER THREE

Rural Credit

Overreliance on Law

The two largest single factors depleting the peasant's income are the exploitation by the moneylender in his double capacity as the credit agency and the marketing agency of the village. — Indian National Congress, Agrarian Reforms Committee[1]

In England we consider the agricultural seasons a failure which do not give 80% of the normal crop. In parts of the Bombay Deccan, I calculated some years ago that, in 1918 there was only 9% of a normal crop, and in 1920 very little more. No normal banking system, as usually understood, can face such a situation. — Harold Mann[2]

Introduction

In the 1860s the American Civil War cut off supplies of cotton to Britain. There were huge profits to be made by growing cotton, and farmers in the Bombay Deccan, in western India, did precisely this. Lenders flocked to finance the costs of cultivation, and a bubble emerged. Borrowers took loans from multiple lenders. The bubble burst after the price of cotton fell. Lenders were no longer willing to provide credit to overleveraged borrowers. In response, Deccan peasants "rioted" in 1875, attacking moneylenders and seizing the documents which recorded their loans. The hypercautious British Raj, already alarmed by claims of large-scale default-related transfer of land from peasants to moneylenders, responded with the Deccan Agriculturists' Relief Act (DARA) of 1879. Its goal was to protect the borrower from unscrupulous lenders who needed strict supervision. Special courts were set up, and judges were given enormous discretion to go "behind the bond," that is, look for bad faith by the lender. The Deccan Agriculturalists' Relief Act also incorporated interest-rate ceilings and limited loan repayment to a maximum of twice the original principal, an Indian credit rule known as *damdupat*.[3]

The Deccan crisis represented the failure of the private moneylenders to provide protection against an aggregate shock, the fall in the price of cotton. That they failed should not have been surprising since they did not have deep pockets. But the Raj identified the problem as primarily one of lender malfeasance. Over the next seventy-five years, it passed a series of legislation to curb the private lender via usury laws, debt relief, and outright restrictions on land transfer following default. After independence, the Indian state took on the task of providing cheap rural credit and relief in the face of aggregate shocks. The policy has helped in poverty alleviation, but at a high cost, some of which is due to rent-seeking. The Indian state also doubled down on legislation to suppress the private lender. This has proved ineffectual. The regime could not eliminate the moneylender because only the moneylender has sufficiently good information to insure the rural poor against idiosyncratic shocks to earnings, that is, misfortunes that are specific to the farmer, or at least very local.

In the last three decades, the new kid on the block is microfinance. It comes in two incarnations in India, the state-subsidized (Self-Help-Group [SHG]) and the usually for-profit Microfinance Institution (MFI). The former has received good press, and there is credible research showing its benefits. The latter has been stigmatized via explicit comparison to the moneylenders. Former Reserve Bank of India governor Y. Venugopal Reddy has said regarding the MFI that "if it is for profit and there is aggressive lending, it's just moneylending." He points out that while moneylenders lend their own money, the MFIs often lend their members' deposits. The MFI is, therefore, just a "leveraged moneylender" and should be subject to the same type of regulation. The newspaper headline accompanying his remarks may have oversimplified his views: "For-Profit MFIs Worse Than Moneylenders."[4] Reddy's comments came in 2010 after the MFI industry went through a crisis remarkably similar to that of Bombay Deccan in the 1870s and ended with an even more draconian regulatory response. We seemed to have come full circle. Cooler heads have now prevailed, and MFI regulation is more sensible.[5] But the risk remains that the crises caused by low and variable incomes will again be overattributed to lender malfeasance and that counterproductive regulation will follow.[6]

We flesh out this argument in the remainder of this chapter. We first discuss the late colonial period and describe the legal and policy regime, which tried to suppress the private moneylender and, to a limited extent, encourage the emergence of credit cooperatives. The next section describes the first two decades after independence when private moneylenders faced even more legal restrictions and state-subsidized finance went mainly to the credit cooperatives, which suffered from rent-seeking. We then move on to the era of state-subsidized public-sector bank expansion, roughly 1975–1991. Bank expansion may have reduced rural poverty, but again, rent-seeking was common. We then discuss the period of India's economic liberalization, starting in 1991: policies have oscillated, with periods of rural banking decline, rural banking expansion, and the growth of microfinance. Throughout, our central argument is relevant. The core problem is that of low and uncertain incomes. In this environment, lenders must either be state-subsidized and exposed to rent-seeking or, to remain financially viable, charge high interest rates and adopt recovery practices that could seem to be cruel. Until insurance markets develop, we have to choose between two evils, and no regulation can change this. The law has only a modest role, to prevent fraud and coercion.

The Colonial Period

In early colonial India (1765–1857), legislation regarding land and credit had modest objectives. The state's overwhelming interest was in collecting land taxes. It did not particularly matter who paid them. The transfer of land from one social group to another, whether by sale or via default on debt, was welcome, especially if the new owner had more capital. However, after the Mutiny of 1857, there was a complete change of attitude, and laissez-faire was abandoned in relation to land and credit. The goal became to maintain social stability by protecting the traditional landowner from the moneylender. In the early twentieth century, when the Indian national movement mobilized against colonial rule, it embraced these attitudes. Independent India then inherited them. This section fleshes out this story.

Although land was transferable even in precolonial India, the early colonial regime clarified ownership titles so that lenders gained confidence in the value of land as collateral. The colonial state also played a much larger role in the enforcement of contracts than had previous regimes. A lender in precolonial times may have had to rely on his or her own devices or the village council to recover money from a debtor. Lending relied heavily on personal connections within a small geographical area. Now, under the British, the lender could approach a district court to recover money. Lenders could migrate to regions where the demand for credit was high, relying on the state to enforce contracts.

There were dramatic changes on the demand side as well. The East India Company wanted India to export agricultural produce—cotton, opium, indigo, tea. Improvements in transportation, especially the introduction of railways in the second half of the century, facilitated this. Exports required greater peasant involvement in the cash economy. A millet farmer who formerly consumed much of his crop might now grow cotton, sell it, and buy food. Since cotton was more resource intensive, the farmer now needed to borrow. Especially in the first half of the nineteenth century, land taxes, collected in cash, were high. This, too, forced the peasant to borrow. Also, compared to preceding regimes, the Raj was more ruthless and effective in collecting taxes. For all these reasons, the demand for credit increased. In relatively poor regions with uncertain rainfall and limited irrigation, the moneylender was often an "immigrant" from another part of British India.

The process we have described in the two preceding paragraphs is called "commercialization," and its effect on the fortunes of the peasantry has been the subject of considerable debate. Commercialization certainly led to an expansion of the area under cultivation, but it may have exposed the peasants to the vagaries of international prices. The combination of market exposure, weather fluctuation, and high land taxation, it is said, forced the peasant to borrow. Often the borrower was unable to repay and needed the lender's forbearance. The borrower typically received it, but when credit bubbles had occurred, with too many lenders and too much lending, or the borrower had otherwise become unviable, the moneylender would foreclose and seize land or refuse to lend any further. This could lead to violence against moneylenders. A prominent example is the Deccan Riots of 1875, which we mentioned in the introduction

For the British, these riots were a political problem. The Raj always consisted of a very small number of Europeans ruling over a subcontinent. They believed the peasantry to be the backbone of Indian society and saw agrarian unrest as threatening their rule. British officialdom also came to embrace an argument that is still highly influential. According to this view, Indian peasants are naive about financial and legal matters, especially in comparison to professional moneylenders. By facilitating borrowing against the land, the Raj had, as one official put it, conferred a "fatal boon" on the feckless Indian peasant.[7] This boon had to be taken back. How would this be done?

As we mentioned above, the British era had seen two innovations that made it easier to lend. One was the operation of a court system, which supported impersonal lending. The second was a clarification of land rights, making it easier to transfer them. In the Bombay Deccan, the Raj chose to alter the way in which courts enforced contracts via the Deccan Agriculturists' Relief Act of 1879, discussed in the introduction. As we mentioned above, two critical elements of this law were interest-rate ceilings and a ceiling on the total repayment, limiting it to twice the original principal. But if the borrower's income is low and variable, the borrower will often default. Interest-rate ceilings may then make lending unprofitable. Moreover, if the borrower eventually repays after a length of time, if the total repayment is limited to twice the principal, the lender's return will be low. DARA drove out the professional, often immigrant, lender who needed to resort to courts and forced the poor peasant to rely on the mercies of his richer neighbors. They had more "informal" ways of enforcing contracts. Thus, an act meant to protect peasants may have increased their vulnerability by making the credit market less competitive.[8]

DARA was by no means the most radical credit-related intervention by the Raj. Many British officials felt that this was too feeble a legislation. It left too many loopholes that the ingenious moneylender could exploit. For instance, the parties could disguise a loan as a repurchase agreement: X could "sell" his land to Y for Rs. 100 and "buy" it back for Rs. 120. The default on the loan would leave the land with the creditor-purchaser. British officials were especially worried about credit when it came to the dealings between moneylenders and tribal populations, which were geographically remote and culturally somewhat distinct from the mainstream of Hindu society. The tribal was considered no match for the far more sophisticated immigrant moneylender. As discussed in chapter 2, the policy adopted in this instance was to ban land transfer by tribals altogether or to limit the transfer to another member of the tribe. Punjab, a politically sensitive border region, enacted a similar policy. The British were particularly concerned about western

Punjab, where the lenders were Hindus and the borrowers were Muslims. There was potential for lender-borrower and Hindu-Muslim tensions to reinforce each other. The Raj passed the famous Punjab Land Alienation Act of 1900, which prohibited the transfer of land from "agricultural castes" to "nonagricultural castes." This was a highly complex piece of legislation, requiring, among other things, district-by-district definition of which castes were "agricultural" and which were not.

Historians have argued that the Punjab Land Alienation Act made life worse for the poor Punjabi peasant for reasons similar to those we have already discussed. The professional "nonagriculturist" moneylender could no longer rely on land as collateral. Now that the professional lender was weaker, poorer farmers depended on richer farmers for loans. The richer farmers were more interested in owning land and more likely to foreclose on mortgages.[9] The Punjab Land Alienation Act was also evaded in clever ways. The "nonagriculturist" who wanted to lend money to an "agriculturist" sought the help of an "agriculturist" friend who would be the ostensible creditor and who would seize the land if the debtor defaulted—a benami transaction. Thus, opacity and corruption were unintended consequences of an effort to protect the borrower.

By the 1930s there was another big player in the picture, the movement for Indian independence. Under M. K. Gandhi, the movement had drawn in the peasantry. After the Depression, when agrarian India went into crisis, farmers were unable to repay their debts. A slew of new legislation was passed, especially by provincial governments, which, following the Government of India Act of 1935, were run by Indians. One set, moneylenders' acts, were in the spirit of the Deccan Agriculturists' Relief Act mentioned above. They imposed interest-rate ceilings and required moneylenders to register, among other measures. The second set was more radical. Various provinces passed debt-relief acts, which required the peasant to repay the moneylender significantly less than was due. In Punjab, the Indian provincial government proposed legislation in 1938 simply extinguishing mortgage debt acquired before 1900 and also extending some of the provisions of the Punjab Land Alienation Act to agriculturist lenders as well. This led to a dramatic decline in mortgage lending, as figure 3.1 shows. To reveal the effect of the legislations on mortgage lending, the figure includes land sales, which did not decline.

Over time in Punjab and elsewhere, it was becoming increasingly difficult for the private lender to operate. Who would replace him? The

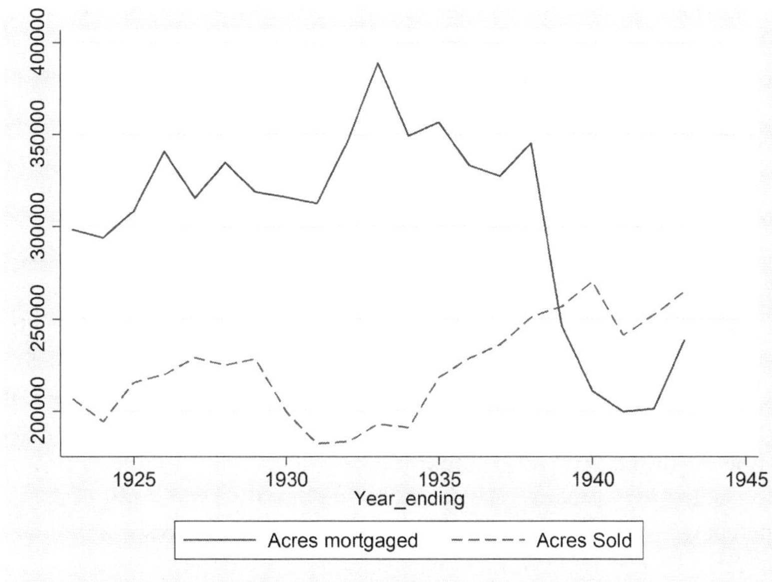

FIGURE 3.1. Mortgages and sales in Punjab (1925–1943)
Source: Authors' computations using Punjab, Board of Economic Inquiry, *Agricultural Statistics of British Punjab* (Lahore: Board of Economic Inquiry, n.d.).

cash-strapped Raj was not inclined to do much. It provided some modest agricultural credit via the Land Improvement Loans Act of 1883 and the Agriculturists Loans Act of 1884. The Raj was forced by terrible famines to be more proactive in the late nineteenth century. The commissions it set up to investigate the causes of these famines and potential solutions had to address the question of credit. It was natural for the commissions to look toward the European experience. Rural credit cooperatives had emerged in several European countries, especially Germany. The rationale for the credit cooperative provided by the Famine Commission of 1901 has a very contemporary flavor, resembling the rationale for microfinance and self-help groups.[10]

> The underlying idea of all Mutual Credit Associations, such as we recommend, is that a number of persons, by combining together, create a new and valuable security, which none of them previously possessed as individuals.... It is simpler for a creditor to deal with a group of fifty or a hundred associated cultivators than with the same number singly; it is simpler for him to obtain

> repayment from the group than from each of the members composing it; it is simpler for the group to make its own arrangements with each member than for the lender to try to do so.

The cooperative would also, in principle, allow members to insure each other against idiosyncratic risk by rescheduling payments or paying for each other. In 1904 the central government passed an act enabling the formation of rural cooperative credit societies. The model was the Raifeissen Society, named after its German inventor. Members would deposit savings as well as borrow. The key feature was unlimited liability, that is, each member was liable for all the debts of the society.

The credit cooperatives were a European transplant with no clear indigenous precedent. Their introduction was top down, with the state rather than the village community taking the lead. So while in principle the cooperative could be driven by the initiative and resources of its members; in fact, government officials played a crucial role. External involvement went hand in hand with another key aspect of the functioning of the cooperatives—they depended heavily on state resources rather than members' deposits.

Though the number of rural credit cooperatives grew rapidly in the colonial period, they did not function very well. The most obvious symptom of this was the high rate of default. Cooperatives worked well in some irrigated regions, but where agriculture was unproductive and risky, cooperatives floundered. Even though the Raj was sometimes willing to use extremely coercive methods to recover loans, after the Depression, many cooperative societies had large percentages of overdue loans (see table 3.1). Besides productivity, three other factors were also relevant. In stratified Indian villages with substantial caste divisions and

TABLE 3.1 **Overdues in Indian cooperatives (1939)**

Province	Amount of loan outstanding in rupees (lakhs)	Percentage of overdues to outstanding loans
Madras	351.99	46.1
Bombay	247.36	51.8
Bengal	396.39	87.4
Uttar Pradesh	75.91	47.7
Punjab	629.40	40.8
Bihar	104.18	92.5

Source: A. I. Qureshi, *The Future of the Cooperative Movement in India* (Madras: Oxford University Press, 1947), 58.

animosities, cooperation was difficult. Also, wealthier peasants, who had resources to offer, were reluctant to join because of unlimited liability.[11] A recent paper has highlighted regulatory problems, which allowed embezzlement and insider lending.[12] At the end of the colonial era, the consensus was that the cooperative movement had failed.

To sum up, the colonial period left four important legacies. The first was a highly negative attitude toward moneylenders and legislation to suppress them. The second was that debt-relief legislation was now part of the policy maker's tool kit. The third was that restrictions on land transfer were common. And the fourth was the existence of state-heavy cooperatives. Given the bad experience with cooperatives in the colonial period, we might have expected policy makers in independent India to be wary of them. In fact, as we explain below, they enthusiastically embraced credit cooperatives while attacking the private lender even more strongly.

Replacing the Moneylender with the Credit Cooperative (1950–1975)

The Indian central bank, the Reserve Bank of India (RBI), had been set up in 1935. After independence, it conducted the All India Rural Credit Survey, a large-scale and ambitious effort to collect evidence that would guide future policy. The committee produced a vast volume of documentation, and its report was hugely influential. The RBI concluded that there was no alternative to the credit cooperative—cooperation had failed because it had not received adequate state support. The cooperative was up against an array of powerful and interconnected forces. The moneylender, the trader, the landlord, and the lower levels of administration were in cahoots, often on the strength of caste-based relationships. A cooperative consisting of poor peasants could hardly compete with them. The RBI argued that "the forces of transformation have to be at least as powerful as those which are sought to be counteracted. Such forces can be generated not by cooperation alone but by cooperation in conjunction with the state."[13]

The paternalistic attitude of the report can be best understood by the analogy it used to explain why the state had to support the cooperative.

> One may consider an institution for the rehabilitation of crippled children struck down by the malady of infantile paralysis. The little patients are stud-

> ied, courses of treatment prescribed and carried out, muscles gradually strengthened and all efforts made to rehabilitate them and send them back to normal life. No one has yet suggested that those children should depend on themselves as much as possible and form themselves into a mutual association for individual rehabilitation.[14]

Given that credit cooperatives had performed poorly during the colonial period, what was the reason for optimism now? The Congress Agrarian Reforms Committee (1949) addressed this issue. The problem, it said, was that credit cooperatives in the colonial period were operating in an unequal and exploitative agrarian structure. This would no longer be the case because land reforms were ongoing: "We believe that reforms would never produce the desired results unless they are simultaneously introduced in sectors organically related to each other."[15]

Given state involvement and subsidized credit, the more powerful members of rural society tried to capture the cooperatives. A legal change facilitated this. The reader will recall that in British India, credit cooperatives had operated under unlimited liability, a factor that tended to keep out the rich farmer, who did not want to be saddled with the debts of his poorer neighbors. This practice began to be abandoned immediately after independence. In 1947–1948 an amendment of the Bombay Cooperative Societies Act (1925) made unlimited liability optional. The RBI made the same recommendation, and over time most Indian cooperatives operated under limited liability.

Between December 1958 and June 1959, Daniel Thorner, whom we have met before in chapter 2, visited 117 cooperatives spread across the country, asking officials to send him to the ones that were working the best. He writes, "In general, I found that the heads of cooperatives were the big people of the villages and that they had their fingers in many other pies as well as cooperatives."[16] The RBI had hoped that the state-supported cooperatives would take on the moneylenders and traders and landlords. In fact, they seem to have often captured the cooperatives. The politician had an outsized role. Punning on the initialism MLA, Thorner noted that in South India, cooperatives were suffering from "emmelaitis."[17]

The number of credit cooperatives and their membership expanded rapidly (see table 3.2), but the system worked poorly. Deposits continued to be a small fraction of loans. Profits on working capital were very low (table 3.3). We have argued that, because of poverty, risk, and rent-

TABLE 3.2 **All-India membership of primary agricultural credit cooperatives (1950–1969)**

Years	Number of primary agricultural credit cooperatives	Average membership	Percentage of rural population covered by active societies	Percentage of borrowing members to total members
1950–1951	115,462	16	—	—
1960–1961	212,129	34	24	53
1968–1969	167,760	57	33	38

Source: S. Ghatak, *Rural Money Markets in India* (Delhi: Macmillan, 1976), 113.

TABLE 3.3 **All-India performance of primary agricultural credit cooperatives (1950–1969)**

Years	Percentage of deposits to working capital	Percentage of overdues to outstanding	Percentage of profit to working capital
1950–1951	12.4	22.1	2.1
1960–1961	5.3	20.3	1.6
1968–1969	7.0	34.6	1.2

Source: S. Ghatak, *Rural Money Markets in India* (Delhi: Macmillan, 1976), 42.

seeking, default rates were high. Table 3.3 confirms this. Careful village-level investigations came to the same conclusions. Perhaps the most reputed studies conducted in the 1970s and 1980s were by ICRISAT (International Crop Research Institute for the Semi-Arid Tropics), whose investigators resided in the village itself and hence had good information. ICRISAT found that there was a "culture" of nonrepayment of loans from cooperatives.[18] By 1971 official agencies ("Institutional Finance") provided only 29% of total credit. Cooperatives provided the bulk of this—20% of all rural credit (table 3.4).

It was not easy for a cooperative (for credit or another purpose) to shake off the state and operate independently. This was put to the legal test in *Daman Singh and Others v. the State of Punjab, 1985*. The petitioners had challenged the state's decision to amalgamate cooperatives, supposedly to make them more effective. They argued that the Indian Constitution guaranteed the right to form associations. This right was violated if the state could merge this association with another one that the citizen had not chosen to join. However, the Supreme Court relied on a provision in Article 31 of the Constitution, according to which amalgamation of two "corporations" in the "public interest" could not be challenged on the grounds that it violated a fundamental right. The court ruled that a cooperative is a corporation, and the petition was dismissed.

Given this, there was clearly a case for new legislation to allow the formation of cooperatives that were more independent of the government. The Brahm Prakash committee proposed a model legislation in 1991. Andhra Pradesh and a few other states passed legislation along these lines. Still, the 2009 High-Powered Committee on Cooperatives recommended the extraordinary step of a constitutional amendment to liberate the cooperative from the state. Article 19, which guarantees various freedoms, would be amended. It would now specifically mention the right to "form and run Cooperatives based on principles of voluntary, democratic member control, member economic participation, and autonomous functioning."[19] The president approved the 97th amendment to the Indian Constitution in January 2012. It is a measure of the state-heavy nature of Indian cooperatives that it required a constitutional amendment to try to change it.

The jury is still out regarding the effect of these legal changes allowing the formation of more independent cooperatives. Credit cooperatives have also received fresh infusions of funds to address debt overhang following the recommendations of the Vaidyanathan Committee (2004). Still, the level of nonperforming assets remains high. In 2011–2012 they were 26.8% for short-term loans by village-level cooperative societies and 36.7% for long-term loans.[20] The problem of the capture of credit cooperatives by politicians and other elites, which Daniel Thorner described in the late 1950s, persists. B. Subrahmanyam, managing director of the National Federation of State Cooperative Banks, recently told the *Economic Times* that cooperative banks are still important to small and marginal farmers despite the "the pernicious influence of politicians."[21]

Meanwhile, what of the professional moneylender?

The Moneylenders

The Government of India succeeded in sidelining the professional moneylenders to some extent. The proportion of credit coming from them fell from 45% to 14% between 1951 and 1971 (table 3.4), though these figures have to be taken with a large grain of salt. In a compelling critique, Clive Bell has pointed out that, taken at face value, the RBI's

TABLE 3.4 **Percentages of main sources of rural credit (1951–2013)**

Source of credit	1951	1961	1971	1981	1991	2002	2013
Cooperative societies/banks, etc.	3.1	9.1	20.1	28.6	18.6	27.3	24.8
Commercial banks, including regional rural banks	0.8	0.4	2.2	28	29	24.5	25.1
All moneylenders							
Professional moneylenders	44.8	14.9	13.8	8.3	9.4	19.6	–
Agricultural moneylenders (rich farmers)	24.9	45.9	23.1	8.6	6.3	10.0	–
Total	69.7	60.8	36.9	16.9	15.7	29.6	33.2

Note: The percentages don't add up to one hundred because we have excluded minor sources. The first six columns are taken from N. C. Pradhan, "Persistence of Informal Credit in Rural India: Evidence from All India Debt and Investment Survey and Beyond" (RBI Working Paper Series, 2013), table 1, p. 6. The last column is from A. Hoda and P. Terway, "Credit Policy for Agriculture in India: An Evaluation" (Indian Council for Research on International Economic Relations Working Paper 302, June 2015), table 1(a), p. 6.

figures for the total volume of debt imply implausible levels of credit contraction that are inconsistent with careful local studies.[22] It is likely that after the passing of antimoneylender legislation, much of moneylending simply went underground.

Various Indian states either retained moneylender legislation from the colonial period or passed fresh legislation to protect borrowers from exploitation.[23] The moneylender was required to obtain a license and maintain accounts in a specific format, was prevented from harassing the borrower, and was limited to a maximum rate of interest. Some states (such as Rajasthan, Tamil Nadu, Bombay, and Karnataka) applied the rule of *damdupat* (described earlier) according to which the court could not award the lender a sum that exceeded the outstanding principal. Courts had wide discretion to reopen and examine a transaction to assess its fairness. The gazetteer of Poona (1954) reported that the Bombay Moneylenders' Act of 1947 was unpopular with moneylenders. Many refused to acquire licenses.

> It is likely therefore that a large number of them have either given up their business or have been doing it illegally. In these circumstances, those to whom moneylenders were an important source of credit now experienced difficulty in obtaining it. In the rural areas there has recently been a marked increase in the number of applications for *tagai* [government] loans which seems to be, at least in part, a result of the contraction of the business of moneylenders.[24]

The fragmentary statistics available are consistent with this impression. For instance, the number of licensed moneylenders in Kolhapur district fell from over eight thousand in 1949–1950 to less than three thousand in 1955–1956.[25]

Various states also passed debt-relief legislation similar to those of the late colonial period. These legislations allowed agricultural borrowers to repay moneylenders less than the amount contracted. For instance, the Mysore Agricultural Debtors Relief Act of 1966 allowed a 40% reduction of debts incurred before January 1, 1941, and a 30% reduction for debts incurred between January 1, 1941, and January 1, 1950. Other legislations included the Gujarat Agricultural Debtors Relief Act of 1972, the Punjab Agricultural Debtors (Relief) Act, 1975, the Andhra Pradesh Agricultural Indebtedness (Relief) Act, 1977, and a slew of similar regulations in other states.[26] Debt relief for farmers continues to be policy relevant in the present day.

The moneylender was viewed not just as an ordinary businessman but as fundamentally antisocial. This perception was made explicit in *Fatehchand Himmatlal and Others v. the State of Maharashtra* in 1977. This case is worth discussing at some length because of the frankness with which a Supreme Court judge explains and justifies his animosity toward the moneylender. The Maharashtra Debt Relief Act of 1975 reduced or liquidated debts to private moneylenders but not debts to the government, banks, or banking companies. The act faced a challenge on the ground that it violated the right to trade. The counsel for the plaintiffs asked, "How is it fair that, if the object of the legislation is to save the victims of rural indebtedness and working-class burdens, that credit institutions should be exempted while noninstitutionalized lenders should be picked out for hostile treatment?" Rejecting the challenge, Justice Krishna Iyer noted that article 301 of the Indian Constitution, which referred to "freedom of trade," also permitted restrictions in "public interest." He wrote,

> There is no merit in the plea. Liabilities due to Government or local authorities are not tainted with the exploitation of the debtor. Likewise, debts due to banking companies do not ordinarily suffer from overreaching, unscrupulousness or harsh treatment.

Clearly, Justice Iyer believed that moneylenders were "ordinarily" unscrupulous. He went on to argue that "some stray moneylenders may be good souls," but the legislature could not make "meticulous exceptions."

It is, of course, true that moneylenders can be bad actors, but if interest-rate ceilings, *damdupat*, and debt relief make legal lending unviable, law-abiding lenders will abandon the profession and only the unscrupulous will remain. The RBI itself noted in 2007 that "the existing ceilings prescribed under the [moneylending] legislations are out of sync with market reality."[27] It recommended that instead of specifying a specific maximum for the interest rate, the law should allow the state government to adjust the maximum according to market conditions. Still, an article in a leading newspaper reported in 2015 that in two districts in Karnataka, moneylenders were being arrested for, among other things, charging interest rates above the legal maximum of 14% for secured loans and 16% for unsecured loans.[28] This is remarkable because until 2014, the RBI's ceiling for interest rates charged by MFIs was 26% (see note 49). Even the not-for-profit Grameen Bank has charged interest rates that amount to 24% per annum.[29] Indeed, the credit cards in the authors' wallets, which potentially provide unsecured loans, have often charged more than 16% per annum, even in the low inflation environment in the United States and the United Kingdom.

There is a stark difference in the treatment of the moneylender and the MFI. In Andhra Pradesh, moneylenders were allowed to charge only 2% points more than the commercial banks.[30] A similar rule applied in Kerala.[31] When the RBI changed MFI interest-rate ceilings in 2014, they were linked to commercial banks as well. But the MFIs were allowed either 2.75 times the base lending rate of the commercial banks or a margin of 10% above costs, whichever was lower (see note 49). It is difficult to understand why moneylenders were treated so much more strictly. There is loan sharking, no doubt, but legislation should not be so strict as to make legal moneylending unprofitable. It is worth noting (table 3.4) that moneylenders (professionals as well as rich farmers) currently provide one-third of rural credit.

The Expansion of Rural Banking (1975–1991)

By the end of the 1960s, given the checkered history of rural credit cooperatives, it was inevitable that the government would look for other alternatives. Indeed, as we have mentioned above, many of the problems faced by cooperatives had been identified during the colonial period itself. Commentators like Anwar Qureshi had suggested that only entities with deep pockets, such as government-supported banks, could effectively operate in India's precarious rural areas.[32] Beginning in the late 1960s, the bank, rather than the cooperative, began to be viewed as the spearhead of rural credit provision. This was part of a broader shift in economic policy.

In 1969 Prime Minister Indira Gandhi came to power and began to govern with an agenda that came to be called *garibi hatao*, or abolish poverty. The state would now intervene in markets even more aggressively than before. One of Indira Gandhi's first steps was to nationalize the fourteen major commercial banks in 1969. Another six were nationalized in 1980. From 1976 onward, a new set of Regional Rural Banks (RRB) opened to serve the rural poor. Banks were given rules for expansion. The focus was to be on opening branches in rural areas or "unbanked" areas more generally. Figure 3.2 shows the expansion of rural branches of commercial banks. Banks also faced targets for how to lend. The government identified "priority" sectors that were to receive specified fractions of bank lending. As table 3.4 shows, the proportion of ru-

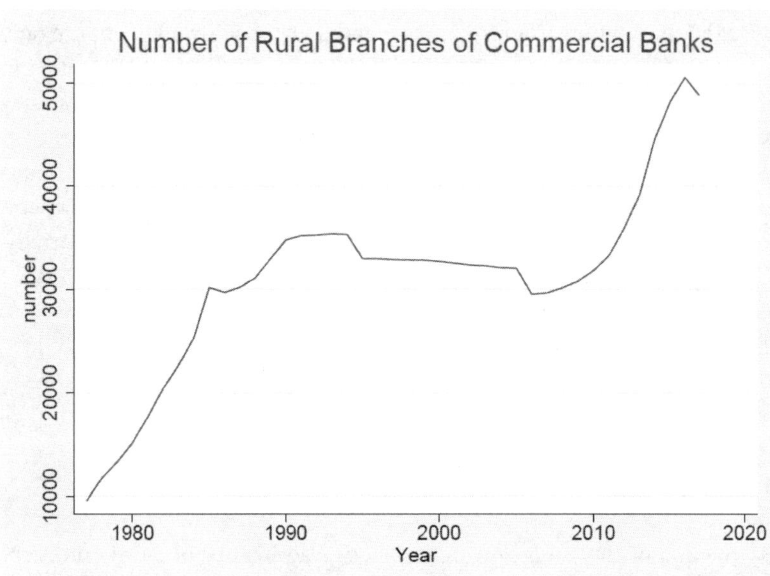

FIGURE 3.2. NUMBER OF RURAL BRANCHES OF COMMERCIAL BANKS
Source: Authors' computation using Reserve Bank of India, "Table 67: Population Group-Wise Number of Branches of Scheduled Commercial Banks," September 15, 2017, https://www.rbi.org.in/scripts/PublicationsView.aspx?id=17842.

TABLE 3.5 **Access to formal and informal credit by landownership in Western Orissa (1981)**

Farm size group	Formal only	Informal only	Both	Not borrowing	Total
Landless laborers	4.2	75.71	2.85	17.14	100
Marginal farmers	4.31	56.03	16.37	23.27	100
Small farmers	32.81	29.68	18.75	18.75	100
Medium farmers	42.5	10	27.5	20	100
Large farmers	60	13.34	10	16.66	100

Source: K. Sarap, "Transactions in Rural Credit Markets in Western Orissa, India," *Journal of Peasant Studies* 15, no. 1 (1987), table 1, p. 86. Cells contain percentages that add up to 100 across the row.

ral credit provided by banks increased from 2% to 28% between 1971 and 1981.

We will discuss four outcomes of the banking expansion. Did government-subsidized credit reach the poor, or was it captured by the better off? Was it effective in reducing poverty? Were banks able to recover their loans? We have highlighted the risk in Indian agriculture: Did government-owned banks also perform an insurance function?

There is significant evidence that though the poor did receive subsidized credit, the better off captured a disproportionate share. This was demonstrated by numerous case studies as well as by careful statistical research.[33] See, for instance, table 3.5. There is also convincing statistical evidence that loans were distributed to influence elections.[34]

Legal and institutional factors were also in play. Banks usually require collateral. The land is the most important asset in rural India, but its distribution is highly unequal despite the huge body of land-reform legislation (chap. 2). This skewed the allocation of credit. Also, as we have mentioned in chapter 2, it is not always easy to establish rights to a piece of land, which increases transaction costs for the lender.

Even those who do not own land often access it as tenants. Surely their crops could have been considered collateral? Tenancy legislation got in the way. As we have seen, some states banned tenancy. Others gave tenants occupancy rights if they could prove residence for a specified length of time. Tenancy went underground, with only oral contracts, to evade such legislation. This made it difficult for a tenant to prove his or her status and thereby obtain a loan against crops.[35]

The influence of bank expansion on rural poverty has been the subject of some controversy because careful pieces of statistical research have come to quite different conclusions. In general, it is difficult to isolate the benefit of major policy changes, like the bank expansion, because they are usually only one piece of a broader package. Also, banks tend to locate in fast-growing areas where they are more likely to be profitable. So, it is difficult to establish causality—is growth occurring because of the banks, or are banks popping up because of growth? In a seminal paper, Robin Burgess and Rohini Pande treated the change in *trend* created by the government's policy of greater expansion in unbanked areas as effectively random.[36] They found, using state-level data, that bank expansion had significantly reduced rural poverty and increased wages.

Anjini Kochar revisited this issue using household-level data from Uttar Pradesh only.[37] Rather than rely on the broad policy discussed above, Kochar looked at the actual rules for implementation of the policy at the level of the district. The government had set up thresholds in terms of the number of persons per bank. Districts that exceeded these thresholds would receive priority in branch expansion. Kochar exploited the discontinuity—areas above the threshold would be favored over areas below it—to isolate bank expansion that could be considered as good as random. She found that rural bank expansion had mainly benefited the better-off sections of rural society in Uttar Pradesh rather than the poor. Moreover, the "directed lending" toward the poor had done little good. The difference in the findings of Burgess and Pande on the one hand and Kochar on the other remain to be clarified.

Ayyagari, Beck, and Hoseini build on Burgess and Pande's work to provide a third perspective on the relationship between bank credit and rural poverty.[38] Indian civil courts are notoriously tardy, and it is rarely worthwhile for a lender to go to them for loan recovery. Recognizing this, in 1993, the Government of India allowed states to set Debt Recovery Tribunals (DRTs) to speed up the process. The loan size had to be large, more than Rs. 1 million (US$20,000 then). The tribunals were set up in different states at different times in no particular order. Therefore, Sujata Visaria could estimate their effect on loan repayment using a difference-in-difference approach.[39] She found that the DRTs substantially reduced delinquency. Drawing on this work, Ayyagari, Beck, and Hosseini use the staggered introduction of the DRTs to predict variation in the total amount of credit disbursed by banks. Using state-level data over the period 1983–2005, they found that the volume of bank credit as a fraction of state GDP ("financial deepening") was important for reducing poverty, more so than the number of banks per capita ("financial outreach").

The DRTs only apply to very large loans, and default continues to be a huge problem. How big depends on how we measure. One standard

TABLE 3.6 **Overdues of various credit institutions as a percentage of demand (1975–1986)**

Agency	1975–1976	1980–1981	1985–1986
Commercial banks	48	47	43
Regional rural ranks	NA	48	51
Short-term cooperative lending	34	43	41
Land mortgage-backed long-term cooperative lending	34	46	39

Source: Adapted from Reserve Bank of India, *A Review of the Agricultural Credit System in India: Report of Agricultural Credit Review Committee* (Bombay: Reserve Bank of India, 1990), 538.

TABLE 3.7 **Age and institution breakdown of agricultural sector overdues (%)**

Age of loan overdue (years)	Commercial bank	Regional rural bank	Short-term cooperative lending	Mortgage-backed cooperative lending
1	11.5	13.1	16.7	16.2
1–4	57.9	65.7	50.4	33.9
4–7	15.5	15.5	20.8	32.8
>7	15.1	5.7	12.1	17.1
Total	100	100	100	100

Source: Adapted from Reserve Bank of India, *A Review of the Agricultural Credit System in India: Report of Agricultural Credit Review Committee* (Bombay: Reserve Bank of India, 1990), 596.

approach has been to look at overdues in relation to "demand," that is, the fraction of currently due payments. By this measure, as table 3.6 shows, public-sector finance, whether a bank or cooperative, performed calamitously. A different approach, taken by the Khusro Committee (Agricultural Credit Review Committee, 1990) was to recognize that much of the money was eventually repaid, as shown in table 3.7. The committee assumed that 1% of all debts overdue less than three years would never be repaid, as would 15% of loans overdue between three and five years and 70% of those exceeding five years. Using this approach, it estimated that of the total loans outstanding, the percentage of bad debts was 4.3%, 4.1%, 8.1%, and 3.3% for the Commercial Banks, the RRBs, short-term cooperative credit, and land-mortgage-backed long-term cooperative credit (provided by Land Development Banks), respectively.

The Land Development Banks should have had high loan recovery rates because the value of the collateral is much larger than the loan amount. However, recovery rates have been low in part because it is difficult to foreclose. Landowners are members of rural communities and have been able to dissuade potential buyers from participating in auctions. The manipulation of land auctions in such circumstances is a phenomenon that goes back a long way in India and elsewhere.[40]

To what extent was bank credit also de facto insurance? The Khusro committee (1990) pointed out that for the first time, public-sector banks were explicitly differentiating between "willful defaulters" ("socially and politically important people") and "nonwillful defaulters" and treating them differently. When natural calamities that reduced output in a certain region by 50% or more occurred, defaulting borrowers were permitted to borrow afresh despite not having repaid. Similar accommodation was provided to small and marginal farmers who were in default to a small extent.[41] Policies to provide accommodation to borrowers who have faced natural calamities have been reiterated recently. They reflect banks explicitly playing the credit-cum-insurance function we have mentioned earlier when it comes to large observable aggregate shocks.[42]

A more controversial and repeatedly adopted policy is an unconditional debt waiver. Here the borrower does not repay, and the government compensates the bank. This is a form of ex post insurance and may be the humane thing to do in the short run, when agriculture is in crisis in a region as a whole. But the evidence suggests that debt waivers are not good policy in part because they undermine the incentive to repay loans. The largest of these debt waivers occurred in 2008, providing relief for more than 40 million households and costing 1% of GDP. Xavier Gine and Martin Kanz find that the debt waiver led to higher subsequent defaults by nonbeneficiaries because, they argue, of the anticipation that debts would be forgiven again. Debt waivers had no positive effect on productivity, wages, or consumption expenditure.[43] They are still, apparently, good politics: in December 2018, a newspaper article declared that, with state elections in the offing, it was "raining loan waivers."[44]

Overall, the bank expansion probably modestly alleviated poverty and provided some de facto insurance at the cost of high default rates. As the Indian economy became more market friendly after 1991, policies changed.

Liberalization and the Rise of Microfinance (1991 Onward)

After 1991 the pace of rural bank expansion slowed down (see fig. 3.2). Over the next decade, the share of rural credit provided by commercial and regional rural banks fell from 29% to 24.5% (table 3.4). The policy has gone back and forth, with a renewed effort to double institutional lending between 2004 and 2006. Still, rural borrowers returned to moneylenders—33% of borrowing was from moneylenders as of 2013 (table 3.4). A new type of financial institution to help the poor has emerged—microfinance. Microfinance has usually been justified as facilitating small-scale nonfarm entrepreneurship. However, since money is fungible, it can also be used to finance consumption.

Microfinance in India began in the late 1980s with the self-help group (SHG) consisting of 10 to 15 women. The SHG is not for profit, often linked to a bank, and receives a subsidy from the government. Membership is growing rapidly, from 9.23 million borrowers in 2003 to 57.85 million in 2013.[45] The SHGs are generally believed to have benefited the poor in terms of conventional economic measures such as consumption and also empowerment more broadly.[46] Several features seem to have contributed to their success. These include solidarity among group members, the combination of savings with credit, and the fact that members of the SHG also cooperate in other dimensions of economic life. However, there are signs that interventions by other government departments undermine this cohesion, and default rates are increasing.[47]

Classic microfinance, with small groups and shared liability along the lines of the famous Grameen Bank of Bangladesh, came to India somewhat later than the SHGs but is now growing rapidly, from 10 million clients in 2006–2007 to 27.5 million in 2012–2013.[48] An important point to note is that Indian MFIs, unlike the Grameen Bank, are usually for profit. The for-profit MFI has been far more controversial than the SHG. Interest rates are often high. As noted, until recently, the RBI permitted annual interest up to 26% per annum.[49] MFIs have also been criticized for using harsh methods in loan recovery.[50] Mihir Shah and coauthors write, "We suggest that while the Microfinance Institution (MFI) model is unsustainable and may actually end up worsening conditions for the poor, the Self-Help Group-Bank Linkage approach has the potential to make a decisive impact on security and empowerment of the most disadvantaged."[51]

In 2010 the microfinance industry received a severe shock in Andhra Pradesh, the Indian state where it was most prominent. The crisis, as well as the regulatory response, are reminiscent of the Bombay Deccan story of the 1870s. The Andhra MFIs had high rates of loan recovery, typical of MFIs in the subcontinent. And they were so profitable that they had attracted foreign capital. The number of lenders multiplied.

Poor urban neighborhoods were being "carpet-bombed" with loans.[52] Borrowers were able to take multiple loans, taking from one lender to repay another. A credit bubble emerged. The bubble burst when some lenders were accused of strong-arm tactics to recover loans and borrowers allegedly committed suicide as a consequence. Local religious leaders began to advocate default, and borrowers complied in large numbers. The Andhra Pradesh government then intervened to regulate the MFIs.

The regulations were draconian. The Andhra Microfinance Act's brief statement of objectives highlighted the need to prevent lenders from using "inhuman coercive measures." Coercion was defined broadly. For instance, it included "any act calculated to annoy or intimidate." The managers and employees of the MFI were liable for three years imprisonment for any coercion. MFIs were forbidden from asking for collateral. The microfinance bill also contained the *damdupat* provision we have seen earlier in DARA (1879): No borrower needed to pay a total amount of interest that exceeded the principal. If the borrower had already done that, the loan was extinguished and the lender was required to repay the excess. Finally, "Fast Track Courts" would be set up to adjudicate disputes.

As repayment rates plummeted, the MFI industry in Andhra was severely affected. Worried that the baby was being thrown out with the bathwater, nine prominent economists felt compelled to write a newspaper article titled "Microcredit Is Not the Enemy."[53] "The new law," they pointed out, "clearly signals that borrowers need not repay their short-term loans." Eventually, the RBI stepped in, better regulation was passed, and the MFI industry is back on track, but MFIs remain controversial.

The effect of microfinance seems to vary by context and by type of borrower in India and across the world. In recent years the randomized controlled trial (RCT) has become the preferred method of analysis. Using this approach, Abhijit Banerjee and coauthors found very modest average benefits when a prominent microfinance lender in Hyderabad, in Andhra Pradesh, expanded its area of operation in informal settlements.[54] However, microfinance was already abundant in Hyderabad. Also, both treatment and control groups were in areas where the MFI lender did not have strong feelings regarding whether or not it opened a branch and thus may not have been representative of the city as a whole. MFIs come across as more useful in the work of Emily Breza and Cynthia Kinnan, who ingeniously use the research opportunity provided by the microfinance crisis in Andhra Pradesh to look at its influence on *other* states. The crisis reduced the aggregate gross loan portfolio of microfinance lenders by 20%, or US$1 billion between 2010 and 2011. They then had to lend less even outside Andhra Pradesh. The resulting decline in the availability of loans reduced consumer spending, investment, and entrepreneurship. Rural wages fell 5%–9%, hurting the bottom fifth of the income distribution.[55]

We began this chapter by pointing out that the for-profit moneylender has historically been perceived as cruel in India. Public-sector banks have been more humane but have needed subsidies and are subject to rent-seeking. We have now seen the same contrast emerge in microfinance, perhaps to a smaller extent—the for-profit MFI appears as exploitative and the subsidized SHG less so. Narasimhan Srinivasan, former chief general manager of the National Bank for Agriculture and Rural Development (NABARD), draws the obvious conclusion:

> The government seems to be making the playing field uneven by subsidizing the operations and cost of funds of one stream of microfinance, that is, SHGs. With customers being common for MFIs and SHGs any reduction in cost of credit should be applied at the customer level and not to the intermediary institution.[56]

The distinction between banks and MFIs is now beginning to blur. For instance, Bandhan, a major MFI operating in West Bengal, has now been given a license to open a private bank. Banks and MFIs are now competing for the same borrowers and are using similar methods for loan recovery. This has probably contributed to the most visible symbol of agrarian distress in India over the past two decades: the high incidence of farmers' suicides. We conclude this chapter with a brief discussion of this issue.

Conclusion

High input costs, low prices, and shocks to productivity have forced farmers into debt. Some have committed suicide after being unable to repay. To whom are these farmers indebted? For the year 2015 the National Crime Records Bureau reported, "Among 3,097 suicides committed by farmers/cultivators due to 'Bankruptcy or Indebtedness',

2,474 farmers/cultivator have taken loan from 'Financial Institutions like Bank/Registered Micro Financial Institutions' [80%] and 302 of them [10%] have taken loan from 'Money Lenders.'" The remainder had taken loans from both moneylenders and formal financial institutions.[57] Abhijit Sen, a former member of the Planning Commission, noted, "The latest data is interesting because all of us thought that moneylenders were the culprits of the piece. Even today, more than half the people take loans from moneylenders." How does he explain the low proportion of moneylender-borrowing-related suicides? "The organized sector is less flexible because rules don't permit them flexibility. The microfinance sector is worse. . . . Many also send goons to the neighbourhood to scare borrowers."[58] The cause-of-suicide figures need to be taken with a large grain of salt, since the police, who record the information, have no particular expertise in this matter. The farmer's family may also be uneasy about blaming the moneylender, who might be in the village and whose help might be needed again.[59] Still, these figures do shed doubt on a traditional narrative that identifies the moneylender as uniquely malevolent. The fundamental problem is that of low and variable incomes in the face of which loan recovery by lenders (institutional or not) who face bottom-line pressures can be harsh. Humane lending can only be state-subsidized lending, which tolerates delayed repayment and sometimes default, with the attendant risks of rent-seeking. The rural credit sector has to tolerate one of these two evils. There is no case for singling out the private noninstitutional lender for especially punitive regulation.

There is surely a role for the legal system, which should not allow lenders to use fraudulent methods to induce borrowing or apply coercion in loan recovery. It also needs to address cases like one that was the subject of recent litigation in which a lender was alleged to be charging more than 10% per month.[60] We can also hope that the Government of India's recently announced high-profile crop insurance scheme (Pradhan Mantri Fasal Bima Yojana, PMFBY) will defeat the conventional wisdom on the challenges of crop insurance, and succeed.[61] In this happy event, the level of default, and therefore controversy regarding methods for loan recovery, may die down, and India might get closer to a "normal banking system," as Harold Mann put it.[62] As of now (July 2020), the jury is still out on the PMFBY, with farmers complaining about breach of contract and some private insurers finding the business unprofitable and leaving the market.[63]

Our argument, that in relation to rural credit the law is trying to do too much, is strengthened by a recent Supreme Court judgment, whose implications have yet to play out. As we have seen, state governments have passed various laws to provide ex post debt relief to farmers who had borrowed from moneylenders. The farmer can be required to pay less than he owed contractually, and the lender takes a "haircut." Also, under the Usurious Loans Act of 1918, a court can rule that the payment received by the lender will be less than the amount contractually owed if the court thinks it is excessive. However, the Banking Regulation Act of 1949 (Section 21A) protects banks from these legislations: "Notwithstanding anything contained in the Usurious Loans Act 1918, or any other law on indebtedness in any state, a transaction between a banking company and its debtor shall not be reopened by any court on the ground that the rate of interest charged by the banking company in respect of such transaction is excessive." In *Jayant Kumar and Others v. Union of India and Others*, the Supreme Court ruled in February 2018 that section 21A would not apply to banks so long as the debt-relief legislation passed by the state specifically mentioned debt to banks. In other words, legislation that reduced the amount courts would award a moneylender could now apply to a bank as well. This may reduce the banks' willingness to lend to rural borrowers.

We have argued in this chapter that India's problems with rural credit arise from rural incomes being low and variable.[64] Many observers argue that the underlying problem is not merely in agriculture itself but also in the fact that India has industrialized very slowly. Employment in manufacturing has stagnated, and there are too many people in agriculture. What accounts for slow industrialization? One common explanation is that it is difficult to acquire land, whether to build a factory, an electricity plant, a road, or to open a mine. The structure of the economy has to change, and land has to be repurposed, but this process is costly and slow. In the next chapter, we note that unlike (say) eighteenth-century England, industrialization in India is occurring in a robust democracy. If land has to change hands, this has to be negotiated rather than done by government fiat. The use of eminent domain has become highly controversial, and the relevant legislation is being vigorously debated and challenged.

CHAPTER FOUR

Democratic Rights and the Limits of Eminent Domain

The accident of a village being situated close to a forest does not prejudice the right of the country as a whole to receive the benefits of a national asset. — National Forest Policy[1]

In India, political democracy has come first. The only course possible for India as a democratic government is to see that the benefits of industrialization as it progresses, are shared with the many. — India, Planning Commission[2]

Don't create an environment in this country where two words, infrastructure and industrialization, become bad words. — Finance Minister Arun Jaitley in Parliament, 2015[3]

Introduction

Structural change is at the heart of the model of development broadly accepted in India and elsewhere. We expect that the share of the labor force and output in agriculture, or the "traditional" sector more generally, will fall over time, and the share of "modern" manufacturing and services will grow. During this process, the modern sector will draw on the resources of the traditional sector. Agricultural land will convert to industrial use. Forests will provide timber for use in the construction of houses or furniture. Land currently used for agriculture and forests may have to be mined. The construction of a dam may flood a village. All this requires reallocation of property rights. In principle, the state can engineer this reallocation using its power of eminent domain. What should be the scope of this power? And how effective are the laws about eminent domain in India? We discuss these questions in this chapter in three contexts: (1) land is privately owned with title, (2) land is owned without title but the owner has customary rights, and (3) a community has customary (undocumented) rights of ownership or use of land or forest.

If a farmer has title to a piece of land, the reallocation to another use can be achieved through the market. Either the state or a private buyer can pay the owner enough to buy the land. The problem, however, is that projects often require the land of many owners, any one of whom can refuse to sell or demand an exorbitant price, making the project impossible. A single person may stop a railroad. The state has to have the right to compel a sale. When and on what terms should the state be allowed to exercise this right?

The situation is more complicated when the traditional user's right is not documented. For instance, a tribal may have been cultivating a small patch of land in a forest for decades but does not have title to that land. Or the residents of a village may for generations have had access to a forest from which they get wood, medicinal plants, and other products, but this right is not documented. The forest is now attractive to a company that makes furniture or paper. If the government leases the forest to this company, it may limit or eliminate the villagers' customary rights. In this instance, it is difficult to use the market mechanism to reallocate rights because there is no well-defined legal right to be sold. When, and on what terms, should the state intervene to transfer rights from customary users to a private company or to itself?

A related issue, of considerable importance in India, has to do with the treatment of historically disadvantaged populations, such as Scheduled Tribes. Their land rights are often undocumented, and they are disproportionately located in forested or mineral-rich areas. According to the Indian Constitution, areas where Scheduled Tribes are numerous (listed in Schedules V and VI) can be governed differently from the rest of the country. Should eminent domain laws be formulated differently for these Scheduled Areas?[4]

We can now summarize the argument of this chapter. The colonial state strongly asserted its rights over land that was not demonstrably privately owned. Even when it was, the government could exercise eminent domain rights via legislation passed in 1894, which we describe below. This state of affairs lasted through the first few decades of independent India. However, as democracy deepened in India, local communities vigorously claimed rights to their land and opposed the acquisition of land for state projects or use by private companies. The devolution of power from the center to the regions also made it necessary to address local concerns to win local elections. Historic new legislation was then passed. However, in an atmosphere marked by conflict and mistrust, the pendulum has swung too far in the other direction, stalling numerous development projects. India has yet to find the right balance between empowering the state to acquire land in the interest of the economy as a whole and respecting the land rights of individuals and communities. We flesh out this argument in the remainder of this introduction.

The British Raj did not face constraints in its exercise of eminent domain, limited only by some protests by dispossessed tribal and peasant populations.[5] For instance, the huge railroad network built by the Raj required extensive acquisition of private land, but this did not prove to be a major challenge.[6] However, barring railways and irrigation, the Raj was not a particularly active state, so it used its eminent domain powers to a modest extent. In the first two decades after independence, the state remained extremely powerful despite universal adult franchise and a more independent judiciary. The state was much more active and developmental, and eminent domain was exercised more often, still without much resistance from the affected population. However, there was a qualitative break from the 1980s on and especially after 1991. Since then industrialization has accelerated, and there are extensive protest movements by the to-be-dispossessed that are supported by educated middle-class activists. In addition, the judiciary is more interventionist. Rural protesters have, in what has been called "legalism from below," agitated for changes in law that they expect will benefit them.[7] Politicians who want their votes have responded by passing historic legislations, such as the Right to Fair Compensation and Transparency in Land Acquisition, Rehabilitation, and Resettlement Act, 2013 (LARR), the Panchayats (Extension to Scheduled Areas) Act, 1996 (PESA), and the Scheduled Tribes and Other Traditional Forest Dwellers (Recognition of Forest Rights) Act, 2006 (FRA). Much of our discussion in this chapter is organized around these three legislations.

Most commentators agree that the colonial-era legal structure inherited by independent India gave too much power to the state. Some reform was necessary. But many have argued that the LARR, PESA, and FRA have gone too far in the other direction—procedures are so demanding and cumbersome that projects that are potentially socially beneficial are held up.[8] And yet at the same time there are concerns about the arbitrary exercise of state power and unjust expropriation of the poor. These problems are interrelated. Because the state lacks credibility and cannot control the behavior of its politicians and officials, laws were written crudely, incorporating restrictions on the discretionary power of the executive. This has led to perverse outcomes. For instance, according to the LARR, a rural owner whose land is being acquired has to be paid up to four times the market price. This is an arbitrary number, which will surely lead to overpayment in some instances. The Forest Rights Act of 2006 also limits the "diversion" of forest land for some developmental purposes to one hectare, another arbitrary number.

The remaining sections of this chapter proceed chronologically. The first section below describes the colonial period. The second section covers the period from Indian independence to approximately 1985, and the third section brings the story up to roughly 2015. Within each section, we first discuss the state's rights to acquire privately owned agricultural land where ownership can be documented. The two major landmarks in this story are a law passed in 1894, which gave the state strong eminent domain rights, and another passed in 2013 (LARR), which curtailed those rights. We then discuss the state's rights over forests where the rights of individuals and communities have often been customary and not documented. Here the landmarks are laws passed in 1878, which asserted the state's rights over forested areas and undercut the rights of local users and communities, and the FRA (2006), which recognizes these rights.

A key feature of structural transformation in India is that it is occurring rapidly in a society with universal adult franchise. This was not true for (say) England in 1750, nor is it true in China in the present day. The Planning Commission had noted in 1958 that "in India, political democracy has come first." Nandan Nilekani, arguably India's leading software entrepreneur, commented in 2006 that "urbanization in the West . . . took place over hundreds of years in countries then with small populations and a limited franchise. In India, the same process is happening at internet speed in the world's largest democracy."[9] It follows that the poor have more voice as the Indian economy undergoes structural change. This has complicated the process, though for good reasons.

The Colonial Period

Land acquisition became an important issue in colonial India in the context of railway construction. The railroad track might, in principle, have to go through titled, privately owned land. Did the state have the right to acquire it compulsorily? If so, at what price? Bengal Regulation I of 1824 allowed the acquisition of land by the state for "roads, canals, and other public purposes."[10] Fresh legislation was passed in Bengal in 1850 to bring railways under the definition of "public purpose" and for land to transfer to a private company.[11] In colonial Bengal, as elsewhere, land acquisition posed some special challenges because land had cultural meaning.[12] For instance, some tribal people feared that the clearing of forests for railways would anger ancestors buried there. Mosques, temples, or burial grounds might lie in the path of a railroad. Moreover, it could be difficult to identify who owned a piece of land and hence who should be compensated. Many of these problems persist into the present day.

Legislation allowing land acquisition in all of British India was passed in 1857 and subsequently modified several times. Eventually, Act I of 1894 was passed and endured into independent India. The 1894 Act allowed the local government to acquire land for a public purpose or for a company that would serve the public interest. The act gave great authority to the state and discouraged second-guessing by courts. According to the act, "whenever it appears to the Local Government that any particular land is needed for a public purpose or for a Company . . . a declaration shall be made to that effect" and "said declaration shall be *conclusive evidence* that the land is needed for a public purpose or for a Company."[13] In an authoritative 1907 commentary on the Act, Sanjiva Row cited case law and noted that the act "does not contain any provision for any objection on the part of the owner to the acquisition itself." The owner's objections are "limited to the amount of compensation and matters connected therewith, such as measurement and area."[14] The act was amended in 1923 to allow a landowner whose property was being acquired thirty days to appeal the decision to the collector (land revenue official), but there was still no recourse to the courts.[15]

What if the state was acquiring the land for a private company? Could the state simply declare that the company's use satisfied a public purpose, acquire the land, and give it to the company? Could it follow the same procedure as when it was acquiring land for its own use? This was not the intent of the legislation. The methods for acquiring land for a private company were laid out in section VII of the act. The local government had to conduct an enquiry, examine witnesses, and conclude whether the company's work would be "useful to the public." The company then had to enter an agreement with the secretary of state for India in council regarding, among other things, "the terms on which the land shall be held by the Company" and the "terms on which the public shall be entitled to use the work."[16] This language suggests that the legislators had in mind public infrastructure but not smaller-scale industrial concerns. H. W. Bliss, an official involved in the framing of the act, noted,

> It is not intended, that is to say, that the Act shall be used for the acquisition of land for any company in which the public has merely an indirect interest and of the works carried out by which the public can make no direct use. The Act cannot therefore be put in motion for the benefit of such a company as a Spinning or Weaving Company or an Iron Foundry.

Bliss also argued that if a company wanted to mine for coal and would pay royalties to the government, "the provisions of the Act might be properly applied." There was surely some ambiguity here. Indeed, Bliss himself noted that though the intention of the act was not to permit the acquisition of land for any company for just any purpose, this had not been clarified "so clearly as desirable."[17] That said, the Madras High Court opined, in a 1925 case, that if a state government did approve acquisition under section VII as being for the public interest, the court could not second guess this.[18] In practice the 1894 act gave the government in late British India enormous power to acquire land, whether for itself or a company.

If land transfers from one user to another who is more productive, there is potential for both parties to gain; the profits of the new owner can be used to make the seller an attractive offer. The 1894 act, however, tied the hands of both government officials and courts. The buyer would pay market value plus an additional 15% to compensate for the forced nature of the acquisition. The act specified that the administration and the courts could not take into consideration "any increase to the value of the land acquired likely to accrue from the use to which it will be put when acquired." This language, which remained part of the act even after the last major amendment in 1984, discouraged the use of profit-sharing methods such as those that have been proposed more recently.

Land acquisition was also complicated during the colonial period by the fact that, following tribal rebellions, the Raj had passed legislation preventing or restricting the transfer of land from tribals to non-tribals. Such legislation was based on the view that the naive and legally unsophisticated tribals were likely to be cheated. One prominent legislation in this regard was the Chota Nagpur Tenancy Act (CNT, 1908), which Mircea Raianu has discussed in the context of one of colonial India's most prominent business successes, Tata Iron and Steel Company (TISCO). The company acquired land for a new township, Jamshedpur, where TISCO's factories would be located.[19] TISCO needed (among other locations) the land of two villages, Sakchi and Bekchi. However, the CNT gave village headmen (*pradhans*) control over their common lands, which they refused to make available to TISCO. This was the "single most intractable obstacle for TISCO in its early years."[20] Such problems with land acquisition were less common during the colonial period because of the (relatively) sparse population. In contrast, in the present day, corporations often seek land in densely populated places with good infrastructure.

Law and policy on forests were even more complicated because the rights of individuals and communities were not documented. Colonial officials considered several issues: the need to clear forests for agricultural use; the use of forests as a resource for shipbuilding, railways, paper mills, and so forth; conservation of forests as a natural resource; and the rights of users who were dependent on forests for food, fuel, firewood, and so forth. There were tensions between these alternative considerations. Officials of the Raj already knew from the European experience that the needs of industrialization could dramatically reduce forested area and have damaging environmental consequences in terms of soil erosion and silting.[21] There was also debate on whether local communities that used the forests did so in a sustainable fashion. For instance, many officials were highly skeptical of shifting cultivation (*jhum*), in which forested areas would be cleared by setting them on fire and cultivated for some time before moving on.[22] The competing view was (and is) that local users are the best managers of forest resources.[23]

Who owned these forests? Were they the property of the state? Did they belong to individual users? Or were they collectively owned by local communities? Who would decide how they were used? In the early nineteenth century, timber from the forests of Malabar and other parts of South India went into shipbuilding and some other commercial uses. British officialdom, which had a tradition of attempting to unearth preexisting Indian law before legislating, went through this exercise with respect to the forests as well. Their "findings" varied not only across space but also for a given location at different points in time—one scholar has gone so far as to say that the law changed every ten years in the nineteenth century. For instance, in Kanara in 1800 it was concluded that the landholders owned the forest and in 1860 that the state owned the forests. The Raj reverted to its previous view in 1874, but there was "another somersault" in 1882 when the Madras Forest Act declared the state the owner.[24]

By the late nineteenth century, even though the rights of landholders or local users were acknowledged, the law shifted decisively toward favoring the state. Ramachandra Guha has argued that the expansion of the railways, beginning in the 1850s, was central to this process.[25] Timber was required for railway sleepers, among other things. Forests in Uttarakhand were felled indiscriminately. In 1862 the governor general proclaimed that the forest administration until the Mutiny was a "melancholy failure," and the Imperial Forest Department was set up in 1864 to ensure sustainable use of forests. The Government Forests Act was passed in 1865 and revised in 1878 as the Indian Forests Act. Many historians view this as a turning point in terms of the assertion of state's rights—a leading scholar has argued that the "bedrock" of the 1878 act "was the assertion that all uncultivated land was the state's property."[26] The key legal innovation here was the creation of a category of "reserved" forests. As the word suggests, this meant that the state reserved forests for its own use and severely curtailed the local population's use rights. There was also another category known as protected forests, which could be subsequently converted into reserved forests. The 1878 act was revised several times, and a new consolidated act was passed in 1927. The Indian Forests Act of 1927 is still the law, though it has been amended, and there is a considerable new body of legislation.

The erosion of the rights of users is not easy to quantify. However, Velayutham Saravanan provides some useful data on Madras Presidency, where the Indian Forests Act of 1878 was not implemented but the Madras Forest Act of 1882 similarly undermined customary rights. Common uses became illegal. As table 4.1 shows, the number of "forest offenses" recorded in the administration reports of the Madras Presidency increased from 2,493 in 1886/1887 to 24,708 by 1930/1931.

The Indian Forest Act did not entirely ignore preexisting rights of users. However, these rights had to be recognized by forest officials before a forest was designated as reserved. The forest department was also given the responsibility for enforcing restrictions on use by the local community. Because local populations viewed the government's restrictions as arbitrary and a violation of their customary rights, they were often in conflict with forest officials. In several cases, there were protests

TABLE 4.1 **Forest offences in Madras Presidency (1886/1887–1930/1931)**

Year	Number of offences
1886/1887	2,493
1903/1904	21,883
1910/1911	26,498
1921/1922	29,040
1930/1931	24,798

Source: V. Saravanan, *Environmental History and Tribals in Modern India* (Singapore: Springer Singapore, 2018), table 3.12, p. 79.

against colonial forest law, and the government granted some concessions.[27] That said, at the end of the colonial period, the idea that the state was the primary owner of forests was firmly in place.

Continuity and Resistance (1950–1985)

Independent India retained all British era legislation not explicitly repealed. The 1894 Land Acquisition Act remained in place, as did the 1927 Indian Forest Act. Moreover, the Indian Constitution had, as we have seen in chapters 2 and 3, allowed states to pass special legislation in areas with large tribal populations to limit the transfer of land from tribals to nontribals. As we mentioned earlier, these areas were listed in Schedules V and VI, the latter pertaining to the northeast of the country. Much of recent controversy over the acquisition of tribal land is regarding Schedule V areas, many of which are in a belt running across the middle of India. We will focus on these regions as opposed to Schedule VI areas.[28]

As we have described, the 1894 Land Acquisition Act had created two separate procedures, one for the acquisition of land by the state for its own use and another for acquisition by the state for a private company. The former merely required that the state declare the acquisition was for a public purpose. It was used, for instance, to acquire land for the now iconic public-sector-owned steel plant in Bokaro following an agreement with the Soviet Union in 1965.[29] Acquiring land for a private company was more cumbersome and required application of Section VII of the act. The spirit of the law, as we have explained, was that the state would not intervene to acquire land for any ordinary industrial concern but only for an enterprise that directly benefited the public. As India began to industrialize more rapidly, state governments sought to avoid section VII, seeking to simplify land acquisition on behalf of companies. The government would declare that the project was in the public interest and make a nominal contribution to the cost of the project, ostensibly positioning itself as a partner to the company. It would then acquire the land, applying procedures as though it were for government use.

Somavanti and Others v. The State of Punjab (1962) is an infamous case in this regard.[30] The Punjab government had acquired land in the district of Gurgaon, adjacent to Delhi, on behalf of Air Conditioning Corporation, a private limited concern that would manufacture refrigeration compressors. The Punjab government, which declared that the project satisfied a public purpose, contributed a mere Rs. 100 toward the land acquisition and then acquired the land directly, avoiding section VII of the act. The landowner's right to appeal the government's decision to acquire within thirty days of notification was nullified because the government invoked the Urgency Clause in the act. When the owners of the land filed suit against the Air Conditioning Corporation and the Punjab government, the defendants' lawyers argued, among other things, that the factory would create jobs and earn precious foreign exchange, which served the public interest. The Supreme Court ruled for the defendants, allowing the Punjab government to sidestep the provisions of Section VII. More importantly, it had allowed compulsory land acquisition for use by an ordinary industrial concern, which, whether desirable or not, was not envisaged by the framers of the 1894 act.

In a different case, *R.L. Arora v. The State of U.P.* (1962), the Supreme Court took a radically different decision when agricultural land was needed for the construction of a textile machinery factory. The court held that the land could not be acquired because the act required that the work be "directly useful to the public and the public shall be entitled to use the work as such for its own benefit," and this condition was not satisfied.[31] There was some political support for this argument, but on the whole, courts continued to defer to governments. Eventually, in 1984, the act was amended. The act specifically required the government to follow the more elaborate procedures of section VII to acquire land for a private company. However, the interpretation of the amendment got entangled in legal minutiae, and some courts even ignored it. The 1984 amendment seems to have had little effect on the land-acquisition process, though it did increase the compensation for the forced nature of the acquisition from 15% to 30%.[32]

Turning to forest rights, in 1952 the Ministry of Food and Agriculture enunciated a National Forest Policy that was "formulated on the basis of six paramount needs of the country." The policy noted the tension between the needs of local residents and those of the Indian economy as a whole, and it came out squarely in favor of the latter. Its perspective is worth quoting at some length.

> Village communities in the neighborhood of a forest will naturally make greater use of its products for the satisfaction of their domestic and agricultural needs. Such use, however, should in no event be permitted at the cost of national interests. The accident of a village being situated close to a forest does not prejudice the right of the country as a whole to receive the benefits of a national asset. The scientific conservation of a forest involves the regulation of rights and the restriction of the privileges of the user, depending upon the value and importance of the forest, *however irksome such restraint may be to the neighboring areas.*[33]

The document also opined that "adequate forest legislation exists in the Indian Forests Act and the Madras Forest Act." These legislations reflected the attitude of a colonial government that did not depend on the votes of the members of the village communities who might be "irked." We will argue in the next section that as Indian democracy strengthened, this decision was no longer politically prudent.

The view that the state owned the forests and had the right to regulate their use is reflected in statistics provided by the Forest Research Institute. As of 1957–1958, of the 7.8 million hectares of forested area in India, 92.3% were state owned, 5.4% were "communal forest area," and 2.3% were privately owned.[34] Reserved forests accounted for 47%, protected forests were 30%, and "unclassed" forests were 22.6%. Thus, there were substantial use restrictions on a large portion of forested area.

The environmental conservation movement, which picked up steam in the 1970s, influenced Indian policy and law. The movement put conservationists at odds with local users as well as industrial interests. The Wildlife (Protection) Act of 1972 not only prohibited the hunting of certain animals but also allowed a state government to create sanctuaries and national parks in areas of "ecological, faunal, floral, geomorphological, natural, or zoological significance."[35] The tension between conservationists and local users is exemplified in *Pradeep Kishen v. Union of India* (1996), in which an environmentalist challenged an order passed by the state of Madhya Pradesh that permitted villagers living near boundaries and national parks to collect tendu leaves, which are used to wrap beedis, sometimes called "poor man's cigarettes."[36] The petitioner contended that the collection of tendu leaves would adversely affect plant and animal life and could also lead to forest fires. Three tribals who sought the court's permission to intervene denied that the collection of the leaves did any harm. Moreover, their subsistence depended on it. The court ruled against Pradeep Kishen on a technicality that the areas in question had not officially been declared national parks or sanctuaries.[37] Another important legislation, the Forest Conservation Act, was passed in 1980 to allow the central government to limit states (provinces) from converting forest land to industrial use. The Forest Conservation Act also impinged on the rights of users. We will discuss it at some length in chapter 5.

There were countervailing forces in defense of local users' rights. A grassroots movement for the protection of users' rights was developing, following the famous Chipko struggle in Uttarakhand, in which peasant women hugged trees to prevent them from being chopped down.[38] Chipko achieved global fame and put the rights of forest users squarely on the agenda. Despite this, the government presented a draft forest policy to the public in 1980 that was viewed as even more draconian than existing law, giving forest guards and officials even more power over local users. After sustained protest, the bill was abandoned. A revised National Forest Policy, more sympathetic to the rights of local users and emphasizing their role in participating in forest conservation, was passed in 1988. Also, in contrast to the National Forest Policy of 1952, it listed "meeting the requirements of fuelwood, fodder, minor forest produce and smaller timber of the rural and tribal populations" as among its "basic objectives."[39] The Forest Policy of 1988 was a leading indicator (as a macroeconomist might say) of basic legal changes that were to follow that curtailed the power of the state.

The State's Rights Challenged (1985–2015)

The Indian economy has grown rapidly since the mid-1980s, and the process of structural change that we described at the beginning of this chapter has accelerated. Agricultural land and forests are increasingly needed for developing infrastructure and for industrial needs, including mining.

Until the 2000s the state's acquisition of private agricultural land was predominantly for infrastructure, with dams being the most visible example. Villages would be inundated after a dam was built. The 1894 act required villagers be compensated, but the state had no legal obligation to resettle them.[40] However, displaced people often prefer to be compensated in land as opposed to cash, which they fear they will fritter away. Governments made promises of resettlement but often failed to honor them. When the two authors of this book were college students in the early 1980s, perhaps the best-known Indian dam (a pair, actually) was the Bhakra-Nangal on the Sutlej river. Prime Minister Jawaharlal Nehru inaugurated it in 1963 and regarded it as one of the "temples" of modern India. We shared this positive view. We did know of complaints, though, that people displaced in the construction of the Bhakra-Nangal dam had not yet been satisfactorily resettled. As we began to write this chapter, we revisited this issue. A quick Google search revealed that rehabilitation was still incomplete. In 2013, the *Times of India*, in a piece titled "50 Years on, Bhakra Oustees Wait for Rehabilitation," reported that many of the displaced people still felt "cheated."[41] On January 4, 2018, the *Times of India* reported again: "CM [Chief Minister]: Will Look into Grievances of Bhakra Oustees."[42] This story was repeated many times over in various development projects that resulted in displacements. It is very difficult to estimate numbers precisely, but according to a widely cited estimate, sixty million people were displaced or project affected between 1947 and 2000. Less than half of the displaced were resettled. Over the period 1951–1995, 35% of evicted households in Orissa were resettled, 29% in Andhra Pradesh, 41% in Goa, and 14% in Kerala.[43] Even when evicted households were resettled, there were often complaints about the quality of land or infrastructure in the new location.[44] Because the government's promises were not credible, people resisted land acquisition.[45]

There was especially strong resistance to a plan to build a series of dams on the river Narmada. The first major dam, the Sardar Sarovar, was expected to bring electricity and irrigation to Gujarat but to inundate villages in Madhya Pradesh. A substantial fraction of those who would be flooded were tribals. The Narmada Bachao Andolan (NBA, Save the Narmada Movement), led by its charismatic leader, Medha

Patkar, was at the forefront of the resistance over a long period beginning in the 1980s. The NBA's stance was uncompromising; it opposed the construction of the dam itself rather than favoring rehabilitation of those evicted.[46] The NBA did not prevail despite enormous efforts on the ground and in court.[47] The Sardar Sarovar dam has finally been built and inaugurated in 2017.[48] Despite its failure to stop the construction of the dam, the NBA played an important role in highlighting the problem of displacement.[49]

Resistance to the acquisition of private agricultural land intensified in the 2000s as the government increasingly intervened on behalf of corporations. Some of the most prominent protests came when governments sought to set up Special Economic Zones. Scholars like Mike Levien have argued that the state was, in some instances, merely acting as a land broker, acquiring land at a low price from the poor and passing it on to corporations.[50] Perhaps the most explosive and nationally visible resistance came from West Bengal.[51] The government of the CPM (Communist Party of India, Marxist) had decided that having firmed up its rural base (see chap. 2), it would now focus on industrialization. In Singur, in Hooghly district, the West Bengal government entered an agreement to provide land to the Tatas, a leading business conglomerate, to build inexpensive cars. Fierce resistance from potential evictees eventually forced the Tatas to relocate their project to Gujarat. In another instance, the West Bengal government agreed to provide land to the Indonesian Salim Group for the construction of a chemical hub in a Special Economic Zone.[52] Following protests, fourteen people were shot and killed by police in March 2007.[53] The CPM subsequently revoked its agreement with the Salim group but still paid an immediate and heavy political price. It lost seats in parliament at the center in 2009. In 2011, after decades of rule in West Bengal, it lost power to the Trinamool Congress, which had opposed the land acquisitions. The electoral message hit home for all political parties. Still, it took considerable negotiation and political maneuvering before the 1894 legislation was replaced by the Right to Fair Compensation and Transparency in Land Acquisition, Rehabilitation and Resettlement Act (LARR) of 2013. This is a drastic overhaul of law pertaining to land acquisition.

The preamble to the act indicates its enormous scope, which was "to ensure, in consultation with institutions of local self-government and Gram Sabhas [village assemblies] established under the Constitution, a humane, participative, informed and transparent process for land acquisition." The act requires that expropriated landowners in rural areas get up to four times the market price of land and two times the market price in urban areas; it makes provision for rehabilitation and resettlement even of affected people who did not own land (e.g., agricultural laborers); if the land is later sold to a third party, the original owner receives 40% of the appreciation; it allows the acquisition of irrigated multicrop land only under special circumstances. Two other provisions have led to the most criticism. These pertain to the Social Impact Assessment and consent from those to be displaced. The acquisition process needs to begin with a Social Impact Assessment by a group including local representatives (e.g., from the Gram Sabha, village assembly), which can take six months. Its report must subsequently be reviewed by an expert group, which also includes representatives of Gram Sabha or Panchayat. If a private company acquires land, 80% of the land losers must consent. The figure is reduced to 70% if it is a public-private partnership. As mentioned above, the LARR requires that when rural land is acquired, *up to* four times the value should be paid as compensation. In practice, it appears that four times the value has become the norm. This number is arbitrary and will make some projects unviable.[54]

A recent survey of land-acquisition legislation across the world has described the LARR as "the most elaborate recent legislative effort."[55] Unsurprisingly, Indian industrialists view the act as extremely cumbersome. A senior official of the Modi government (which replaced the government that formulated the LARR) complained that land acquisition would take four to five years.[56] He advised states to pass their own amendments, which some have done. For instance, an amendment in Gujarat exempts defense projects, rural infrastructure, affordable housing for poor people, industrial corridors, and infrastructural projects, including public-private partnerships where the land continues to vest with the government.[57] This was along the lines of a 2015 amendment to the LARR, which failed to pass the Rajya Sabha (upper house). State governments are also resorting to land banks that accumulate property, which can then be made available for specific projects depending on need.

The state's rights to forest land have been challenged at a fundamental level partly via the effort to give teeth to the idea of Panchayati Raj. From at least the 1850s some intellectuals, both British and Indian, had valorized village-level governance as embodied in the Panchayat (literally, a council of five). It was argued that leaders at this level would be more aware of community needs and would better serve their interests. Also, as is well known, for M. K. Gandhi, the self-governing and self-sustaining village was an ideal. However, the writers of the Indian Constitution believed that at that fraught moment in the nation's history, a centralized state was needed to hold it together. Panchayati Raj did not become law. Instead, it was included as a desideratum in the Directive Principles section of the Constitution. This intention came to fruition, beginning with what has been called Indian democracy's "second wind," via the seventy-third amendment to the Indian Constitution in 1993.[58] We have seen earlier that areas listed in the Fifth Schedule of the Indian Constitution are governed differently, with a particular emphasis on retaining land within the tribal community. It followed that the Panchayati Raj legislation would need to be modified to apply to Fifth Schedule areas. After pressure from activist groups, the Panchayats (Extension to Scheduled Areas) Act was passed in 1996.[59] We will, like everyone else, call it PESA.

When PESA was passed in 1996, it gave considerable power to the Gram Sabha.[60] N. C. Saxena, a former member of the Planning Commission, and Jayanti Ravi have argued that PESA was "unprecedented" in that it gave "radical self-governance powers" to the tribal community and recognized "traditional community rights over natural resources."[61] This meant the Gram Sabha would have to be consulted before land acquisition for development projects. The Gram Sabha would also manage the use of forest resources, including the lucrative nontimber forest produce.

The importance of PESA was reinforced in an important court case, *Samata v. The State of Andhra Pradesh*, in 1997. As we have discussed above, states are permitted to pass regulation preventing transfer of land to nontribals in Schedule V areas. Andhra Pradesh had passed such a law in 1959, which had been amended in 1970. A central legislation, the Mines and Minerals (Development and Regulation) Act of 1957, was also relevant. The issue was, Could the state of Andhra Pradesh lease government-owned land in a Schedule V area to a (nontribal) mining company? The Supreme Court ruled it could not. In a wide-ranging decision, it reaffirmed the rights of the Gram Sabha to preserve community resources.[62]

Though radical on paper, PESA was ineffective, at least in the early years.[63] Saxena and Ravi went so far as to say that it was "almost forgotten," and "academics, administrators, policymakers, and even parliamentarians remain unaware of it."[64] Another scholar has argued that the Ministry of Environment and Forests continued to view the forests within Scheduled Areas as being under its jurisdiction.[65] Moreover, PESA did not apply to forests in non-Scheduled Areas.

The vulnerability of forest-dwelling populations became even more visible after the Ministry of Environment and Forests issued a circular on May 3, 2002, calling for a "time bound programme for the eviction of encroachers from the forest lands." This was a response, possibly based on a misinterpretation, to a Supreme Court order under a famous case, *Godavarman Thirumulpad v. Union of India*, which related to the application of the Forest Conservation Act of 1980.[66] The evictions were carried out harshly, with some reports that elephants had been used to crush homes.[67]

After a series of protests, the Congress government passed the Forest Rights Act (FRA) in 2006, which applies to forest-dependent populations, whether or not they are Scheduled Tribes.[68] The FRA has been called a "game-changer."[69] The orientation of the act is evident from the language of its preamble. The state is not conferring rights; it is merely acknowledging existing rights that have been unfairly denied to forest-dependent populations, thereby correcting "historical injustice." The FRA sought to document private ownership rights as well as community rights. A Scheduled Tribe forest dweller who could prove that he or she had resided on a piece of land since 2005 could now get a title for up to four hectares. For married people, the title would go to both spouses. By 2015, 1.5 million titles had been granted.[70] In an echo of land-reform legislation (see chap. 2), the forest dwellers who received land could not transfer it.

More controversially, the FRA also allowed for the recognition of community rights to the use of forests and "habitat" (natural resources more broadly). The Gram Sabha was given a central role in the implementation of the act. It was required to set up a forest rights committee with provisions for the representation of Scheduled Tribes and women.[71] The committee would receive and examine claims for both individual and community rights. After hearing the interested parties, it would forward the claim to higher-level committees in which again Scheduled Tribes and women would be represented.[72] A key provision of the FRA is that if the land is required for a development project, this needs approval from the Gram Sabha.

Unlike PESA, which was largely ignored, the Forest Rights Act is more visible and has had a real effect. Civil society organizations have mobilized to support its implementation. It also has significant support within the Government of India. We have alluded earlier to the fact that the Government of India is not monolithic. The Ministry of Environment and Forests has, as the name suggests, been the controlling authority for forest policy. It has been responsive to various pressures, including those from industrial lobbies. The Ministry of Tribal Affairs, in contrast, is more squarely focused on tribal interests. The FRA is under the aegis of the Ministry of Tribal Affairs, which partly accounts for the momentum toward implementation.[73]

The FRA has some limitations, even given its stated objectives. For instance, forest dwellers who are not from Scheduled Tribes have to prove residence for 75 years to receive titles to land, which is a tall order. There are also complaints that Gram Sabhas have been coerced or manipulated to give consent to development projects. Also, the FRA only explicitly gives village communities rights over nontimber forest products. The Forest Department continues to control rights to timber. More generally, a confusing array of legislations, each with their own lobbies, now apply to the use of forests. These include the Forest Act of 1927, The Wildlife Protection Act (1972), the Forest Conservation Act of 1980, PESA, and the FRA, not to mention numerous state-level legislations

Some positive effects of the FRA have been widely acknowledged. For instance, once given title to land, forest dwellers have been able to grow and sell bamboo to paper mills at good prices.[74] However, the Forest Department still claims the right to regulate and issue permits for the movement of bamboo across states. The rules vary depending on whether the bamboo in question comes from a forest area or nonforest area. As Bibek Debroy has pointed out, it is not clear how someone in possession of bamboo can prove where it came from.[75] There is some evidence from Maharashtra (see table 4.2) that the number of forest offenses has declined after the FRA was passed, but of course we shouldn't entertain the post hoc argument—afterwards doesn't mean because of. The Maharashtra government has also produced a statistical analysis showing a twenty-five-year trend of decline in forest offenses that it attributes to, among other things, greater participation of local people in forest management.[76] This remains an important area for future research.

The influence of the FRA was tested in a major case decided by the Supreme Court in 2013, *Orissa Mining Corporation v. Union of India*. The disputants were the Government of Orissa (Orissa Mining Corpora-

TABLE 4.2 **Forest offences in Maharashtra (2005–2014)**

Year	Injury by fire	Unauthorized felling	Unauthorized grazing	Other cases	Total
2005–2006	2,002	36,748	1,795	6,374	46,919
2006–2007	2,685	33,337	1,909	5,807	43,738
2007–2008	3,253	35,715	1,801	9,401	50,170
2008–2009	3,853	43,782	1,899	8,487	58,021
2009–2010	2,418	31,702	1,645	6,805	42,570
2010–2011	3,045	26,315	1,444	5,389	36,193
2011–2012	4,670	23,972	1,058	5,079	34,779
2012–2013	2,718	21,609	1,017	8,723	34,065
2013–2014	2,235	20,400	1,033	6,407	30,075
2014–2015	2,729	22,450	981	4,456	30,616

Source: Government of Maharashtra Forest Department, *A Statistical Outline* (Nagpur: Office of the Principal Conservator, 2016), 33.

tion) and the Ministry of Environment and Forests. The Vedanta Corporation, a large multinational, had built an alumina refinery in the Kalahandi district of Orissa (now Odisha). It sought to obtain bauxite from the Niyamgiri hills, which were held sacred by the Dongria Kondh, a Scheduled Tribe vigorously opposed to the proposed mining. The Ministry of Environment and Forests (MOEF) set up a committee to examine the project. The committee came out against it not only because it violated community rights but also because it was environmentally destructive.[77] The MOEF then refused to allow the project to proceed, and the decision was challenged in the Supreme Court by the Government of Orissa.

The Supreme Court invoked both PESA and the FRA and ruled that a key question was whether the mining project would violate the rights of the Dongria Kondh to worship their deity, Niyam Raja. It directed the Government of Orissa to place the matter before the Gram Sabhas. The Government of Orissa sought the views of the Gram Sabhas of twelve villages. All of them rejected the mining proposal, and hence the MOEF refused clearance.[78] In 2016 the Supreme Court rebuffed a subsequent effort by Orissa Mining Corporation to reopen the case.[79]

While PESA and the FRA involve Gram Sabhas in protecting community resources, they do not give Gram Sabhas rights over the minerals underneath the land—the state still manages those as trustee.[80] There will always be some intractable cases like the one just discussed, but one obvious step is to share the benefits of the mining with the Gram Sabha. A 2015 Amendment to 1957 Mines Act requires that mining companies donate a portion of royalties to a District Mineral Foundation that will work for the benefit of affected local people. Critics have described the amendment as leaving the tribals with the glass "half-full" because it did not highlight the need to get the consent of Gram Sabhas, though it did acknowledge the need for decisions to be consistent with the FRA.[81] A substantial sum of money has accumulated, and, as we write (June 2020), there is talk of using these funds to ameliorate the effect of COVID-19.[82]

The LARR and the FRA have foregrounded the fundamental issue we raised in the introduction to this chapter: how will structural change occur in an economy in which democratic processes have protected the property rights of the poor in the "traditional" sector? It is clear now that in India, unlike eighteenth-century Britain or present-day China, the state's right to acquire land for infrastructure or industry has been significantly curtailed. The transfer of land, and natural resources more generally, from one use to another will have to be negotiated rather than imposed by the state. How will this play out?

Conclusion

The LARR and the FRA were responses to complaints that the state had too much power to acquire land or limit how it was used.[83] A corrective was necessary. Still, these legislations have some puzzling aspects. For instance, why does the LARR specify that rural land be acquired at four times the market value? It is true that land markets can be distorted by restrictions on sales to nonfarmers and by requiring permission to transfer to nonagricultural use. Further, high stamp duties on transactions can motivate underreporting of the price.[84] Still, the premium could be decided on a case-by-case basis. The issue here may be a lack of trust in government officials. Jairam Ramesh, the minister of rural development at the time the bill was passed, explicitly states the intention to rein in the executive branch of government, noting that "the new Act . . . puts in place a comprehensive formula for the calculation of compensation that completely removed the discretion of the authorities."[85]

Why does the FRA recognize previously informal (private) ownership rights of forest dwellers but then disallow the sale of these rights? Here there is continuity from the colonial period—the shared opinion, from colonial-era officials to present-day activists, that tribals are not sufficiently sophisticated to negotiate land markets and will lose out by participating. This is related to a broader debate about whether tribal lifestyles should be protected or whether they should be assimilated into mainstream society.[86]

The LARR and the FRA are still playing out, and much may have changed by the time this book is in print. At this point, five types of outcomes are possible. First, some projects are being stalled—a recent paper provides a figure of US$9 billion.[87] Second, some projects are still feasible because of exemptions. In the LARR, thirteen prior enactments on land acquisition for highways, railways, and electricity continue to be honored.[88] Even within the LARR, restrictions on acquiring multi-crop irrigated land are loosened for projects that are "linear in nature"—canals, roads, and so forth.[89] Also, as we have noted, some states have amended the LARR.[90] Third, in some cases, coercion and intimidation are being used to get the consent of individuals or Gram Sabhas. Fourth, critics of fresh legislation, such as the Compensatory Afforestation Fund Act (2016), have argued it undercuts the goals of the FRA and the LARR and facilitates land grabs by the state.[91] And fifth, a development that is the most promising. Here, contrary to the spirit of the 1894 Land Acquisition Act, the original owner is given a share of the benefits from the enhanced productivity in the new use of the land. This is a feature of the 2015 amendment to the Mines Act (see above) and is also part of "land-pooling" arrangements being proposed in some states. In land-pooling arrangements, the state acquires more land than needed for (say) urban housing. The original land losers are compensated by giving them plots whose value has increased because of development. The jury is out on these specific methods, but the broad strategy of benefit sharing between original and new owners should facilitate land acquisition while respecting the local rights of individuals and communities.

We will end this chapter with a comment on property rights and the stage of development. One of the most controversial decisions by the US Supreme Court in recent years was in *Kelo v. City of New London* in 2005. The town of New London, in Connecticut, sought to acquire private residential property for commercial development, that is, use by other private parties. When Suzette Kelo and others resisted, the case eventually went up to the Supreme Court. In a 5–4 decision, the court ruled in favor of the town. The judgment was written by Justice Stevens, a stalwart of the American "left." The dissent, from the "right," was written by Sandra Day O'Connor. The *Kelo* decision was hugely controversial, and many state-level legislations have diluted its influence.

Therefore, it is interesting to hear from Jairam Ramesh and Muhammed Ali Khan that the dissent in *Kelo* provided "compelling arguments for why acquisition for private parties (particularly companies) was an overreach on the part of the Government."[92] Thus, the framers of the LARR, which in India is considered a "left" legislation aimed at protecting the property rights of the poor, were influenced by arguments from the conservative wing in the US Supreme Court. It may be that a robust defense of private property against seizure by the state is appropriate in the United States, which already has a highly developed infrastructure and industry and has urbanized. India's needs may be different.

In this chapter, we introduced the debate on the rights of forest dwellers and users, alluding only briefly to forest conservation as a driver of legislation on this issue. Forest conservation itself is part of a larger dialogue on environmental degradation, which, beginning in the 1970s, has become a significant concern in India and elsewhere. We will argue in our next chapter that in relation to the environment, more than in any other area, the Supreme Court itself has taken the lead in shaping the law.

CHAPTER FIVE

Environmental Law

Judiciary Takes Center Stage

India has been blessed with a culture of foresighted judges who brought a sea change in environmental law. These judges have not only made precedent—they have made history. — M. C. Mehta[1]

Seven of the top 10 most polluted cities in the world are in India. — M. Jamrisko[2]

Introduction

We have seen that in relation to rights in land, the law goes back a very long way. In contrast, much of environmental law has emerged in the last few decades. Courts have been unusually important in interpreting the law and even in implementation to the point where they have been accused of violating the separation of powers between the legislature, the executive branch, and the judiciary. How has this come to be, and what are the potential consequences? We address these questions in this chapter.

As we have seen in chapter 4, there was important colonial-era legislation in some areas of environmental law. However, after independence, industrialization, urbanization, and population growth have made environmental issues—pollution being a prominent example—far more salient. The problem of pollution illustrates one of the biggest challenges facing environmental law and governance. There is, to begin with, the classic problem of the divergence between private and social cost. For instance, the benefits of operating a factory accrue largely to the employer and the workers, whereas the effect of the factory pouring sewage into a river may be borne by users faraway downstream. In principle, the government could require the factory to treat the sewage before it is released, or in an extreme case close the factory. But governments respond to the pressure of constituents. There is then the problem of organizing collective action by constituents. If the factory is closed, the losses will be felt intensely by the owner and the workers, whereas the benefits will spread across river users over a large area, each of whom will benefit to only a modest extent. It is likely that the pressure to keep the factory open will be more organized and intense than the opposition to it.

Moreover, the costs of closing the factory (especially in terms of job losses) will be felt immediately, before the next election, whereas the benefits, such as better health of water users downstream, may be long term. Inaction may be the government's politically expedient option. Finally, even if a law is passed requiring factories to treat sewage before releasing it, they have to be inspected to verify that they are obeying the law. This creates opportunities for corruption. This is a particularly relevant matter in India, with its history of "license-permit Raj." Competition between states (provinces) also plays a role. States compete for capital and infrastructure and are ready to relax forest and pollution law.

All this creates an opening for the courts. Supreme Court judges don't face elections and can make decisions based on a comprehensive analysis of social costs and benefits. This can, in principle, make judges better decision makers than legislatures. They can also compel (or at least instruct) governments to enforce the law. Of course, for this to happen, environmental problems have to be brought to the attention of the courts, which are not set up to govern. Also, the intervention of courts is constrained by the Constitution. In India both these constraints on the courts have been eased since the late 1970s. After the end of the Emergency, during which the Supreme Court had sullied its reputation by kowtowing to the executive, it was now ready to play a more progressive and activist role.[3] The Supreme Court relaxed rules about locus standi, the right to approach a court. A concerned citizen not directly affected by the problem at hand was permitted to file a petition. Moreover, this could be done in a highly informal way, perhaps even with a postcard. This allowed an explosion of Public Interest Litigation (PIL).[4] While PIL is a means for improving citizens' access to justice, it has also greatly enhanced the court's ability to use its discretion to intervene in public policy, a more controversial outcome.

The Supreme Court was able to respond forcefully to this PIL because of a fundamental change in its interpretation of Article 21, the Right to Life in the Indian Constitution. The text of article 21 merely says that "No person shall be deprived of his life or personal liberty except according to procedure established by law." This was a conservative formulation, highlighting what the government could *not* do. Moreover, the Constituent Assembly had avoided the term *due process*, which carries the implication that a procedure established by law needs to be substantively fair. This changed after the famous *Maneka Gandhi v. Union of India*, a case involving denial of a passport. The court decided that the implications of Article 21 had to be considered jointly with those of Article 14 (equal protection under the law) and Article 19 (which guaranteed various freedoms, including the right to pursue an occupation). As a legal scholar has said, the court's interpretation gave a "visa" to the notion of due process, which had hitherto been left out.[5] It also opened the door for the right to life to be interpreted as involving human dignity more broadly rather than as just physical existence. This permitted a series of landmark judgments in which citizens' rights to a healthy environment were recognized, and a whole body of environmental law developed. The court also took it upon itself to ensure that justice was actually done on the ground. Much more than before, it involved itself in the enforcement of its decisions.

The legislature was not entirely passive. There *was* one impetus to act on the environmental front: visible and dramatic disasters. In such situations, the status quo was no longer politically advantageous, and the legislatures acted. The Bhopal gas tragedy, which we discuss below, is perhaps the most prominent example of a disaster motivating legislation.

In tracing the evolution of environmental law, to retain focus, we primarily discuss only two major issues—forest conservation and pollution. Unlike other chapters in this book, we do not have a separate section on the colonial period. We have already discussed the most important colonial-era legislation regarding forests, the Indian Forests Act of 1927, in chapter 4, and there was very limited legislation on pollution during the colonial period.[6]

The remainder of this chapter is organized as follows. The first section focuses on legislation and its motivations, the second on the accomplishments of the Supreme Court in shaping environmental law, and the third on the court's role in law enforcement. Here we argue that success and failure aside, some of the court's decisions seem to violate the separation of powers between the legislature, the executive branch, and the judiciary. In the final section of the chapter, we suggest that court activism in environmental law has reinforced a tendency that has been a traditional feature of postindependence Indian economic policy—neglect of market mechanisms, which has encouraged rent-seeking.

The Origins of Legislation

By the early 1970s international organizations like the United Nations, the International Union for the Conservation of Nature (IUCN) and the World Wildlife Fund (WWF)were highlighting environmental problems. The influential United Nations Conference on the Human Environment (in Stockholm in 1972) saw "growing evidence of man-made harm in many regions of the earth: dangerous levels of pollution in water, air, earth, and living beings; major and undesirable disturbances to the ecological balance of the biosphere; destruction and depletion of irreplaceable resources," and so forth. The report made a distinction between developed and developing countries, noting that "in the industrialized countries environmental problems are generally related to industrialization and technological development." In contrast, in developing countries, "most of the environmental problems are due to underdevelopment." Still, developing countries had to recognize "the need to safeguard and improve the environment."[7]

India passed the Water (Prevention and Control of Pollution) Act of 1974. It set up a Central Water Board and corresponding provincial state-level boards. The state boards could set industrial effluent standards and monitor sewage and treatment facilities. Violators could be punished under the act's provisions. However, citizens could approach courts only through or with the sanction of the state pollution board. In 1981 a parallel Air (Prevention and Control of Pollution) Act was passed. Again, courts could be approached only through the pollution board. Abraham and Rosencranz argued in a 1986 paper that the air and water acts were ineffectual.[8] Often government-owned factories were causing the pollution, hence government-appointed members of pollution boards faced conflicts of interest.

Moreover, the boards could not directly impose fines but had to pursue cases via public prosecutors in India's slow-moving courts. The acts give the pollution board little involvement in deciding the location of industrial sites. They had to be consulted only after the site was chosen and approved by the appropriate ministry, at which point it was politically difficult to refuse a permit. There was no requirement to consult the public before projects were approved.[9]

A major industrial disaster jolted the status quo. In the early morning of December 3, 1984, vapor containing methyl isocyanate was released from a pesticide factory owned by the Union Carbide Corporation. The factory was in a crowded neighborhood of Bhopal city in central India. The vapor killed two thousand people and injured three hundred thousand more, with serious long-term health effects for many of those affected. The immediate cause of the accident was the seepage of water in a tank that stored the chemical, causing a sudden increase in heat, a blowup of safety valves, and the release of the chemical into the atmosphere. However, the exact composition of the toxic gas is still not known; there were symptoms of acute cyanide poisoning among some victims.[10]

The enormity of the disaster dwarfed legal action. Indeed, the Government of India unsuccessfully sought to have the case tried in the United States, arguing that the Indian legal system was slow moving and could not handle the litigation.[11] It proved almost impossible to fix liability. Inquiries by the company and writings by company officers alleged that the tragedy happened because of sabotage by a disgruntled employee and blamed the state government for poor pollution control standards and monitoring. Inquiries conducted by the government and NGOs alleged that emergency procedures were inadequate and almost nonexistent on that night because of a series of breakdowns that the company's engineers knew of. For some time before the disaster, the plant, licensed to manufacture pesticides based on methyl isocyanate, was running at a loss. It was alleged that at the time of the accident, the plant might even have been producing substances that it was not authorized to make. Criminal suits failed. The Government of India, apparently in an effort not to scare away foreign investment, did not pursue the extradition of Warren Anderson, the then chief executive of the company who was declared a "fugitive from justice" by a Bhopal court.

Civil suits failed to provide an adequate remedy because the disputes settlement system was quickly clogged up. The local courts were cluttered with compensation suits. The government set up "special courts," which settled a fraction of the hundreds of thousands of cases filed. There were many fraudulent claims. The government filed a suit of US$3 billion, while the company filed a countersuit. Five years after the tragedy, in an out-of-court settlement, Union Carbide agreed to pay US$470 million in damages. The average amount paid to the families of those who died fell far short of standards established in commercial industrial disasters elsewhere. Corrupt officers, it was said, took a cut on the amount.

Though the victims suffered injustice, the accident had a far-reaching effect on environmental law and activism. Within India, public awareness of chemical pollution increased, and so did the will to frame stricter environmental regulations. In the late 1970s, the government of the Madhya Pradesh state had permitted Union Carbide India to build a pesticides plant in a crowded neighborhood.[12] At that time, no one seriously cared about laws on environmental governance and the siting of factories. After Bhopal, these laws were much better enforced. Both Indian and global NGOs stepped up campaigns against toxic chemicals, partly directed at the parent firm of Union Carbide, Dow Chemical. The Indian subsidiary of the firm was eventually sold. But the derelict factory site is still said to contain toxic waste that the decontamination effort did not fully remove.

Following the Bhopal disaster, the Department of Environment, which had been set up in 1980 (and subsequently became the Ministry of Environment and Forests and is now the Ministry of Environment, Forest, and Climate Change) was pressured by the public as well as the office of the prime minister to act. A new umbrella legislation, the Environment (Protection) Act, was passed in 1986. It strengthened the capacity of the central government to set emission standards and additional rules, seek information from factories, and open laboratories for testing environmental quality. The punishment for violating the provisions of the act included imprisonment for up to five years. An important reform allowed citizens the right to file suits directly, without going through the pollution boards. Rules subsequently passed in 1992 and 1994 (and amended several times) established the criteria for a new project to get an environmental clearance from the Ministry of Environment and Forests. An environmental impact assessment had to be done, and public hearings had to be held. The public's right to obtain information was recognized.[13] The public hearings have been a convenient point of entry for concerned NGOs. Unsurprisingly, the quality of the environmental impact assessment and the fairness and openness of the public hearings have been controversial and the subject of litigation.[14]

A separate stream within environmental law, forest conservation, has emerged as a particularly charged area. As we have seen in chapter 4, forest law was the subject of controversy even during the colonial period, with three competing interests—the imperatives of industrialization, forest conservation, and the rights of local users. The most important legislation emerging from the colonial period was the Indian Forest Act of 1927, which prioritized industrial needs and revenue generation. The focus on industrialization was reemphasized in the Forest Policy of 1952. User rights and conservation were still subordinate. In chapter 4 we discussed the struggles over rights of local users culminating in the passing of the Forest Rights Act of 2006. Here we will focus on the tension between industrialization and forest conservation centered on the Forest Conservation Act of 1980. Again, the impetus for the legislation came from social movements.

Forest conservation came to national and international attention in the early 1970s via the Chipko movement. Chipko was a protest against the government by peasants in Uttarakhand because it was allocating timber rights to industrial concerns while neglecting their needs for firewood, fodder, and other forest products. Their anger was also driven by the understanding that deforestation caused by commercial logging was partly responsible for flooding. Chipko was embraced from a variety of perspectives. For one of its charismatic leaders, Sundarlal Bahuguna, the problem was modern industrialization itself, which was a "butcher of nature." The thinking of M. K. Gandhi and contemporary commentators like E. F. Schumacher influenced this understanding. For Chandiprasad Bhatt the problem was the nature of the development process, which was "biased towards the city and big industry and against local and ecological self-reliance."[15] The name Chipko (to stick or to hug) came from one of the strategies adopted by women to use their bodies to prevent tree felling. For some ecofeminists, this suggested a natural affinity between women and nature. Whatever the interpretation, in Chipko a local/regional movement for conservation and user rights gained national and international visibility. Its forty-fifth anniversary was recently celebrated by a Google Doodle.[16] Chipko dramatically raised the profile of deforestation as a policy concern in India. In Indian federalism, the center has been relatively powerful compared to the states. This came to be true with regard to forest conservation as well, with the center, in particular Prime Minister Indira Gandhi, supporting Chipko and other movements. After she appointed a committee to study the matter, in 1981 the government imposed a fifteen year moratorium on commercial felling in the Uttarakhand Himalaya.[17]

In another highly visible controversy, in 1970 the Kerala State Electricity Board proposed a hydroelectric project that would damage a species-rich moist evergreen forest known as the Silent Valley. The forest was uninhabited, so the issue, in this case, was purely conservation, not local users' rights. The Silent Valley project attracted large-scale protests in which two NGOs, the Kerala Shastra Sahitya Parishad (Kerala Science Writers Forum) and Friends of the Trees, played a key role. Prominent environmentalists like Salim Ali and Madhav Gadgil spoke up as did other public figures. The International Union for Conservation of Nature opposed it. However, the Kerala government and various political parties in the state remained committed to the project. Some viewed the protest against the project as an "imperialist plot to keep Kerala backward."[18] Writing while the controversy was ongoing, Darryl D'Monte wrote in 1982 that "if the Silent Valley remains intact today, it is primarily due to the concern of the Prime Minister," who was "sensitive to international opinion."[19] With Indira Gandhi's intervention, the project was canceled in 1983, and the Silent Valley was declared a national park in 1984.[20]

Legal developments reflected the changing understanding of the central government. The forty-second amendment to the Indian Constitution, in 1976, declared that the state and its citizens had the duty to protect the environment and wildlife. These were Directive Principles, not directly justiciable, but they proved to be influential. The amendment also transferred "forests" and "protection of wild animals and birds" from subjects that were prerogative of the states to the concurrent list, in which both state and center had a say. In 1980 the Forest Conservation Act (FCA) was passed, requiring states to seek the permission of the center before diverting land from forest to nonforest use. This legislation and the Supreme Court's interpretation of it (discussed below) have had an enormous influence on forest management in India. Shekhar Pathak, an environmental activist and scholar, has commented that "the Forest Conservation Act of 1980 and the very creation of the environment ministry [in 1985] are due to the consciousness created by Chipko."[21]

The FCA gave enormous power to the central government vis-à-vis the states. At its core is the very broad instruction that "no State Government or other authority shall make, except with the prior approval of the Central Government, any order directing . . . that any forest land or any portion thereof may be used for any non-forest purposes." Growing tea, coffee, and even medicinal plants is a nonforest purpose. The FCA also clarifies that the center's approval is required for any state to dereserve (i.e., allow public use of) a reserved forest. The act allows the central government to set up an advisory committee to help it make decisions on projects involving forest felling. The Forest Advisory Committee has now become an important policy player.

The FCA and especially the Environment (Protection) Act were umbrella legislations. Their implementation required the enactment of more specific rules, and their role in dispute resolution had to involve the judiciary. As India industrialized, more environmental problems emerged. While governments were preoccupied with economic development and electoral prospects, a growing body of NGOs highlighted environmental issues and repeatedly approached the Supreme Court with public interest litigations. The Supreme Court was highly responsive.

The Supreme Court Shapes Environmental Law

International trends influenced Indian law and jurisprudence. The global conversation that began in Stockholm in 1972 had expanded and developed a set of principles to govern the environment-development relationship. Polluter pays, the precautionary principle, public trust, intergenerational equity, and sustainable development are perhaps the most prominent. These were highlighted in high-profile international conferences and declarations, including the UN World Charter for Nature (1982), the UN Rio Declaration (1992), and the Kyoto Protocol (1997). Sustainable development became a global action point through the UN document *Our Common Future* (1987).

When India joined these initiatives, these principles had to be made operational. While the central government joined international treaties, the actual responsibility for pollution control, forest conservation, or biodiversity protection rested on the state governments, which followed the rules with varying levels of commitment. NGO's began to approach the judiciary on environmental issues using the relaxed rules for locus standi and procedure.

As mentioned above, a broad reading of Article 21 (the right to life) was central to the Supreme Court's postemergency progressive stance.

In a series of important judgments, the court concluded that a healthy environment, including clean air and water, are essential dimensions of the right to life. The court also invoked the amendments to the Constitution in 1976 that obliged the state and the citizenry to protect the environment and wildlife. This allowed the court to bring contemporary ideas regarding environmental management into law and push the government and corporations to provide relief to victims of environmental damage.

An early indication that the Supreme Court would take a broad view of the right to life came in a 1985 litigation, *Rural Litigation and Entitlement Kendra v. State of U.P.* The petition was to shut down limestone quarries because they were polluting the environment. The court recognized that the businesses would lose their investment but argued that "it is a price that has to be paid for the right of people to live in a healthy environment with minimal disturbance of ecological balance." In *Subhash Kumar v. State of Bihar* (1991), the Supreme Court declared that "the right to live is a fundamental right under the Constitution and it includes the right of enjoyment of pollution free water and air for enjoyment of life." In *Virendra Gaur v. State of Haryana* (1994) the Supreme Court declared that "environmental, ecological, air, water, pollution, etc. should be regarded as amounting to violation of Article 21." In *Narmada Bachao Andolan v. Union of India* (2000), the Supreme Court declared that "water is the basic need for the survival of human beings as enshrined in Article 21 of the Constitution of India and can only be served by providing a source of water where there is none." Finally, in *A.P. Pollution Control Board (II) v. Prof MV Nayudu* (2001) the Supreme Court looked back in satisfaction and declared that it was "one of the first Courts to develop the concept of right to 'healthy environment' as part of the right to life under Article 21 of our Constitution."

With these underpinnings, the court passed a series of rulings outlining the principles under which environmental cases would be adjudicated. In *Indian Council for Enviro-Legal Action v. Union of India* (1996), the defendants were companies that had polluted the groundwater, aquifers, and streams with toxic effluents. The petitioners' lawyer, the eminent M. C. Mehta, tells an entertaining story regarding the turning point in the case. Mehta took a bottle of water from the affected area, around a village called Bichri in Rajasthan, to the Supreme Court. The water was dark brown, and when the judge saw it, he asked whether it was rum.[22] The point was made, and Mehta won the case. This anecdote aside, the case is important because the court explicitly invoked the polluter pays principle—the companies would pay for the cleanup. The court noted that the OECD (Organisation for Economic Co-operation and Development) had developed the polluter pays principle in the 1970s and that it was now embedded in treaties signed among members of the European Community.

The Supreme Court declared the precautionary principle the law of the land in *Vellore Citizens Welfare Forum v. Union of India* (1996), in which petitioners complained against toxic emissions of tanneries in Tamil Nadu. The precautionary principle calls for prudence in view of risks of possibly irreversible future consequences of current decisions. *Possibly* is a significant word, for the principle urges precaution even when the effects of current decisions are not scientifically known or proven. A key implication is that the burden of proof falls on the actor (e.g., the firm) rather than the petitioner.

The Supreme Court invoked the public trust doctrine in *M. C. Mehta v. Kamal Nath* (1996). The family of Kamal Nath, then Minister of Environment and Forests, owned a vacation resort named Span, adjoining the Beas river. Some forest land had been used for this purpose with the approval of the Ministry of Environment and Forests under the Forest Conservation Act of 1980. The river had overflowed its banks and had flooded the resort. In response, Span Resorts had decided to block the river five hundred meters upstream and divert it to one kilometer downstream. *The Indian Express* reported this risky undertaking with the headline "Kamal Nath Dares the Mighty Beas."[23] In ruling for the plaintiff, the court noted acerbically that it could not have been a coincidence that an application for additional diversion of forest land, which had been held up, had been approved only after Mr. Nath became a minister. More to the point, the court used Roman, English, and American precedent to argue that the doctrine of public trust applied in this case. The doctrine states that some resources of broad social value—a forest, a waterway, a seashore—should never be privatized. The sovereign should hold them for use by the general public. The company was ordered to return some of the lands it had acquired and to bear the cost of repairing the damages. The court concluded by declaring that the public trust doctrine is "part of the law of the land."

The Supreme Court brought this body of law together in *N. D. Jayal v. Union of India*, a 2003 case brought by opponents of the Tehri dam on Bhagirathi river in Uttarakhand. Though the court ruled against the plaintiffs, it endorsed the principle of sustainable development as a "sine qua non for the maintenance of symbiotic balance between the rights to environment and development." It argued that "the concept of 'sustainable development' is to be treated as an integral part of 'life' under Article 21" and that "weighty concepts like intergenerational equity, public trust doctrine and precautionary principle . . . could only be nurtured by ensuring sustainable development." By 2010 when the National Green Tribunal came into being (more on this below), the principles we have discussed were firmly embedded in Indian law. The act creating the tribunal declared it would, "while passing any order or decision or award apply the principles of sustainable development, the precautionary principle, and the polluter pays principle."[24]

Thus, the Supreme Court of India has played an extraordinary role in the development of Indian environmental law, perhaps more than in any other field. Not only has it been more active, it has also reaffirmed social justice and fundamental rights in legislation, whereas in several other areas of corporate law, the old commitment to social justice has also been diluted.[25] However, there is still the perennial problem of enforcement of the law. The Supreme Court has taken this head-on.

The Supreme Court as Enforcer of Law

The Supreme Court has taken the view that it needs to not only pass judgments to protect fundamental rights guaranteed by the Constitution but also to ensure that these rights are honored in practice. To do this, it has often kept cases open for long periods, even decades, while passing a series of important interim orders. It has approached government agencies to conduct studies or has set up expert committees to investigate the subject at hand. To manage the workload of a large number of cases, it has even delegated its own decision-making authority. Eventually, given the sheer volume of environment-related cases, the National Green Tribunal was set up in 2010 to deal with cases expeditiously. The aim was to produce a decision within six months of filing. The National Green Tribunal is not bound by the Code of Civil Procedure of 1908. Instead, it relies on the "principles of natural justice." It is also not required to follow the rules of evidence, as described in the Indian Evidence Act of 1872.

This flexibility is meant to ease the process for petitioners approaching the court. Also, as mentioned above, it applies the principles of sustainable development, the polluter pays, and the precautionary principle.

The results of all this effort have been a mixed bag—we see success but also failure and judicial overreach. In some instances, the court has been saddled with the consequences of the government's failure to streamline the process by which a project is approved. We will discuss examples of each of these types of outcomes sequentially.

One of India's biggest ongoing environmental challenges is to reduce pollution in the river Ganga. More than four hundred million people are said to be dependent on the Ganga in some form or the other. The Supreme Court's extensive involvement in its cleanup has been described by the eminent activist-lawyer M. C. Mehta in his book *In the Public Interest*. Mehta's interest in the Ganga as a legal matter began when, in 1984, a half-kilometer stretch of the river caught fire after a lit cigarette was thrown in it. A giant factory owned by BHEL (Bharat Heavy Electricals Limited), a public-sector undertaking, was dumping untreated waste into the river. The effluents, which were floating on the surface, had caught fire. Mehta's investigations showed that this was by no means an isolated incident. He filed a petition with the Supreme Court to save the "Holy Ganga, Our Forsaken Mother." The core argument was that millions of people depended on the Ganga for drinking water, for bathing, cooking, and irrigating their crops. If the river was poisoned, their right to life was being threatened. The court took an expansive view of the matter, beginning by asking government agencies for a list of all industries that were polluting the river and municipalities that were pumping in sewage through the entire length of the Ganga. Eventually, the court split the case, considering pollution and municipal waste separately. Around the same time (1985), the Government of India had inaugurated its own cleanup effort, the Ganga Action Plan. Mehta describes the Supreme Court's engagement with Ganga Action Plan I and then Ganga Action Plan II but concludes (in 2009) that after twenty-five years of litigation, it was "far from protected." He was right. In 2014 he was back at the National Green Tribunal on the issue of pollution of the Ganga.[26] That said, Mehta praises the Supreme Court's intervention, arguing that it had undermined a culture of impunity. When the case had begun, many industrialists had gambled that the task was too large for the Supreme Court. It had proved them wrong, and "from that point on every industry had to wonder whether the court would come calling at its factory gates."[27]

Statistical evidence on the effect of regulation and the Supreme Court's interventions is only beginning to emerge. Shareen Joshi and coauthors have shown that judgments in the Ganga cases ordering tanneries and the municipalities in Kanpur to take antipollution measures improved river quality and reduced infant mortality downstream.[28] The Ganga action plan of the Government of India extended to other rivers in 1995 under the National River Conservation Plan. A recent careful statistical study by Greenstone and Hanna could not identify any positive effect of these regulations.[29] A Supreme Court order in 1995 required installation of catalytic converters in new gasoline-fueled cars in four major cities and the policy extended to forty-five others in 1998. Greenstone and Hanna find that this significantly improved air quality but had no discernible effect on infant mortality.[30] A 1998 Supreme Court order requiring Delhi's buses to switch to compressed natural gas (CNG) has been shown to have improved air quality and reduced concentrations of particulate matter, sulfur dioxide, and carbon monoxide.[31]

The Supreme Court's efforts at enforcement have sometimes failed when it has clashed with state governments allied with powerful local interests. We see long and drawn out battles of attrition involving nonimplementation of court orders and repeated litigation. A good example of this is protracted struggle regarding illegal construction and mining in the Aravalli Hills of Rajasthan and Haryana, where the forest range has been described as "the most degraded zone in India."[32] The litigation began in 1985, but as recently as 2018, the *Indian Express* carried the extraordinary headline "Supreme Court Shocked over Disappearance of 31 Hills in Aravalli Area of Rajasthan."[33] The Forest Survey of India had sampled 128 hills or hillocks of which 31 were missing. Referencing an incident in the Hindu epic the *Ramayana*, an exasperated Justice Lokur asked the counsel of the government of Rajasthan, "Have the people become Hanumaan that they are running away with hills?"[34] In another 2018 judgment, the court noted "irreversible damage" in the Aravallis. It criticized the government of Haryana for its "complete lack of any concern for the environmental and ecological degradation carried out in the Aravalli hills by influential colonizers . . . and what appears to be a very strong mining lobby in Haryana."[35]

At times the judiciary has overreached. Perhaps the clearest example of this is the famous Godavarman case. In September 1995 the Supreme Court was approached by T. N. Godavarman Thirumulpad, who complained of illegal felling in the Nilgiri forests in Tamil Nadu. The Supreme Court combined this with another writ petition, considered the case of fundamental importance, and in December 1996 delivered an interim order of extraordinary scope.[36] The court first clarified the domain of the Forest Conservation Act (FCA) by using an expansive definition of "forest" and "forest land."

On the one hand, the court declared that a forest "must be understood according to the dictionary meaning." On the other hand, "forest land" would include "not only forest as understood in the dictionary sense, but also any area recorded by the government as forest irrespective of ownership." This would mean that the FCA would apply to any land that satisfied *either* the dictionary definition *or* had been recorded as a forest by the government.

With this definition in hand, the court then issued a series of instructions, some applicable to the whole country and some to specific states. First, the court declared that all sawmills and "mining of any mineral" that was ongoing should be stopped unless prior approval of the central government had been sought. The felling of trees in any forest was suspended "except in accordance with the Working Plans of the State Governments, as approved by the Central Government." In the "tropical wet ever-green forests of Tirap and Changlang in the State of Arunachal Pradesh, there would be a complete ban on felling of any kind of trees therein." Moreover, "all saw mills, veneer mills and plywood mills in Tirap and Changlang in Arunachal Pradesh and within 100 Kms. from its border in Assam" would be closed immediately. There was a "complete ban on the movement of cut trees and timber from any of the seven North-Eastern States to any other State of the Country" with an exception for timber required for defense or any other government purpose. In the state of Himachal Pradesh and hill regions of Uttar Pradesh and West Bengal, there would be "no felling of trees permitted in any forest, public or private."

The Godavarman decision was at odds with many existing laws and practices at the state level. The Supreme Court had to be approached for a variation in each case. In her insightful analysis of this case, Shomona Khanna reports that in the nineteen years following the Godavarman decision, there were 3,700 such applications.[37] The court set up a special Forest Bench that met for at least two hours each week. It also sought special help and set up a Central Empowered Committee, which was described as a "Committee for all the forest areas in the whole of India to give directions, hear objections, and take decisions so that there is no need to approach this Court from time to time."[38] State-level empowered committees were also set up. The Supreme Court chose to keep the Godavarman case open and hear numerous forest-related matters under its umbrella. It is sometimes simply called the Forest Case.

The Godavarman decision and the subsequent steps have been praised by some conservationists. They include among its accomplishments the court's decision in 2002, following the recommendation of the Central Empowered Committee, to close down the mining operations of Kudremukh Iron Ore Mining Company Limited, a large and profitable government-owned company, because of the damage it was doing to rich tropical rainforest in the Western Ghats of Karnataka.[39] Others, while acknowledging the severity of the problem of deforestation, have argued that the Godavarman decision was flawed in several respects. There is the basic constitutional question of separation of powers—was the Supreme Court taking on the powers of the executive? Armin Rosencranz and Sharachchandra Lele took issue with the Supreme Court's definition of "non-forest." They noted that logging is considered forestry all over the world and argued that "to equate sawmills with mining, as the December 1996 order does, is really extreme."[40] A study in the northeastern state of Meghalaya noted that the ban on felling in forests had affected the livelihood of two hundred thousand people who had no alternative. The revenues of state governments in the northeast had fallen sharply.[41] In fairness, we should note that the tension between forest-protecting legislation and local livelihoods is not unique to this case. In his sympathetic discussion of the Chipko movement, Thomas Weber notes that "as laws were enacted to protect ever larger portions of the Himalayan catchment area from the axe, the supply of the necessary raw materials to the industries set up by the Chipko workers dried up."[42]

A more recent example of judicial overreach is in a dispute regarding mining for coal. The minister of state for environment and forests during the period 2009–2011, Jairam Ramesh, had, compared to his predecessors, given much greater weight to environmental considerations, thereby incurring the wrath of even some of his fellow ministers. There was considerable tension between the coal and environment ministries. In the case of a coal block, usually referred to as PEKB, Ramesh showed flexibility and decided to overrule the advice of the Forest Advisory Committee (FAC) and provide the necessary forest clearance.[43] He offered six reasons for the decision, beginning with the claim that the mines were in a fringe area of the forest. When a resident of Chhatisgarh, Sudiep Shrivastava, challenged the decision at the National Green Tribunal, he invoked the Lafarge decision (discussed below), according to which application of the FCA has to defer to the Forest Policy of 1988 and view the forest as a "national asset which has to be properly safeguarded for providing sustained benefits to the community."[44] Therefore, the "diversion of forest land for any non-forest purpose should be subject to the most careful examination by specialists from the point of view of social and environmental costs and benefits." The petitioner claimed that the environment ministry had not abided by this exhortation, and the National Green Tribunal (NGT) seems to have agreed when it concluded that "the FAC did not examine all the relevant facts and circumstances while rendering its advice and to cap it the Minister acted arbitrarily and rejected the FAC's advice for reasons having no basis in any authoritative study or experience in the relevant fields." It instructed to ministry to seek the FAC's advice on seven specific questions and reconsider the matter.[45]

The judgment is striking in that it not only accused the environment ministry of failing to perform due diligence, it even chastised its philosophical predispositions. The NGT quoted a 2012 Supreme Court judgment that argued that "environmental justice could be achieved only if we shift away from the principle of anthropocentric to ecocentric." In the former, the "non-human has only instrumental value to humans," whereas in the latter, the "non-human has intrinsic value."[46] The problem in this instance (the NGT argued) was that the ministry had been anthropocentric rather than ecocentric. The Supreme Court had previously made the same argument in *Centre for Environmental Law, World Wildlife Fund for Nature-India v. Union of India and Others*, where it had invoked Article 21 of the Indian Constitution, the right to life. We are economists, not legal scholars, so we will not dispute the legal point. As we have noted, the Supreme Court's creative and progressive interpretation of Article 21 in a variety of settings has been widely celebrated. Our sense, though, is that the criteria by which development-conservation tension will be negotiated, including the extent to which it will be anthropocentric or ecocentric, should be decided via debate within India's democratic institutions, not as a legal matter.[47]

Another example of judicial extravagance occurred when the Uttarakhand High Court, in *Mohd. Salim v. the State of Uttarakhand*, in March 2017, declared the Ganga a living person. The judgment emphasized the religious significance of the river. The decision was appealed by the state government on the grounds that it would lead to numerous practical complications. For instance, if a person drowned in the river could a claim be brought against it? Fortunately, in July 2017 the Supreme Court stayed the Uttarakhand High Court's decision.[48]

By the early 2000s forest conservation law had significantly complicated the process of getting permission to begin a project. This was especially true for mining, which often requires clearing the forested area. One part of the problem was that multiple environmental legislations were relevant, and there was no single window that a company could approach. After the company satisfied the state government, it still required an "environment clearance" from the Ministry of Environment and Forests in the central government. One might have suspected that environmental clearance would only be given if the project satisfied the conditions of the Forest Conservation Act. But this was not the case—a separate "forest clearance" had to be sought for which the ministry, as we have seen above, would rely on advice from a Forest Advisory Committee.

Meanwhile, there was still no clear definition of the term *forest*. This led to an important case, *Lafarge Umium Mining Limited v. Union of India*, under the Godavarman umbrella. In 1997 Lafarge had obtained environmental clearance for mining limestone in Meghalaya, declaring in its application that the area was not forested. Lafarge did not seek a separate forest clearance. The problems began when the chief conservator of forests visited the site in 2006 and found that the mining area was surrounded by "thick natural vegetation cover with sizeable number of tall trees." He recommended the project should stop since it had not been approved under the Forest Conservation Act. After considerable back-and-forth, involving, among other things, discussion of a Meghalaya law defining an area with twenty-five trees per acre as a forest, the Supreme Court allowed the project to continue on the grounds that it was a fait accompli. This was a controversial decision.[49]

The Lafarge case, read in conjunction with the Vedanta/Niyamgiri Hills case discussed in chapter 4, clarifies the legislator's problem. If a project is complex and its details emerge over a period of time, there are two risks. The first is that the government or the courts may stop the project after the company has sunk a significant sum, which is then lost. The second is that, precisely because a significant sum has been invested, the pressure to go through with the project is immense. In practice, it appears that typically the process may be delayed substantially but not stopped altogether. In other words, we get a delay plus fait accompli. Of course the requirement for government permission at several stages also creates the opportunity for rent-seeking. In 2017 a former minister was formally charged with having taken bribes to provide clearances under the Forest Conservation Act.[50]

Conclusion

As the quotation at the beginning of this chapter shows, the Supreme Court's efforts to protect the environment have been widely applauded. Its incorporation of internationally accepted principles of environmental law was a major accomplishment. Its efforts to enforce the law have also had some salutary practical outcomes. That said, activists have complained that in some major controversies, such as the construction of dams on the Narmada and Bhagirathi rivers, the court has come down on the side of development despite acknowledging environmental risks.[51] We have also discussed at length the issue of judicial overreach. Still, on balance, our assessment is favorable. It appears that unlike governments contemplating reelection, Supreme Court judges have been able to take a long-term view of the trade-off between growth and environmental damage.

However, there is still reason for concern when courts start to do a good part of what governments should. There is, to begin with, the question of allocation of the government's time and budgetary resources. Consider an instance in which the Supreme Court orders the cleanup of a particular stretch of river in response to a public interest litigation. What is the opportunity cost? Given the government's resources are not infinite, this cleanup will come at the expense of some other expenditure by the government. Will another river be neglected? Or will a health program receive fewer resources than it otherwise would have had? Allocation of budgets involves trade-offs, and evaluating these is the task of policy makers, not judges.

A long-standing critique of Indian economic policy is that it has not relied sufficiently on market mechanisms and has instead used quantitative restrictions and bans. This applies to environmental regulation as well. Shreekant Gupta noted that a command-and-control approach, imposing uniform standards across firms, does not account for their different costs of abatement. In contrast, an emissions tax would lead to more abatement by firms that could do this more cheaply. Using data from five states (Maharashtra, Gujarat, Andhra Pradesh, Uttar Pradesh, and Tamil Nadu), he estimates that command-and-control methods would cost between 26% and 169% more than an emissions tax approach for a 50% reduction in emissions.[52] Using plant-level data from Surat, Michael Greenstone et al. estimate that a cap-and-trade policy would lower abatement costs by 39% compared to concentration standards that mimic existing norms.[53] Unsurprisingly, complaints about rent-seeking, so common in the context of restrictions in trade and industrial licensing, have emerged in the sphere of command-and-control environmental regulation as well.[54] A 2013 cover story in the weekly *India Today* colorfully argued that "red tape has become a green noose and is strangling development."[55] In a 2013 seminar in Delhi regarding the proposed National Environment Appraisal and Monitoring Authority, the prime minister of India himself declared that the new institution would remove the "hated license-permit Raj."[56] To the extent that courts make policy, this tendency to rely on bans or other blunt instruments will be reinforced. Courts cannot be expected to develop taxation or trading mechanisms.

CHAPTER SIX

Law in a Labor-Surplus Economy

The biggest killer is the Industrial Disputes Act, which says that if you are a manufacturing firm with 100 workers or more, you cannot dismiss any of [the workers] under any circumstances unless you get prior approval from government. — Arvind Panagariya, 2014[1]

This isn't the time to make labour reforms. We can't . . . put labourers in the hands of corporates. States are creating such a situation that there is no rule of law. — Bharatiya Mazdoor Sangh[2]

Introduction

The situation of Indian workers in (say) 1985 presented a paradox. On the one hand, Indian and international media often reported on the plight of "bonded laborers," that is, people who are forced to work for a particular employer because they are indebted to him. On the other hand, businessmen complained that workers had too many legal protections. Once hired, they were difficult to fire. This rigidity was making them turn to more capital-intensive methods of manufacturing. This puzzle—simultaneous existence of unfree and apparently overprotected workers—can be quickly resolved if we recognize that both were small parts of the labor force. The protected workers were in the so-called organized sector, especially factories employing more than one hundred workers. The bonded laborers were the very poorest people, often agricultural workers. The majority of Indian workers, in the unorganized sector, were not coerced to work but neither were they protected in any meaningful way by the law and the state. Their problems were low wages and unemployment in an economy where labor was abundant and capital and land were relatively scarce.

Over the last few decades, this picture has slowly changed. Rapid economic growth has created new opportunities, and while bonded labor remains a problem, there are probably fewer workers trapped in this way, though this is difficult to measure accurately. At the other end of the spectrum, as the Indian economy has liberalized, there has been a slow decrease in the job security given to workers in the organized sector. This erosion has been stealthy rather than overt or loud. But perhaps the biggest change is not at the extremes of the labor market—it is in the hitherto largely ignored unorganized sector. As Indian democracy has become more substantive, citizens are demanding more from their governments. Workers in the unorganized sector are receiving attention (and programs and benefits) from political parties because they vote. The most prominent legislation of this type is a radical and ambitious rural employment guarantee, unique in its scope, which has created a "Right to Work."

Indian workers' legal status still varies hugely. Two sets of laws—pertaining to the rural employment guarantee and job security for organized sector workers—are fiercely debated. Just about the only consensus in policy circles and the academic literature is that there is a need for simplification—there are too many laws. To coherently describe how this complex picture came to be, we have organized this chapter as follows: we begin at one end of the spectrum, the bonded laborer, and end at the other, the relatively protected organized sector worker. With this description under our belt, we can ask, How much is labor law protecting workers from exploitation, and, Is labor law constraining economic development? The answers to these questions are not easy to summarize precisely because workers' legal status varies so much, so we will postpone this discussion until the concluding section of this chapter.

Unfree Labor

The welfare of India's poorest and most socially disadvantaged workers was never a priority for the British colonial rulers of India. Indeed, in the early colonial period, the East India Company used forced labor, drawing on locally prevalent practices as well as methods used in Britain.[3] In the second half of the nineteenth century, the Raj passed notorious legislation permitting indentured labor, putting the weight of the state behind the enforcement of such contracts. The Workman's Breach of Contract Act of 1859 permitted imprisonment of a worker who had taken an advance from an employer but had quit before his contract ended.

The act was rescinded only in 1926. Responding to the demands of European planters in Assam, the Raj even passed special legislation permitting them to privately arrest "absconding" employees, a right that existed until 1908. Eventually, the Raj passed legislation banning forced or bonded labor relationships under various names across the country such as *vetti* and *kamiauti*, but these efforts were ineffectual.[4]

When the Indian Constitution was being debated and written, members of the Constituent Assembly considered the problem of forced labor to be sufficiently important to warrant Article 23 of fundamental rights: "traffic in human beings and begar and similar forms of forced labour are prohibited and any contravention of this prohibition shall be an offense punishable in accordance with the law."[5] Because this is a fundamental right, violations can be taken to the Supreme Court.

Forced labor in India often takes a specific form—bonded labor. Why? In a precarious agrarian economy, a worker will encounter financial difficulties because of drought, harvest failure, unemployment, ill health, and the like. Lacking savings and access to formal banking, he or she will need to go to an informal lender. Lenders usually want collateral, but the worker doesn't have any. Therefore, he or she will take the loan and promise to work in exchange. If the debt is to be repaid via labor, the wage will be less than the market wage. Moreover, the borrower may put his or her family to work as well. It is also likely that the employer will prevent the worker from finding work elsewhere until the loan is repaid. Therefore, there will probably be a coercive aspect to this relationship. Over and above this, the worker's weak financial situation as well as lower caste status may expose him or her to physical abuse, poor working conditions, or other indignities. Intimidation or fraud may also be used to keep the worker indebted because the arrangement is so useful to the employer.[6] Thus, the "bonded labor system" has four components: debt, a long duration of employment, below-market wage, and coercion.[7]

Despite the mention in the Constitution, no specific national-level legislation was passed until the 1970s, when Prime Minister Indira Gandhi positioned herself as a champion of the poor. Consistent with this, the Bonded Labour System (Abolition) Act of 1976 declared such arrangements illegal. The freed worker's debt would be extinguished. The state would try "as far as practicable to promote the welfare of the freed bonded labourer by securing and protecting the economic interests of such bonded labourer so that he may not have any occasion or reason to contract any further bonded debt."[8] The act remains in place. In 2016 the central government made its scheme for rehabilitation of bonded laborers more generous.[9]

It was not easy to implement the provisions of this act because, to begin with, it was difficult to tell who was a bonded laborer. How could a laborer prove that he or she had borrowed money from his or her employer? Most likely, cash had changed hands without any documentation. Even if it could be proven that the worker had taken a loan, how could the worker demonstrate that this had led to coercion? The act of 1976 put the onus on the employer—given the existence of debt, the employer had to prove that it did not lead to bondage.[10] Identification of bonded labor was complicated by the fact that in rural India there is a common category of workers known as attached laborers who have annual contracts. The daily wage of the attached laborer is lower than that of the "casual" laborer who is hired on a daily basis, but the attached laborer is assured of employment. In return, the employer is guaranteed that he or she will have labor on hand when essential, for instance, during the harvest season.[11] An attached laborer could well have borrowed from his or her employer. If this is so, the employer may well use some type of coercion to prevent the worker from leaving the job before the loan is paid off. This makes the distinction between an attached laborer and bonded laborer blurry.

Given this ambiguity, it is difficult to estimate the number of bonded laborers. The bureaucracy and the politicians often represent society's upper echelons, are likely to be sympathetic to the employer rather than the laborer, and will be reluctant to report a crime. It is also likely that investigators will find it hard to get reliable information on whether the worker is being coerced and how much the worker is being paid. In the discussions preceding passing of the Bonded Labour System (Abolition) Act of 1976, twenty-one states declared that they had no bonded laborers at all.[12] In 1977–1978 India's well-regarded National Sample Survey reported that there were 345,000 bonded laborers in India. The Gandhi Peace Foundation, a respected NGO, studied ten states and estimated there were 2.6 million in 1981.[13] According to the Ministry of Labour and Employment, by 2007–2008, 287,000 bonded laborers had been identified.[14] It is difficult to take these estimates seriously—the best we can say is that the problem persists, but has diminished, as figure 6.1 shows.[15]

Arguably the best-known bonded labor case is *Bandhua Mukti Morcha v. Union of India* (first decided in 1983), simultaneously a cause for

FIGURE 6.1. NUMBER OF BONDED LABORERS REHABILITATED
Source: Authors' computation from India, Planning Commission. *A Report on Bonded Labour Rehabilitation Scheme under Centrally Sponsored Bonded Labour System (Abolition) Act, 1976 in the States of Madhya Pradesh, Orissa, Rajasthan, Tamil Nadu and Uttar Pradesh*. New Delhi: Planning Commission 2010, A1–A2.

celebration and despair.[16] On the one hand, the Supreme Court used (indeed perhaps contorted) the law to provide the worker maximum benefit under the provisions of the Indian Constitution. On the other hand, its recommendations were very poorly implemented. The story begins with Swami Agnivesh, an activist, taking up the cause of workers employed in stone quarries in Haryana, just outside Delhi, in the early 1980s. Swami Agnivesh brought the matter to the attention of Bhajan Lal, then chief minister of Haryana. Bhajan Lal was not sympathetic and, for his pains, Swami Agnivesh himself was accused of being Naxalite (Maoist) and was arrested, a fairly common tactic used to harass activists. He had better luck with the Supreme Court. On February 25, 1982, Agnivesh wrote to Justice Bhagwati, who, as we saw in chapter 4, was an activist judge and a pioneer of Public Interest Litigation. Bhagwati attended to the matter immediately, and the Supreme Court held hearings from March 1 to March 3, 1982. The court appointed a two-man committee, which submitted a damning report in June 1982, and the court issued its decision in 1983.[17]

The first question was whether the Supreme Court could act in this context—for this to happen, a fundamental right had to be violated.[18] Among the various arguments Justice Bhagwati used was one that he imported from a previous decision, *PUDR v. Union of India*, 1982. The issue there concerned the treatment of workers involved in the construction of the stadiums and other facilities for the Asian Games (1982). Some workers were receiving less than the minimum wage. This was a violation of the Minimum Wages Act of 1948. But was this a violation of a fundamental right? Bhagwati argued that "there is no reason why the word 'forced' should be read in a narrow and restricted manner so as to be confined to physical or legal 'force' particularly when the national charter, its fundamental document, has promised a new socialist republic."[19] He argued that anybody who worked for less than a minimum wage was being forced, by economic if not physical compulsion. This was a violation of Article 23 of the Constitution, a fundamental right.[20] So the Supreme Court could act.[21] Bhagwati's argument, though well intentioned, was dubious. Minimum wage violations are very common in India, and by his argument a large fraction of the labor force is "forced."

Bhagwati's second legal innovation was more defensible. The Haryana government had argued that there were no bonded laborers in the state. Even if they were forced, they were not bonded—there was no evidence that the transaction began with a loan. If this point had been conceded, there would have been no need for the Haryana government to rehabilitate the workers as required by the Bonded Labour System (Abolition) Act of 1976. Justice Bhagwati argued, fairly in our view, that the laborer could not be expected to provide proof of indebtedness. Given his "poverty, illiteracy, and social and economic backwardness," formal procedural requirements would have to be waived.[22]

The court ruled in favor of Bandhua Mukti Morcha (Swami Agnivesh) and issued twenty-one instructions to the Central Government and the Government of Haryana to free the laborers and improve working conditions for those who remained. What did not happen next was remarkable. The depressing saga of resistance by the Government of Haryana, delay, adjournment, and the appointment of one committee after another, is described in detail by Arun Shourie, who wrote as late as 2001 that the case was ongoing. Meanwhile, the activists had repeatedly approached the Supreme Court, which had responded by issuing fresh orders, to little effect. Writing nine years after Shourie (in 2010), Ramesh Tiwari commented that "more than 25 years have passed and there is still non-compliance of the court's directives."[23] Human rights lawyer Upendra Baxi reported that, feeling let down, Swami Agnivesh had contemplated a mock funeral procession for the Supreme Court's decision in *Bandhua Mukti Morcha v. Union of India*.[24]

Bandhua Mukti Morcha v. Union of India starkly revealed the limits of legislation and court action when the structural location of workers vis-à-vis employers is weak. Shourie pointed out that the bonded laborers were not in a remote location. They were just outside Delhi, India's capital. And this was not some minor tribunal; it was the Supreme Court. But the court had been thwarted by the mine owners and their associates, who were "in many ways the real government of India."[25]

The prevention of coercion is of course a basic obligation of the state. However, as we have already seen, the state itself can use its authority in ways that hurt the poor. We need legislation to clarify the limits of state power. The Forest Rights Act of 2006, which we discussed in chapter 4, is a good example. The Street Vendors Act of 2014 is a potentially important legislation in the same spirit. It takes away the presumption of unconstrained state power in urban spaces. In the next section we will describe the process by which this Street Vendors Act came into being and its future prospects.

The Right to Livelihood: Street Vendors

The street vendor is ubiquitous in urban India. They sell anything from food to books to clothing. The vendor is usually on the sidewalk, if there is one, or perhaps even on the street itself. Often vendors have no legal status at all and can work in their locations as long as the local police and officials allow. They are at their mercy and pay substantial bribes. However, Indian cities also have systems of licensing for street vending. In this section we will trace the evolution of law pertaining to street vending, following a few important cases from Delhi and ending with national-level legislation.

In the first few decades after independence, the vendors were in a very weak position, de jure as well as de facto, and courts were not sympathetic. Beginning in the 1980s, with the support of middle-class activists and lawyers, the vendors approached the Supreme Court, which was now more responsive to the poor. After extensive Supreme Court intervention and foot-dragging from the government, national-level legislation was passed in 2014. Implementation remains a huge challenge.

Our story starts with an appeal to the Supreme Court of a Punjab High Court decision by a vendor named Pyare Lal, who sold potato chips in a high-traffic central Delhi neighborhood called Janpath. Pyare Lal claimed to have been working in that location since 1950. After joining an association of vendors who lobbied for legal status, he had received a permit known as tehbazaari from the New Delhi Municipal Committee (NDMC) in 1963. The NDMC had subsequently concluded that the vendors needed to be relocated and given new permits. Pyare Lal was not given an alternative site. He approached the court on the grounds that his fundamental right to a trade was being violated and the NDMC's decision was discriminatory and unconstitutional. As in any such dispute there were many issues relevant to the specific case at hand—in this instance the NDMC argued that Pyare Lal's food preparation was unhygienic, a rationale the court accepted. More significantly, the Supreme Court concluded that while the NDMC had been kind in allowing Pyare Lal to operate, there was no fundamental right involved—"it cannot be said that persons in India have a lawful right to pursue street trading."[26] This meant that street vendors were dependent on state benevolence; they did not have intrinsic rights to practice their trade.

Over time, as we have seen in earlier chapters, the public discourse changed, and courts became more supportive of the poor. *Olga Tellis v. Bombay Municipal Corporation* (1985) was a seminal decision. The case had to do with the right of the Bombay Municipal Corporation to evict squatters. The petitioners did not argue that people had a right to squat. Instead, they argued that they had the right to make a living. They lived on the sidewalk because their work was nearby, serving Bombay's better-off population. If they were evicted, they would lose their livelihood because they would live too far away to get to work. The Supreme Court allowed the eviction, with instructions for relocation. However, more important from a legal point of view was their view that the right to life (Article 21 of the Constitution) included a right to livelihood. The judgement said that

> The State may not, by affirmative action, be compellable to provide adequate means of livelihood or work to the citizens. But, any person, who is deprived of his right to livelihood except according to just and fair procedure estab-

> lished by law, can challenge the deprivation as offending the right to life conferred by Article 21.[27]

Olga Tellis did not provide the precise legal foundation for the case we will discuss in the next paragraph, but it reflects the tone, the changed legal-moral sensibility with which matters like this would be adjudicated.[28] In addition to affirming a right to livelihood, the court argued that "human compassion must soften the rough edges of justice in all situations."[29]

In *Sodan Singh v. New Delhi Municipal Committee* (1989) the Supreme Court explicitly rejected its previous view in *Pyare Lal* that street trading was not a fundamental right. The court argued that street trading provides citizens a useful service. It is a legitimate activity, and as such the right to practice it is protected by the Indian Constitution's affirmation of the right to a trade.[30] This is of course subject to reasonable restrictions so that it does not tread on other fundamental rights. The court's position in this and other cases was that a systematic regulatory framework needed to be developed for when and where street vendors could operate. Over the next two decades, the Supreme Court was approached repeatedly, and it nudged recalcitrant municipalities to lay down rules. National policies were articulated in 2004 and 2009. In 2010, in *Gainda Ram v. M.C.D.* (Municipal Corporation of Delhi), the Supreme Court argued that municipal rules were not sufficient. If a fundamental right (to street trading, in this instance) was to be restricted, another law was needed. In 2014 the Street Vendors (Protection of Livelihood and Regulation of Street Vending) Act was passed. The act allows for the appointment of Town Vending Committees (TVCs) in which 40% of the members will be street vendors' representatives. Areas of the city where they may not operate are identified. In areas where they can operate, the maximum number is specified. Each vendor is given a certificate that is proof of his or her right to work in a specific location. The right can be bequeathed but not sold.[31] Up to 2.5% of the population of a city can be certified in this way.

The Street Vendors Act is viewed by its supporters as "historic" legislation, "the first of its kind in the world and human history." The act may benefit as many as twenty million vendors across the country.[32] However, at this point in time implementation is weak, and it remains to be seen when and where the law will have a substantial influence.[33] It is too early to tell.

As *Olga Tellis* had clarified, while the State could not arbitrarily *interfere* with the right to a livelihood, it had no *obligation* to provide work to every citizen. Perhaps the most radical labor legislation passed in independent India is a 2005 act that created such an obligation in the rural areas.

A Right to Employment?

It is now common in Indian policy circles to use the expression "right to work." How did this emerge? The story starts with a series of devastating famines in the late nineteenth century. Initially, the Raj took a disastrous laissez-faire approach. This reflected callousness toward Indian life as well as unwillingness to incur unnecessary expenditures. As the death toll mounted, it became necessary to develop a systematic policy to anticipate and respond to famines. One decision was to begin public works to provide employment to the needy in a location close to the village. This would be manual labor at a low wage rate. It would attract only the desperate, so it would not cost too much. People could also stay at home rather than congregate in relief camps, which spread disease and increased the death toll. This form of workfare became part of the Famine Code, the first draft of which was submitted in 1880.[34]

Hunger and malnutrition, long features of Indian rural life, persisted past independence. But independent India has differed from colonial India in one crucial way—there has never been a famine. Amartya Sen famously argued that this is because India is a democracy. A famine is a huge and visible failure of government, which will have to pay a price in the next election. Even the most incompetent or callous government will, from self-interest if for no other reason, act to prevent famine.[35] Sen's explanation fits the case of the massive drought in Maharashtra in the early 1970s. Even though there was a sharp decline in output, there was no famine because of effective government interventions. One of these was a public works program that employed the needy. The program proved popular and remained in place even after the famine was over.

What was the effect of public works in nonfamine years? In addition to directly providing income to the poor, it had some other benefits. In a competitive labor market, if the demand for labor increases the wage rate will rise. Therefore, even private-sector employers will have to pay more. Even in a noncompetitive labor market, an improvement in the outside option will increase the bargaining power of the worker. In the Maharashtra program there were other social benefits as well. Many of the beneficiaries were women. Participation in the program also made some workers politically active and more willing to approach the government for other needs.[36]

There was, inevitably, the problem of corruption. Government officials intercepted some of the wages. Ghost workers were invented and their wages were pocketed. In principle, the scheme could have created valuable assets (roads, irrigation, and repairs), but it was much criticized on this score. Various government departments had to coordinate to ensure that the workers were employed at productive tasks, and this proved difficult. Still, the Maharashtra program became an act in 1977.

By the early 2000s the Indian economy was growing rapidly, but employment had not kept pace. Agriculture had grown slowly, and rural distress was an important political issue. In this context, the government introduced NREGA (National Rural Employment Guarantee Act), following the Maharashtra example. This was deliberately formulated as an act rather than just another government policy so that the worker was given a legal entitlement and the government could be held accountable. Also, an act would make it harder for a later government to end the program; it would require parliament to pass an amendment.[37] NREGA guaranteed one hundred days of employment per year to the adults in a family. As often happens in India, Mahatma Gandhi was later added to the title. The program is now known as MGNREGA.

MGNREGA has run into one thorny legal issue. To keep costs in check, governments would like to keep wages low. Can they be lower than the minimum wage? In *Sanjit Roy v. the State of Rajasthan*, decided in 1983, the Supreme Court ruled that employment provided for famine relief could not pay less than the minimum wage. Justice Bhagwati relied on the argument we have described above, that employment at less than the minimum wage is in effect forced labor, which is ruled out by Article 23 of the Constitution. In his concurring judgment Justice Pathak appealed to Article 14, regarding equal treatment—workers in a famine-relief program could not be treated differently from others. This issue has come up again, but it remains unresolved.[38]

MGNREGA is expensive, costing 0.8% of GDP in 2009–2010.[39] It is controversial for the same reasons as the Maharashtra program, and it is viewed by some as unproductive make-work. Jagdish Bhagwati and

Arvind Panagariya christened it a "Rural Inefficiency Act."[40] That said, there is growing evidence, using various statistical methods, of the benefits of MGNREGA to the rural poor.[41] Indeed, two Indian states, Kerala and Madhya Pradesh, have launched Urban Employment Guarantee schemes in 2010 and 2019 respectively. It is too early to assess their effect. It is clear, though, that the idea of a legally binding right to (some) employment is here to stay.

We have journeyed from the coerced worker (bonded laborer) to one who is allowed to work (street vendor) to one who is guaranteed some work (rural laborer). Our last stop is the worker in the organized sector, a subset of workers who have received legal protection from being fired from their jobs. The organized sector has seen the most legislation, the most conflict, and the most resistance to change. Our next section argues that these features are interrelated.

Organized Labor

In principle, we can think of labor law in the organized sector in four categories: wages, working conditions, social security and welfare, and dispute resolution/labor-management relations.[42] Dispute resolution has been by far the most controversial, and we organize this section around this thread. There are four phases. First, in the late colonial period, a basic legal structure was put in place reflecting the growing participation of Indians in governance and their desire to maintain industrial peace in the face of an often-militant labor movement. Then, in the early postindependence decades, there was a compact wherein Indian business received protection from international competition and was, in return, willing to pay the higher costs imposed by more regulation. This compact broke down in the 1970s and 1980s as industrial growth slowed and strikes and lockouts increased. After 1991, and especially in the 2000s when the Indian economy "liberalized," many economists and policy makers agreed that labor law needed to be simplified and rationalized. They continue to be particularly vociferous on the need to get rid of firing restrictions. Others question how much bite this particular set of regulations has, and the unions, irrespective of political affiliation, are fiercely opposed to changes. The jury is out on when substantial and sustainable reforms will occur.

Colonial Roots: The Origins of State Management of Industrial Relations

Factory-based manufacturing began in India in the 1850s, but legislation came slowly. A series of Factory Acts were passed beginning in 1881 regulating hours, working conditions, women's work, and so forth. The Raj's motivation was partly to raise costs for Indian industry so as to protect British rivals. Laws and the basis for them changed in the interwar period. The immediate reason was a sharp rise in disputes in the factories. The cotton textile mill industry was troubled because of lack of modernization, a poor welfare record, and Japanese competition in the Indian market. When large-scale disputes broke out, the Employers and Workmen's (Disputes) Act, 1860, which allowed summary adjudication of employment contract violations by magistrates, was effectively the only law available. But this law, which did not provide for arbitration or a negotiated settlement, proved inadequate in the face of large-scale industrial unrest.

Reforms in 1919 gave Indians more say in governance, a reward for participation in World War I. Textile factory workers joined political movements in the interwar period. For example, the nationalist leader M. K. Gandhi was influential in the establishment of the Textile Labour Association of Ahmedabad city. Industrial disputes threatened to take on a political aspect, involved nationalist and communist unions, and often pitted Indian workers against British employers or Indian employers who donated money to the same parties with which the workers were affiliated.

The government at all levels was now more willing and more able to legislate on worker issues. The Indian Trade Unions Act, 1926; the Indian Railways Act, 1930; the Tea Districts Emigrant Labour Act, 1932; and the Payment of Wages Act, 1936, were instituted. These laws were meant to create an institutional mechanism for dispute resolution and collective bargaining. However, driven by anxieties that labor disputes were getting out of hand, the main nationalist party, Congress, drove a movement toward political (i.e., government-controlled) rather than institutional mechanisms for avoidance and resolution of disputes. In 1937 reforms installed elected Indian governments in the provinces. Provincial legislation in Bombay (the Bombay Industrial Disputes Act of 1938) Province endorsed the government's role as an arbitrator in the textile industry and effectively installed politicians as protectors of the unionized workers. Soon after its success in the 1937 elections, the Congress committee announced that "it is the imperative duty of the Government to intervene in the conflict and to secure speedy settlement of the dispute on the basis of the recognition of the workers' rights and satisfaction of their just demands."[43]

During World War II the government became more actively involved in labor disputes, a result of the Defence of India Rules, which prohibited strikes and lockouts. In 1946 and 1947, nearly two million workers struck work in each year, leading to thirteen and sixteen million man-days of work lost, respectively. There had been unrest earlier—in particular the years 1921 and 1928–1929 were bad years for industrial relations—but nothing like this had happened before. Wartime inflation was the direct impetus behind these strikes, and the chaos of transfer of power from British to Indian hands made managing it difficult.

Independence came amid this chaos.

The Developmental Foundation of Labor Law (1947–1965)

Recent research on Indian labor law in the organized sector has tried to distinguish between states that have prolabor or probusiness legal regimes. This classification scheme does not help us understand the design of the legal regime in the years after independence when the government was both prolabor *and* probusiness. The policy makers and framers of law did not think that these two sympathies were contradictory. Almost no employer complained that the labor law was against their interest. In these years American sociologists were debating the character of Indian industrialization. In their view Indian labor law was not necessarily prolabor in sentiment. It was rather a developmental law—"the urgencies of development have been compelling considerations in shaping Indian legislative practice in labor matters."[44] In that spirit, Morris D. Morris, author of the first systematic history of textile labor in Bombay, observed that the basis of trade unionism and trade union legislation was to maintain a disciplined labor force rather than foster collective bargaining at the workplace.[45] Numerous statements scattered in five-year-plan documents and reports gave voice to another developmental imperative: employment was precious and needed to be protected.

Large employers like factories and mines did not complain about the proemployment bias in legislation because they shared in the developmental ideology and received a big privilege in return. They received protection, too, in the form of high tariffs. Given protection in the final market, the average firm could bear excess labor cost (i.e., sustain labor productivity below levels that were internationally competitive) and afford some overstaffing. This implicit quid pro quo simultaneously addressed (in principle) two overarching aims of development policy: industrialization with domestic resources and social justice.

Almost immediately after independence, a consolidated law was enacted to deal with industrial disputes, and the government was firmly installed as a negotiator, adviser, and arbitrator. As a direct legacy of the preindependence links between politics and unions, the Industrial Disputes Act, 1947, created a formal role for the government in the dispute settlement process. It set out the platforms where negotiations would take place. The works committees, for example, formed on the shop floor, did not have government participation but followed certain guidelines set out by the act. The government had a direct role in appointing conciliation officers, boards of conciliation, and courts of enquiry if disputes persisted. It could then enforce and oversee arbitration proceedings and send disputes to labor courts, industrial tribunals, and national tribunals. Although the federal government took the lead in legislation, state (province) governments managed disputes except for cases of "national importance," which were heard by national tribunals. Provincial governments had engaged in negotiating labor disputes before independence both in Bombay and in Calcutta, where most industrial workers were. It was in keeping with this tradition that the states continued to perform a similar role after independence. The Supreme Court was the final court of appeal, but only when a constitutional issue was involved.

The most common grievance related to wages. Wage revision followed a routine administrative process in the government. In private industrial enterprise such a routine process was either absent or disregarded, making strikes and lockouts more likely. The strike is the weapon of the worker, the lockout or unannounced closure of a factory the weapon of the employer. In both cases, the government had the legal power to step in and force arbitration on the parties, though this was not always used or effective.

Although a few pieces of legislation dominated the field, a spate of amendments and specific laws ensured that by the early 1960s, labor issues were covered under multiple heads. There were sector-specific laws that covered fully or partly issues relating to labor; there were laws pertaining to wages and welfare provisions; and there were laws covering bargaining and disputes (see table 6.1).

TABLE 6.1 **Laws relating to labor (ca. 1965)**

Year	Factories, mines, plantations, railways, transport	Wages, working conditions, compensation, insurance, provident fund, welfare	Collective bargaining and dispute resolution
1890	Indian Railways Act		
1923		Workmen's Compensation Act	
1926			Trade Unions Act
1932	Tea Districts Emigrant Labour Act		
1934		Dock Labourers Act	
1936		Payment of Wages Act	
1938		Employers' Liability Act	
1939	Motor Vehicles Act		
1942		Weekly Holidays Act	
1943		War Injuries (Compensation Insurance) Act	
1946		Mica Mines Labour Welfare Fund Act	Industrial Employment (Standing Orders) Act
1947		Coal Mines Labour Welfare Fund Act	Industrial Disputes Act
1948	Dock Workers (Regulation of Employment) Act; Factories Act	Coal Mines Provident Fund and Bonus Schemes Act; Employees' State Insurance Act; Minimum Wages Act	
1949			Industrial Disputes (Banking and Insurance Companies) Act
1951	Plantations Labour Act		
1952	Mines Act	Coal Mines (Conservation and Safety) Act; Employees' Provident Funds Act	
1958	Merchant Shipping Act		
1961	Metalliferous Mines Regulations Act; Motor Transport Workers' Act	Iron Ore Mines Labour Welfare Cess Act; Maternity Benefit Act	
1963		Personal Injuries (Compensation Insurance) Act	
1965		Payment of Bonus Act	

As Morris predicted, the presence of trade unions did not foster collective bargaining at the enterprise level. In 1947 trade unions were common only in two fields, textiles and railways, where the majority of the employees were members of unions. Outside these two fields unions were not common, and union members formed a minority of the workforce. Most unions were affiliated with "federations" that were arms of the main political parties. Again, for political reasons, union membership was concentrated in three states: Maharashtra, West Bengal, and Kerala. Both Maharashtra and West Bengal were relatively more industrialized until the 1960s. Also, in West Bengal and Kerala, where the communists were a strong force, there was fierce competition between the left-affiliated unions and their rivals, which encouraged more people to join one union or another.

The ties with political parties gave the Indian trade union movement an unusual character and had two features that made the union movement unstable and employers potentially hostile. First, observers noted that "white-collar politicos run unions with the help of unskilled activists in the factories[,which] contrasts sharply with the Western experience where skilled workers spearheaded the union movement and insisted that wage-skill differentials be respected."[46] The power of labor depended on numbers rather than on skills, experience, or hierarchy of workers. The numbers fixation made recruitment into unions competitive and often violent. Second, the presence of many potentially rival politically affiliated unions in one large workplace acted as an obstacle to collective bargaining.

The Collapse of the Paradigm (1970–1991)

The government-mediated quid pro quo—employers would get protection from competition and workers would get job security—was becoming unsustainable from the time an industrial depression set in, roughly from 1970. In practice, retrenchment was made substantially more difficult. When the employment-protection ideology was under serious strain, employment in the organized sector was subject to well over forty central laws relating to hours, security, wages, safety, and layoffs. According to legislation passed in 1982, any firm with at least one hundred workers on its rolls and wishing to downsize or close had to first seek permission from a government body. Such permission was rarely given or given quickly.

A spate of industrywide strikes showed that organized labor was unhappy. Employers in cotton textiles, jute textiles, and engineering, all being industries staring at bankruptcy, were unwilling to offer workers anything substantial. Under the industrial licensing and import licensing regime in place, these older factories were deemed to have a weak claim to obtain a license, the favored sectors being metals, machines, and chemicals. Therefore, most of these had not modernized at all. Many employers, of course, were happy to close shop and use workers as the excuse.

The most traumatic instance of institutional failure took place in January 1982 when the Bombay cotton mill workers went on a strike. The biggest mass strike in history, the strike officially lasted eighteen months and at its peak involved more than two hundred thousand workers. As expected by law and the ideology of protecting workers, the government, the police, the press, and the unions all became quickly embroiled in solving the crisis. Even the peasants became involved by donating food to workers. The result was grimmer than anyone had imagined at the start of the strike. Law proved powerless to force an arbitration. Grassroots organizations talking to workers were ineffective. Donations dwindled. Class solidarity collapsed. The leadership alienated itself from the workers. A slow judiciary and cooked-up employment registers deprived many thousands of their jobs and dues when some of the mills reopened in 1983.

Anyone would think that after this colossal waste of time and spirits, labor law would get a serious look. This did not happen. Institutional reform was just not an option on the table. Amazingly, industrial growth revived in the 1980s. From the mid-1980s the trade regime allowed freer import of equipment for modernization. Investment and industrial growth revived, but employment did not. Called "jobless growth," the episode seemed to suggest that the legal obstacle to letting workers go had encouraged employers to avoid hiring even though wages were low.[47]

The economic reforms of the liberalization era began with this backdrop of industrial revival and employment stagnation. The 1980s did not really open up the economy to imports and foreign investment. Once these changes were introduced, there were two important consequences. Rationalization was thrust on many incumbent corporations, and the mindset changed. No aspect of the old developmental ideology and instruments was sacrosanct anymore.

Questioning Law and Reform by Stealth (1991–2016)

In the first ten years after the liberalizing reforms began, labor law did not emerge as a priority. But with more open markets, incumbent industries needed flexibility to rationalize employment. Economists explained why labor laws needed change. The case rested on two sets of arguments. First, labor laws obstructed rationalization. The laws provided little flexibility for downsizing, made closure difficult, and locked up assets that could otherwise be sold and recycled into investment. Second, the overall quality of jobs fell. Laws being designed to protect insiders, employers often hired more people on contract for auxiliary work. The terms of these contracts were often harsh. For example, in the case of contract employment, no severance pay is mandatory.

In practice it was not easy to implement drastic reform. Resistance from the Ministry of Labour as well as state governments, who were in charge of the implementation of law, was often fierce. The attempt to find a consensus during the proceedings of the Second National Commission of Labour (2002), for example, did see agreements between the stakeholders on social security measures, but there was little stomach for reform of employment law.

There were legal ways to bypass the obstacles posed by employment law, such as contract labor, as mentioned above, but they could not be used in every situation. Two other such escape options, voluntary retirement and ancillarization of services, were used extensively in the 1990s.[48] A National Renewal Fund was announced in 1992–1993 to subsidize retrenchment, retraining, redeployment, and compensation due to closure. Through the 1990s, voluntary retirement schemes were implemented in almost all major corporate firms and public-sector units with minimal or no resistance from labor.[49] Many firms subcontracted previously integrated processes and services to other firms, shedding permanent workforce in the process.[50] The unionized component of the workforce fell in the process. In different contexts, this backdoor rationalization was called "casualization," "informalization," and "feminization." Feminization points to the fact that the core workforce tended to be more male than casual work, which allowed women to balance home and paid work better. The state-backed unions and industry-wide bargaining both declined.[51] The bargaining regime changed from one where, thanks to their ties to political parties, unions played a role in national politics to a more decentralized one where firm-specific unions had little or no relationship with political groups.[52]

In 2014 the election of a new federal government in India revived public discussion of labor law reform. Not much was achieved in the next four years. The media concluded that this government, like its predecessors, was not keen on major changes. The three main obstacles to retrenchment of workers remained in place. These were the Chapter V-B of the Industrial Disputes Act, which required a unit of a sufficient size (one hundred workers) intending to retrench workers to seek the government's permission; the Contract Labour (Regulation and Abolition) Act, 1970, which prohibited enterprises from the use of contract labor as a strategy to meet uncertain demand conditions (though exceptions were allowed for retrenchment forced by disasters or power failures); and the requirement of larger units to comply with more than forty-four labor laws and be subject to inspections in this regard. The persistence of these issues meant that legal consultants to foreign investors wishing to take over a business were in high demand. The laws were also generally projected in the media as deterrent to takeovers.

Interestingly, there were again several escape routes. First, several state (province) governments amended the scope of these laws in their domain. These laws being federal laws, states had to comply with them. But states overseeing enforcement could raise the size threshold for units before the regulation kicked in. Between 2016 and 2018, this was done by the governments of Maharashtra, Rajasthan, Haryana, and Assam. Second, the federal government started a campaign to attract foreign investment to India, and as part of the package of offers exempted start-up companies from inspections under several laws, including the Industrial Disputes Act and the Trade Unions Act. In February 2017, the Ministry of Labour announced "ease of compliance" measures. A few significant judgments (especially *Steel Authority of India v. National Union Water Front Workers*, Supreme Court, 2001) in cases under the Contract Labour Act went "against the historical rhetoric of the Act."[53] In the Steel Authority case, the contract workers demanded regular employment and cited previous state government orders directing similar conversion of contract jobs into regular jobs to support the claim. The judgment made it clear that the conversion or "absorption" of contract labor was not a right. Several judgments in the same spirit made contractual employment easier from the employer's side.

Backdoor reforms or reforms by stealth were not novel steps in India, but perhaps nowhere else did such steps cause more anxiety than in this sphere. It is widely believed that there has been a general decline in job quality in India. As recently as May 2018, "there is a clear public perception that there is a job crisis. . . . The rising incidence of vulnerable jobs like contract, casual, fixed term jobs and the disturbing wage differential between standard and non-standard workers have further dented faith in . . . labour policies. . . . Many regional labour law reforms have removed chunks of workers out of the purview of basic labour laws . . . [,] thus ensuring the creation of non-standard jobs."[54]

Trade unions, irrespective of party affiliation, oppose the easing of firing restrictions. The central government has recently proposed four labor codes to consolidate and simplify the plethora of existing legislation. The code pertaining to industrial relations is especially controversial. The Bharatiya Mazdoor Sangh (BMS; Indian Workers' Organization) has close ties to the ruling party, as does a publication called the *Organiser*. In June 2019 it was reported in the *Organiser* that

> BMS has rejected totally the controversial Industrial Relations Code as it will only create jungle law in the industrial sector. Many of the existing workers' rights are being curtailed, like Government deciding the criteria of office bearers of trade unions, restricting the right to strike, allowing arbitrary dismissal of workers, excluding apprentices, raising the exclusion of Chapter VB from 100 to 300 workers and the like provisions.[55]

Our best guess is that, in the medium term, labor law will be simplified without fundamentally changing existing restrictions on firing workers (but see the postscript to this chapter).

Conclusion

We have not discussed several important aspects of labor law, partly to avoid overwhelming the reader with legal detail. One important omission is the treatment of women. Perhaps the most important legislation in this regard is the Equal Remuneration Act of 1976, which, as the name suggests, requires that women be paid the same as men for the same work. Legislation in defense of women can backfire because it has to contend with deep-rooted cultural biases regarding women's work. Samita Sen has argued persuasively that unionization contributed to a decline in women's work in factories.[56] Policies that favor women, such as maternity benefits, can become a reason, or a pretext, for not hiring women or for letting them go.[57]

There are also many worker-welfare initiatives since the 1980s that have been driven by "competitive populism."[58] By the 1980s, especially in Kerala and Tamil Nadu, the efforts to woo voters led to the passing of legislation providing insurance and welfare benefits to informal workers. At the national level the most prominent legislation is the National Health Insurance Scheme (Rashtriya Swasthya Bima Yojana), introduced in 2008.[59] There are also initiatives under way to protect domestic workers.

Considered in total, has labor law in India effectively protected the poor from exploitation? Clearly, the answer is no, and this is no surprise. In a labor-surplus economy, labor is in a structurally weak position. An agricultural worker who has few employment prospects and limited access to credit may *choose* to enter a bonded labor contract—a law banning such arrangements may merely push them underground. A law recognizing the rights of a street hawker may not discourage an official from asking for a bribe. For such legislation to be effective the poor need to be aware and organized. We have seen this before, especially in the context of land reforms.

Has labor law been a constraint on economic growth? This claim has been repeatedly made in the context of manufacturing. Academic research on the effects of labor regulation picked up when Timothy Besley and Robin Burgess, in a 2004 paper, used data for 1958–1992 to show that states that adopted relatively proworker policies had lower output, productivity, investment, and employment in the organized sector.[60] Others modified their methodology and qualified the conclusion, finding that proworker states had lower labor demand elasticity or that proworker states had higher incidence of disputes.[61] Aditya Bhattacharjee argued that Besley and Burgess had underestimated the variation in legal regimes across states and that a proworker stance mattered less than enforcement and judicial attitudes.[62] Another relevant finding was that proworker regimes were relatively friendly toward women workers.[63] Although it is said that tough labor laws push more jobs into the informal or unorganized sector, one later study did not find much of the effect of labor regulation on this variable.[64] There is some evidence regarding the differential impact of demand shocks on employment in states with "proworker" regulation as compared to "proemployer" or "neutral" regulation: firms in proworker states seem to rely more on adjusting the number of contract workers as opposed to permanent employees.[65] Hiring and firing contract labor is a way of evading labor regulation.

According to an official in one of India's leading human resource companies, restrictions on firing workers matters less now because firms are allowed to hire workers for renewable fixed terms.[66] A senior government official has also pointed out that "not much has happened" in states that have made firing easier.[67] As we have noted several times, in a highly regulated environment it is difficult to tease out the effect of one constraint. That said, most observers would probably agree that taken together, the array of labor laws faced by Indian industry is a form of "regulatory cholesterol."[68]

Labor regulation is of course only one of the ways in which law affects the operation of business. As Indian economic policy has transitioned toward a more sympathetic view of markets, foreign trade, and foreign investment, the legal environment has also changed. As the reader will see in the next two chapters, the transition has been easier and met with less resistance than in the case of land or labor law, but older attitudes are still influential.

Postscript

We revised this manuscript one last time in the early stages of the COVID-19 crisis. The pandemic is having a surprisingly large influence on labor law in the short run, though its long-run effect is unpredictable. We will end this chapter with a brief discussion of what has already happened and what it might mean.

In May 2020, three large states in India announced radical changes in labor laws, in one case a freeze on the application of most rules. The announcement came as the COVID-19 pandemic was on the rise in India. The "reform" was a confusing response to the disease, and the timing of it made the media take notice. Why should a pandemic induce relaxation in labor laws? The expected aim was stimulation of investment and employment to counteract the effects of an inevitable recession. Retrenching employees would now become easier, the logic went, encouraging employers to hire more freely. As we have seen, labor laws come in great variety, covering, among other topics, conditions of employment, wages, social security, and job security. The announcement on job security provisions attracted the most attention in the press. In fact, the reform did not just address this; it also took steps to reduce transaction costs in other ways, such as by enabling digital contracts.

Cutting across the left-right divide, the move generated less enthusiasm among economists and the corporations than might have been expected. Whereas three states changed laws, most did not, and the federal labor laws did not change either. Moreover, India was already on the brink of an economic recession before the pandemic started. Many economists held that the recession was a problem of weak demand. If it was a demand problem, supply-side reform would not only not help but could be damaging. If labor laws were restrictive before, surely there was a surplus labor pool in employment to begin with, and a reform would see some of those people lose their jobs before hiring began. That outcome would depress wages, already under pressure, and worsen the recession. Another common view in India was that the recession stemmed from a weak banking system reluctant to lend. In this chaotic mix, the pandemic caused massive disorder via migration of unemployed workers and unpaid debts. When work starts again, jobseekers will return, banks will be even weaker, and investment slow to recover. In other words, employment terms will take a hit anyway, even without the reformers adding their support.

A striking feature of the early COVID-19-period reforms is that much of labor law has been simply jettisoned rather than modified, especially in Uttar Pradesh.[69] This situation, in which minimal health standards and the right to form trade unions or earn minimum wages have been undercut, is clearly not sustainable. In addition to protests from unions, there are probably going to be legal challenges.[70] The International Labor Organization has joined the criticism.[71] Ironically, it is possible that the backlash will, if anything, slow down the reform process, which had been proceeding more systematically via the development of the four labor codes we mentioned above.[72]

As we have mentioned, the rural employment guarantee program (MGNREGA) has been controversial and sometimes viewed as a poor use of resources. However, the COVID-19 crisis has generated unemployment on a large scale, including that of rural migrant workers returning home from cities, and made MGNREGA more salient. The current government, which has often been lukewarm toward MGNREGA, has increased the budget for it by 65%.[73]

CHAPTER SEVEN

Politicians' Burden?

The Evolution of Company Law

SICA [Sick Industrial Companies Act] is probably the world's most powerful legislation to aid industrial restructuring. — *Report of the Committee on Industrial Sickness and Corporate Restructuring*, 1993[1]

[The] necessity to bring Indian law on corporate insolvency in tune with globally acceptable practices and procedures . . . will involve . . . repeal of SICA. — Committee on Law Relating to Insolvency and Winding Up of Companies, 2000[2]

Introduction

This chapter tells a story about corporate law. Development policy and legal regimes became closely interdependent in late-twentieth-century India. From the 1990s policy changed. While changing policy was relatively easy, changing the laws was not. The story is about that predicament.

When India was a colony of Britain, the legislators copied British corporate law. The main body of law was the Companies Acts, which regulated birth, operation, and death of joint-stock limited-liability companies.[3] Competition law was not a serious concern, probably because the largest business houses, besides being British in origin, were exporters in a big world market and had little power to influence the market. The parity in law between Britain and India encouraged investment and international trade. In principle, disputes could be heard in either country. A lawyer trained in England had enough expertise to practice in India. The Companies Act seemed to be adequate to deal with corporate governance until the very end of colonial rule, when a few scandals led the legislators to reform laws relating to the managing agency system, an institution popular in some formerly colonial territories. The Companies Act, 1936, addressed that task.

Independence in 1947 did not bring about an immediate change in this setup. But by the late 1960s, it was obvious that the adoption of a radical and protectionist industrial policy with an accent on capital goods production at home had made a change in corporate law inevitable. This was so because the policy favored industries like metals, machines, and chemicals, which required high doses of capital that only a few business groups could undertake. Creation of monopolies now emerged as a new worry. On the other side, older industries like textiles, which were denied government patronage, were going bankrupt. The potential loss of jobs in an economy with few good jobs posed political risk. Could these businesses be saved with better governance? Governance, in this way, added another worry.

The two major interventions to take shape in response to these new needs were the Monopolies and Restrictive Trade Practices (MRTP) Act, 1965, dealing with competition, and the Sick Industrial Companies (Special Provisions) Act (SICA), 1985, dealing with insolvency. Both these laws narrowed the field for the Companies Act. The MRTP antitrust law was a response to the idea that the Companies Act had no provision to target restrictive practices, and SICA worked on the assumption that although the Companies Act did have provision to deal with insolvency, the need of the hour was that the state should gently nurse sick firms back to health. That was something the Companies Act could not deliver.

When India liberalized its economy in the 1990s, these two protectionist-era laws quickly became a burden. Promoting investment rather than regulating it was the new mantra. The government had failed to nurse insolvent firms back to health. SICA merely delayed insolvency proceedings while locking up capital in unproductive assets. But if the diagnosis was clear enough, the medicine was not easy to find. Rolling back these laws would not have been easy to push through the parliament because it would invite criticisms from trade unions and socialist lobbies. Besides, it was not clear that the problem lay with the laws alone. The system of dispute settlement needed new ideas.

The chapter describes this three-stage evolution of corporate law—

through the colonial, protectionist, and liberal regimes—and returns to the interdependence between policy and corporate law in the conclusions. Let us start with the colonial legacy.

The Colonial Inheritance

Legislation in the fields of property and commerce derived from different motivations in colonial India. Whereas in both cases, the promotion of market exchange was a distant goal, in the sphere of property, the desire to maintain social and political stability often made legislation cautious, bound by Indian tradition or interpretations of tradition, and generally conservative. But in commercial law, the state was proactive and freely borrowed legal precepts from Britain and Western models. In the second half of the nineteenth-century legislation in these areas applied to contracts, companies, negotiable instruments, trusts, transfer of property, promissory notes, evidence, wills and probates, and specific relief, all of which drew on English rather than Indian precedence.

Law relating to companies covered three main organizational forms: partnership, the joint-stock company, and the managing agency. Until 1850 partnership was the general form of ownership and management, which made raising finance and hiring managers difficult. Joint-stock limited liability was recognized in the 1850s and legislated from the end of the decade. Thereafter, the equivalence of British and Indian corporate law encouraged foreign investment in India, especially industrial investment. India's precocious industrialization—the country was the largest producer of machine-made cotton textiles and steel in the tropical world until World War II—owed partly to this equivalence.

Having said that, a type of business organization that Indian firms routinely used, managing agency, remained underlegislated until 1936. The managing agency was a firm that managed other firms. Typically, the agency was a partnership and the managed firm a joint-stock company; the contract between them allowed the owners to maintain control even with a small shareholding and thus save on capital. Several British agency firms in Calcutta also saved on managers in this way. A small pool of partners and managers managed many companies, sometimes companies that they had not started or had no ownership stake in. By contrast, Indian firms were usually majority family owned. For them, the agency firm was an additional means of control over the management of the company.

Agency created a moral hazard problem. The agent, with the security of a fixed commission, could take undue risks on behalf of the managed firm. There were occasional conflicts of interest as well, when partners in the agency had other firms that did business with the managed company. These problems were well known.[4] But there were no major corporate scandals to shake the legislators' faith in the soundness of the arrangement despite little oversight. Furthermore, there was no British precedence available to use as a model legislation for managing agency. The system was used in some parts of the British Empire, but rarely in Britain itself. It is not surprising, then, that this field was underlegislated. Nevertheless, allegations of misuse of the agency contract broke out during and immediately after World War II. Independent India inherited this crisis, and managing agency became the first area of reform.

Thus, Indian law was a copy, though not exact, of the British law. What kind of motives drove the legislators when they copied British laws for India and with what effect? The historiography of Indian company law suggests that legislation in British India carried a pro-British bias. Corporate law was perhaps the best example of a colonial institutional transplant because the regime wanted to make the operation of British capitalists easier. This reading, which owes to Radheshyam Rungta's pioneering work on corporate history, has been recycled into many subsequent works.[5] From this foundation it is easy to conclude that "all of these had the effect of adversely impacting local business forms."[6]

While Indian law was no doubt a transplant, we should be cautious about guessing why it copied English precedent and what the effects of that decision were on Indian business. The legislators did not understand Indian business forms, but neither did Indian businesses demand a different law to suit their preferences. A simpler interpretation of the transplant is that the companies' law, from the late 1850s, was geared to the joint-stock limited liability form of company organization; that idea had no indigenous roots. The idea came from elsewhere, and therefore the associated laws came from elsewhere too. With or without colonialism, it had to be a transplant. A desire to integrate finance and industry and an ongoing globalization process motivated legislation and the impulse to borrow institutional precedents. In the nineteenth century, little difference would be recognized anywhere between colonialism and globalization or between the adoption of British imperial law and the adoption of global standards. In this way, as India borrowed from Britain, Indian corporate and contract law was transplanted into the colonial territories that the Empire acquired later.

At the time the joint-stock limited liability was formally introduced in India, British firms operating in India were probably more familiar with the practice of raising money from stock markets, whereas most Indian firms raised investment money from trading profits and borrowings. However, soon after the laws came into place, bourses formed in India, starting with Bombay in 1875. Indian-owned cotton mill shares were the most heavily traded item in the Bombay Stock Exchange for decades thereafter, and Indian interests controlled the three main exchanges in Bombay, Calcutta, and Madras. Indian dominance of the stock markets was so absolute that a series of hostile takeovers in the turbulent 1940s and 1950s saw control of many British companies change over from foreign to Indian hands. Nearly all British as well as Indian trading firms also had associates in London and Liverpool, and such associations would need legal parity. Thus, the lobby for legal transplant, if there ever was one, would have been as much Indian as British by ethnic origin.

While formally corporate law after 1947 was a colonial legacy, the business world in which it was applied was changing rapidly from the 1950s.

How the Inheritance Changed (1947–1970)

Company law deals with the birth, operation, and the end of a company; defines the company; and sets rules by which the company transacts with its owners, associates, and clients. All of this is routine and should help the firm raise capital and enter contracts more easily. Corporate law also deals with two nonroutine matters—market dominance and power, and corporate governance—when one company's scale of operation and actions have adverse implications for competition or for shareholders. Regarding dominance by one firm or a cartel, legislation declared its commitment to protecting the interests of weaker firms. On governance within the firm, legislation declared its commitment to protection of shareholder interest against deliberate self-serving actions of managers or majority shareholders. With industrial companies that employed large numbers of people, the regulators often served the interests of employees, especially when bankruptcy became imminent. For about thirty years after independence, a regulatory regime took shape that served these three types of interest.

However, as we show later, the economic policy regime pushed legislators to serving these with special laws that overlapped with the scope of the Companies Act. The economic policy pursued import-substituting industrialization; preferred diversification toward metals, chemicals, and engineering from a mainly light industrial base dominated by textiles; and attributed a leadership role to the government in managing investment. The government took control of financial services and permitted import, diversification, and expansion by private companies under a license. The scope of private investment was relatively small, smaller than that of public investment, and government companies enjoyed many exemptions from regulatory action. State control over banking, licensing of investment and foreign collaboration, and restraints on foreign investment reduced the importance of private corporate investment in national investment and practically ended inflow of foreign money into the private corporate sector. The range of strategic actions the companies could undertake to expand or diversify was limited, and these needed permission from ministries every time. In the new world, there were few global firms. The private capitalist enterprise was to operate in well-defined areas. The government had expanded its executive powers via fresh legislation, and these powers were shared with courts of law. Either the judges had to fall in line or routine corporate processes such as investment, debt recovery, contract enforcement, and insolvency would take years. From the 1960s these matters did take years to resolve.

In one reading, postcolonial corporate law should be seen as "autochthonous."[7] The principal indigenous element was the wish to extend and deepen state regulation and oversight over private companies via antitrust laws and licensing requirements imposed on investment, import of technology, trading activities, foreign investment and collaboration, repatriation, and hiring abroad. This drive is often called *socialist*, but the term is imprecise. Socialism as a political ideology might explain the desire to regulate big companies to some extent via antitrust laws. Socialism per se does not explain restrictions imposed on foreign investment and trading. Hostility toward openness owed also to the legacy of economic nationalism in the last years of colonial rule. In addition, governmental commitments to spend on infrastructure, subsidies and redistributive programs, and its own companies induced the state to partially nationalize the financial system and regulate flows of investment funds. The counterpart was a set of restrictions and licensing requirements imposed on investment in the private corporate sector. How far these restrictions were "socialist" or "developmental" can be disputed.

With this overview of the transition, we now go to a chronological account of how the colonial inheritance changed. The first major field of reform was the managing agency clause in company law.

Taking On the Managing Agency (1952–1970)

The main target of reform in the 1950s and 1960s was the managing agency. A Company Law Committee (1952) made a series of recommendations on reforming companies that were targeted at curbing the managing agent's role and authority. These included restrictions on the election of agents or those connected with the agency as directors of a company, limits on the duration of agency contract to fifteen years (ten in the case of renewal), and restrictions on the role of "associates" of the agency firm. M. L. Shah, a member of the committee and a dissenter to the main report, called these moves "hasty and panicky" responses to "administrative inaction in preventing chances of abuse" during the World War II.[8] Such criticism had basis. The nationalist politicians disliked the managing agency partly because of its long association with the Indo-British firms that they did not like much. A new Companies Act passed in 1956 changed certain provisions of the managing agency system, but despite a growing demand to abolish it, it did not go that far.[9] Low-key debate continued for the next eighteen years, after which managing agency was abolished. When it was abolished in 1970, the system had become almost a dead letter. What was the legal issue with its operation?

As we mentioned, managing agency involved a contract between a trading or a producing company and a managing company. The managing company undertook the management of the business for a commission. Almost all Indo-British firms in Calcutta and Bombay were run in this way. The company usually had public shareholding, whereas the managing agent firm was usually a partnership. If the companies made profits, two benefits followed. The company could raise money in the stock market more easily, and the agency cashed in on the reputation of the company in the shape of a higher commission. Sometimes the agent had a small stake in the company, but there were many cases where it did not, and companies were transferred from one agent to another. These renegotiations occurred smoothly because the managers of the agent company and those of the company formed a relatively homogeneous social set, or a network. For example, the majority of the managers in Calcutta were Scotsmen. Still, the Indo-British firms in Calcutta were run by a network of managers and partners not usually related by blood or marriage. The Indo-British firms were not family firms in this sense.

Most Indian companies were family firms; that is, a family closely held control and supplied top managers to the business. When these companies managed trading operations, a managing agency contract was rarely used, and management as well as the capital came from a network of friends and associates. Capital in trade turned over quickly and did not pose complicated management problems. Factories, however, needed long-term investments. The banks financed trade and did not make long-term investments. Industrial companies, therefore, depended on the stock market. Managing agencies were closely controlled by families and usually had a controlling stake in the business companies they managed. But the reputation of the agent made it possible to raise money from shares more easily than otherwise. Where one family owned both the managing agency and the managed business, the agency contract gave the family a further handle to control the managed company. This added security made hostile takeovers difficult. Thus, the contract worked differently for different sets of firms, depending on whether the partnership firm was made up of family members or professional managers and on whether or not the same entity controlled both managing agency and managed business.

A conflict of interest was latent in this type of arrangement. The agent could use its power to start doing business deals with the managed company, say, as creditor or as trader. Many Indian companies did this routinely. Few Indo-British firms did it. When such conflicts existed, the risks of the trading or credit business passed on to the managed company and eventually the shareholders. This was the main governance issue with the managing agency. It is not clear, however, that this was a devastatingly damaging problem. Such conflicts can just as easily occur in companies managed by boards.

As we mentioned before, managing agency was not regulated until the 1936 Companies Act. The act sought to reduce conflicts of interest but was otherwise a light touch on agency. Soon after independence, further reforms set the maximum number of companies a managing agent could control far below the level that some of the larger agencies in Calcutta were used to controlling. Regulation also forced agencies to become corporate entities. These two moves forced most firms working within the system to go to the stock market and exposed the Indo-British companies to takeover risk. A spate of takeovers did happen, though how many of these were hostile and how many were hastily negotiated with Indian partners and associates it is hard to judge.

In the interim, political sentiment turned against the managing agency system. When the 1936 Companies Act amendments were debated, the Indian Merchants' Chamber of Bombay, a leading organization of Indian members, acknowledged occasional abuses and then noted that "it is not in keeping with any sense of proportion to attribute exaggerated importance to this problem."[10] In the 1950s, by contrast, politicians alleged that the agents "were only anxious to grab their commission" at the expense of workers and the tax office and that the government was too "weak-kneed" to deal with these powerful corporations.[11] In the late 1960s the political attack on managing agency turned fierce. Now there was no doubt where the sentiment was coming from. In 1967 a leading socialist, Madhu Limaye, asserted that managing agency had become "a factor accentuating the trend towards concentration of wealth and economic power in a few hands . . . in the interest of industrial development the Government should check managing agents taking away the lion's share of profits."[12]

In other words, legal reform of the managing agency system had started (in the 1930s) with a view to improving corporate governance. In the 1960s, in contrast, managing agency had become a symbol of monopoly power. Its abolition was the first step in the march of India's unforgiving antitrust regulation.

Long before its formal abolition in 1970, the managing agency had become redundant. A government-sponsored survey of the operation of managing agency, the first and the only one of its kind, in 1955, found that 17% of the companies were under agency contract. Large Indo-British companies dominated this set so that half of the paid-up capital in the corporate sector was in the hands of a managing agency. These proportions fell rapidly as the British companies divested. In March 1964 the *Times of India* quoted a report on the private corporate sector to say that of the twenty-five thousand odd companies operating, a little over 5% still used the managing agency contract.[13]

If the abolition of the managing agency was only part political in intent, the two most significant pieces of legislation between 1965 and 1985 were more explicitly so, and they created a field of state intervention in competition and governance for which there was no precedence so far.

New Objectives (1965/70–1992)

The shift from a relatively open and deregulated economy of colonial times to a regulated and closed economy of the postcolonial times created many losers, especially among the old textile firms and the Indo-British export-oriented firms. At the same time, the policy helped domestic business groups already well placed to make investment commitments to diversify into chemicals, metals, and engineering, and in this way grow bigger. There was a credible perception in the media and among economists that government policy to license private industrial investment allowed a few groups to lobby, bribe, or influence politicians and corner licenses.

During the 1960s and the 1970s, both these problems—concentration of business power and corporate bankruptcy—invited intervention. The growing size of business groups required antitrust laws. With regulation of market power, regulators had a notion of an ideal world without any big business present. The Indian Constitution had provided this guidance with its commitment to reduction of abuse of power and economic inequality. Dominance was defined with reference to the size of firms rather than specific actions of the firms like horizontal and vertical agreements. The larger the firm, the more likely it would be subjected to a deeper and harsher set of regulations governing expansion, management, intercorporate links, and diversification. Dominance and the abuse of dominance became synonymous. Likewise, bankruptcy, or so-called *sickness*, the word implying that insolvency had a cure, again demanded separate laws. The jobs under threat inside sick industrial firms, almost all in the metropolitan cities, alarmed politicians in the cities and even encouraged formation of new political parties.

Regulating Monopolies

The initial thrust of competition law in India was on equity and followed constitutional directives. Article 38 of the Constitution allows for state intervention to redress unjust inequalities in the control of resources, wealth, and income. This was the basis for state regulation of corporate power.

A series of reports on concentration of economic power in the 1960s and the abuse of the licensing system revealed that the industrialization policy had not met the goal of attaining "social justice." These reports showed that business groups used a common instrument to create an empire of connected firms: investment by one company in another. In 1960 the economist and statistician P. C. Mahalanobis submitted a government-sponsored report on income and wealth distribution. Two more reports on intercorporate investment and the industrial licensing system soon followed. In 1965 a Monopolies Inquiry Committee was set up, and in the same year, the parliament passed the Monopolies and Restrictive Trade Practices (MRTP) Act. The law restricted expansion, mergers, and acquisitions by large companies. A list of large companies was prepared for the purpose, and practically any decision these companies took with implications for their scale or the nature of business needed approval from the MRTP commission set up in 1969.

The commission implicitly accepted that the government monopolies were there to serve development and justice and should not be subjected to regulation. The commission defined dominance as the power to influence prices in a market. The benchmark of dominance was size. Large industrial firms were targeted in order to prevent "a few industrialists" from succeeding "in the creation of industrial empires."[14] Although more intrusive in the scope of regulation, the MRTP Act did not possess strong instruments to enforce compliance. It passed "cease and desist" directions when an infringement was judged, and failing compliance, submitted an appeal to the court.

If compliance was poorly enforceable, a large company could still be restrained from mergers and acquisitions by other means. The Controller of Capital Issues, for example, examined all applications by companies seeking to make investments in other companies and refused many. The Foreign Exchange Regulations Act (FERA, 1973) made it nearly impossible for a foreign firm to buy a stake in an Indian firm. Throughout the 1980s the government financial institutions had been investing in big companies with the result that no transfer of control could be feasible without their agreement. The combined effect of the regulations was that mergers, acquisitions, and takeovers were rare except when managed by quasi-government agencies.

Insolvency and the Government as a Supermanager

The Companies Act contained clauses on corporate insolvency, defined as the situation where a company was unable to pay its debts and had its capital eroded in the process of paying debts. A section (433 of the act of 1956) defined insolvency, and another section (434) set out grounds for declaration of insolvency. These sections acknowledged that insolvency could constitute a case for winding up the company. If a company wanted to wind up and made an application to a court of law, the court would consider the matter, consider disputes related to unpaid liability, pass an order on winding up the company, and appoint a liquidator to complete the process. If this seems straightforward enough, the disputes over debts made the proceedings exceedingly complicated, because creditors complained that the default was willful or the amount of the debt was disputed. Sometimes the very fact of a debt was disputed in the absence of sufficient documentation.

It is helpful at this stage to distinguish the two very different ways that the insolvency issue appeared before legislators. One of these was large-scale contagious bankruptcy of many firms in one industry. The Companies Act seemed powerless to deal with the situation when whole industries went bankrupt with potential loss of employment and shareholder capital occurring on an industrial scale. A whole new judicial and institutional framework was needed that would monitor insolvency. The Sick Industries legislation met that need.

The second situation was individual and isolated examples of insolvency, usually involving noncorporate firms, when bilateral negotiations between creditors and debtors monitored by the court would deal with the proceedings well enough. These were bilateral disputes, usually between small firms and an individual large creditor or supplier. The situation would be much more complicated with large corporations that had many creditors, aggrieved shareholders, and the banks as creditors. It would then be almost impossible for the court to admit a petition for insolvency from one stakeholder alone. The two situations overlapped often, for some of the sick firms were noncompanies with small numbers of creditors, no shareholders, and little job loss. But in principle, the two fields were distinct.

Let us consider the bilateral disputes first and the industrial sickness issue next. In some of the widely cited insolvency cases, the creditor is the petitioner or appellant seeking a dissolution of the company and recovery of dues from it. The points debated were the fact of a debt, ability to pay, and the amount of the debt. In *Madhusudan Gordhandas and Co. v. Madhu Woollen Industries Pvt. Ltd.* (1972), the Supreme Court ruled that if the fact of the debt was established, disputation over the exact amount of the debt could not stand in the way of a winding up order.[15] In a 2000 case the creditor's appeal was dismissed on the ground that the debt was disputed.[16] In *Sharda Bhandari v. Ananya Electroniks Ltd.* (Delhi High Court, 1992), the petitioner was a woman whose husband had acquired a plot in an industrial estate and was murdered before the business started. She had rented out the plot to a company that did not pay the contracted rent. The petitioner made an application for the company to be declared insolvent, which was allowed after seven years of court battle.[17] These cases suggest that declaring insolvency and bankruptcy did exist as options for firms that could not carry on and that the judges accepted the claim as consistent with law. But, then, these cases involved smaller firms and were stand alone in nature. Some of these cases took a long time to settle, probably more because of the inadequate judicial infrastructure than inadequacy of law. When insolvency affected many firms simultaneously in an industry, law seemed to break down with spectacular effect.

From the 1970s insolvency appeared before legislators as a macro- rather than firm-specific problem. The textile (cotton and jute) industry had been in difficulty for a long time. These old industries had to deal with restrictions on imports of technology. Exporting firms lived with overvalued exchange rates, and cotton mills faced restrictions on capacity as a concession to handloom weavers. Foreign firms were discriminated against by policies on repatriation and recruitment of foreign personnel. They were taken over by or sold off to often incompetent and dishonest businesses. When insolvency appeared in a few isolated firms, the concerned state or central government announced nationalization and was cheered by the media and the unions for its boldness and socialist sympathies. In the 1970s insolvency spread throughout the entire cotton and jute textile industries, involving hundreds of thousands of workers and hundreds of factories. But the generosity of the state came with a big fiscal bill. Over the 1980s the annual growth in the number of large-scale units reporting sick was 5%, and the rate of increase in credit outstanding was 18% (11% in real terms). The rates were higher when small-scale units were added to the list.[18] The National Textile Corporation started in 1968 to run sixteen nationalized cotton textile mills; by 1995 it owned and managed 119 mills. The company ran at a huge loss. A few nationalized former managing agencies had jute mills under them. Besides these, the National Jute Manufacturers Corporation started in 1980 to own and manage five large jute mills. The corporation did not expand very much after that. It was never a commercial success. And the appetite for nationalization was already waning. A different solution had to be found.

The Companies Act failed to offer a solution. Relevant provisions of the Companies Act enabled insolvency. The government wanted to avoid that outcome. SICA offered a way out. It acted on the premise that insolvency could be avoided under honest and efficient management. The act made provisions for setting up a Board for Industrial and Financial Reconstruction (BIFR) and an appellate Authority for Industrial and Financial Reconstruction (AIFR). These regulatory bodies under the Ministry of Finance had the charge of nursing sick corporations back to health, "sick" being defined as a situation when accumulated losses had eroded the entire net worth of a company. They had the legal power to override other laws, proceedings, and orders in relation to a company. These bodies started working from 1987.

The task before this judicial-administrative system was enormous. For most companies that were sick, like textile mills, rehabilitation was a pointless exercise while the business environment remained restrictive. Trade and tariff policy had made import of new technology difficult, trading was discouraged, capacity expansion not permitted, and retrenchment of surplus labor was not easy. In short, modernization of operations was nearly impossible for many old firms. The board was expected to make an inventory of liabilities, assets, shareholders, and creditors for every one of the companies, then design a plan of revival and hand over the company to an "operating agency" for implementation of the plan. The operating agency included another set of government actors—banks—who were also usually the large creditors to the company. The key part of any revival package was infusion of fresh capital. Since the banks were charged with supervising recovery and supplying credit at the same time, there was conflict of interest and occasional complaints of collusion between banks and owners. Fresh borrowing at the usual high rates of interest placed a weak company under undue strain anyway. As the Report of the Committee on Industrial Sickness and Corporate Restructuring (1993) noted, the overriding powers of the

BIFR meant little, for its orders could be stalled by stay orders filed in the courts. The board lacked knowledge of the firms and usually had to work with the existing management. Too often, owners used SICA to "evade recovery" and "delay and prolong proceedings for recovery," because under the act, banks could not proceed to recover dues while a restructuring plan was in motion.[19]

In the next twenty years, about seven thousand cases came before the board. Many were large industrial companies that had been in operation for decades. At the end of twenty years, the board could claim to have rehabilitated 7% of the companies referred and recommended about 18% for winding up. The remaining 75% of the companies were in some sort of limbo.[20] The average time taken to wind up was well over ten years, and in 12% of the cases, over thirty years.

Why was the process so cumbersome? The ideological climate made saving employment a worthy aim to pursue, and the regulators surely shared that sentiment with the officers. On a technical plane, there was another issue: regulatory overlap. From 1985 corporate insolvency for industrial companies became the subject matter of two acts at the same time—liquidation being handled by the Companies Act, and recovery and restoration by SICA. A short and simple insolvency process would require a short and simple debt-recovery process. Because of the regulatory overlap, debt recovery became costly, and therefore liquidation took much longer than otherwise. Because of the existence of "an extremely generous rehabilitation policy for insolvent industrial debtors, dependent in part on the provision of rescue finance by Indian banks and financial institutions," nonbank creditors faced high transaction costs in recovering debts.[21] This problem could affect both voluntary and compulsory liquidation—the courts could in either case intervene to stop the process "in the public interest."

The legal regime did not just impose a cost in time, it also entailed "a systematic drain of scarce public funds," though to our knowledge no precise estimate seems to exist of the cost to the exchequer.[22]

The Road to Reform after 1992

The post-1992 legal reforms in these areas were not due to foresight. They were an afterthought, an adjustment. The process started with policy shifts making it easier for Indian companies to trade, import

TABLE 7.1 **Laws governing corporations (1947–1992)**

Law	Regulator/adjudicator	Jurisdiction	Reform
Capital Issues Control Act	Controller of Capital Issues	Vetted and approved new issues	Repealed in 1992, the regulator abolished. Functions absorbed by the Securities and Exchange Board of India
Companies Act, 1956	Ministry of Company Affairs, Company Law Board, Registrar of Companies	Dealt with disputes arising from registration, incorporation, operation, and winding up of companies	
Securities Contract (Regulation) Act, 1956	Ministry of Company Affairs	Operation of the stock exchanges and securities transactions	
Monopolistic and Restrictive Trade Practices (MRTP) Act, 1969	MRTP Commission	Antitrust and anticompetition activities of companies	Repealed in 2002, functions absorbed and redefined by the Competition Commission of India
Foreign Exchange Regulation Act (FERA), 1973	Courts, Reserve Bank of India	Foreign exchange transaction, repatriation	Repealed and replaced by Foreign Exchange Management Act, 1999
Sick Industrial Companies Act (SICA), 1985	Board of Industrial and Financial Reconstruction	Insolvency and bankruptcy	Replaced by Insolvency and Bankruptcy Code

technology, enter foreign collaboration, and make investments (some of these moves had started in the mid-1980s). The result was explosive growth of companies, a sharp rise in the share of private investment in domestic product, and a rise in market capitalization. Along the way, a few crises took place.

As Omkar Goswami observes, despite the nineteenth-century origin of company law in India and the growth of companies thereafter, *corporate governance* was an unheard-of term until the 1990s.[23] In that decade an episode of stock market speculation exposed the weakness of oversight in the financial market at least. But similar abuses had happened before and did not draw robust response from legislators. Insider trading and benami (operating through front parties) transactions in the stock market were almost a routine matter in the 1950s and long after that.

That these transactions did not lead to a major stock market run had owed more to the unattractiveness of stocks generally. The liberalization and an investment boom encouraged speculators, and insider traders found the game warming up. Further, government control over industrial finances exercised via ownership of leading banks and finance companies made almost every major corporate investment decision a political matter. These negotiations were secret.

Earlier, the ruling economic philosophy made sure that bad governance was not seen as such and therefore did not need a law to deal with it. Simply put, the government believed that its oversight of the companies via nationalized finance was for the public good. The government did not fear insider trading either. Such insider deals as there were had resulted in takeovers of the politically irrelevant British managing agencies. Such cases became rarer from the 1960s. The office of the Controller of Capital Issues made sure that there was regulatory oversight on nearly all large-scale equity transactions. When stock market raids reared their head in the media again with Swraj Paul's takeovers of two Indian companies in the 1980s (see chap. 8), the government stepped in to stop the deals.

Between 1985 and 1990, the belief that the government could continue to act as a supermanager was shaken. Scathing assessments of SICA destroyed confidence in the government. The financial system partially denationalized. Companies moved to raise equity in large volumes. The office of the Controller of Capital Issues was abolished. The sick industries initiative was a spectacular failure. The government-owned and nationalized businesses did exceptionally badly in the new regime. So did several of the older Indian business groups, which had significant political weight in New Delhi. The liberalizers had no one to fight anymore. But this was still an adjustment after the fact.

What had changed?

The 1993 Companies Bill and the Competition Act 2002

Although separated by a decade, we will discuss these two acts together because they served similar aims. The economic liberalization and revival of private investment in the 1990s put pressure on parliament to work toward a business-friendly legal regime. The process of starting and running companies was made simpler than before. For example, the

1993 Companies Bill, which aimed to be a "recodification" as opposed to an amendment, simplified the process of incorporation and the winding up of companies. Companies would be able to alter their objectives without seeking permission from the Company Law Board, a quasi-judicial body. The bill also took steps to standardize accounts and ensure disclosure of information to shareholders.[24] The bill lapsed, but it had set out an agenda for reform.

The 2013 Companies Act aimed to achieve more clarity on entrenchment clauses. Entrenched clauses are provisions that are generally difficult to override with a simple majority. The term derives from constitutional law. In company law the articles of association are an example of a potential entrenchment clause. Earlier, changes in the articles of association required conditions that were difficult to meet. This provision was relaxed. The act made representation of a foreign partner or investor in a domestic company where it had a stake no longer subject to judicial approval. Share transfers between public companies, again subject to regulatory and court approval earlier, became contractual, and the contracts acknowledged a variety of options.[25]

The major fields where reforms were needed were competition and insolvency, for the fall of the MRTP and SICA had created a vacuum. In the 1980s a limited regulatory reform in these areas revived private investment. Licensing policy was not given up but retracted a little. Imports were made easier. And inflow of foreign money into joint ventures with Indian companies increased. In an unannounced way, the overriding aim of regulation began to change. Already, the Supreme Court had introduced the distinction between dominance and abuse of dominance.[26] Dominance states a fact; abuse of dominance says that dominance had been achieved by unfair means. The MRTP commission had defined certain actions as means to achieve dominance. The court observed that the actions were not necessarily anticompetitive or taken for that purpose.[27]

In the 1980s again, amendments made to the MRTP act had introduced a chapter on unfair trade practices, thus turning the attention of regulators away from the size of firms and toward the actions of firms. With the economy opening to foreign trade and investment, a spate of mergers, acquisitions, and joint ventures took place. Blanket restrictions on such strategies seemed to make little sense anymore even though the MRTP could technically be applied to stop these. Implicitly, the priority shifted from targeting all large companies, designated rightly or otherwise as monopolies, to targeting cartelization. The changes were neither abrupt nor radical, but overall, the regulatory stance on the so-called monopolies had started to shift. The number of trade practices orders and investigations declined. The new doctrine was to consider the effect and the intention of firms rather than the size of firms. These ideas had been present before, but they now began to drive legal reforms. A series of Supreme Court judgments in the early 2000s reiterated that regulatory intervention was justified only when an abuse of dominance was proven.[28]

Although it took some time—between 1985 and 2000—the conceptual leap from the old to the new was so great that expertise built up over forty years of the operation of the old regime was made redundant. There was little resistance to the transition to a new framework thereafter. The Competition Act (replacing MRTP) was the first systematic expression of the new thinking.

The Competition Act 2002 defined anticompetitive activities and set penalties for these offences. The regulatory body, the Competition Commission, would conduct investigations, decide penalties, and enforce the law. The Competition Appellate Tribunal, popularly known as COMPAT, heard appeals. With this move, legislation in effect acknowledged that regulation of companies needed to assess conduct more than equity in the sense in which the Constitution defined it. This was neither a smooth nor a unidirectional change. Economic inequality grew after the liberal reforms. The judges could not forget that redressing inequality was one of the original aims of the Constitution and behind state intervention in markets in general. From time to time, therefore, case laws reflected this reversal.[29]

The Competition Commission had its work cut out. With few relevant past cases available, it set out to define market, competition, dominance, and control afresh. These efforts led to a strong body of jurisprudence while creating inconsistencies as well. It let government companies off lightly. It passed orders that could be seen as "shifting the burden of defining the relevant product and geographic market onto the Supreme Court."[30] Some matters were too complex for the law. In the most common kind of cases—called bid rigging, including cover bidding, where bidders for a tender colluded among themselves or submitted bids that were meant to fail—identifying the signs of collusion or unlawful information exchange proved difficult. In one early case—a dispute between real estate firms and cement manufacturers—the exis-

TABLE 7.2 **Laws governing corporations (1992–)**

Law	Regulator/Adjudicator	Jurisdiction
Securities and Exchange Board of India Act, 1992	Securities and Exchange Board of India (SEBI)	Regulation of stock markets, investor protection
Securities Contract (Regulation) Act, 1956	Securities and Exchange Board of India	
Competition Act, 2002	Competition Commission of India	Anticompetition activities
Recovery of Debts due to Banks and Financial Institutions Act (1993)	Debt Recovery Tribunals (see table 7.3)	
Foreign Exchange Management Act, 1999	Courts, Reserve Bank of India	Foreign exchange transaction, repatriation
Insolvency and Bankruptcy Code, 2016	Tribunals (see table 7.3) and Insolvency and Bankruptcy Board of India	Insolvency and bankruptcy

tence of a price-fixing cartel was assumed on allegedly weak and circumstantial grounds.[31] A recent study of the commission's work asked how successful the setup has been in regulating public-sector units and reported a mixed outcome. In some cases the commission did subject the government-owned units to the same rules as others. However, many government agencies also enter the market as buyers, sometimes using discretionary rules, and "the Commission's responses to a lack of competitive neutrality shown by public buyers are relatively mild" and more advisory than interventionist.[32] Overall, however, the Competition Commission received a favorable assessment from experts.

While mergers and acquisitions were made simpler, being an easier issue to address politically, the closure of a company was a much more sensitive matter.

Insolvency: Toward the Bankruptcy Code of 2016

It was common knowledge that the regulatory regime embodied in SICA had failed. The idea that the government had the managerial competence to nurse companies back to health was unrealistic. And SICA overlapped with the scope of the Companies Act. In 1999 a committee appointed to reform insolvency law recommended repeal of SICA and the BIFR and recommended establishment of a National Company Law Tribunal. Instead of the courts, this body would decide applications for winding up according to the provisions set out by the Companies Act. In common with international practice, the tribunal would appoint official liquidators and take care of the recovery of assets and repayment of dues as quickly as possible. The move signified two things. At one level, it was a legal reform, a desire to reduce regulatory overlap and simplify process. At another level, it signified the loss of a key faith on which the developmental state ideology had stood: that the state had the intellectual and financial capacity to act as a supermanager, discipline errant owners, rescue companies from their hands, nurse bankrupt firms back to health, and act as the benevolent father figure to surplus employees.

From the 1990s economists and chambers of commerce lobbied for a comprehensive law on bankruptcy that would make it easier for sick companies and firms to wind up rather than carry on indefinitely, remove the regulatory overlap between SICA and the Companies Act, and take matters away from the slow-moving courts when possible. Almost fifteen years of debate later, a bankruptcy code was made into law in 2016. Under the new bankruptcy regime, the National Company Law Tribunal tries corporate cases and Debt Recovery Tribunals personal cases (involving debt above a certain size, discussed in chap. 3), and an Insolvency and Bankruptcy Board would regulate the insolvency professionals and the process.

The bankruptcy code represented a sharp turn away from a pattern of judicial intervention in bankruptcy cases that favored debtors over creditors and survival of the firm over contract enforcement. The code and the tribunal that applied the law instead gave due weight to the creditors' claims and stressed speedy enforcement. A stocktaking of cases a year after the code came into effect found that "of the 110 cases that we reviewed, 75 percent of the cases were triggered by creditors."[33]

Since assets of bankrupt companies tend to devalue quickly, speedy handover is essential to the efficiency of any bankruptcy code. The new code set 270 days as the maximum limit for resolving disputes over payments. When the code came into effect in 2018, several steel companies were declared bankrupt and offered for sale. Two acquisitions, Tata Steel's of Bhushan Steel and Vedanta's of Electrosteel, were conducted with little difficulty. The code was tested because the firms were deep in debt to the banks. However, another large takeover process—Binani Cements—got caught up in a court case because one promising bid by Dalmia Cements (February 2018) was superseded a month later

TABLE 7.3 **Tribunals for adjudication of corporate disputes (2018)**

National Company Law Appellate Tribunal	2016, adjudication of company law cases and corporate insolvency cases. Replaced the Company Law Board, 1956, which earlier dealt with company matters; and replaced the Competition Appellate Tribunal, 2002, which had in turn replaced monopolies and restrictive trade practices legislation
Debt Recovery Tribunals	Adjudication of noncompany and unlimited liability company insolvency and bankruptcy cases
Securities Appellate Tribunal	1992, to hear appeals against orders of the Securities and Exchange Board of India or other officers dealing with securities
Intellectual Property Appellate Board (see chap. 8)	1958, to hear appeals against decisions referring to the Indian Patents Act; its role was redefined after India signed TRIPS in 2005 and again after the Copyright (Amendment) Act, passed in 2012

by another one. That the regulator allowed the second bid as an afterthought set a potentially awkward precedent because it could defeat the purpose of the act, which was speed.

Interestingly, although the regulatory overlap was addressed with the repeal of SICA, liquidation could still be difficult because the speed of debt recovery depends also on the quality of banking. If the corporate governance of banks is generally poor, the oversight by creditors of borrowers is poor too. Even the banks' incentive to recover their money could be weak, as was the case in relation to many sick industrial firms.[34] Government-owned banks have been known to make unwise and often willfully bad decisions to lend money to dubious borrowers. These debts are not easily recoverable because the borrowers do not have the assets to cover these. As we are going to press, the problem of bad corporate debt or "nonperforming assets" in government-owned and some private banks has become large in scale and politically charged. If this problem is of a serious order, a more competitive and transparent banking industry should encourage speedier liquidation. More information will be exchanged, private banks will have the incentive to monitor the borrower, and overall the creditor's knowledge of the borrower's conditions will improve. There is evidence that this association between competitive banking and ease of bankruptcy has emerged in India.[35]

Corporate Governance: Toward Voluntary Guidelines 2009

Corporate governance theory builds on the types of agency costs that arise in a joint-stock, limited-liability company. Where managers do not own the company at all and shareholding is too dispersed for the owners to oversee management, the agents might take undue risk with the assets of the company. Where managers are majority shareholders of a family firm, the agents might use company assets for personal gain at the cost of the minority shareholders. These two scenarios are sometimes identified as the American and the Asian models respectively.[36] The third problem, tunneling, refers to the practice when majority shareholders or persons in control of a company with governance structures that make deployment of cash flows difficult divert assets to other companies or future businesses, usually for personal gain. The losers are the minority shareholders and the companies. There is indirect evidence to suggest that tunneling opportunities might encourage closer control and the formation of diversified business groups, both enduring features of the Indian corporate world.[37]

Two common characteristics of Indian companies compromised good governance. First, most companies were closely held. And second, the majority shareholders were usually families, which would mean that some decisions were not publicly discussed or transparent. This situation made it relatively easy for the owners to divert funds to "related parties" or investments that profited them rather than the company. And in doing so, owners could manipulate the appointment of nonfamily or "independent" members and the audit process. Certain clauses of the Companies Act made it mandatory for companies to disclose the qualification and interests of the directors and made transactions between entities in which the directors have interest and the company illegal.[38] But it was not difficult to bypass these rules. However, no significant steps were taken to address corporate governance in family firms until the 2000s.

In 2008–2009, India's biggest corporate fraud broke out. It involved the then fourth largest information technology services firm, Satyam Computer Services. The founder and head of the company was said to have diverted the company's assets by inflating its cash reserves and creating fictitious employee accounts and then spending the money on insider trading, real estate, and family-owned enterprises. The amounts involved were very large, but the nature of the alleged crime was nothing new. In the 1970s government economists fretted over intercorporate investment (tunneling) from the worry that it was too easy for directors of a company to divert the resources of the company to other companies or to the stock market for insider trading and hostile takeovers. The fundamental problem was not an absence of legal provisions that made such actions a crime. These provisions existed on paper. The problem was the opaque nature of personal control and the ease with which the opacity could be sustained through the appointment of friends, relations, and loyal associates as auditors, as finance managers, and as directors. If family and personal control remained, these actions became more likely. And if the actions remained more likely, they could potentially be used for the wrong reasons. Tightening up law would help little to remove that prospect. A campaign for corporate responsibility had a better chance.

Nevertheless, the Satyam scandal did produce a legacy relating to corporate governance. The legacy can be seen when two versions of the Companies Act reform effort, an abortive one in 2008 and the successful one in 2013, are compared. Both expressly committed to a simpler probusiness act. But between the two versions, the campaign for corporate responsibility had gained hold in the media and took concrete shape in insistence on the "independence" of directors and auditors. The Companies Act 2013 went further along these lines.

In 2009 the Ministry of Corporate Affairs issued a document called "Voluntary Guidelines." The code, among other things, emphasized that independent directors should be truly independent and recommended the creation of an audit committee in the board to ensure independence of the audit process. India had been familiar with corporate fraud for a long time. But two immediately preceding scandals, one involving Satyam Computer Services, discussed above, and the other Nagarjuna Finance, acted as a push. In both cases, independent directors had been influenced to sanction use of the company's money (in the latter case collected from depositors) in making shady investments. The code recognized that the two most common ways the controlling shareholders could manipulate finances were working through independent directors and working through the auditors. Laudable as the goal was, "independence" proved hard to define in precise terms. The fact that these were guidelines rather than regulatory laws with an enforcement clause attached raised the question of whether these would have any effect at all in India. One view was that Indian companies would not take voluntary codes seriously.[39]

A different set of governance issues emerged in relation to corporate finance. There were two sources of these problems: rapid rise in market capitalization and nationalized banks.

Financial Market: Incomplete Regulation

From the 1990s Indian companies demanded more options in methods of raising capital, and the demand was granted quite simply by aligning India with global practice. One area of reform was the increase in options about the types of equity. Indian companies could earlier raise preference and common shares. In 2000 more combinations of voting and returns were allowed. Buybacks and stock options were introduced. In 2000 again, depository receipts were allowed, and cross-border listing norms were liberalized.[40] The scope of such instruments was expanded to include global depository and American depositary receipts. Since the economic liberalization began, companies started raising more money from the stock market, and market capitalization levels increased. From 2003 especially, foreign institutional investment in India's equity joined this process. The licensing norms for issuing such instruments were liberalized in 2014. Restrictions (and sometimes ambiguity), however, persisted in matters of taxation, convertibility into equity, eligibility of a company to issue depository receipts, and disclosure and governance norms. Although global depository receipts became hugely popular, since 2017 concerns have been raised that they are sometimes used for money laundering.[41]

These changes raised the importance of the stock markets in India's economic transformation. Was the institution ready for the challenge? The oldest stock exchange in the country, the Bombay Stock Exchange, or BSE, was owned by individuals who had trading rights in the exchange, a situation that was widely seen as detrimental to its governance. By contrast, the National Stock Exchange, or NSE, is owned by financial institutions and is more professionally managed. From its start in 1992, the Securities and Exchange Board of India, or SEBI, worked to separate ownership and trading rights in the BSE and other regional exchanges where the problem existed.

If these steps addressed conflicts of interest, they did not stop insider trading. Government-owned banks were especially vulnerable to being abused in this process. In two successive frauds in ten years, bankers' trust came into question. Commercial banks were required to maintain a statutory holding of government securities, which offered low rates of interest. Money tied to such transactions was diverted to the stock market through the operational departments. The procedure involved an instrument called the bankers' receipt (BR), which was issued by a bank selling securities to another bank. Banks also made payment by banker's check for purchase of securities. The BR was issued in anticipation of an actual transfer of securities but involved a transfer of the money. Many transactions took place through brokers. The money was deposited in a broker's account and could be immediately invested in the stock market. If all went well, the money was returned before the transfer of securities took place.

In 1992, in what became known as the Harshad Mehta scam, the National Housing Bank issued a check to the stockbroker Mehta for securities. It was subsequently discovered that the bank had no record of receiving these securities. In turn, Mehta instructed his bank to make a payment to another party against this check, and the money ended up in the stock market.[42] Mehta already had a reputation for bullish bets. His biggest bet, however, was funded by staggeringly large amounts of money diverted in this way. A string of brokerage firms affiliated with him would sell the shares at inflated prices. In 2001, the Ketan Parikh scandal involved an almost identical tool but a different set of government banks.

Fixing responsibility was never an easy matter in these cases. No law had been broken. Individuals followed the banks' procedures. The bankers had failed to perform their "fiduciary duty." No one knew whether this was a criminal liability or that mens rea (criminal intent) was implicated. Still, the transfer of the funds was a failure of the internal management audits of the banks and technically also a failure of the Reserve Bank of India, for securities transactions needed to be reported to and approved by its Public Debt Office. However, BR issues did not get reported to the central bank.[43] The RBI was also implicated because it was the regulator of the banks, including the government banks.

The substantial response to the 1992 scam was the new regulator of stock markets, SEBI, which had been created in 1988 and became an independent regulator by a parliamentary act in 1992. One of its key preventive interventions was the introduction of the so-called Clause-49 norms, which set out requirements on disclosure, independence of the board and audit, and accounting standards. This was introduced in 2002, ten years after SEBI started as a regulator and soon after the passing of the Sarbanes-Oxley compliance rules in the United States. A few years earlier, in 1994, the RBI set up the Board for Financial Supervision, an office to supervise governance norms in banks. Initially these norms addressed capital adequacy and liquidity; in the 2000s these were expanded to include disclosure, accounting, and composition of the boards.

Banks and Financial Companies

Government banks had other problems to deal with. Industrial sickness hit many of them hard and left them with a load of bad debts for, among others, the reason that the government regulators often arm-twisted them into joining consortium loan schemes in favor of doubtful debtors. The Securitisation and Reconstruction of Financial Assets and Enforcement of Security Interest (SARFAESI) Act, 2002, provided for a definition of bad loans (nonperforming assets) in financial companies, created mechanisms to differentiate the quality of loans and to securitize loans, and made recovery and reconstruction of assets easier.

One of the means, tried elsewhere with mixed experience, is an asset reconstruction company that securitizes loans and sells them to financial companies. Reconstruction companies began to be created around 2010, but they had little chance of making a difference to the health of the banks. Security receipts formed less than a quarter of the size of bad loans because half of the bad loans had been given to small firms and peasants under an administrative fiat known as priority sector lending, and these could not be easily securitized.[44] Asset valuation and getting lenders together were also complicated issues. Perhaps when the banks are government owned, the best chance of a successful deal involves political intervention of some kind, which had created the problem of bad loans to begin with.

One area where corporate governance failed repeatedly was the so-called nonbank finance companies or NBFCs. With the banks doing the government's bidding, the financial regime allowed for large excess demand to develop in such important but overlooked businesses as commodity trading, hire purchase, leasing, and housing finance. All except the regulators knew that exceptionally high rates of interest were to be had in some of these markets if money was carefully invested. The NBFCs emerged to collect public deposits on promise of higher-than-official rate of interest and to invest the money in the high-return markets such as trading and stock market speculation. Not all NBFCs entered high-return, high-risk markets, but many did. Their business not only carried risks, it was also occasionally exposed to political interference. Given the extremely cumbersome system of land law in most states, political influence helped to conduct the real estate business but exposed the deposits to demands from the benefactors.

In practice some of these firms have often willingly or unwillingly ended up as Ponzi schemes. There is no evidence that the people who promoted the most disastrous such schemes necessarily started with wrongful intent. The big gap between government-regulated low interest on bank deposits and market rate of interest in unregulated commercial loans was enough incentive to draw both honest operators and wise depositors into the game. However, short-term investments could carry high risk.

The RBI is the regulator of such businesses. A Prize Chits and Money Circulation Schemes (Banning) Act, 1978, had been in place, and an investigative agency, the Serious Fraud Investigation Office, had existed since 2003. Still, preventive checks have never been very robust in this sphere. The regulatory laws consisted of a set of specific directions that the RBI introduced. These directions introduced restrictions on raising finance and penalties for default to depositors but did little to reduce either the attraction of these unserved markets or the risks that these entailed. Within an individual NBFC, the passage from sound to unsound business practice occurs so silently that the regulator is routinely caught unprepared. In the early 1980s West Bengal saw several companies collapse; the most famous ones were Sanchayita, Sanchayani, Favourite, and Overland. In the 2010s, again, the collapse of Sarada and Rose Valley underlined the failure of law to act as a preventive check.[45]

Conclusion

The historiography of postcolonial corporate law is caught up in a debate about whether the Indian system was a "legal transplant" from Britain or not. The question overstates the importance of the source of law and overlooks the importance of the context in which laws are applied.

This chapter started by showing that the colonial legacy changed in meaning after 1947. Whereas the purpose of British-Indian corporate law was to promote trade and investment links between Britain and India—hence the transplant—that aim was dropped after 1947. Integration with the world economy was no longer a priority, and therefore parity between international law and Indian law was not a conscious goal either. If there was parity, it was because there was no need to change the status quo. In this scenario the Companies Act became a passive body of law. It existed but did not generate reformist passion. All the excitement flowed from interventions that were supposed to serve developmental and equity goals. The Companies Act served neither. The two main areas where developmental and equity consideration prevailed were antitrust law and the insolvency process. Investment barriers were raised, and insolvency was made difficult by means of special laws that encroached on the operation of the Companies Act.

These interventions depressed investment in the private sector and encouraged investment in the government sector, where capital yielded considerably less value. Directly or indirectly, they raised the cost of capital in India. In the mid-1990s, on the eve of the first round of liberal reforms, the ratio of private investment (gross fixed capital formation in the national accounts) in gross domestic product was 10%, and foreign investment was 1%. These proportions had moved up and down a lot in the previous decades, but not decisively upward. In the early 1990s reforms, capital controls were eased, even removed, and private enterprise in the financial system was allowed more freely. Reforms relating to foreign investment, stock markets, and domestic credit were introduced at the same time. After the reforms, the share of private investment began to move upward, exceeding 20% by 2015. Foreign direct investment rose gradually to exceed 10% by 2013. There were corresponding increases in foreign portfolio investment, domestic credit, and market capitalization as proportions of GDP.

These results were achieved not entirely by changing policy but also by changes in statutes. There were three types of change. First, reforms in corporate law since 2000 reintroduced elements of global practice into Indian law. But legislative reform would mean little if disputants had to rely on the conventional courts of justice where disputes took years to settle. An escape route was created by the addition of tribunals where corporate cases could be settled more quickly. In short, if reglobalization was one of the three elements of the ongoing shift, tribunalization was another. The third element was the emergence of corporate governance as a field of legislation and public discourse on jurisprudence; it was also the focus of tribunalization.

The reintegration of India into the global economy since 1992 created new and specific challenges that did not fall into the realms of competition and governance. One of these challenges was takeovers, mergers, and acquisitions. Before the reforms, the corporate world dominated by family firms openly displayed paranoia about takeovers and wanted regulators to take steps to prevent them. Business and the legislature found common ground on this cause. As a result, mergers and acquisitions were difficult to achieve in practice. But globalization and a sudden increase in competition made these obstacles pointless and dangerous. The next chapter discusses the response to the challenge.

CHAPTER EIGHT

Globalization with a Nationalist Face

Mergers, Acquisitions, and Intellectual Property

The village neem tree has become a symbol of Indian indigenous knowledge, and of resistance against companies, which would expropriate this knowledge for their own profit. — Vandana Shiva[1]

Introduction

Chapter 7 began with a quotation from a report in 2000 on insolvency procedure. The authors, a committee headed by Supreme Court justice V. B. Eradi, stressed the need to make the Indian system of corporate laws compatible with global practice. In areas like mergers, acquisitions, and intellectual property rights, the project would involve shedding protectionist biases that had erected barriers to mergers, acquisitions, and a competitive intellectual property regime. The reformist drive took off, but with strings attached, as this chapter will show.

Domestic firms lobbied for reform in competition and insolvency law (chap. 7). In contrast, with mergers, acquisitions, and intellectual property, the impulse to reform came from the rapid globalization of the economy in the 2000s. Of course, any country that wanted to receive foreign investment would need to align its laws with global conventions. But there was more to it. As it embraced openness, India was transforming into an exporter of services, and legal reform was a condition to participate in services trades more deeply. For example, trade in information-technology-based services required appropriate systems of intellectual property protection.

Mergers and acquisitions had been permitted earlier, but these were enormously difficult to carry out in practice. Acquisitions required administrative and court sanctions. Political sentiment frowned on these. A hostile takeover of an Indian company by a foreign one was politically unworkable. Mergers were easier, and there were more mergers than acquisitions in the prereform years.[2] The number was still small because the courts moved slowly. Clearly, any worthwhile reform would require a change in law, process, and sentiment at the same time. The bottom line of this chapter is that there was a credible change in law and process but not in sentiment.

The key new laws in question are a Takeover Code, adoption of the Trade-Related Aspects of Intellectual Property Rights (TRIPS), and the move toward an investor-friendlier foreign exchange regime. All these changes happened between 1999 and 2015, and therefore, this chapter is quite contemporary in focus. But there are exceptions. Intellectual property protection, for example, had the necessary laws and the dispute settlement mechanism from colonial times (see also table 7.3). Globalization changed the context for their application.

This chapter travels the road leading to these legislations. Its organization is thematic, with a description of prehistory in each case.

The conclusion offers a broader assessment. Did an easier legal process to implement corporate restructuring enhance shareholder value? Did de jure change in institutions bring about de facto changes in the ease of making investment decisions? While the thrust of the reform was to move farther away from an insular and protectionist regime toward one aligned with international practice, was there a real convergence in business conditions? Two fields where nationalist sentiments had ruled—takeover and copyright—are good testing grounds for the question. We conclude that we need more time to know how substantive the changes were.

Mergers, Acquisitions, Takeovers

Prehistory (1947 to Swraj Paul)

In the 1950s a spate of takeovers saw the control over some of the largest European managing agencies, and more often companies managed by them, pass on to Indian control. The circumstances of these transfers are little known. It is plausible that a few of these were hostile takeovers engineered by a bidder-broker alliance then common in Calcutta. However, on several occasions, large shareholders and directors of the companies appeared willing parties. We say "appeared" because deals of this nature were hardly ever documented. Public shareholders had almost no say in these transfers. Some of the companies taken over were so badly managed and had so much of their assets stripped by the new owners that the episode caused a scandal, and instances of hostile takeovers became rare.[3]

Negotiated mergers, however, continued on a low-key basis. A series of mergers were managed by the state on behalf of bankrupt companies. Amendment of corporate tax law to make such mergers attractive to the bidder helped the process, though the instances of such mergers were too few to make a difference to the scale of the problem. Around 1970 the impending abolition of managing agency led to a series of mergers. The acquisition of two large Indo-European conglomerates, Williamson Magor and Duncans, by two Indian groups based in Calcutta was also completed in the 1970s. Both were negotiated acquisitions.

Overall, mergers and acquisitions were not common at all before the 1980s, and hostile takeovers of Indian firms by foreign ones were completely unknown.[4] In this torpid scenario, the move by two foreign firms to acquire Indian companies through the stock market came as a shock. These two attempts took place in 1984–1985 and in 1999. In 1984, the Britain-based businessman Swraj Paul tried to acquire DCM (Delhi Cloth Mills) and Escorts. In 1999, the chemical multinational ICI tried to acquire Asian Paints. Paul's bid was striking because it targeted two large family-run Indian companies and because it was a hostile takeover, something the market had not seen in a long time. The Controller of Capital Issues allowed Paul's purchase to go through. But the media, the economists, and the politicians did not let this pass quietly, and they generally took an anti-Paul stance. The boards of the companies being taken over refused to register the shares, and a large minority shareholder, the government-owned Life Insurance Corporation, supported the boards. The takeover bid became a nationalist and emotive issue, led to a court case, and was eventually settled out of court through political intervention, with the owners buying up Paul's shares at a premium. The ICI–Asian Paints bid also failed because of political intervention through an office called the Foreign Investment Promotion Board.

These episodes tested the legal and regulatory framework governing hostile takeovers. There were no formal barriers in either case, but the bids still failed. The reason for failure was the government approvals process, directly through offices and indirectly through government-owned companies called development finance institutions that held shares of private companies. The prospect of political interference left room for public opinion and political sentiment to influence the process. In neither case did the public shareholders' preferences matter nor were they seriously considered.

Hostile takeovers apart, even friendly mergers remained extremely rare from 1947 to 1990. The reason for this was the heavy transaction cost—but no outright prohibition—imposed by law on such moves. The Monopolies and Restrictive Trade Practices (MRTP) Act that restrained capacity expansion or the emergence of "monopolies," the presence of government shareholders in the boards who usually preferred the status quo, foreign exchange regulations, and the rule that such deals would have to be approved by the High Court added to the transaction cost.

The Transition of the 1990s

The steps to open the Indian economy in the 1990s made mergers and acquisitions more likely for companies exposed to a new type of competition. Although the MRTP was relaxed in 1991, FERA (Foreign Exchange Regulation Act) was still in place, and the law had not really had time to adapt to the reality of a surge in foreign investment. The Foreign Exchange Regulation Act of 1973 in effect made foreign investment unattractive for the investors thanks to a range of restrictive clauses on ownership and repatriation of profits. In 1999 a new law, the Foreign Exchange Management Act (see below), eased the restrictions. But already in the 1990s the regulators were losing the heart to strictly apply FERA. In the early 1990s the foreign corporations in India sometimes adopted a new strategy hoping that the government agencies would not interfere. Several of these were actions by multinationals to preempt competition from other multinationals by taking over domestic brands. For example, Brooke Bond India, an affiliate of Hindustan Lever, acquired control of Kothari General Foods to stave off Nestle (1992). Hindustan Lever also bought Tata Oil Mills in response to a marketing alliance between two soap makers, Godrej Soaps and Proctor and Gamble.[5] Such acquisitions by large firms accelerated steadily from the second half of the 1990s as several deals were arranged that involved companies that had faced difficulties because of trade liberalization.

FEMA, 1999, and the Companies Act, 2013 (2000–2015)

In 1999 a crucial legislation was passed (Foreign Exchange Management Act [FEMA]) that made it much easier to raise funds to acquire assets and in turn encouraged a series of large deals involving Indian firms, foreign firms, or subsidiaries of foreign firms. The approval process for such deals was simplified in the Foreign Exchange Management (Transfer or Issue of any Foreign Security) Regulations, 2004. The act permitted an Indian company to acquire companies abroad by using its foreign currency account held abroad or drawing funds from an authorized currency dealer or by issuing depository receipts. From 2006 both the number and the value of mergers and acquisitions, mainly the latter, rose sharply. A few very large deals dominated the total value of transactions.

Whereas the increased mergers and acquisitions activity touched all types of business, the majority of these occurred in the services (rather than manufacturing), especially financial services. This phenomenon is well known in the empirical literature, but a compelling explanation does not seem to exist.[6] Services like trade and finance possess certain historically inherited features that could explain this. First, before the reforms, they were both heavily repressed by the government, which partly nationalized trade and finance and imposed barriers to entry for the private sector in these fields. In part, the heightened activity in the services reflects a catch-up with international standards after a decades-long falling behind. Second, worldwide, the share of services in consumption and GDP grew from the early 1990s. The end of government-controlled exchange rates and the telecommunications revolution created a huge impetus for the development of financial services. India emerged as a leading exporter of services. A final factor was the brand sensitivity of some financial services (such as insurance). Indian banks and financial companies were very small by international standards. To deliver retail services they sometimes needed more reputed foreign partners.

The Limited Liability Act, 2008, was an important reform for the service industry and for partnerships between Indian and foreign entities. A limited-liability partnership leaves the individual partners exempt from joint liability for the actions of other partners. The lobbyists for the new law included chambers that represented the interests of the large multinational firms.[7] However, the limited-liability provision of the law was clearly more compatible with new businesses like information technology services because it made it easier for larger partnerships to form, helped with the induction of partners with complementary skills or expertise but who were not friends or relations of other partners, and helped cross-border partnerships.

The 2013 Companies Act shifted the burden of external approval of deals from the High Court to the National Company Law Tribunal (NCLT). Traditionally, the courts heard the creditors' case in all suits where a company ended its life or merged into another. Doing this business in the courts involved enormous delays because the courts were too busy with other matters. The start of the NCLT in effect shifted these cases to a dedicated bench.

In the new regime, a domestic market deal started with a series of internal approvals by the audit committee, the board, and the shareholders. Then it sought approval from the NCLT, which in turn consulted the Registrar of Companies, the Income Tax Department, the Reserve Bank of India, the Securities and Exchange Board of India (SEBI), and the Competition Commission, among the more important parties. Under certain conditions, acquisition of the shares of a listed company entailed an open offer to the public shareholders. Therefore, the stock exchanges and SEBI are involved. The Reserve Bank restricted the scope of leveraged buyouts and overseas foreign exchange entitlements. The legal process unfolded at the same time and could be protracted, especially over tax implications and the pricing of shares.[8] The Competition Commission assessed whether or not a merger or acquisitions could have "appreciable adverse effect on competition," usually by means of globally accepted benchmarks.

The combined result of these changes in the company law, foreign exchange regulations, and securities regulations was a spate of friendly mergers and acquisitions between 2000 and 2015, though the drive lost momentum toward the end of this time span. The drive weakened as the low-hanging fruits had all been picked and the shock of a range of reforms wore off.

How successful were these mergers and acquisitions? Three large-scale mergers in the aviation industry created more problems than they solved. These were the merger of Kingfisher Airlines and Air Deccan (2006–2007), Air Sahara and Jet Airways (2006–2007), and Indian Airlines and Air India (2012). Two of the companies leading these deals went bankrupt, and the third deal survived because the companies involved, also bankrupt, were government owned. In banking, mergers have often been enforced on the more profitable partner by the regulator, the Reserve Bank of India, following frauds, but the experience has been somewhat happier. Several large acquisitions attracted media interest because these involved a foreign firm or large business groups. Examples included the acquisition by HDFC Bank of the Centurion Bank of Punjab (2008), the Oriental Bank of Commerce of Global Trust Bank (2004), Tata Power of Welspun Renewables (2016), Kotak Mahindra Bank of ING Vysya Bank (2014), Vodafone of Hutchison Essar (2006), and HDFC Ergo of L&T General Insurance (2016).

FEMA made acquisitions by domestic firms of subsidiaries of multinationals in India much easier. Examples of such acquisitions include Reliance Communications of MTS India (2016). Indian firms acquired companies or assets abroad, like Tata Steel of Corus (2007), Tata Motors of Jaguar Land Rover (2008), Hindalco of Novelis (2007), Videocon of Daewoo (2006), and Suzlon Energy of REPower/Senvion (2009). In oil and steel, a few large-scale mergers represented the government's decision to privatize operations or cut losses. Most large-valued cross-border deals occurred in pharmaceuticals, telecommunications, petroleum, and power. Some of the overseas deals were partial, that is, aimed to acquire brand names.[9] This incomplete list does not include cases of mergers within a business group.

These were cases of negotiated settlements to protect profits in an industry where competition had increased. Given the shadow of the Swraj Paul fiasco, an interesting question for the analyst was, Did the law make hostile takeovers any easier than before?

Hostile Takeovers

In 1994 a takeover code was framed in view of the new needs. This turned out to be controversial legislation. It wanted to do what takeover codes should do in all cases: protect minority shareholders (usually by the clause that the buyer discloses intentions and offers to buy shares at an attractive price from anyone wishing to sell) and make hostile takeovers easier in law by specifying the conditions when it can happen. The code turned out not to be flexible enough to do that. In 2011 another takeover code came into being wherein SEBI would oversee takeovers subject to rules. The new takeover code made hostile takeovers easy in law but still difficult in practice.[10]

The code also examined whether friendly acquisitions followed existing government restrictions on sector-specific foreign investment. Foreign investors were a significant new player in the mergers and acquisitions scenario. While foreign portfolio investment increased, India retained limits and quotas imposed on foreign direct investment in several fields such as print media and aviation. This was retained with the political aim to reduce foreign control over some Indian businesses that could be classified as being in the national interest. Behind the rhetoric of national interest, lobbies like Indian newspaper magnates and politicians rooting for the state-run aviation company worked hard against openness and competition.

The biggest acquisition in a hitherto protected segment was the Etihad Airways' purchase of 24% of the stakes in an Indian aviation company, Jet Airways, in 2013, after the limits were liberalized.[11] Immediately, the government ministries and regulatory bodies started a discussion about whether the purchase entailed a shift of control. Control was defined somewhat differently between the relevant laws depending on the aim of the act in question. Nevertheless, the difference complicated the discussion. Etihad in its turn was keen not to be seen as the controlling party because signatories to the International Air Transport Agreement can withdraw privileges offered to a company if it is not owned by nationals of the country. Eventually, the acquisition was approved on the reassurance that Etihad did not exercise control. The conclusion was in the company's favor and speedy enough, but the process was hardly reassuring for the future investor in the aviation industry.[12]

In practice, the takeover code did not face a big test because hostile takeovers of Indian firms by foreign entities remained rare even as merger and acquisition activity increased. Why were they rare? There were natural barriers to hostile takeovers. For example, despite increasing capitalization of Indian companies, close family control over companies persisted. The promoter shareholding in companies was generally high. The rapidly rising share prices from the early 2000s acted as another obstacle.[13]

It is also likely that potential raiders did not want to push their luck, fearing a political backlash. Overall, the thrust of the reforms was on formalizing the approvals process so that neither the judges nor the officers under ministerial control could have a direct say in the matter. But formal legal reform did not make hostile takeovers any more politics free than in the past. A large investment proposal would still have to clear the Foreign Investment Promotion Board that vetted proposals in protected areas, the Competition Commission, and SEBI. The law did not stop these moves. But when the question arose as to who "controlled" the Indian company, politics could still step in. The existence of several layers of approval process involving the regulators, which ostensibly acted as a safeguard for shareholders, also indirectly acted as a barrier to hostile takeovers because the regulators were not immune to sentiments.

A different sort of political imperative was at play in intellectual property protection.

Knowledge Protection

The history of intellectual property protection in India is usually divided into three stages. During 1950–1970 a constitutional guarantee to private property and the basket of colonial laws, including those on trademarks and the Indian Patent and Designs Act, 1911, provided the framework of the law. Indian legal theory and practice in these years were broadly equivalent to international standards. For example, the 1911 act recognized product patents, as did international law.

The Patents Act, 1970, changed the game substantially by recognizing the process of production as a ground to claim the originality and the usefulness of an idea that had potential industrial application. Apparently innocuous, the recognition of process as patentable gave a huge boost to the domestic pharmaceutical industry. Under the product-patents regime protected by the 1911 Act, principal patent holders in the pharmaceutical industry after 1947 were American and European multinational companies who enjoyed the benefits of a restrictive trade regime by producing patented goods in India. Now domestic firms reverse engineered well-known international brands. They reproduced similar products with a modification of the process and patented the new product. Thus began the second phase in the history of intellectual property protection, the era of divergence from international law. The 1970 Act was one of three measures—the Foreign Exchange Regulations Act (1973) and the Drug Price Control Order being the others—that reduced the freedom of multinational pharmaceutical companies and strengthened domestic producers.[14]

Economists claimed that the Indian Patents Act was expected to foster innovation by domestic producers. No doubt this was one of the expectations behind the creation of process patents. The number of bulk drugs (intermediaries) produced at the end of the 1980s was indeed impressive. The growth of formulations (medicines sold in retail) was also noteworthy. Indian firms were also remarkably successful in capturing the export market for standard drugs in the developing world. And yet, if innovation is defined as the discovery of new cures, the industry did little of that sort of research. Such research was simply too costly in knowledge, money, and time for a protectionist law to enable. The end of the 1980s was a crunch time in international negotiations around intellectual property. The pressure was intense on India to join the convention to discuss a global service trade regime. In this scenario, the moral right of the industry to continue to claim a privileged patent regime became unstable.[15]

As India reembraced globalization in the 1990s, it no longer had a choice about the patent regime. The reintegration in the world trade system subjected it to the provisions of TRIPS. The key provision was restoring equivalence of law. The subsequent twenty odd years saw a shakeout in the pharmaceutical industry. The reintroduction of product patents in 2005, it was expected, would encourage research in India. This did happen to some extent but not in drugs development. The coincidence of the shift in the patent regime and the end of patents on a range of drugs helped the Indian industry find a new and worldwide market. The knowledge it had gained during the process patent regime helped in making a successful transition.

The new administrative setup, however, was quite chaotic. The legal and regulatory system that governed the industry was far from perfect. The Competition Commission resolved cases of cartel activity with little precedence. The drug approvals body did not coordinate with the patents authority. Drug price controls remained and often caused confusion.[16] The new environment did not dramatically improve drugs development innovation.

Not long after India complied with TRIPS, two court cases in India tested the new legal regime. Both were heard at the Intellectual Property Appellate Board, and one went to the Supreme Court. In one of these cases (*Bayer v. Natco*, 2013), a provision called compulsory license was the matter in dispute. The compulsory license was a provision that allowed the government to permit the production of a patented drug by a domestic firm without consulting the patentee if a case could be made that the drug was lifesaving, too expensive, and the patentee was neither producing it in the country nor importing it in adequate quantity. Bayer challenged the compulsory license taken out by Natco to produce Nexavar, a drug Bayer had patented for the treatment of advanced liver cancer. Natco made a case that the grounds for a compulsory license had been satisfied. The price of the patented version was fifteen times that of the licensed domestic version, and probably for that reason, it was not easily available in India. The appellate board rejected Bayer's argument for full compliance with international law; the main ground for doing so was that the promised lower price by the licensee was "in public interest."

In *Novartis AG v. Union of India*, the issue at stake was "evergreening," or extending the life of a patent about to expire, by using "new forms of known substances" (in the language of the act). Although applicable to all manufacturing innovation, the clause had a significant influence in the pharmaceutical industry. An application for a patent on Novartis's Gleevec, used for the treatment of chronic myeloid leukemia, had been submitted soon after India joined the World Trade Organization (1998) and awaited decision. The appellate board revived the case after 2005 and found merit in the claim that there was an innovation in the product but not a substantial innovation over the older version of the drug. The Supreme Court rejected the company's appeal but seemed to hold an "indeterminate position on what constitutes a 'known compound,'" the key issue in evergreening.[17]

The alignment of Indian law on patents with international law renewed controversy over the rationale of the US patent regime for pharmaceuticals. The issue at stake was of fundamental importance to drugs patents. Major innovations in pharmaceuticals are costly in time, money, and risk; the award of strong patent protection to successful innovation is fair and just incentive to the innovator. In the retail market for medicines, the pursuit of fairness could end up with drugs that saved lives and cost twenty times more than a cheaper copy. To permit the production of such copies serves welfare, especially in a poor country. The old law in India privileged welfare, while the new law privileged fairness, with escape clauses. Thus, while laws changed to allow patented production, patented production created a new dynamic of disputation between these two sides of the argument.

Bayer and Novartis were both early examples of that dynamic. The decisions can be seen to have privileged welfare considerations over fairness, effectively strengthening the case for domestic production of patented drugs. Elsewhere in the book, we have talked about how the Supreme Court sometimes took on an activist, social-justice-oriented role focusing on, say, the right to life or other fundamental rights. Many political activists, nongovernmental organizations, and economists share the sentiment that openness and commercialization threaten some of these rights. Intellectual property disputes could not stay immune to tensions like these.

The new regime of patent law made the implementation of a patent or a license mandatory. Apparently there was no insistence on the enforcement of that implementation clause. Several studies show that after a court battle was over, the winner in a patents dispute did not start using the patented process in production. Rules insisted that they had to submit reasons for the delay in doing so or suffer a penalty. They did submit reasons on a prescribed form, but cursorily. It seemed no one took the paperwork related to enforcement seriously enough.[18] Filing a patent had often been misused to preempt competition, and lax enforcement made that use more likely.

In the courts, international patent holders could more easily than before challenge and stall an Indian firm from using a version of the invention.[19] For Indian companies globalizing their operations, dealing with national patent law was an inevitable process. Two well-cited cases with different outcomes, both fought in the United States, revealed how the process might work. Both cases turned on the provision in US law that a patent application will not be successful if "the subject matter as a whole would have been obvious at the time of the invention" (Supreme Court in *KSR v. Teleflex*, 2007). The Indian pharmaceutical company Lupin's appeal against an earlier decision by a district court favoring the German multinational Aventis for a blood pressure drug was heard after the 2007 decision. The appeal was upheld on the point that Aventis's claim that the key innovation was nonobvious could not be sustained, for the drug that Aventis patented came from a family of drugs used for the purpose. In *Forest Laboratories v. Ivax Pharmaceuticals and Cipla*, patent infringement was accepted on the same ground that the claim that the patented innovation was "obvious" in relation to the state of the art was not established. Forest Laboratories and Ivax (Cipla's associate in this case) are American companies, and Cipla is an Indian one.

These cases showed that the 2007 judgment had "in effect raised the bar regarding patentability"; that is, a patent claim now needed a stronger justification and was more challengeable on the "obviousness" point. This shift made generics producers hopeful in challenging patents.[20]

One key advantage of the convergence between Indian law and global law was that India could now access a wider range of intellectual property protection, including geographical indications. This increased access was demonstrated in two international cases, one involving turmeric and the other neem, both vegetable products used as medicines or insect repellents in traditional Indian medical practices. There were attempts in the United States to patent turmeric and an attempt in Europe to patent neem. The neem case triggered nationalistic backlash in India (see epigraph at the head of this chapter). The attempts to patent neem were successfully challenged by India on the ground that the inventions lacked originality.[21] India also made bids to secure rights for Basmati rice, Darjeeling tea, Alphonso mangos, and Kolhapuri chappals (a type of footwear) and made joint bids with other countries to secure the stronger geographical indications protection then available only to wines and spirits.[22]

The welfare consideration about patents was in effect a worry that patented products would be sold at excessive prices. One of the measures to avoid that outcome was to specify what a patentable innovation was. For some of the most common applications, this question is the hardest to settle. Computer programs used in an invention fell in this gray area. Before 2016, patent law did not sharply distinguish software and hardware. A draft Guidelines for Examination of Computer Related Inventions prepared in 2016 did rethink the law but retained an old provision that for a claim to novelty to be sustained, an invention would involve a change in the hardware. In view of a Madras High Court judgment in the same year (*Ericsson v. Intex Technologies*) that "any invention" in which a technical contribution can be established is patentable, the revised draft guidelines dropped the distinction.[23]

Given India's impressive advances in information technology services since 2000, economists asked the question, Could copyright protection strengthen the industry? There was industry interest in the question, too, and the main industry association lobbied for legal reforms in this area. The backdrop to that interest was Indian participation in innovations in the United States and technological changes (such as the shift to system on a chip) that entail "the historical shifting between integrated and ever more fragmented organizational modes of production in the electronics industry."[24] The number of Indian origin persons and firms filing patent applications in the United States was rising rapidly from 2000 to 2004.[25] But there was little activity in India. Software is hard to patent because, among other reasons, it changes form quickly, and a program consists of too many parts for the originality to be precisely identified. Most software that is patented is in the nature of specific industrial applications and is patented by the firm that sponsors the application.[26]

Outside the pharmaceutical industry, where patent rights disputes represented the lingering shadow of India's protectionist patents regime of the past, disputes were surprisingly rare. A calculation showed that between 1970 and 2000, only ten cases of patent infringement and revocation were heard in the higher courts, not enough to supply work for more than a few dozen lawyers. Twelve more cases were heard between 2000 and 2008, an acceleration no doubt, but there was still a surprising lack of activity in this area.[27] Most patent specialists helped people file applications rather than argue in court.

But if the numbers were small, some cases drew a lot of attention for the prospect that they could set a precedent for the future. In 2002, Bajaj Auto Limited filed a patent for a twin-spark ignition in one of its motorcycle brands. In 2007, TVS Auto, a rival, filed a case for revocation of the patent. TVS was marketing a model of a motorcycle with a similar ignition. Bajaj sought an injunction on TVS. The Madras High Court decided the case in favor of TVS on the grounds that the company had a license with an Austrian firm for the innovation and did not infringe on the patent. On an appeal, the order of the Supreme Court, confusingly, upheld Bajaj's patent and allowed TVS to continue with sales of the rival brand. The Supreme Court used the legal rule known as the doctrine of equivalents, where patent infringement was granted even though the tool or the process that infringed on the patented tool or process was not a copy nor a derived form. It appears that the intention was to deliver substantive justice even though procedurally the case for a patent infringement was not obvious.

The Bajaj-TVS dispute had interesting spillover. While the case was in court, TVS patented another invention relating to motorcycles, and a new dispute between the two firms started. The Supreme Court observed the unnecessary delay in processing the case and advised tribunals and courts to hear intellectual property cases quickly and settle these within four months. The legal professionals alternately hailed and regretted the fact that unconventional material (a blog post, articles in obscure printed books without citation of sources) was used in cases like these as evidence.

Foreign Investment and Private Equity

Along with the revival of domestic private investment, globalization thrust on the legislators a need to address a whole new field—which emerged only with the inflow of foreign portfolio investment—in the form of private equity and venture capital. A robust stock market was an irresistible attraction for global finance to come to India (usually via intermediaries based in Mauritius and Singapore).[28] These huge movements in the business world made mergers, acquisitions, and takeovers more likely, and private equity was often the enabling agent. Previously, regulatory law discouraged such investments. New laws enabled them at first by reducing transaction costs like licensing and registration of investment funds and following up with tribunals.

Until the end of the 1990s, the Government of India was caught up in a dilemma between opening doors to foreign investment and serving nationalist sentiments. In 1999 FEMA replaced FERA, and by simplifying repatriation rules encouraged the inflow of capital. But as mentioned before, quotas remained in place, restricting investment in areas that needed competition, including civil aviation and newspapers. Procedurally, an interministerial body called the Foreign Investment Promotion Board vetted applications by foreign direct investors. However, since the Board had to coordinate the views of a large number of ministries and other regulatory bodies, its decisions were often delayed. In 2017 the board was abolished. The permissions process remained in place but was subjected to new guidelines on speedy disposal of applications. The institutions in charge faced no credible penalty for not complying with these guidelines.

The introduction of FEMA in 1999 and subsequently easier licensing rules for investors (an investing company needed only to register with SEBI) led to a surge of funds into Indian companies from 2003. Restrictions on exit of money continued. But the prospect of capital gains in the stock market was irresistible. Private equity firms' interest in India was growing rapidly in the 2000s as well because mergers and acquisitions activity had warmed up.

Far from being celebrated, foreign institutional investment caused new anxieties about the source of funds. The 2013 revision of the Companies Act imposed hard disclosure requirements on such investments, which encouraged indirect methods of investment. One such indirect method was the rights issue, where initially the new shares went to the existing shareholders and were subsequently transferred to the private equity firm. The board of the issuing company managed the process so that control remained in its hands, and yet no laws were broken. Among legal professionals, there is a view that government regulation is still onerous and opaque. The persistence of controls encouraged start-ups, venture capital firms, and technology firms to register in cities like Singapore rather than in India.[29]

By 2010 private equity investment was large in scale and specialized as seed funds, venture capital funds, private equity funds, real estate or technology, and debt or equity. Investment regulation framed by the Securities and Exchange Board of India dealt with venture capital, and while it did have rules on disclosure of information, registration, transparency, and tax avoidance, it did not deal enough with conflicts of interest between managers and owners. In 2011 a move began to create a comprehensive regulatory regime with a finer classification of funds and class-specific investment conditions. The evolution of the first draft of 2011 into a full system of regulations and consultations in 2015 illustrated a pattern of regulatory catch-up that was often present in the financial market and involved both the central bank and SEBI taking the industry on board in the negotiations process.[30]

Openness made reforms necessary in another field, international contracts, that touched on cross-border transactions.

International Contracts

From the 1990s the practice of international firms outsourcing services to Indian suppliers began to increase. In the 2000s the scale grew rapidly. At the same time, the scope of such contracts expanded and diversified. Regulation or the lack of it played a big role in the making of the offshoring revolution, especially in the information technology and knowledge industries. The lack of regulation in the United States, the main client, and government activism often bypassing a protectionist trade regime in the supplying regions, especially India, contributed to this growth.[31] Foreign firms set up bases in India to manage offshoring. However, as growth stabilized and other countries entered the fields, regulatory issues emerged.

All forms of foreign investment raise two types of contractual issues, one involving the contract between the foreign and domestic partners or affiliates, and the other one between these firms and the tax authorities. In the case of service exports, the two issues frequently intertwine. That is, whereas tax authorities worldwide follow the general rule that income generated in goods and services produced in the country is liable to be taxed, with services the portion of the income generated in the country is harder to determine than in the production of goods. Typically, the foreign contracting firm or the front office would outsource a part of a package of services to the back office, and what value that package added to the total product could not be easily identified in the accounts. Further, activities like data processing and technical support were classified as preparatory or auxiliary to the main activity. In principle, only a main income-generating activity was taxable, not auxiliary services.[32] The conceptual issue was whether the foreign firm could be seen to buy services or produce services in Indian soil through outsourcing operations. Production was the taxable activity, buying was not.

The Competition Commission had to deal with disputes involving the traditional service providers, such as taxi companies, and online service providers, such as online taxi-hailing companies like Uber and its Indian rival Ola. Hoping to expand the consumer base and capture network economies, online service providers often priced their services below the level that was profitable for them. Network economy refers to the value accruing to the firm from there being a rise in the number of users. By traditional competition law, which does not account for network economies, this pricing strategy can be challenged as an anticompetitive strategy and abuse of dominance. In the case of the taxi-hailing firms, there is little dispute that market dominance did exist. But they also made large losses. Whether discounting was an abuse of dominance or a strategy to capture network effects was not clear.[33]

Conclusion

In the first fifteen years of the new millennium, there was business-friendly legislation in response to evidence that businesses had benefited from globalization but needed alignment between Indian law and global law to sustain the gains. The broad trend of legislation in response to these changes was the same as that discussed in chapter 7: reduce regulatory overlap, shift the approvals and dispute resolution system away from ministries and to regulators, reduce the say of conventional courts and judges, and create a parallel judiciary along with a parallel jurisprudence. Whereas earlier the goal of tribunals was to make things harder for the companies, now the goal was to make things easier.

In the short run, the huge surge in Indian stock markets bears witness to the ability of Indian corporations to attract fresh capital and thus raise shareholder value. Corporate restructuring was a key step to make that happen. Would the gains last? In the long run the shareholder value due to mergers, acquisitions, and hostile takeovers should depend on how easy or difficult it is to trade in company reputation. The prevalence of family firms, identification of reputation with families rather than companies, and a persistent antiglobalization streak within mainstream Indian politics seemed to make anything other than friendly deals still difficult.

Did de jure change in institutions bring about de facto changes? The general aim of the de jure change was convergence between international law and Indian law. In intellectual property, this was done under external push; in takeovers and mergers, restoring parity was a more endogenous process. Questions remain over how deep the convergence was. Although the Takeover Code was modeled after the United Kingdom City Code, the similarity was only in form; the contexts of application of the code were significantly different. The high level of promoter family control of shareholding in India ensured that the chance of a hostile takeover succeeding was small with or without the defense mechanisms allowed in law.[34] Intellectual property, too, warrants only a cautious form of optimism. In some other fields, such as taxation (not included in the book), political considerations played a more explicit and arbitrary role when globalization created new challenges for the fiscal administration.[35]

In other words, postreform India did witness a radical structural break in thinking about corporate law. And yet it was not a clean break, and the old anxieties persisted into the operation of the present regime.

In this and the preceding chapters we have discussed the various sources of law, particularly as it pertains to property and contract: the colonial legacy, developmental goals, the "socialist" influence, the strengthening of Indian democracy, the activism of the courts, the liberalizing impulse, and the need to align with global practices. We have not yet discussed a key topic: the religious roots of law, which are particularly relevant when it comes to the rights of women and caste-based discrimination. Religion-based law also applies to certain trusts and endowments, which manage some important public assets. This class of issues is important but also highly complex, warranting a detailed treatment of its own, beyond the scope of this book. We will comment briefly in the next chapter.

CHAPTER NINE

Property

Equity versus Religious Norms

We understand the difficulties involved in bringing persons of different faiths and persuasions on a common platform. But, a beginning has to be made if the Constitution is to have any meaning. Inevitably, the role of the reformer has to be assumed by the courts. — *Mohd. Ahmed Khan vs Shah Bano Begum*, Supreme Court, 1985

Introduction

A conflict between equality and freedom was fundamental to disputations over how property should pass on between generations. The conflict had its roots in the colonial-era practice of framing property rights with reference to religion. Religion-based rules had built-in inequalities, especially between men and women. Legislation in colonial times supplied escape routes from these inequalities without making religious law invalid. For example, the judges sometimes ruled using "justice, equity, and good conscience" when religious law seemed to discriminate by gender or the caste of the parties. Legislation after independence added new weapons like the Constitution, a democratic legislature, and a Supreme Court, which upheld equality. But the Constitution, the judiciary, and the legislature also at times upheld personal law, citing the freedom to follow tradition or religion in matters of succession within a family. The struggle between equality and freedom, therefore, proved a messy one, as this chapter will show.

The colonial legacy included an elaborate system of rules for succession and inheritance of private property. British-Indian law was territorial and did not discriminate by caste, ethnicity, or gender. However, by accepting that customs and religion might govern inheritance and succession of property, it indirectly allowed differences between men and women, between Hindus and Muslims, and between castes to persist. The problem was well known to legislators, publicists, and jurists for a long time and was addressed sometimes in case laws and sometimes in legislation that provided an escape route for the holders of weaker rights under religious law. However, no radical departure from the foundation of law in religion and custom happened. The colonial rulers were probably afraid of making a radical changes and did not think that personal law deserved such top-down intervention.

In 1950, after the end of colonial rule, the Constitution preserved a potential for conflict between freedom of religion and fundamental human rights. One set of articles (mainly Article 26) guaranteed that a religious group should have the right "to manage its own affairs in matters of religion," though the Constitution did not get into the details of what these affairs might be. Another set of articles guaranteed that all citizens have equal right of treatment in law (14–16) and be subject to a uniform civil code (44). Women's right to property was already weaker than men's in both Hindu and Muslim law according to the orthodox reading of the religious codes. What should happen when religious freedom (26) and gender equality (14–16) came into conflict? Should Article 44 resolve the tension?

The democratic polity often debated such matters. The conflict was more serious and more open in independent India. Legislators now acted with a heavier hand. And once again, legislators retreated from an explicit rejection of religion and custom as the source of personal law while providing escape routes. In that respect, the colonial and postcolonial strategies of reform of personal law were qualitatively similar though different in the degree of intervention. One of the more famous occasions in which personal law was framed with reference to religion and fundamental rights coming into conflict was the Shah Bano case settled in 1985, which we will discuss at some length below.

Nevertheless, we do see attrition in religion-based personal law. Over the seventy years covered in this book, there was a convergence between personal law and the public principle of equality on several fronts, partly by legislative change and partly by reinterpretation of traditional law. A silent revolution in society may have contributed to the convergence. For example, the fact that middle-class families are smaller than in 1950 and that women marry later and work more than they did before increased the pressure on families to ensure that daughters were not deprived of succession because of a quirky law.

Another not-so-silent revolution also contributed to the convergence of personal law and public principle. Personal law applies to the succession and inheritance of physical assets. But the Indian economy relies increasingly on the production of services. The top end of that services pyramid is formed by companies that command valuable and patented intellectual property and supply services in the world market. The base of that pyramid is formed of millions of workers—a substantial number among them being women—who supply skilled and unskilled services for wages. For those reasonably well placed on that ladder, inheriting parental property is less a crucial matter than before because it is easier now to get a mortgage and own property. The services and the knowledge revolution did not exist in colonial times, and it was inchoate for much of the postindependence years. But it was rapidly changing Indian society and the position of women in the workplace in the new millennium.

This chapter on property rights deals with succession and inheritance of physical property, the field in which we observe a gradual and tortuous process of extraction from colonial roots.[1]

Women's Rights to Property

A woman's right to property was a persistent source of disputation in colonial India. Three issues repeatedly emerged: women's right to inherit property by virtue of birth in the family, the head of the family's right to will (testamentary right), and the terms on which a divorce was settled.

Directly, the propensity for disputation had owed to the decision of the colonial government to follow Indian tradition. However, in certain fundamental areas, Indian law agreed with contemporary English law. In the case of a divorce, both sets of law recognized separate rights and not joint rights over all assets. That is, women had rights over their own earnings and inheritances. Divorce in the nineteenth century was rare in both cases, not because families were happier but because both personal law and property law made divorce an almost impossible option for women. But whereas succession rules were more equitable in England in that the law privileged the testamentary power of the owner, in Indian law, wills and testaments were overridden by the right of the joint family.[2] The nature of the family's right to jointly held property varied by religion and custom.

Further, the Indian joint family, thanks to the spiritual benefit or pious obligation principle, recognized agnate successors (related by blood or adoption wholly through males) as the inheritors of property, leaving females with a right to maintenance.[3] When a woman was widowed and did not have a son, the family could renege on the right to maintenance or maintain or perform it with indifference. Such cases were numerous. So were attempts by a woman about to lose a husband to hurriedly adopt a son, a decision that required the husband's consent and was often challenged in court by the family.

Therefore, and as *Law and the Economy* has shown, the deference of colonial law to Hindu tradition created two types of inequity—women's right as a "coparcener" and testamentary rights of individual members of a joint family. Coparceners are coowners of the family estate, that is, individuals with the right to demand a partition of their share upon the death of the head of the estate. While all schools of Hindu law contained versions of the coparcener idea, the nature of women's membership in it varied, the Mitakshara school being the least favorable to women. A limited form of reform was introduced via two legislations: the Hindu Women's Right to Property Act XVIII of 1937, and the Hindu Law of Inheritance Act, 1929. These recognized certain types of female successors as the equivalent of coparceners. The reference to scriptures was often given up in the courtroom, but because litigation was expensive in time and money, only a fraction of the disputes reached the court. Besides, the problem was deeper than case laws could address. Legislation could not ideologically commit to Hindu law and yet deliver equality.[4] Judgments and legislation redressed the imbalance but without rendering any part of the traditional law invalid.

The overlapping of new and old principles increased the disputatious tendency in succession laws. In Hindu joint families, women's rights to succession became subject to much controversy and conflicting judgments in the nineteenth century. The disputes came not only from the iniquitous nature of religious law but also from differences of opinion within religious law. The Mitakshara ruled that the right to property by birth accrued to male successors alone on certain ritual grounds. Known as pious obligations, these rules were elevated to legal obligations in colonial law, empowering male heirs significantly. An exception was made for the property the wives were bestowed by their own families or received as gifts, which made dowry and gold ornaments a critical part of the marriage transaction and valuable in protecting the future well-being of the wives.

Through case laws and legislation, the rights of wives to property were recognized. However, the rights of females as coparceners remained poorly defined. Legislation began with the Indian Succession Act 1865, which applied to the Jews and the Europeans, followed by the Hindu Wills Act, 1870, and finally the Indian Succession Act, 1925, which consolidated the Hindu Wills Act, the Indian Succession Act, the Probate and Administration Act, 1881, and the Parsi Intestate Succession Act, to create a framework for both unwilled and willed succession for all people except Muslims. For Muslims, a 1772 Regulation (II) had already upheld the primacy of the sharia in personal and inheritance matters but as modified by local customs added during the nineteenth century through case laws and legislation.

There is not enough jurisprudence available on precolonial times to say how closely colonial law approximated Indian indigenous practice. The measures that the colonial regime introduced are more visible. Although different schools within Hindu law differed on the nature of women's property, there was a convergence in practice between them, and the consensus was for retaining discrimination. On the other hand, classes, regions, and castes followed different customs. Only Hindu upper castes followed scriptural law closely in their own customs. Others did not.[5]

This was the situation in 1949, when the Indian Constitution was drafted. The Constitution had three provisions that were relevant to the subsequent evolution of the framework of property law. First, Article 372 made the rule that all colonial laws were valid unless repealed or changed. The article gave formal sanction to personal laws. Second, Article 15(1) stated that the state shall not discriminate against any citizen on grounds only of religion, race, caste, sex, or place of birth. And third, Article 13 stated that laws inconsistent with or in derogation of the fundamental rights including that set out in 15(1) will be void.

It was now left to the judges how to resolve the apparent contradiction between Article 372 and Article 13 or 15(1). If polygamy was sanctioned by personal law, would that practice violate Article 15(1)? In *State of Bombay v. Narasu Appa Mali* (All India Report, 1952, Bom. 84), the judges held otherwise. The case followed the petition of several Hindu men to challenge a Bombay state law prohibiting bigamy among Hindus. The argument was that the prohibition violated personal law, which sanctioned men to take more than one wife to ensure the generation of a male heir. The court considered a counterargument that Article 15(1), which made discrimination on the basis of sex unlawful, also made polygamy under personal law unconstitutional since under that law men could take more than one wife whereas women could take only one husband. The judgment rejected the petition, arguing that the state had the right to legislate on marriage practices. It became famous by then saying that personal law such as marriage practices were not unconstitutional. Personal law was not "law in force." The Constitution had used this expression to mean "laws in force in the territory of India immediately before the commencement of this Constitution," which, if in violation of fundamental rights, would be void. The judges held that polygamy was not unconstitutional or discriminatory, being "based on considerations which were very vital and compelling to those who believed and who still believe in the sanctity of their personal law." Indirectly, the judgment strengthened the case for retaining a different personal law among the Muslims. It took the court forty years to decide that the Article 15(1) did extend to personal law (A.I.R. 1992 Bom. 215).

The 1952 case underscored the fundamental anomaly that polygamy was allowed by both personal law and law in force for Muslims. The judges did not think much of the anomaly between Hindu and Muslim personal law, but it came back to haunt politics in the 1980s. We will discuss several cases involving Muslims below.

Division of property after divorce involved types of a fundamental right that neither the Constitution nor existing laws recognized clearly. One rationale was that the "relationship [of being married] has generated needs which the other party should meet."[6] For example, children borne of a marriage need to be cared for even after the marriage ends. Another rationale was that marriage entailed the creation of a common pool shared between the husband and the wife, regardless of individual inheritances, so that the dissolution of the marriage entailed an equal division of the common pool. Personal law did not recognize these principles. In the case of divorce, again, Indian legislation was held back by a commitment to personal law. English law in principle recognized joint property and made the court responsible for division (after 1973). In India, the legislation did not explicitly recognize joint property, though the right to "maintenance" was defined independently of religious references and probably enforced better than before. The judges often struggled with the notion of separate property, which was more explicitly defined for women than for men. In principle, if women had exclusive rights to what they received from their parental home or husbands, the husbands ought to have exclusive rights to what they received from their families. But this in itself would be iniquitous because one-time gifts may not sustain lives. Income will, but usually men have better prospects of earning an income.

In 1956, in one of the first major reforms, the Hindu Succession Act recognized the daughter as a "class I heir" of her father's property, Class I referring to direct descendants and surviving spouse. At the same time, the act recognized the testamentary rights of individual members of the family. In numerous other ways the 1956 Act failed to change the discriminatory tone of the succession law. There was strong resistance in the parliament to repeal the more controversial body of Hindu law, the Mitakshara, a move for which the framers of a new Hindu Code Bill had asked.[7] The power to legislate was divided between the center and the states so that some states enacted more equitable law than the center.

Legislation on agricultural property was a state subject, whereas other types of property were legislated at the center. That cleavage was again a colonial legacy. This is the reason we have more than one chapter on property in this book. To cut a long story short, reforms in governance carried out in 1935 gave the right to legislate on agricultural land to the provinces. Locally, there was a strong sentiment against transfer and fragmentation of agricultural land, which translated into two things—legal restrictions on the use of agricultural land for nonagricultural uses, and restrictions on succession of agricultural land. In details, the succession rules varied a lot. But in effect, they made women's right to inherit weak and the right to will or gift weak too.[8] State laws were amended in four states—Andhra Pradesh (1986), Tamil Nadu (1988), Karnataka (1990), and Maharashtra (1994)—to redress this inequality in inheritance of agricultural land. The 2005 amendment of the Hindu Successions Act generalized the principle.

In practice there remained considerable ambiguity about the status of personal law. The right-by-birth principle was followed in certain states in a modified form. The right by birth meant that individuals had property rights by being born in a family. Men had these rights, but they were weaker for women. The framers of the Hindu Code Bill recommended that the right-by-birth principle be dropped, which faced stiff resistance from Hindu campaign groups.[9] Also, case judgments often ruled in favor of personal law.[10] The state acts on succession, while making daughters equal as heirs to father's property, weakened the rights of the married daughters on the assumption that they would already have received a dowry at marriage.

Only as late as in 1996, the Supreme Court ruled in a case that when personal rights and fundamental rights contradicted one another, the fundamental rights would prevail. The Hindu Succession (Amendment) Act, 2005, made equality the universal rule. Unlike in the 1950s, the move attracted little public protest. There was not much pressure anymore to retain religious references or much reason since several states had already discarded the principle. The so-called pious obligation of males was dropped without much resistance. The clauses sanctioning, even elevating, dowry to a legitimate transaction, were dropped, too, though only through parliamentary intervention.

Certain provisions of traditional law had been underlegislated before and remained so in these reforms. The subject of the reunion was one of these. Reunion refers to the intention of a successor to keep her share of property joined with the shares of other successors. In family firms, the reunion was a crucial matter. It was traditionally governed by fairly clear instructions in Hindu law that only males could unite property. Although by default, Hindu law still ruled in reunion, in practice the reference to tradition became rarer.

Improved access to property has benefited women. As we have mentioned above, some states amended Hindu inheritance law to give women equal rights to property even before the passing of national level legislation in 2005. Klaus Deininger, Hari Nagarajan, and Aparajita Goyal compared outcomes for women whose fathers died before the prowomen amendments were passed with outcomes for women whose fathers died after the amendments were passed. They concluded that the amendments led to greater inheritance of land by women. Women whose education decisions were made after the amendments were passed received more education.[11] Perhaps unsurprisingly, these changes in inheritance law also had some perverse effects, as long-standing gender inequity was challenged. Sonia Bhalotra and coauthors find that the inheritance reforms aggravated son preference in that, if the firstborn was a daughter, this reduced the probability that later children were girls, suggesting higher female feticide.[12] Siwan Anderson and Garance Genicot found that the inheritance reforms increased suicide rates for both men and women. They conjecture that this was due to increased conflict among married couples.[13] Clearly, law has changed faster than attitudes.

Muslim Personal Law

Two colonial-era laws formed the body of Muslim personal law in India. These were the Shariat Application Act, 1937, which made the Shariat rather than common law applicable to the Muslims, and the Dissolution of Muslim Marriages Act 1939, which was a specific law applicable to divorce, embodying the same principle. The former was short on specifics. In both, the rights of men and women differed on matters of marriage and divorce. But women's property right was defined somewhat more explicitly with Muslim women than their Hindu counterparts.

The persistence of personal law made for a difference between rights to control and inherit property between Hindu and Muslim women. The difference did not have a uniform character. Until 2006, the Hindu schools of thought curbed women's rights to control joint family estate; by comparison, Muslim women had more rights to manage a property. On the other hand, reforms in Hindu succession rights defined the rights of daughters to inherit a share of the estate better than corresponding rights for Muslim women. While both Hindu and Muslim law evolved after 1950, the influences differed. In Hindu personal law, the convergence process to a nondiscriminatory civil code was faster because the influence of orthodox Hindus declined. Among Sunnis, the Muslim Personal Law Board formally protected the boundaries between sharia and a universally applicable civil code, though that boundary was becoming unstable all the time because of the influence of transnational Islamic law, intracommunity reform movements, and landmark cases.

One of these cases occurred in 1955, the Calcutta High Court judgment in *Anjuman Ara v. Nawab Asif Kade*. This judgment recognized the testamentary rights of Muslims as equivalent to the rights of any other community. At the time hailed as a significant step, its subsequent effect on practice was limited. A 1960 Allahabad High Court judgment in a case involving polygamy and cruelty to the first wife (*Itwari v. Asghari*) set out the principle that "cruelty" was a universal, that there was no such thing as Hindu cruelty and Muslim cruelty, and therefore, it needed a uniform response.[14] However, the implications of this judgment in the economic sphere were limited.

Two other judgments, by contrast, figure prominently in recent jurisprudence as game changers: the 1985 *Mohd. Ahmed Khan v. Shah Bano Begum* maintenance case, and the 2014 *Shabnam Hashmi v. Union of*

India judgment, both delivered by the Supreme Court. In the 1985 case the court accepted the right of a divorced woman to alimony from her husband. The Muslim Personal Law Board disputed the decision, and the ruling party listened and passed the Muslim Women (Protection of Rights on Divorce) Act, 1986, which weakened the alimony rights. When similar cases reappeared in court more recently (*Shamima Farooqui vs Shahid Khan*, 2015), the Supreme Court upheld the spirit of the Shah Bano judgment. On this occasion, the All India Shia Personal Law Board accepted the verdict as fair. The judgment in *Shabnam Hashmi v. Union of India* affirmed the right to adopt a child when religious personal law denied or disputed that right.

If the Shah Bano case was not directly about property, disputes over the right to adopt were almost always about property. Adoption in personal law was historically a means to retain the freedom of the male property holder to make a bequest within the family and ensure that the widow would be looked after well. Neither option was available when the property was owned by a joint family whose rights were set by religious law. Hindus wanting to adopt struggled to gain this right in the nineteenth century and managed to get a limited right (male head could adopt a male). The Hindu Adoptions and Maintenance Act, 1956, removed these limits. A 1972 Adoptions Bill technically made the benefit of this unrestricted adoption available to all religions. The judgment in *Shabnam Hashmi v. Union of India* referred to this option and upheld the right of a Muslim mother to adopt. The Muslim Personal Law Board objected to the judgment that it conflicted with the sharia. "The most resounding objection was that adoption would alter inheritance patterns."[15] On this occasion, however, the political opposition was considerably muted.[16]

An unresolved tension in the Constitution was the one between the right to religious freedom and the desirability of a uniform civil code. This tension produced perhaps the most significant public debate on law in the late-twentieth century.

A Uniform Civil Code? Article 44 of the Indian Constitution

Article 44 in the Directive Principles of the Constitution asks for a uniform civil code for all religions. Its inclusion in the Directive Principles means that it is not enforceable as law. A justifiable rule as such, it co-exists with other oddities such as a ban on cow slaughter (Article 48), suggesting that equity was not always the motivation behind the drafting of the Directive Principles. That ambiguity enabled religious groups to resist the enforcement of Article 44.

The Supreme Court's Shah Bano judgment in 1985 (see above) became famous because it asked for Article 44 to be made into a law. The Shah Bano case had involved the family of Muhammad Ahmed Khan, an advocate based in Indore in central India. Khan had married his first cousin Shah Bano in 1932 when still a student, and another first cousin in 1946. Disputes over property, among other matters, led Khan to drive out Shah Bano from his house in 1975. In 1978 Shah Bano filed a divorce petition and a demand for maintenance under Section 125 of the Criminal Procedure Code of 1973, which dealt with the right to maintenance of divorced women. Khan divorced Shah Bano by unilateral "triple talaq"—instant divorce by saying talaq (divorce) three times. He argued in court that he had paid compensation permitted by religious law and was not obliged to pay maintenance.[17] The courts upheld Shah Bano's right to maintenance in 1980. On Khan's appeal, the case came to the Supreme Court. The ground for the appeal was that under Muslim personal law a divorced woman was not entitled to maintenance beyond a designated "waiting period" and that the Section 125 of the Criminal Procedure Code did not apply. The Supreme Court did not accept this argument. In the final judgment, Justice Chandrachud (later Chief Justice of India) said that the demand for a uniform civil code was justified, one that Muslim reformers had previously made; by failing to implement it the government had left it to the court to do so.[18]

The point of law was apparently simple. Both personal law and the Criminal Procedure Code accepted the rule that a wife was entitled to maintenance. In personal law, the wife ceased to be a wife after divorce; in the Code, the status of being a wife for maintenance purpose continued after divorce. Not all jurists of Islamic law accepted the interpretation of the sharia that a wife ceased to be a wife after a triple talaq divorce. There was also a view, which the court embraced, that the code and sharia were convergent on this issue.

The judgment made the statement that Article 44 should be a law as an obiter dictum, that is, as a nonbinding opinion. This opinion and the jurisdiction of the Criminal Procedure Code in relation to religious law raised a storm in the press after the judgment was published. When the judgment was published, several Muslim jurists and reformers supported the interpretation of the sharia that had led the judges to justify the application of the Criminal Procedure Code to the Muslims. Asghar Ali Engineer, India's most famous campaigner for liberal Islam, wrote in favor. Baharul Islam, a former justice of the Supreme Court and later the architect of legislation on the rights of disabled persons, justified the judges' reading of the sharia.

But Justice Chandrachud had not made the reformer's task easy, having quoted the nineteenth-century British orientalist Edward Lane that "the fatal point in Islam is the degradation of women." The majority view among Muslim community organizations was against the legal stand the court had taken, and they castigated the judges for daring to reinterpret the Qur'an. Prominent Muslim politicians across parties said this in speeches, and their tone was increasingly strident. The Urdu press was at first ambivalent but later took a hard and critical line. The English press almost without exception defended the judges and backed a uniform civil code. The fact that the most vocal supporters of this campaign included leftist intellectuals and Hindu right-wing leaders, normally mutual enemies, did little to give moral support to the campaign. Except the Christians to a limited extent, other minority religious groups, with or without personal laws of their own (the Parsis had one, the Sikhs did not), did not strongly support the demand for the Article 44 to be made a law.[19]

As we have seen, the Muslim Women (Protection of Rights on Divorce) Act, 1986, ended the debate for the time being. The act made it practically impossible for a Muslim woman to seek maintenance under the Criminal Procedure Code. The press held Prime Minister Rajiv Gandhi responsible for bringing about what many across the religious divide thought was a regressive law. It was also rather a sudden step, for until shortly before the act was brought to the Parliament, Gandhi had spoken in public against the sentiment that had turned a court judgment into a battle for identity. Gandhi, however, was not playing a strong hand.

The act started or fueled a political debate. Indeed, the judgment and the act turned into a political watershed in India. While Muslim personal law had been a concern of the jurists, it now became a political battlefield. The duty to defend the law seemingly unified a community that had otherwise been quite divided. The movement isolated prominent reformist intellectuals and activists like Ashgar Ali Engineer, Danial Latifi, and Nusrat Bano Roohi. On the other hand, writers and intellectuals affiliated with Hindu nationalism, or those who became absorbed in its fold later, articulated the view that the political mainstream had pandered to the views of conservative Muslims hoping for electoral gain. The argument became a rallying point for mobilization of support for Hindu political revival.

In the courtroom, the Shah Bano judgment had a curious effect. The act had accepted the demand that the right to maintenance would be limited to the waiting period but added that the court would decide on a "reasonable and fair" provision applicable to that period. Several High Court judgments first passed in Kerala and later elsewhere, interpreted "reasonable and fair" generously in favor of the divorced wife. A writ petition before the Supreme Court (*Danial Latifi v. Union of India* 2001) upheld the principle that reasonable and fair could include consideration of the future well-being of the divorced person irrespective of the waiting time.

In 2005 the government instituted a large-scale inquiry (known as the Sachar Committee) on the social and economic situation of the Muslims in India and found that they fared worse than other communities on matters such as education and the quality of life. The inquiry was not directly about the law. Several independent studies followed its report to cover this aspect and found that there was deprivation also in the sphere of law. Even as many Muslim women believed that the personal law ensured justice in principle, in practice, the community-based dispensation of justice did not work to their favor.[20] In recent years, activist organizations have fought battles in the court and the legislature to end practices such as triple talaq (instant divorce). In 2017, in a 3–2 decision, the Supreme Court declared triple talaq unconstitutional (also see note 16).

Besides case law and national politics, the contestation over personal law led to another type of effect. It raised the question, How far could the judges go in asserting the right to interpret religion? This question was always present in India from the time the British first framed property right with reference to religion. But a despotic colonial state did not need to worry about too much backlash or the limits of legislative reach. During the nineteenth century, judges and case laws departed from a strict interpretation of personal law and the practice of consulting religious experts in the courtroom and moved toward a broadly liberal-secular interpretation of personal law. There was neither a political nor an intellectual movement driving such actions. Change happened organically in the courtroom rather than via interventions. After 1947 the Constitution and the democratic setup took this contestation to a new level and exposed the judges to conflict with political opinion. Judgments that now departed from religious law needed to justify that action with reference to the Constitution. This was more than isolated acts of "judicial activism"; it entailed appropriating "the authority to define 'essential' practices of a religion."[21]

Another area of ambiguity over religion was rights framed with reference to caste.

Caste and Economic Rights

Although the reference to Hindu scripture could consolidate caste autonomy and elevate conventions within castes to the status of law, it did not also shape the relationship between castes in any explicit way. As far as one can see, the judges did not accept the principle that intercaste disputes could be addressed based on claimed customs of any one caste.[22] Discriminatory access to public services and institutions was not sanctioned. Access to temples and wells was a trickier problem. While the law did not recognize caste rights in these matters, discriminatory rights were often packaged as customary law as well as personal law, which the state did recognize.

The Constitution (1950), the Hindu Code Bill (1955–1966), and the Untouchability Offences Act (1955) made discrimination based on caste and untouchability an offense against the Constitution and a criminal act. Prosecuting someone for untouchability was almost impossible since Brahmanic and religious law sanctioned many forms of pollution by touch that could be claimed as customary and not obviously disabling to the other party. Though the laws made inherited practices open to challenge, in practice complaints were rare because many members of the oppressed castes or Dalit communities were not fully aware of their rights.

In the colonial period, certain specific legislation on caste discrimination and occasionally case laws applied equality when there was a dispute between members of different castes over property matters. After independence, the Constitution framed a general principle. Article 46 of the Constitution states the commitment to deliver economic justice to the Scheduled Castes, Scheduled Tribes, and other weaker sections of the society. Probably the most frequent form of disputation on a property between castes concerned lands on which members of Scheduled

Castes and Tribes had an inherited customary property right. The government occasionally implemented affirmative action in colonial times. The Madras Depressed Class Land Act 1892, for example, had designated twelve million acres of land for certain castes and limited the freedom to transact in these lands between castes. Similar legislation was passed after independence in several states (see chap. 2). However, as the urban real estate market exploded and cities began to expand, documents came into the courts that showed that property so designated had passed on to outsiders (i.e., not Scheduled Caste or Tribe groups). The mode of transfer may have been legal, that is, it made use of the limited freedom available in law, but when these transfers happened and whether the parties were fully aware of their legal rights remained unknown. On several occasions, however, the transfer was obstructed by activist groups and right holders.[23]

Laws against discrimination and for affirmative action exist in India mainly to improve access and reduce barriers to entry of the underprivileged people into education and jobs.[24] A large literature now exists on the transformation of caste through political activism, affirmative action, and economic change.[25] Economic change has been particularly rapid in the last twenty-five years since India's market reforms started. Unlike in landholding, caste matters less in recruitment into urban service-based jobs not least because the labor force is more mobile and migratory than before, whereas the significance of caste is usually understood locally, and affirmative action rules are set by the states for its domiciled population.

These processes raise the question, Will caste eventually disappear? Several recent studies on the transformation of caste revisit this issue and find that caste as a bundle of prejudice and discrimination has not disappeared and is not likely to anytime soon, but there are now many more cases where these constraints are overcome. For example, a study done in 2002 on Punjab after the Green Revolution (from 1970) found that while hierarchical relationships persisted because landholders had become better off and the landless people needed to depend on the landowners for their livelihood, in the long run, job openings in the towns had reduced dependency.[26] Using data from the National Sample Survey over the period 1983–2005, Viktoria Hnatsovka and coauthors have shown a decline in the gap between Scheduled Castes and Scheduled Tribes and others in terms of wages, education, consumption expenditure, and occupational status.[27] There is also evidence of improvement in social status and dignity of the Dalits.[28] However, Ashwini Deshpande and Rajesh Ramachandran, also using National Sample Survey data, find that Scheduled Castes and Tribes have caught up except in higher education and prestigious occupations.[29] Lakshmi Iyer and coauthors have found that Scheduled Castes and Tribes are underrepresented in enterprise ownership, with only a small improvement between 1990 and 2005.[30] The general pattern seems to be that historically disadvantaged groups have gained but are still struggling to enter the top echelons.

A final issue we need to consider is the role of religion in the management of joint property.

Trusts and Endowments

Joint property survives outside the joint family in the form of endowments. The legal means to manage these are the Indian Trusts Act and the Waqf Act for Muslims. The trustee or waqif are the custodians and not owners of a property. The concept behind the law is that the custodian has limited power to divide or alienate property and to use it for private gains, and the custodian has the power only to use it in a manner authorized by the person or group that gave it over to the trust. Custodianship was universally adopted in the maintenance of religious endowments. Trusteeship could be used also in any situation when a property served a collective purpose. The idea of custodianship was an old one in India and manifested in different ways. British-Indian jurists recognized this fact.[31] When formal law of property was first codified, it recognized ownership and not trusteeship, thus weakening the legal status of endowments. The Indian Trusts Act (1882) was a response to this anomaly. The Waqf Act followed in 1923 in recognition of specific features of the waqf that made the institution distinct from English laws of endowments.[32]

Shortly after independence, the zamindari abolition acts led to the confiscation of waqf property managed by landlords, which were then informally taken over by government departments and private parties. The remaining waqfs came in two sets: some tied to major shrines and monuments were managed by the Archaeological Survey of India, whereas the majority of the urban waqfs were managed by individuals approved by the Waqf Board. The former set earned a good income from tourists. The others did not. A study of Uttar Pradesh reveals that communication between the custodians, the Waqf Board, and the people who often lived on the property and paid rent was so defective that the waqf found it difficult to make ends meet.[33]

From well before independence, there were complaints about the governance of the trusts, including waqfs. Unlike in a commercial business, where the directors could pay a penalty for misgoverning, in a trust, the trustees did not expect to lose much if the trust did not deliver expected benefits to the community. Conflicts of interest, therefore, were rife. Soon after 1947 the states of Delhi, Bihar, West Bengal, Uttar Pradesh, and Jammu and Kashmir passed their own legislation to regulate the waqfs in these states. These were superseded by federal legislation in 1954 and a more comprehensive act in 1995.

There have been many legal disputes around trusteeship. While few of these questioned the idea behind it, many questioned its uses. Competence of the trustee and conflicts of interest are common grounds for disputation. Muslim waqfs were usually located in towns and cities, and when real estate prices increased rapidly, waqf lands were secretly sold to politically connected individuals.[34]

With some religious endowments, the Parsis for example, trustees maintained the boundary between the sphere of the religious community and the uniform civil code, giving rise to disputation over whether there should be a boundary at all.[35] One recent court case takes us back to a perennial issue of contradiction between personal law and universal principles.[36] The judgment reveals the reluctance of individual judges to create a radical departure from a convention started by British-Indian law to leave personal law alone.

Conclusion

Colonial Indian law of transfer of property initially followed religious codes. Almost without exception, the varieties of Hindu and Muslim codes in force gave men more rights, women fewer, and empowered the family over individual members in it, in effect empowering male heads of families. The courts then heard disputes between the holders of stronger and weaker rights and often settled the cases in favor of the latter. There was nothing like an announced policy to weaken the religious foundation of these laws. In fact, the framework of Muslim personal law was created during legislation passed as late as the 1930s. Disputants had the option of staying within the tradition as formally defined by coded law or to depart from it if past judgments seemed to support their case. The outcome of this confusion was a judiciary overloaded with appeals.

In 1947, soon after independence the dynamics changed. The Indian Constitution made a commitment to equality of rights, uniformity in law, and substantive equality, given India's history of caste and gender repression. Regulations and affirmative action addressed caste, whereas legislators addressed the issue of women's property right. Legal reforms notwithstanding, jurists and activists believe that not enough was done to create parity between men and women over the transfer of property rules, at least partly because few politicians dared to speak against tradition. But the conflict between tradition and equality was out in the open. In the 1980s it energized and polarized mainstream politics. A political solution to conflicts like these was never going to be easy. The coalitions were often unstable and ill fated, like the one between the communists and Hindu conservatives during the movement over Article 44. However, as in colonial times the Supreme Court and the High Courts, through case laws, allowed for a flexible reading of personal law. The outcome is a clear trend toward equity.

CHAPTER TEN

Conclusion

If India copies England, it is my firm conviction that she will be ruined. — M. K. Gandhi[1]

The Hindu Nationalists were the first to caution the people against the danger of the foreign economic imperialism. — Dattopant Thengadi[2]

This book began with a stylized fact that few would dispute: doing business in India is difficult, and the existing laws seem to add to the difficulty, not ease it. This is a puzzle, an anomaly, for an emerging economy trying to achieve rapid economic growth to create gainful jobs for the vast number of poor people who struggle to earn a living. Their title to property is sometimes poorly recorded, and in the labor market, they face exploitation. The state and the legislators were aware of these issues and were well intentioned, but somewhere along the way the intentions did not translate into an efficient legal system. What went wrong? And what was done to correct the wrong?

In 1947 the newly independent state of the Indian Union had inherited a rich legacy of property and contract laws from British colonial rule and with it some dysfunctionality. Colonial property law aimed to be market friendly by strengthening the ownership right and mortgage value of private property, but in practice it encumbered these rights with many restrictions, ostensibly to accommodate Indian tradition into the system but in truth to avoid discontent in the countryside. Contract and corporate law, by contrast, borrowed freely from Britain and were effectively institutional transplants. However, they worked in a setting that had some peculiar features that British law did not have to deal with.

One of our theses is that the colonial legacy persisted into postindependence India in land and credit law. It did not persist just as a relic of the past but because in land, the legacy entailed poor and incomplete registers of ownership and user rights. The state began with a land-reform policy that involved recognizing the rights of the tiller whether or not these rights were registered legally. Locally powerful actors often hijacked the operation of the policy in part because of poor maintenance of land records. Access to credit posed a huge obstacle to the conduct of agriculture as a business. The poor were denied credit because they had little collateral, the interest rate was high, and they faced a high risk of seasonal fluctuations in the tropical environment. To protect the security of the poor in the credit market, the independent state greatly strengthened a colonial legacy of debt laws that allowed mortgages but restricted asset transfers. The regime drove the private market in credit underground, viewing it as intrinsically exploitative.

As we noted, this was not the effect of a passive carryover of a colonial problem. The state in independent India had been actively making laws and policies. The overriding intention was to reduce inequity in a famously hierarchical social setup. The Constitution of India formalized this ideology. The framers of the Constitution, not least B. R. Ambedkar, the leader of the oppressed castes, took the opportunity to create a document that made an uncompromising commitment to equality in all forms. In the courtroom, when land reform or credit regulation came under disputation, the judges could draw on these dictates of the Constitution. Why, then, did any dispute occur at all? Paradoxically, the Constitution also committed to fundamental rights to property and trade, and the state was infringing on those freedoms.

In commercial and corporate law, where the colonial legacy was more international to begin with, the state introduced the new element of equity, though not entirely by choice. If land reform was one of the pillars of development policy in the 1950s, import-substituting industrialization was the other one. The process involved encouraging capital-goods production in India—that is, industries like metals, machines, and chemicals—and reduced priority for traditional industries like tea, mining, and textiles. About fifteen years into its operation, big business and monopolies emerged in the capital goods, and bankruptcy started to spread in the traditional manufactures. The legislators stepped in with a monopoly regulation law and laws on insolvency that effectively delayed or avoided bankruptcy to protect precious jobs. In both cases, freedom of enterprise to deploy capital was curtailed, sometimes with disastrous results.

Such, more or less, was the state of affairs in the mid-1980s, when India started to deregulate its economy and allowed freer play to private enterprise. Private enterprise was not happy with the laws as they stood. Acquiring land for industry was caught up in a cumbersome system of rights that varied from one state to another. The employment of labor was constrained by inflexible regulation. Deploying capital from unprofitable to profitable fields faced the insolvency laws, which did not want bankruptcy to occur. New challenges such as environmental stress and the overreach of the state in acquiring common property for developmental purposes added to an already complicated legal and regulatory environment.

Like in the first thirty years after independence, development policy and legal regimes became closely interdependent in the three postreform decades. But while changing policy in the more recent years was relatively easy, changing the laws was not. The postreform story is not one of undoing past errors. The pressure to change laws was enormous, but so was the backlash. The legislators responded in corporate law by a combination of legal reform and the creation of a parallel system of courts. The states (provinces) moved at different speeds reforming the land law to make it more investor friendly. Microfinance allowed the market to creep back in credit transactions, raising the old specter of exploitation of poor debtors by powerful creditors.

Where was the judge in all this? In the statist regime that was in place between 1950 and 1985, politics more or less prevailed. The judges, by and large, spoke the language of politics and sided with the ideological mainstream of the time. However, there were significant exceptions to this pattern, especially in the Supreme Court, where constitutional law was debated. A few landmark judgments, especially concerning land reform, forced politicians and legislators to innovate, leading, as we have seen, to the removal of the Fundamental Right to property. In more recent times, the court's activist role has expanded in scope, especially in environmental law. In turn, the activism in environmental law has reinforced a tendency that has been a traditional feature of postindependence Indian economic policy—neglect of market mechanisms, which has encouraged rent-seeking.

The story is unfinished. That said, the history we write suggests the institutional framework for capitalism in contemporary India is changing in five ways. First, the interdependence between law and policy has reduced. Reforms have delivered more freedom to the courts, not always the traditional lower court and high courts and not usually by changing the laws, but also by creating specialized tribunals that follow their own codes and procedures. Second, the burden of colonial law has been reduced among other reasons because land and credit are provincial subjects and provinces compete fiercely for investment in modern industry and services. Third, the rhetoric of equity is less universal than it was in the 1970s. Instead of retreating across the board, the equity concern has moved away from capital-labor or creditor-debtor disputes into specific types of issues concerning caste, gender, and the environment. Fourth, civil society organizations are taking a larger role in the battles for fundamental rights or equity.

The fifth field of change concerns the legal infrastructure, by which we mean the courts, the legal profession, and the reach of the judicial system and possibly the costs of dispute settlement in time and money. The massive backlog of pending cases in the courts shows not only that the laws are dysfunctional but that the state has underinvested in the infrastructure for a very long time. The history of that failure goes back to the colonial era. The lower courts still function much the same way that they did thirty or forty years ago. Where is there a change then? The main field of change is in the legal profession. There has been an explosion of new schools for law education, which have turned out new graduates. With a few exceptions, the new breed of lawyers deals with corporate cases. With the globalization of India's corporate sector, the demand for legal professionals who have some familiarity with international practice and can write contracts for foreign companies has increased. Few lawyers trained in this fashion go into litigation, as their predecessors did a generation ago.

As we write, the Government of India is taking steps toward creating an environment that facilitates efficient allocation of capital. Perhaps the most visible manifestation of this is the Insolvency and Bankruptcy Code of 2016, which its supporters believe is, for the first time, holding India's well-connected business magnates accountable. An economic adviser to the finance ministry has argued that this is the "equivalent of the French Revolution. The insolvency and bankruptcy code is the equivalent of the guillotine."[3] This is perhaps an overstatement—there are still many glitches. However, the code is undoubtedly a step forward.

The Government of India is also seeking to improve the Ease of Doing Business, as measured by the World Bank, streamlining and simplifying various procedures.

That said, it is worth remembering that, compared to (say) the United States, almost the whole political spectrum in India is more skeptical of markets and less open to foreign trade and investment. We have frequently alluded to the allegedly socialist inclinations of India's early Prime Ministers, especially Indira Gandhi. However, as the two quotations at the top of this chapter suggest, other political traditions in India do not embrace capitalism wholeheartedly either. In the case of M. K. Gandhi, his rejection of capitalism was embedded in a repudiation of industrial modernity as such. Capitalism and economic interactions with the West are viewed with suspicion by many even in India's current ruling dispensation, often described as Hindu Nationalist. Dattopant Thengadi has been described as the "most influential thinker" in the RSS (Rashtriya Swayam Sevak Sangh, National Volunteer Organisation), a key supporter of the government.[4] Thengadi writes, "Our nation has evolved concepts, institutions, and orders which are unique in many respects. . . . We cannot accept capitalism based upon the principle of 'production for profit,' which brings into operation the Law of Supply and Demand leading to regulation of production by prices, nor can we accept communism."[5] He also recommends the adoption of "the golden rule: No retrenchment without alternate employment."[6] The trade union BMS (Bharatiya Mazdoor Sangh, Indian Workers Party), also affiliated with the ruling party and RSS, opposing what it views as efforts to weaken protections for workers, recently commented, "Ease of living is equally important along with ease of doing business."[7] It is, therefore, no surprise (see chap. 6) that the controversial restrictions on firms firing or reallocating their workforce remained in place. The RSS-affiliated Swadeshi Jagran Manch recently opposed the entry of Walmart; the *Deccan Chronicle* reported that the "the SJM [Swadeshi Jagran Manch] batted for getting new regulations in place to protect small and medium traders."[8] The importance of private capital has been recognized, and the language has changed. Still, ambivalence toward market mechanisms, trade, and foreign investment continues to influence law and policy.

Acknowledgments

This is the second of two volumes. We would like to thank Price Fishback, the editor of the series, for his consistent support and feedback, over a long span of time, on two wide-ranging projects. Two anonymous referees provided invaluable comments. Sudiksha Joshi, Evelyn Mahon, Sudeshna Nandini Pahari, and Sanjeev Sambasivan provided excellent research assistance. Amitabh Pande provided detailed comments that greatly helped the revision. We have also benefited from regular and ongoing exchanges with Latika Chaudhary and Bishnupriya Gupta.

We have also separately incurred many debts. Tirthankar would like to thank Padam Khaitan for a wide-ranging and helpful conversation on the subject of the book. Sudakshina and Mrinmoyee were always a source of support. Anand would like to acknowledge the Interlibrary Loan office at Williams College, whose help has been critical. Gaurav Datt, Steve Nafziger, Mukul Sharma, and Aseem Shrivastava read parts of the book and provided useful comments. Participants at Cornell University's "Law, Economics and Conflict: Contemporary Challenges" conference in 2018, especially Kaushik Basu and Jonathan Conning, helped improve chapter 3. Discussions with Sanjay Anandaram, Jerry Caprio, Doug Gollin, Benugopal Mukhopadhyay, Jogin Sengupta, and Nagendra Venkaswamy were helpful. Swamy would also like to thank his family in Bengaluru, Delhi, and Munsiari and Jyotika, whose presence sustains his life and work.

Notes

Chapter One

1. India, Planning Commission, *The New India: Progress through Democracy* (London: Macmillan, 1958), 31.

2. India ranks 77th out of 190 countries in the World Bank's measure of ease of doing business. It performs particularly poorly on registering property (166th) and enforcing contracts (163rd). See World Bank, "Ease of Doing Business in India," https://www.doingbusiness.org/en/data/exploreeconomies/india.

3. European officers in the army and the civil administration numbered 6,400 in 1875 (European soldiers were 64,500) in a workforce of about 120 million and a population of about 200 million. Based on data from F. J. Atkinson, "A Statistical Review of Income and Wealth in British India," *Journal of the Royal Statistical Society* 65, no. 3 (1902): 209–83.

4. D. Washbrook, "Law, State and Agrarian Society in Colonial India," *Modern Asian Studies* 15, no. 3 (1981): 649–721. *The Raj* is a common and handy reference to the British Empire in India (1858–1947). The word derives from the Sanskrit word *rajya*, meaning state or government. Princely states and landlord estates in Northern India often used it to refer to themselves.

5. Government revenue in India amounted to 6.7% of GDP in 1910. The proportion was 11% in Japan and 9% in the United Kingdom. These proportions convert into a revenue per head in India that was one-third that in Japan and one-seventeenth that in Britain. Even in comparison with the British, Dutch, and French colonies in Asia, British India was a poor government. See Tirthankar Roy, "Why Was British India a Limited State?," in *Fiscal Capacity and the Colonial State in Asia and Africa, c. 1850–1960*, ed. A. Booth and E. Frankema (Cambridge: Cambridge University Press, 2020).

6. R. Guha, "Forestry in British and Post-British India: A Historical Analysis," *Economic and Political Weekly* 18, no. 44 (1983): 1882–96; T. Sanjiva Row,

The Land Acquisition Act, 1894: Act 1 of 1894, With Case-Law Thereon (Madras, M. E. Press, 1907).

7. P. S. Appu, *Land Reforms in India: A Survey of Policy, Legislation, and Implementation* (New Delhi: Vikas, 1996); P. C. Joshi, *Land Reforms in India: Trends and Perspectives* (Bombay: Allied Publishers, 1975); D. C. Wadhwa, *Agrarian Legislation in India (1793–1966)* (Poona: Gokhale Institute of Politics and Economics, 1973).

8. For overviews of early Indian economic policy, see A. Panagariya, *India: The Emerging Giant* (New York: Oxford University Press, 2010), chaps. 1–4; R. Guha, *India after Gandhi: A History of the World's Largest Democracy* (New York: Harper Perennial, 2008), chap. 10.

9. Upendra Baxi, "Taking Suffering Seriously: Social Action Litigation in the Indian Supreme Court," *Third World Legal Studies* 4 (1985): 107–32.

10. For a quick overview of the liberalization process, see S. Aiyar, "Twenty-Five Years of Indian Economic Reform," Cato Institute, policy analysis 803, October 26, 2016, https://www.cato.org/publications/policy-analysis/twenty-five-years-indian-economic-reform.

11. See R. Jagannathan, "UPA Land Act is Creating 20,000 Rural Crorepatis Every Year and Making Infrastructure Unviable," *Swarajya*, January 17, 2018, https://swarajyamag.com/ideas/upa-land-act-is-creating-20000-rural-crorepatis-a-year-and-making-infrastructure-less-viable.

12. "Insolvency and Bankruptcy Code, 2016," India Brand Equity Foundation, Brand India, May 2016, https://www.ibef.org/research/india-study/insolvency-and-bankruptcy-code.

13. B. Balakrishnan, "Resistance to FDI a Hangover of the Past," *The Hindu*, BusinessLine, December 1, 2011,https://www.thehindubusinessline.com/opinion/columns/bhaskar-balakrishnan/resistance-to-fdi-a-hangover-of-the-past/article20371402.ece1.

14. This is in the spirit of the burgeoning literature on growth diagnostics. See D. Rodrik's "Diagnostics before Prescription," *Journal of Economic Perspectives* 24, no. 3 (2010): 33–44.

15. India's ranking in the World Bank's ease of doing business category is frequently discussed.

16. N. Sundar, "Law, Policies, and Practices in Jharkhand," *Economic and Political Weekly* 40, no. 41 (2005): 4459–62. For a broader discussion of the role of law in creating focal points see K. Basu, *Republic of Beliefs: A New Approach to Law and Economics* (Princeton, NJ: Princeton University Press, 2018).

17. S. Cole, "Fixing Market Failures or Fixing Elections? Agricultural Credit in India," *American Economic Journal: Applied Economics* 1, no. 1 (2009): 219–50.

18. Based on National Judicial Data Grid data, https://districts.ecourts.gov.in/, accessed June 1, 2018.

19. See M. Chemin, "Does Court Speed Shape Economic Activity? Evidence from a Court Reform in India," *Journal of Law and Economics* 28, no. 3 (2012): 460–85; "Do Judiciaries Matter for Development? Evidence from India," *Journal of Comparative Economics* 37, no. 3 (2009): 230–50; A. Amirapu, "Justice Delayed Is Growth Denied: The Effect of Slow Courts on Relationships Specific Industries in India" (Working Paper 1706, School of Economics Discussion Papers, University of Essex, 2017); J. Boehm and E. Oberfield, "(Un)ease of Doing Business: How Congested Courts Hinder Firm Productivity," *VoxDev*, February 7, 2019, https://voxdev.org/topic/institutions-political-economy/unease-doing-business-how-congested-courts-hinder-firm-productivity; S. Ghosh, "Corporate Investment and Political Federalism: Does Judicial Efficiency Matter?," *Indian Economic Review* 35, no. 1/2 (2018): 263–85. There is recent research on the effect of debt tribunals on speedy resolution of debt disputes. See S. Visaria, "Legal Reform and Loan Repayment: The Microeconomic Impact of Debt Recovery Tribunals in India," *American Economic Journal: Applied Economics* 1, no. 3 (2009): 59–81; U. Lilienfeld-Toal, D. Mookherjee, and S. Visaria, "The Distributive Impact of Reforms in Credit Enforcement: Evidence from Indian Debt Recovery Tribunals," *Econometrica* 80, no. 2 (2012): 497–558.

20. See S. Aiyar, "Gujarat Tribals Turn Bamboo Plantation Owners," *Times of India*, Swaminomics (blog), January 24, 2016, https://timesofindia.indiatimes.com/blogs/Swaminomics/gujarat-tribals-turn-bamboo-plantation-owners/.

21. See T. Roy and A.V. Swamy, *Law and the Economy in Colonial India* (Chicago: University of Chicago Press, 2016), chap. 4.

22. As the book goes to press, fear over an impending economic recession in the wake of the COVID-19 pandemic led to quick-fire labor law reform in three states of India. Whether for the bad timing or the manner of the reform, the move has been controversial.

23. An Indian medicinal tree known as neem has been the source of much controversy. See BBC, "India Wins Landmark Patent Battle," *BBC News*, March 9, 2005, http://news.bbc.co.uk/2/hi/science/nature/4333627.stm.

24. *Zamindari* refers to the system of taxation where the zamindars are the designated taxpayers. The abolition of zamindari, which we will discuss in detail, was more complex than this simple description. Many zamindars were able to circumvent the law and retain large tracts of land.

25. See chapter 2 for examples from Bihar.

26. R. J. Herring, "Abolition of Landlordism in Kerala: A Redistribution of Privilege," *Economic and Political Weekly* 15, no. 26 (1980): A59–A69.

27. B. Lewis, N. Agrawal, C. Gadi, D. Goyal, J. Kulkarni, A. Tawakley, S. Viswanathan, et al., *India: The Growth Imperative*, report, McKinsey Global Institute, October 1, 2001, http://www.mckinsey.com/insights/india/growth_imperative_for_india.

28. "A Bad Idea: Niti Aayog Rightly Rejects Farm Loan Waivers," *Times*

of India, December 20, 2018, https://timesofindia.indiatimes.com/blogs/toi-editorials/a-bad-idea-niti-aayog-rightly-rejects-farm-loan-waivers/.

29. Government of India, The Right to Compensation and Transparency in Land Acquisition, Rehabilitation and Resettlement Act, 2013. http://legislative.gov.in/sites/default/files/A2013-30.pdf.

30. A. Banerjee, P. Bardhan, K. Basu, M. Datta-Chaudhuri, M. Ghatak, A. S. Guha, M. Majumdar, D. Mookherjee, and D. Ray, "Beyond Nandigram: Industrialization in West Bengal," *Economic and Political Weekly* 42, no. 17 (2007): 1487–89.

31. See R. Jagannathan, "Forest Rights Act Needs to Go: Tribals Aren't Part of a Tiger Reserve," *Firstpost*, September 12, 2014, https://www.firstpost.com/india/the-forest-rights-act-needs-to-go-tribals-arent-part-of-a-tiger-reserve-1707317.html.

32. R. Allen, *Enclosure and the Yeoman: The Agricultural Development of the South Midlands 1450–1850* (New York: Oxford University Press, 1992).

33. On reform by stealth, see P. Bardhan, "Nature of Opposition to Economic Reforms in India," *Economic and Political Weekly* 40, no. 48 (2005): 4995–98.

34. This expression is used by Rina Agarwala as well as K. P. Kannan. See R. Agarwala, *Informal Labor, Formal Politics, and Dignified Discontent in India* (Cambridge: Cambridge University Press, 2013); K. P. Kannan, "The Welfare Fund Model of Social Security for Informal Sector Workers: The Kerala Experience," Working Paper 332 (Thiruvananthapuram: Centre for Development Studies, 2002).

35. T. S. Papola and J. Pais, "Debate on Labour Market Reforms in India: A Case of Misplaced Focus," *Indian Journal of Labour Economics* 50, no. 2 (2007): 183–200.

36. For a succinct description of the MRTP, see G. Chikermane, "70 Policies: Monopolies and Restrictive Trade Practices Act, 1969," Observer Research Foundation, India Matters, August 6, 2018. https://www.orfonline.org/expert-speak/43035-70-policies-monopolies-and-restrictive-trade-practices-act-1969/.

37. R. Desai, "India's Data Localization Remains a Key Challenge for Foreign Companies," *Forbes India*, April 30, 2019, https://www.forbes.com/sites/ronakdesai/2019/04/30/indias-data-localization-remains-a-key-challenge-for-foreign-companies/#5f37ecdbe0a3.

Chapter Two

1. Indian National Congress, Agrarian Reforms Committee, *Report of the Congress Agrarian Reforms Committee*, 2nd ed. (New Delhi: All-India Congress Committee, 1951), 7.

2. Indian National Congress, Agrarian Reforms Committee, 11.

3. Our view is in the mainstream. See L. I. Rudolph and S. H. Rudolph, *In Pursuit of Lakshmi: The Political Economy of the Indian State* (Chicago: University of Chicago Press, 1987), 315, 318.

4. India, Planning Commission, *Report of the Task Force on Agrarian Relations* (New Delhi: Planning Commission, 1973), 11.

5. B. Lewis, N. Agrawal, C. Gadi, D. Goyal, J. Kulkarni, A. Tawakley, S. Viswanathan, et al., *India: The Growth Imperative*, report, McKinsey Global Institute, October 1, 2001, 4, http://www.mckinsey.com/insights/india/growth_imperative_for_india.

6. This section is based on chapters 3 and 4 of our previous book, *Law and the Economy in Colonial India* (Chicago: University of Chicago Press, 2016).

7. Some scholars argue that the state remained the ultimate owner of the land; the zamindar received a right to the revenue subject to payment of taxes. See A. Bagchi, review of *Law and the Economy in Colonial India*, by T. Roy and A. V. Swamy, *Business History Review* 91, no. 2 (2017): 424–28.

8. S. Henningham, "Bureaucracy and Control in India's Great Landed Estates: The Raj Darbhanga of Bihar, 1879 to 1850," *Modern Asian Studies* 17, no. 1 (1983): 35–55.

9. G. Austin, *The Indian Constitution: Cornerstone of a Nation*, 2nd ed. (New Delhi: Oxford University Press, 1999), 111

10. O. P. Aggarwala and S. K. Aiyar, *The Constitution of India* (Delhi: Metropolitan Book, 1950), 50.

11. For discussion, see, for instance, H. C. L. Merillat, *Land and the Constitution in India* (New York: Columbia University Press, 1970), and N. Wahi, "The Fundamental Right to Property in the Indian Constitution," in *The Oxford Handbook of the Indian Constitution*, ed. S. Choudhry, M. Khosla, and P. B. Mehta (Oxford: Oxford University Press, 2017).

12. See paragraph 48 of the case report.

13. Merillat, *Land and the Constitution in India*, 130.

14. Quoted by V. K. Ananth, *The Indian Constitution and Social Revolution: the Right to Property since Independence* (New Delhi: Sage, 2015), 129.

15. Ananth, 201

16. J. Singh, "Separation of Powers and the Erosion of the 'Right to Property' in India." *Constitutional Political Economy* 17, no. 4 (2006): 303–24; Wahi, "Fundamental Right to Property"; Ananth, *Indian Constitution*. For a lucid account of the legal back-and-forth, see S. Rajagopalan, "Our Founders and the Right to Property," *Pragati*, July 24, 2017, https://www.thinkpragati.com/opinion/1849/founding-fathers-right-property/. This is one of an eight-part series.

17. F. T. Januzzi, *Agrarian Crisis in India: The Case of Bihar* (Austin: University of Texas Press, 1974), 30n2.

18. India, Land Reform Planning Committee, *Implementation of Land Reforms: A Review by the Land Reforms Implementation Committee of the National Development Council* (New Delhi: Planning Commission, 1966), 47.

19. The relevant case history is summarized in *Bimal Kumar Sinha v. State of Bihar and Others*, para. 12. Also see Januzzi, *Agrarian Crisis in India*, 32.

20. Daniel Thorner, *The Agrarian Prospect in India: Five Lectures on Land Reform Delivered in 1955 at the Delhi School of Economics* (Delhi: Allied, 1976), 31–32.

21. A. Sinha, "Legal Loopholes: To Landlords' Rescue." *Economic and Political Weekly* 13, no. 42 (1978): 1758–60.

22. India, Land Reform Planning Committee, *Implementation of Land Reforms*, 45.

23. India, Land Reform Planning Committee, 47.

24. Thorner, *Agrarian Prospect in India*, 48.

25. The 450,000 and 230,000 figures are from India, Planning Commission, *Report of the Task Force*, app. 1, 30. The 17.77% figure is from P. S. Appu, *Land Reforms in India: A Survey of Policy, Legislation, and Implementation* (New Delhi: Vikas, 1996), app. 4.3.

26. Thorner, *Agrarian Prospect in India*, 50.

27. Nikita Sud, "From Land to the Tiller to Land Liberalization: The Political Economy of Gujarat's Shifting Policy," *Modern Asian Studies* 41, no. 3 (2007): 607.

28. G. Shah, "Caste and Land Reforms in Gujarat," in *Land Reforms in India: Performance and Challenges in Gujarat and Maharashtra*, ed. G. Shah and D. C. Sah (New Delhi: Sage, 2002), 131.

29. Appu, *Land Reforms in India*, 173.

30. P. K. Choudhary, "Land Reforms in Bihar: Need for a Fresh Appraisal," in *Land Reforms in India: Bihar—Institutional Constraints*, ed. B. N. Yugandhar and K. G. Iyer (New Delhi: Sage, 1993), 25.

31. Quoted in Appu, *Land Reforms in India*, 173.

32. India, Land Reforms Implementation Committee, *Implementation of Land Reforms*, 51.

33. V. M. Dandekar and G. J. Khudanpur, *Working of the Bombay Tenancy Act, 1948: Report of Investigation* (Poona: Sangam Press, 1957), 5.

34. R. V. Bhuskute, "Overview of Land Reforms in Maharashtra," in *Land Reforms in India: Performance and Challenges in Gujarat and Maharashtra*, ed. G. Shah and D. C. Sah (New Delhi: Sage, 2002), 49.

35. Bhuskute, 50.

36. Bhuskute, 69.

37. H. C. Hart and R. J. Herring, "Political Conditions for Land Reform: Kerala and Maharashtra," in *Land Tenure and Peasant in South Asia*, ed. R. E. Frykenberg (New Delhi: Orient Longman, 1977), 247.

38. Sud, "From Land to the Tiller," 610.

39. Kerala Land Reforms (Amendment) Act, 1969.

40. For Bombay, see Dandekar and Khudanpur, *Working of the Bombay Tenancy Act*, 5.

41. 1970 KLJ 1060.

42. K.T. Jacob, *Tiller Gets the Land in Kerala* (New Delhi: Communist Party of India, 1970), 13.

43. For a harsher assessment of the majority's view, see R. J. Herring, *Land to the Tiller: The Political Economy of Agrarian Reform in South Asia* (New Haven, CT: Yale University Press, 1983), 197–98.

44. Jacob, *Tiller Gets the Land*, 19.

45. Jacob, 19.

46. Herring, *Land to the Tiller*, 211.

47. Section 21B, West Bengal Land Reform Act of 1955, amended 1977.

48. S. Chattopadhyay, "Notes: Operation Barga," *Social Scientist* 8, no. 87 (1979): 43.

49. The text of the circular is in the case note for *Biswanath Ghosh v. State of West Bengal*.

50. R. Khasnabis, "Operation Barga: A Further Note," *Economic and Political Weekly* 17, no. 36 (1982): 1469.

51. B. Dasgupta, "Sharecropping in West Bengal: From Independence to Operation Barga," *Economic and Political Weekly* 19, no. 26 (1984): A89.

52. P. Bardhan and D. Mookherjee, "Subsidized Farm Input Programs and Agricultural Performance: A Farm Level Analysis of West Bengal's Green Revolution, 1982–1995," *American Economic Journal: Applied Economics* 3 (2011): 192.

53. J. H. Conning and J. A. Robinson, "Property Rights and the Political Organization of Agriculture," *Journal of Development Economics* 82, no. 2 (2007): 416–47.

54. Bihar High Court. *Report on the Administration of Civil Justice in the State of Bihar during the Year 1960* (Patna, Bihar: Superintendent Secretariat Press, 1961), 10.

55. India, Land Reforms Implementation Committee, *Implementation of Land Reforms*, 55.

56. India, Planning Commission, Report of the Task Force, app. 3, 96.

57. G. Iyer, "Evaluation of Land Ceiling Measures in Bihar," in *Land Reforms in India: Bihar—Institutional Constraints*, ed. B. N. Yugandhar and K. Gopal Iyer (New Delhi: Sage, 1993), 95.

58. A. K. Singh, "Determination of Farzi Transfers and Transactions in Gaya District," in *Land Reforms in India: Bihar—Institutional Constraints*, ed. B. N. Yugandhar and K. Gopal Iyer (New Delhi: Sage, 1993), 122.

59. Singh, "Determination of Farzi Transfers," 122. Also see David Geary,

"The Decline of Bodh Gaya Math and Afterlife of Zamindari," *South Asian History and Culture* 4, no. 3 (2000): 366–83.

60. Appu, *Land Reforms in India*, 308.

61. L. Srinivas, "Land and Politics in India: Working of the Urban Land Ceiling Act, 1976," *Economic and Political Weekly* 26, no. 43 (1991): 2482–84.

62. Srinivas, "Land and Politics in India," 2482.

63. S. Singh, "On Repealing the Urban Land Ceiling Act," *Economic and Political Weekly* 41, no. 8 (February/March 2006), 698–99.

64. For a time-line of repeal in various states, see Asset Yogi, "Urban Land (Ceiling and Regulation) Act 1976 / Repeal Act 1999—Hindi," YouTube video, 13:04, posted May 19, 2018. https://www.youtube.com/watch?v=9oLer1aej9s.

65. S. Ashar, "State Closer to Unlocking Vacant Plots Exempted under Urban Land Ceiling Act." *Indian Express*, November 5, 2017, https://indianexpress.com/article/cities/mumbai/state-closer-to-unlocking-vacant-plots-exempted-under-urban-land-ceiling-act-4924263/; S. Ashar, "Top Business Families to Benefit, Govt to Free Up Exempted Vacant Lands," *Indian Express*, August 21, 2018, https://indianexpress.com/article/cities/mumbai/top-business-families-to-benefit-govt-to-free-up-exempted-vacant-lands-5318294/.

66. M. Das, B. L. Mishra, D. Samanta, and B. Mishra, *Land Governance Assessment Framework for Bihar: Final Report* (Patna, Bihar: Chandrgupt Institute of Management, 2014), 2.

67. H. Kumar and R. Somanathan, "The Right to Shelter: An Evaluation of the Land Transfer Program to Mahadalits" (IGC project report, May 2016).

68. T. Paulini, *Agrarian Movements and Reforms in India: The Case of Kerala* (Saarbrucken: Breitenbach, 1979), 295.

69. Herring, *Land to the Tiller*, 213. To be sure, Dalits are still hugely disadvantaged in land ownership in Kerala. As prices have boomed, land has become even less accessible. See C. R. Yadu and C. K. Vijayasuryan, "Triple Exclusion of Dalits in Land Ownership in Kerala," *Social Change* 46, no. 3 (2016): 393–408.

70. PTI, "President Ram Nath Kovind Likely to Nod for Karnataka Land Reform Amendment Bill in Day or Two," *Financial Express*, October 10, 2017. https://www.financialexpress.com/india-news/president-ram-nath-kovind-likely-to-nod-for-karnataka-land-reform-amendment-bill-in-day-or-two/889084/.

71. D. Bandopadhyay, "Unfinished Tasks," *Economic and Political Weekly* 38, no. 27 (2003): 2841.

72. Kumar and Somanathan, "Right to Shelter," 15.

73. S. Bhalotra, A. Chakravarty, D. Mookherjee, and F. Pino, "Property Rights and Gender Bias: Evidence from Land Reform in West Bengal," *American Economic Journal: Applied Economics*, 11, no. 2 (2019): table 4, p. 226.

74. D. C. Wadhwa, *Guaranteeing Title to Land: The Only Sensible Solution* (Pune: Gokhale Institute of Politics and Economics, 2002).

75. P. Mishra and R. Suhag, "Land Records and Titles in India," PRS India,

September 2017, http://www.prsindia.org/policy/discussion-papers/land-records-and-titles-india.

76. K. Deininger and A. Goyal, *Going Digital: Credit Effects of Land Registry Computerization in India (English)*, Agricultural and Rural Development (ARD) Case Study (Washington DC: World Bank, 2012).

77. A. Kotwal, K. P. Krishnan, T. N. Ninan, and I. Patnaik, "141 Panel Discussion: The Way Forward for the Indian Economy," Ideas for India, January 29, 2019. https://www.ideasforindia.in/topics/miscellany/the-way-forward-for-the-indian-economy.html.

78. Ministry of Tribal Affairs, *Report of the High-Level Committee on Socio-economic, Health, and Educational Status of Tribal Communities of India.* (New Delhi: Ministry of Tribal Affairs, 2014), 279–80.

79. Ministry of Tribal Affairs, *Report of the High-Level Committee*, 283.

80. K. N. Nair and V. Menon, "Lease Farming in Kerala: Findings from Micro Level Studies," *Economic and Political Weekly* 41, no. 26 (2006): 2732, 2734.

81. B. Goswami and M. P. Bezbaruah, "Incidence, Forms and Determinants of Tenancy in the Agrarian Set-up of the Assam Plains," *Economic and Political Weekly* 62, no. 2 (2013): 60–68.

82. S. D. Sawant, "Comparative Analysis of Tenancy Statistics: Implications for Concealed Tenancy," *Artha Vijnana* 23, no. 1 (1991): 12–23.

83. K. Deininger, S. Jin, and H. K. Nagarajan, "Efficiency and Equity Impacts of Rural Land Rental Restrictions: Evidence from India," *European Economic Review* 52, no. 5 (July 2008): 892–918.

84. B. Tripathi, "Liberalising Land Leasing Necessary for Growth, Says Tajamul Haque," *Business Standard*, updated March 31, 2018, https://www.business-standard.com/article/economy-policy/liberalising-land-leasing-necessary-for-growth-says-tajamul-haque-118033100560_1.html.

85. See section 42 of *The Maharashtra Land Registry Code, Act 41*, 1966, https://lawsofindia.blinkvisa.com/pdf/maharashtra/1966/1966MH41.pdf.

86. S. Rajagopalan, "India Needs to Trust Its Farmers and Set Them Free," *Livemint*, updated March 20, 2018, https://www.livemint.com/Opinion/Ur1gpECTWdd3VnbpuuUD9O/India-needs-to-trust-its-farmers-and-set-them-free.html.

87. Sandeep Ashar, "Maharashtra: Norms for Non-agricultural use of Farmland Relaxed," *Indian Express*, January 11, 2017, https://indianexpress.com/article/india/maharashtra-norms-for-non-agricultural-use-of-farmland-relaxed/; N. Sud, "The State in the Era of India's Sub-national Regions: Liberalization and Land in Gujarat," *Geoforum* 51 (2014): 233–42.

88. S. H. M. Sastry, "Karnataka Opens Up Land Purchase for All," *Deccan Herald*, June 11, 2020. https://www.deccanherald.com/state/top-karnataka-stories/karnataka-opens-up-agricultural-land-purchase-for-all-848465.

89. Financial Express Online, "This Portal by Yogi Adityanath Government

Will Tighten the Noose around Land mafia in Uttar Pradesh: Here Is How," *Financial Express*, June 24, 2017, https://www.financialexpress.com/india-news/this-portal-by-yogi-adityanath-government-will-tighten-the-noose-around-land-mafia-in-uttar-pradesh-here-is-how/733857/.

90. Indo-Asian News Service, "UP: Azam Khan Declared Land Mafia by Yogi Adityanath Government," *India Today*, July 19, 2019, https://www.indiatoday.in/india/story/up-azam-khan-declared-land-mafia-by-yogi-adityanath-government-1571131-2019-07-19.

91. India, Ministry of Rural Development, "Draft National Land Reforms Policy," July 2013, 13.

92. A. Banerjee, P. J. Gertler, and M. Ghatak, "Empowerment and Efficiency: Tenancy Reform in West Bengal," *Journal of Political Economy* 110 (2002): 239–80

93. Bardhan and Mookherjee, "Subsidized Farm Input Programs," 186–214.

94. The poverty gap measures the average depth of poverty as a percentage of the poverty line. T. Besley and R. Burgess, "Land Reform, Poverty Reduction, and Growth: Evidence from India." *Quarterly Journal of Economics* 115, no. 2 (2000): 424.

95. For instance, if the middle class gains at the expense of both the rich and the poor, the Gini coefficient may remain stable.

96. T. Besley, J. Leight, R. Pande, and V. Rao, "Long-Run Impacts of Land Regulation: Evidence from Tenancy Reform in India," *Journal of Development Economics* 118 (2016): 72–87.

Chapter Three

1. Indian National Congress, Agrarian Reforms Committee, *Report*, 2nd ed. (New Delhi: All India Congress Committee, 1951), 85.

2. Harold Mann, "Review of the General Report of the Committee of Direction: All India Rural Credit Survey," *Indian Economic Review* 3, no. 4 (1957): 76–80.

3. For an analysis of this rule, see M. Oak and A. V. Swamy. "Only Twice as Much: A Rule for Regulating Lenders," *Economic Development and Cultural Change* 58, no. 4 (2010): 775–803.

4. G. Nayak, "For-Profit MFIs Worse Than Money Lenders," *Economic Times*, November 23, 2010, https://economictimes.indiatimes.com/opinion/interviews/for-profit-mfis-worse-than-money-lenders/articleshow/6973551.cms.

5. S. Menon. "Microfinance Industry Is out of an Unprecedent[ed] Crisis, Thanks to Regulations, Diligent Borrowers," *Economic Times*, April 19, 2016. https://economictimes.indiatimes.com/industry/banking/finance/microfinance

-industry-is-out-of-an-unprecedent-crisis-thanks-to-regulations-diligent-borrowers/articleshow/51886097.cms.

6. The parallel between the Deccan crisis of the late nineteenth century and the recent MFI crisis is described in more detail in L. Chaudhary and A. V. Swamy, "Microfinance and Predatory Lending: The Same Old Story?" *Ideas for India*, October 19, 2012, https://www.ideasforindia.in/topics/money-finance/microfinance-and-predatory-lending-the-same-old-story.html.

7. W. B. Oldham, referring to his tenure as deputy commissioner of the Santhal Parganas, lamented that the tribals had been given "this new and fatal boon of transferability." India, Department of Revenue and Agriculture, *Selection of Papers on Agricultural Indebtedness and the Restriction of the Power to Alienate Interests in Land*, vol. 3 (Simla: Government Central Print Office, 1898), 303.

8. For an analysis of the impact of DARA on borrowing, acreage, and investment, see L. Chaudhary and A. V. Swamy, "Protecting the Borrower: An Experiment in Colonial India," *Explorations in Economic History* 65 (2017): 36–64.

9. The professional moneylender did not want to hold land; it tied up capital.

10. Quoted in a speech by deputy governor of the Reserve Bank of India, R. Gandhi, "Rural Cooperatives-Repositioning," keynote speech at the National Conference of Cooperative Banks, Lucknow, February 9, 2016, https://www.bis.org/review/r160217a.pdf.

11. See A. I. Qureshi, *The Future of the Cooperative Movement in India* (Madras: Oxford University Press, 1947), 143.

12. M. Nath, "Do Institutional Transplants Succeed? Regulating Raiffeisen Cooperatives in South India, 1930–60," *Business History Review* (forthcoming).

13. Reserve Bank of India, *All India Rural Credit Survey: Report of the Committee of Direction*, vol. 2, *The General Report* (Bombay: Reserve Bank of India, 1954), 279.

14. Reserve Bank of India, 279.

15. Indian National Congress, Agrarian Reforms Committee, *Report*, 50.

16. Daniel Thorner, *Agricultural Cooperatives in India: A Field Report* (New Delhi: Asia Publishing House, 1964), 3.

17. Thorner, 83.

18. P. J. Bhende, "Credit Markets in the Semi-Arid Tropics of Rural South India," ICRISAT, Economics Program Project Report 56, Patancheru, Andra Pradesh, 1983, 19.

19. S. G. Patil, *Twelfth Report of the High-Powered Committee on Cooperatives* (New Delhi: Ministry of Agriculture, 2009), vii.

20. R. Srinivasan, *State of Rural Finance in India: An Assessment* (New Delhi: Oxford University Press, 2016), 84.

21. See G. Seetharaman, "The Biggest Lessons for India from the PMC Bank Fiasco," *Economic Times*, October 13, 2019. https://economictimes.indiatimes

.com/industry/banking/finance/banking/the-biggest-lessons-for-india-from-the-pmc-bank-fiasco/articleshow/71557920.cms.

22. C. Bell, "Interactions between Institutional and Informal Credit Agencies in India." *World Bank Economic Review* 4, no. 3 (1990): 297–327

23. According to the Indian Constitution, the states had the right to regulate moneylenders. The relevant legislations include the Kerala Moneylenders Act 1958, the Karnataka Moneylenders Act 1961 and the Rajasthan Moneylenders Act 1963. A full list is provided by the Reserve Bank of India in its 2007 publication, *Report of the Technical Group to Review Legislations in Money Lending* (Bombay: Reserve Bank of India, 2007), 70. https://www.thehinducentre.com/multimedia/archive/03217/78893_3217517a.pdf. We have relied on this source for this paragraph.

24. Bombay (India: State), *Gazetteer of Bombay State: Poona District* (Bombay: Government Central Press, 1954), 359.

25. Government of Maharashtra, *Maharashtra State Gazetteers: Kolhapur District* (Bombay: Directorate of Government Printing, 1960). https://gazetteers.maharashtra.gov.in/cultural.maharashtra.gov.in/english/gazetteer/KOLHAPUR/home.html.

26. V. Kumar provides a useful overview in "Hollowness of Relief Laws," *Cochin University Law Review* (1997): 100–111.

27. Reserve Bank of India, *Report of the Technical Group*, 44.

28. V. Kundapura, "Crackdown on Moneylenders: 40 Arrested in Kolar, Chickballapur. *The Hindu*, July 17, 2015. These interest-rate ceilings were put in place in 2003. See Indian Department of Cooperation, "Karnataka Money Lenders and Pawn Brokers Act 1961 and Rules 1965," Sahakara Sindhu, Department of Cooperation, Government of Karnataka, http://sahakara.kar.gov.in/faqML&PB.html.

29. See David Roodman, "Quick: What's the Grameen Bank's Interest Rate?" Center for Global Development, September 24, 2010, https://www.cgdev.org/blog/quick-whats-grameen-banks-interest-rate.

30. P. S. Kumar, "Law against Lenders Rarely Enforced," *Hans India*, August 22, 2017. https://www.thehansindia.com/posts/index/Hans/2017-08-22/Law-against-lenders-rarely-enforced/320732.

31. K. C. Gopakumar, "Provision in Law against Moneylenders Rarely Enforced," *The Hindu*, updated May 23, 2016, https://www.thehindu.com/news/national/kerala/provision-in-law-against-moneylenders-rarely-enforced/article6024791.ece.

32. Qureshi, *Future of the Cooperative Movement*

33. See Bhende, "Credit Markets"; A. Kochar, "The Distributive Consequences of Social Banking: A Microempirical Analysis of the Indian Experience," *Economic Development and Cultural Change* 59 (2011): 251–280.

34. S. Cole, "Fixing Market Failures or Fixing Elections? Agricultural Credit

in India," *American Economic Journal: Applied Economics* 1, no. 1 (2009): 219–50.

35. Under the recent Kisan (farmer) Credit Card scheme, tenants with oral leases can borrow against them. We have been unable to locate evidence on how often this actually happens.

36. The deviation from trend was the "instrumental variable" for the number of banks. R. Burgess and R. Pande, "Do Rural Banks Matter? Evidence from the Indian Social Banking Experiment," *American Economic Review* 95 (2005): 780–95.

37. Kochar, "Distributive Consequences."

38. M. Ayyagari, T. Beck, and M. Hoseini, "Finance, Law, and Poverty: Evidence from India," *Journal of Corporate Finance* 60 (2020), art. 101515.

39. The difference-in-difference approach can be understood with the following example. Let x be the change in repayment rates in state A after a DRT was introduced. Let y be the change in the repayment rate over the same period in state B where a DRT was not introduced. $x - y$ can be interpreted as the effect of the DRT on repayment rates under some conditions. The reader can find the details in Sujata Visaria's paper, "Legal Reform and Loan Repayment: The Microeconomic Impact of Debt Recovery Tribunals in India," *American Economic Journal: Applied Economics* 1, no. 3 (2009): 59–81

40. We are grateful to Benugopal Mukhopadhyaya for this point. For the colonial period, see Roy and Swamy, *Law and the Economy in Colonial India* (Chicago: University of Chicago Press), chap. 4.

41. Reserve Bank of India, *A Review of the Agricultural Credit System in India: Report of Agricultural Credit Review Committee* (Bombay: Reserve Bank of India, 1990), 555.

42. The Reserve Bank of India issued a "Master Circular" collating existing rules in 2014.

43. They do a difference-in-difference analysis comparing districts that had more and less program exposure. X. Gine and M. Kanz, "The Economic Effects of a Borrower Bailout: Evidence from an Emerging Market," *Review of Financial Studies* 31, no. 5 (2018): 1752–83.

44. S. Bera, "8 States. Rupees 1.2 trillion. It's Raining Farm Loan Waivers, but Are Farmers Really Gaining?" *Livemint*, December 21, 2018. https://www.livemint.com/Politics/zL8mErALC6vw96u5wcKlaP/8-states-19-trillion-Its-raining-farm-loan-waivers.html.

45. Srinivasan, *State of Rural Finance in India*, 109, fig. 13.1.

46. K. Deininger and Y. Liu, "Economic and Social Impacts of an Innovative Self-Help Group Model in India," *World Development* 43 (2013): 149–63.

47. Srinivasan, *State of Rural Finance in India*, 110.

48. Srinivasan, 109, fig. 13.1.

49. In 2014 the Reserve Bank of India altered the rules: the maximum rate

charged would be the lower of the cost of funds plus a 10% margin or 2.75 times the base rate of commercial banks. Economic Times Bureau, "RBI Removes 26% Interest Rate Cap on MFI Loans," *Economic Times*, February 8, 2014, https://economictimes.indiatimes.com/news/economy/finance/rbi-removes-26-interest-rate-cap-on-mfi-loans/articleshow/30004542.cms.

50. "Women Allege Coercive Loan Recovery by Microfinance Firms," *The Hindu*, updated January 6, 2017, https://www.thehindu.com/news/national/karnataka/Women-allege-coercive-loan-recovery-by-microfinance-firms/article17000680.ece.

51. M. Shah, M., R. Rao, and P. S. Vijay Shankar, "Rural Credit in 20th Century India: An Overview of History and Perspectives," *Economic and Political Weekly* 42, no. 15 (2007): 1351–64.

52. See K. Gokhale, "A Global Surge in Tiny Loans Spurs Credit Bubble in a Slum," *Wall Street Journal*, August 13, 2009.

53. A. Banerjee, P. Bardhan, E. Duflo, E. Field, D. Karlan, A. Khwaja, D. Mookherjee, R. Pande, and R. Rajan, "Microcredit Is Not the Enemy," *Financial Times*, December 13, 2010.

54. A. Banerjee, E. Duflo, R. Glennerster, and C. Kinnan, "The Miracle of Microfinance? Evidence from a Randomized Evaluation," *American Economic Journal, Applied Economics* 7, no. 1 (2015): 22–53. In later work, A. Banerjee, E. Breza, E. Duflo, and C. Kinnan find that microfinance can help entrepreneurs who are already running a business. See "Can Microfinance Unlock a Poverty Trap for Some Entrepreneurs?," National Bureau of Economic Research Working Paper No. 26346, October 2019, https://www.nber.org/papers/w26346.

55. E. Breza and C. Kinnan, "Measuring the Equilibrium Impacts of Credit: Evidence from the Indian Microfinance Crisis," *VoxDev*, June 22, 2018, https://voxdev.org/topic/finance/measuring-equilibrium-impacts-credit-evidence-indian-microfinance-crisis, accessed August 10, 2019.

56. Srinivasan, *State of Rural Finance in India*, 113.

57. See India, National Crime Records Bureau, *Accidental Deaths and Suicides in India* (New Delhi: Ministry of Home Affairs: 2015), 267.

58. D. Tiwary, "In 80 per Cent Farmer-Suicides Due to Debt, Loans Taken from Banks, Not Moneylenders," *Indian Express*, January 7, 2017. https://indianexpress.com/article/india/farmer-suicides-due-to-debt-in-80-per-cent-cases-loans-taken-from-banks-not-moneylenders-4463986/.

59. We thank P. Sainath for this point.

60. State of Maharashtra & Ors v. Sarabgdharsingh Shivdassing, 2010. This is discussed by M. Menon and Uzramma, *A Frayed History: The Journey of Cotton in India* (Delhi: Oxford University Press, 2018).

61. There are many challenges. Plots are dispersed, and it is difficult to assess damage. There is asymmetric information between farmer and insurer. And

there is correlated risk, which the insurer may be unable to manage. See H. P. Binswanger-Mkhize, "Is There Too Much Hype about Index-Based Agricultural Insurance?" *Journal of Development Studies* 48, no. 2 (2012): 187–200.

62. See the epigraph at the beginning of the chapter.

63. S. Bera, "Crop Insurance Flaws Fuel Farm Distress," *Livemint*, November 19, 2019, https://www.livemint.com/news/world/crop-insurance-flaws-fuel-farm-distress-11574185759756.html.

64. There are many factors at play besides those discussed in this chapter, such as poor regulation of product markets, problems with irrigation and water management, and the need to introduce better crop varieties.

Chapter Four

1. The National Forest Policy of 1952 is reproduced in Forest Research Institute, *One Hundred Years of Indian Forestry*, vol. 2 (Simla: Government of India Press, 1961), app. 3. The quoted text is on page 330.

2. India, Planning Commission, *The New India: Progress through Democracy* (New York: Macmillan, 1958): 31.

3. Jaitley was speaking in Parliament in support of an amendment to the Land Acquisition Act of 2013. ANI News, "Jaitley Defends Clauses of Proposed Land Bill, Part-1," YouTube video, 3:15. Posted February 26, 2015. https://www.youtube.com/watch?v=wxmWdrJUQB0.

4. We focus our discussion on Schedule V areas, where land-related issues have been particularly controversial, rather than on Schedule VI areas.

5. R. Guha, "Forestry in British and Post-British India: A Historical Analysis," *Economic and Political Weekly* 18, no. 45/46 (1983): 1940–47.

6. S. Sarkar, "Land Acquisition for the Railways in Bengal, 1850–62: Probing a Contemporary Problem," *Studies in History* 26, no. 2 (2010): 103–42.

7. K. N. Choubey, "The State, Tribals, and the Law," *Social Change* 46, no. 3 (2016): 367. Also see N. Sundar, "Law, Policies, and Practices in Jharkhand," *Economic and Political Weekly* 40, no. 41 (2005): 4459–62.

8. See PTI, "Land Acquisition a Difficult Task in India: Panagariya," *Times of India*, August 1, 2015. https://timesofindia.indiatimes.com/india/Land-acquisition-a-difficult-task-in-India-Panagariya/articleshow/48308944.cms.

9. See J. Johnson, "Lunch with the Great Leveler," *Financial Times*, July 21, 2006. For discussion on this point, see A. Shrivastava and A. Kothari, *Churning the Earth: The Making of Global India* (New Delhi: Penguin 2012), 170–71. Also see A. Sarkar, "Development and Displacement: Land Acquisition in West Bengal", *Economic and Political Weekly* 42, no. 16 (2007): 1435–42.

10. V. Ananth, "The Evolution of the Land Acquisition Act," *Livemint*, March9, 2015. https://www.livemint.com/Politics/T2tN2OWzJIy9SuFgsGsmHN/

The-evolution-of-the-Land-Acquisition-Act-from-1824-to-2015.html. Also see Sarkar, "Development and Displacement."

11. Sarkar, "Land Acquisition for the Railways."

12. Sarkar, "Land Acquisition for the Railways." The rest of this paragraph is based on this source.

13. T. Sanjiva Row, *The Land Acquisition Act, 1894: Act 1 of 1894, With Case-Law Thereon* (Madras: M. E. Press, 1907), 14, emphasis added.

14. Sanjiva Row, *Land Acquisition Act*, 15.

15. See K. Y. Danyal, "Land Acquisition in India- Past and Present." http://docs.manupatra.in/newsline/articles/Upload/FF6D173D-E5C5-4954-A73A-9D77708DD9B6.pdf.

16. See Sanjiva Row, *Land Acquisition Act*, sec. 40, p. 74, and sec. 41, p. 75.

17. These remarks by Bliss are widely cited. See C. Gonsalves, "Judicial Failure in Land Acquisition for Corporations," *Economic and Political Weekly* 45, no. 32 (2010): 37–42; E. Krishnan, "Private Speculations and the Public Interest: N.C. Kelkar's Land Acquisition Bill," *Social-Legal Review* 78 (2012): 78–105; A. Mandke, "Land Acquisition for "Companies": Part II or Part VII?" *PL Web Jour* 15 (2004), http://www.ebc-india.com/lawyer/articles/850.htm.

18. Krishnan, "Private Speculations and the Public Interest," 96.

19. M. Raianu, "A Mass of Anomalies: Land, Law, and Sovereignty in an Indian Company Town," *Comparative Studies in Society and History* 60, no. 2 (2018): 367–89.

20. Raianu, "A Mass of Anomalies," 378.

21. A. Pathak, *Law, Strategies, Ideologies: Legislating Forests in Colonial India* (New Delhi: Oxford University Press, 2019). For a discussion of "state conservationism" in India, see R. Grove, *Green Imperialism: Colonial Expansion, Tropical Island Edens and the Origins of Environmentalism, 1600–1800* (Cambridge: Cambridge University, 1995), chap. 8.

22. See M. Gadgil and R. Guha, *This Fissured Land: An Ecological History of India* (New Delhi: Oxford University Press, 1992): 151–52.

23. M. Gadgil and R. Guha, *This Fissured Land*, 218–19.

24. A. Pathak, *Law, Strategies, Ideologies*, 1–2.

25. R. Guha, "Forestry in British and Post-British India: A Historical Analysis." *Economic and Political Weekly* 18, no. 44 (1983): 1882–96.

26. K. Sivaramkrishnan, "Colonialism and Forestry in India: Imagining the Past in Present Politics," *Comparative Studies in History and Society* 37, no. 1 (1995): 13.

27. S. Lele and V. Saberwal show that the Havik Brahmins of Uttara Kanara district in present-day Karnataka were able to negotiate generous user rights to forests to support their cultivation of areca nut. See "Locating Local Elites in Negotiating Access to Forests: Havik Brahmins and the Colonial State 1860–1920," *Studies in History*, n.s. 20, 2 (2004): 273–303. In Kumaon, local commu-

nities were allowed to form Forest Committees (Van Panchayats) after a widespread campaign to burn forests under the control of the forest department. See R. Agrawal, "Van Panchayats in Uttarakhand," *Economic and Political Weekly* 34, no. 39 (1999): 2779–81, and R. P. Tucker, *A Forest History of India* (New Delhi: Sage, 2012), chap. 3. Also see the introduction to S. Lele and A. Menon, eds., *Democratizing Forest Governance in India* (New Delhi: Oxford University Press, 2014), 4.

28. Have regions designated as Scheduled Areas benefited from this? A recent study, using the census from 2001, finds that there were few differences between villages on either side of a border defining a Scheduled Area within ten kilometers of it. See S. Gulzar, N. Haas and B. Pasquale, "Does Political Affirmative Action Work and for Whom? Theory and Evidence on India's Scheduled Areas," *American Political Science Review* 114, no. 4 (2020): 1230–46. The effect of Scheduled Area classification is an important area for future quantitative research.

29. India, Press Information Bureau, "Land Acquisition for Steel Plants," March 18, 2013. http://pib.gov.in/newsite/PrintRelease.aspx?relid=93899.

30. AIR 1963 SC 151.

31. The quoted text is reproduced by C. Gonsalves, "Judicial Failure in Land Acquisition for Corporations," *Economic and Political Weekly* 45, no. 32 (2010): 38.

32. J. Ramesh and M. A. Khan, *Legislating for Justice: The Making of the 2013 Land Acquisition Law* (Delhi: Oxford University Press, 2015), 56.

33. Forest Research Institute, *One Hundred Years of Indian Forestry*, 2:330, emphasis added.

34. Forest Research Institute, 2:39.

35. This text of the act is quoted in S. Divan and A. Rosencranz, *Environmental Law and Policy in India: Cases, Materials, and Statutes*, 2nd ed. (Delhi: Oxford University Press, 2001), 329.

36. See Down to Earth, "The Tendu Leaf," June 28, 2015, https://www.downtoearth.org.in/coverage/the-tendu-leaf-12528.

37. Before this could be done, the government had to buy out the land rights of any landowners under the 1894 Land Acquisition Act. Divan and Rosencrantz, *Environmental Law and Policy in India*, 335. Also see the full case report, paragraph 17, in AIR 1996 SC 2040.

38. We discuss Chipko in chapter 5.

39. The text of the Forest Bill of 1988 is reproduced in R. N. Choudhry, *Law of Forests in India* (1999; repr., New Delhi: Orient, 2002). The quoted text is on page 1716.

40. See the introduction to J. Drèze, M. Samson, and S. Singh, eds., *The Dam and the Nation: Displacement and Resettlement in the Narmada Valley* (Delhi: Oxford University Press, 1997), 1–25.

41. TNN, "50 Years on, Bhakra Dam Oustees Wait for Rehabilitation," *Times of India*, India News, October 22, 2013, https://timesofindia.indiatimes.com/india/50-years-on-Bhakra-Dam-oustees-wait-for-rehabilitation/articleshow/24504585.cms.

42. TNN, "CM: Will Look into Grievances of Bhakra Dam Oustees," *Times of India*, January 4, 2018, https://timesofindia.indiatimes.com/city/shimla/cm-will-look-into-grievances-of-bhakra-dam-oustees/articleshow/62362448.cms.

43. W. Fernandes, "Liberalisation and Development-Induced Displacement," *Social Change* 36, no. 1 (2000): 109–123. The statistics cited are on page 113.

44. U. Ramanathan, "A Word on Eminent Domain," in *Displaced by Development: Confronting Marginalization and Gender Injustice*, ed. L. Mehta (New Delhi: Sage, 2009), 133–45.

45. On credibility, see A. Banerjee, P. Bardhan, M. Datta-Chaudhry, M. Ghatak, A.S. Guha, M. Majumdar, D. Mookherjee, and D. Ray, "Beyond Nandigram: Industrialisation in West Bengal," *Economic and Political Weekly* 42, no. 17 (2007): 1487–89.

46. See introduction to Drèze, Samson, and Singh, *Dam and the Nation*.

47. We discuss the relevant case in chapter 5.

48. See Amrita Ray, "Sardar Sarovar Dam LIVE: PM Narendra Modi Inaugurates Narmada Dam on Birthday." NDTV, updated September 17, 2017, https://www.ndtv.com/india-news/sardar-sarovar-dam-live-pm-narendra-modi-to-inaugurate-narmada-dam-on-birthday-1751278.

49. For a celebration of the NBA, see S. Visvanathan, "Chronicle of a Struggle Retold," *The Hindu*, updated March 29, 2016, https://www.thehindu.com/opinion/lead/chronicle-of-a-struggle-retold/article7504666.ece.

50. M. Levien, *Dispossession without Development: Land Grabs in Neoliberal India* (New Delhi: Oxford University Press, 2018).

51. For a discussion of various flash points, see the chapter with this name, as well as appendix A2, in S. Chakravorty, *The Price of Land: Acquisition, Conflict, Consequence* (New Delhi: Oxford University Press, 2013).

52. "The Nandigram Story till Now," *Livemint*, March 19, 2007. https://www.livemint.com/Politics/I1CAfbH2Und58UkVckctVP/The-Nandigram-story-till-now.html..

53. "The Nandigram Story till Now."

54. See R. Jagannathan, "UPA Land Act Is Creating 20,000 Rural Crorepatis Every Year and Making Infrastructure Unviable," *Swarajya*, January 17, 2018. https://swarajyamag.com/ideas/upa-land-act-is-creating-20000-rural-crorepatis-a-year-and-making-infrastructure-less-viable. For a creative proposal on "discovering" prices via auctions, see M. Ghatak and P. Ghosh, "The Land Acquisition Bill: A Critique and a Proposal," *Economic and Political Weekly* 46, no. 41 (2011): 65–72.

55. See J. Lindsay, K. Deininger, and T. Hilhorst, "Compulsory Land Acqui-

sition in Developing Countries: Shifting Paradigm or Entrenched Legacy?," in *Eminent Domain: A Comparative Perspective*, ed. I. Kim, H. Lee, and I. Somin (Cambridge: Cambridge University Press, 2017), 125.

56. PTI, "Land Act Bit Draconian, Frame Own Laws: Arvind Panagariya to States," *Economic Times*, September 10, 2015, https://economictimes.indiatimes.com/news/economy/policy/land-act-bit-draconian-frame-own-laws-arvind-panagariya-to-states/articleshow/48901548.cms.

57. For the text of the amendment, see Government of Gujarat, "Right to Fair Compensation and Transparency in Land Acquisition, Rehabilitation and Resettlement (Gujarat Amendment) Act, 2016 (Gujarat Act No. 12) of 2016," August 8, Bare Acts Live, 2016, http://www.bareactslive.com/Guj/guj373.htm.

58. The phrase second wind is used by Peter D'Souza, "Decentralization and Local Government: The 'Second Wind' of Democracy in India," in *India's Living Constitution: Ideas, Practices, Controversies*, ed. Z. Hasan, E. Sridharan, and R. Sudarshan (London: Anthem, 2005), 370–404.

59. See Choubey, "State, Tribals, and the Law."

60. For the text of the act, see India, Ministry of Tribal Affairs, "The Provisions of the Panchayats (Extension to Scheduled Areas) Act, 1996, No. 40 of 1996," December 24, 1996, tribal.nic.in/actRules/PESA.pdf.

61. N. C. Saxena and J. Ravi, "Realising Potential of Panchayati Raj in India," Working Paper id:202, eSocialSciences, 2005, http://www.esocialsciences.org/Download/repecDownload.aspx?fname=Document1109200540.1757013.pdf&fcategory=Articles&AId=202&fref=repec.

62. For a summary of the judgment, see Samatha vs State of A.P. And Ors, July 11, 1997, InforMEA, https://www.informea.org/en/court-decision/samatha-vs-state-ap-and-ors.

63. PESA does seem to have allowed Scheduled Areas to benefit more from the Pradhan Mantri Gram Sadak Yojana (Prime Minister's Rural Roads Scheme), introduced in 2000. There is also some evidence that the National Employment Guarantee Scheme (discussed in chap. 6) was more effective in Scheduled Areas because of PESA. See Gulzar, Haas, and Pasquale, "Does Political Affirmative Action Work and for Whom?"

64. Saxena and Ravi, "Realizing Potential," 4.

65. M. Sarin, "Undoing Historical Injustice: Reclaiming Citizenship Rights and Democratic Forest Governance through the Forest Rights Act," in *Democratizing Forest Governance*, ed. S. Lele and A. Menon (Delhi: Oxford University Press, 2014), 119.

66. The *Godavarman* case has stretched over decades and is a saga in its own right. Many believe it has led to overreach by the Supreme Court, which has been accused of micromanaging in addition to adjudicating. We discuss this case in chapter 5.

67. For a contemporaneous press report, see: R. Dhavan, "Evicting 10 Mil-

lion Tribals," *The Hindu*, September 19, 2002, https://www.thehindu.com/todays-paper/tp-national/tp-tamilnadu/evicting-10-million-tribals/article27870371.ece.

68. Ministry of Tribal Affairs, Government of India, *Forest Rights Act, 2006: Act, Rules, and Guidelines* (2014), https://tribal.nic.in/FRA/data/FRARulesBook.pdf.

69. Sarin, "Undoing Historical Injustice," 125.

70. G. Seetharaman, "How Community Rights under the Forest Rights Act Could Transform the Lives of Millions of Forest Dwellers," *Economic Times*, August 9, 2015, https://economictimes.indiatimes.com/news/economy/policy/how-community-rights-under-the-forest-rights-act-could-transform-the-lives-of-millions-of-forest-dwellers/articleshow/48405279.cms.

71. At least two-thirds of the members should be Scheduled Tribes and at least one-third women.

72. Chap. 4, clause 8 of the act.

73. Sarin, "Undoing Historical Injustice," 127.

74. S. Aiyar, "Gujarat Tribals Turn Bamboo Plantation Owners," *Times of India*, Swaminomics (blog), January 25, 2016, https://timesofindia.indiatimes.com/blogs/Swaminomics/gujarat-tribals-turn-bamboo-plantation-owners/.

75. B. Debroy, "Legislation on Forests in India Have a Colonial and Complicated Legacy: Bibek Debroy." *Financial Express*, January 11, 2018, https://www.financialexpress.com/opinion/legislation-on-forests-in-india-have-a-colonial-and-complicated-legacy-bibek-debroy/1010169/.

76. Maharashtra Forest Department, "Brief Review and Statistical Analysis of Forest Offence Cases during Last Quarter-Century (25 Years)," n.d., https://mahaforest.gov.in/report_file/1424264710Report%20-%20Analysis%20of%20Forest%20Offence%20Cases.pdf.

77. N. C. Saxena, S. Parasuraman, P. Kant, and A. Baviskar, *Report of the Four Member Committee for Investigation into the Proposal Submitted by the Orissa Mining Company for Bauxite Mining in Niyamgiri* (New Delhi: Ministry of Environment and Forests, Government of India, 2010).

78. See M. Tatpati, A. Kothari, and R. Mishra, *The Niyamgiri Story: Challenging the Idea of Growth without Limits?* (Pune: Kalpavriksh, 2016), 11.

79. The Orissa Mining Corporation approached the Supreme Court to have the Gram Sabhas consider the issue again. G. Seetharaman, "The Story of One of the Biggest Land Conflicts: No Mine Now, but Is It All Fine in Niyamgiri?," *Economic Times*, updated April 18, 2018, https://economictimes.indiatimes.com/industry/indl-goods/svs/metals-mining/theres-no-mine-but-is-it-all-fine-on-niyam-hills/articleshow/63763978.cms?from=mdr.

80. Gram Sabhas do have to be consulted in the case of "minor minerals."

81. For contrasting views of the amendment, see B. Karat, "A Glass Half Empty for Adivasis." *The Hindu*, May 1, 2015, https://www.thehindu.com/

opinion/op-ed/a-glass-half-empty-for-adivasis/article7162260.ece; B. Biswas, "Will MMDR Amendment Act, 2015 Change the Mining Situation in India?" *AlCircle* (blog), May 5, 2015, https://blog.alcircle.com/2015/05/05/will-mmdr-amendment-act-2015-change-mining-situation-india/.

82. See S. Banerjee, "Utilising District Mineral Foundation Funds to fight the COVID-19 Crisis in India: Current and Future Opportunities," Brookings Institution India Center, April 6, 2020, https://www.brookings.edu/blog/up-front/2020/04/06/utilising-district-mineral-foundation-funds-to-fight-the-covid-19-crisis-in-india-current-and-future-opportunities/.

83. Indeed, some of its supporters argued that Maoist movements have been fueled by the state and corporations running roughshod over the rights of farmers and forest dwellers.

84. See M. Pal, "Rehabilitation of the 'Project Affected': Eminent Domain and Just Compensation," in *Law and Economics*, vol. 2, *Practice*, ed. S. Gangopadhyay and V. Santhakumar (New Delhi: Sage, 2013), 1–18.

85. Ramesh and Khan, *Legislating for Justice*, 11.

86. For the protection argument, see R. Guha, "Savaging the Civilized: Verrier Elwin and the Tribal Question in Late Colonial India," special issue, *Economic and Political Weekly*, 31, no. 35–37 (1996): 2375–89. For the opposing view, R. Jagannathan, "Forest Rights Act Needs to Go: Tribals Aren't Part of a Tiger Reserve," *Firstpost*, September 12, 2014. https://www.firstpost.com/india/the-forest-rights-act-needs-to-go-tribals-arent-part-of-a-tiger-reserve-1707317.html. Amita Baviskar argues that this is an unhelpful dichotomy—tribals already *are* engaged with mainstream society and the economy but need to be able do so on their own terms. See A. Baviskar, "Displacement and the Bhilala Tribals of the Narmada Valley," in *The Dam and the Nation: Displacement and Resettlement in the Narmada Valley*, ed. J. Drèze, M. Samson, and S. Singh (New Delhi: Oxford University Press, 1997), 108.

87. I. R. Chowdhury and P. R. Chowdhury, "Holdout and Eminent Domain in Land Acquisition," *Indian Economic Review* 51, no. 1/2 (2016): 1–19.

88. These are listed in the Fourth Schedule of the LARR.

89. Section 10 (4).

90. Regarding the LARR, see A. Bharadwaj, "Did you know Gujarat and Rajasthan Passed Land Acquisition Bills?," *Newslaundry*, April 29, 2016, https://www.newslaundry.com/2016/04/29/did-you-know-gujarat-rajasthan-passed-land-acquisition-bills.

91. M. Karthik and A. Kodiveri, "The Great Indian Land Grab Being Carried Out in the Name of Compulsory Afforestation," *The Wire*, January 30, 2018. https://thewire.in/environment/great-indian-land-grab-carried-name-compensatory-afforestation.

92. Ramesh and Khan, *Legislating for Justice*, 27.

Chapter Five

1. M. C. Mehta, *In the Public Interest: Landmark Judgements and Orders of the Supreme Court of India on Environmental and Human Rights* (New Delhi: Prakriti, 2009), xxxi.

2. M. Jamrisko, "The World's Dirtiest Air Is in India," *Bloomberg*, Business, March 4, 2019, https://www.bloomberg.com/news/articles/2019-03-05/the-world-s-dirtiest-air-is-in-india-where-pollution-costs-lives.

3. During a notorious twenty-one-month period between 1975 and 1977, Prime Minister Indira Gandhi used a provision in the Constitution that allowed the government to assume exceptional powers in the national interest and declare an emergency. During this period civil liberties were suspended, and many activists and opponents of Indira Gandhi were jailed.

4. Justice Bhagwati, a pioneer in this regard, describes his motivations in "Justice Must Be for the Common Man," YouTube video, 8:02, posted by "MyLaw," August 2, 2011, https://www.youtube.com/watch?v=OrXO8CAi98E.

5. Z. Mody, *Ten Judgments That Changed India* (New Delhi: Shobha De Books, 2013), 42.

6. For examples of pollution-related legislation in colonial India, see S. Gupta, "Environmental Policy and Governance in a Federal Framework: Perspectives from India," in *Environmental Policies in Asia: Perspectives from Seven Asian Countries*, ed. J. Huang and S. Gupta (New Jersey: World Scientific, 2014), 21.

7. All the quotations in this paragraph are from page 3 of the conference report: United Nations, *Report of the United Nations Conference on the Human Environment*, Stockholm, June 5–16, 1972, http://www.un-documents.net/aconf48-14r1.pdf.

8. C. M. Abraham and A. Rosencranz, "An Evaluation of Pollution Legislation in India," *Columbia Journal of Environmental Law* 11, no. 1 (1986): 101–18.

9. For discussion of implementation of the air and water acts, see S. Ghosh, "The Environment," in *Regulation in India: Design, Capacity, Performance*, ed. D. Kapur and M. Khosla (London: Bloomsbury, 2019): 203–27.

10. W. Bogard, *The Bhopal Tragedy: Language, Logic and Politics in the Production of a Hazard* (San Francisco: Westview Press, 1989); D. Kurzman, *A Killing Wind: Inside Union Carbide and the Bhopal Catastrophe* (New York: McGraw-Hill, 1987).

11. C. M. Abraham and S. Abraham, "The Bhopal Case and the Development of Environmental Law in India," *International and Comparative Law Quarterly* 40, no. 2 (1991): 334–65.

12. S. Pargal and M. Mani suggest that some of the crowding emerged after the plant was located. See "Citizen Activism, Environmental Regulation, and the Location of Industrial Plants: Evidence from India," *Economic Development and Cultural Change* 48, no. 4 (2000): 831.

13. See "Understanding EIA," Centre for Science and Environment, https://www.cseindia.org/understanding-eia-383.

14. M. P. Ram Mohan and H. Pabreja, "Public Hearings in Environmental Clearance Process: Review of Judicial Intervention," *Economic and Political Weekly* 51, no. 50 (2016): 68–75.

15. These summary characterizations of Bahuguna and Bhatt are by Ramachandra Guha, whose 1989 book includes arguably the most influential discussion of the Chipko movement. Quoted text is from R. Guha, *The Unquiet Woods* (1989; repr., New Delhi: Oxford University Press, 2001), 182.

16. "Chipko Movement Turns 45, Google Celebrates with a Doodle," *Times of India*, Panache, March 26, 2018. https://economictimes.indiatimes.com/magazines/panache/chipko-movement-turns-45-google-celebrates-with-a-doodle/videoshow/63463018.cms.

17. A. Mitra, "Chipko: An Unfinished Mission," *Down to Earth*, June 7, 2015, https://www.downtoearth.org.in/coverage/chipko-an-unfinished-mission-30883.

18. D. D'Monte, "Storm over Silent Valley," *India International Centre Quarterly* 9, no. 3/4 (1982): 295.

19. D'Monte, 296.

20. For a timeline of events, see S. Dattatri, "Silent Valley: A People's Movement That Saved a Forest," Conservation India, September 25, 2015, http://www.conservationindia.org/case-studies/silent-valley-a-peoples-movement-that-saved-a-forest.

21. Mitra, "Chipko: An Unfinished Mission."

22. Mehta, *In the Public Interest*, 303.

23. The *Indian Express* on February 26, 1996, quoted on the first page of the judgment.

24. In section 20 of the act.

25. On the origin of judicial activism, see P. Leelakrishnan, "Law and Sustainable Development in India," *Journal of Energy and Natural Resources Law* 9, no. 3 (1991): 193–206.

26. India Environment Portal, "Judgement of the National Green Tribunal Regarding Ganga River Pollution," India Environmental Portal, July 13, 2017, http://www.indiaenvironmentportal.org.in/content/445260/judgement-of-the-national-green-tribunal-regarding-ganga-river-pollution-13072017/.

27. Mehta, *In the Public Interest*, 121.

28. See S. Joshi, "Ganga Pollution Cases: Impact on Infant Mortality," Ideas for India, February 26, 2016, https://www.ideasforindia.in/topics/environment/ganga-pollution-cases-impact-on-infant-mortality.html.

29. See M. Greenstone and R. Hanna, "Environmental Regulations, Air and Water Pollution, and Infant Mortality in India," *American Economic Review* 104, no. 10 (2014): 3038–72.

30. That is, the effect was negative (good) but not statistically significant. Greenstone and Hanna, 3063.

31. U. Narain and A. Krupnick, "The Impact of Delhi's CNG Program on Air Quality" (RFF Discussion Paper 07–06, 2007).

32. J. Pananchikal, "Why the Aravalli Forest Range Is the Most Degraded Zone in India," *Outdoor Journal*, September 20, 2018, https://www.outdoorjournal.com/featured/environment/aravalli-forest-range-degraded-zone-india/.

33. PTI, "Supreme Court Shocked over Disappearance of 31 Hills in Aravalli Area of Rajashan," *Indian Express*, October 23, 2018, https://indianexpress.com/article/india/supreme-court-shocked-over-disappearance-of-31-hills-in-aravalli-area-of-rajasthan-5414912/.

34. PTI, "Supreme Court Shocked."

35. *M.C. Mehta v. Union of India and Others*, September 11, 2018.

36. *T.N. Godavarman Thirumulkpad v. Union of India and Others*, December 12, 1996.

37. S. Khanna, "Boundaries of Forest Land: The Godavarman Case and Beyond," in *Democratizing Forest Governance in India*, ed. S. Lele and A. Menon (New Delhi: Oxford University Press, 2014), 225–60. See p. 228.

38. Khanna, 228.

39. S. Dattatri, "The Kudremukh Saga- A Triumph for Conservation," Conservation India, March 26, 2010. http://www.conservationindia.org/case-studies/the-kudremukh-saga-a-triumph-for-conservation-2. The judgment is available at https://indiankanoon.org/doc/282585/?type=print.

40. A. Rosencranz and S. Lele, "Supreme Court and India's Forests," *Economic and Political Weekly* 43, no. 5 (2008), 11–14.

41. M. Ramnath, "Impact of Ban on Timber Felling," *Economic and Political Weekly* 37, no. 48 (2002): 4774–76.

42. Thomas Weber, *Hugging the Trees: The Story of the Chipko Movement* (New Delhi: Penguin India, 1989), 119.

43. PEKB stands for Parsa East and Kanta Basan, which is located in Hasdeo-Arand coalfield in the state of Chattisgarh. For a more detailed discussion of the Hasdeo-Arand coalfield see D. Kumar, *Defending the Green Realm: The Forest Conservation Act of India in Theory and Practice* (Bangalore: Institute of Social and Economic Change, 2015), 101–12.

44. *Sudeip Shrivastava v. State of Chhatisgarh*, March 24, 2014

45. For more recent developments pertaining to the Hasdeo-Arand coalfield, see D. Gupta and B. Paul, "Chhattisgarh's 'No-Go Area' for Coal Mining Faces the Prospect of Being Opened Up," *The Wire*, October 5, 2018. https://thewire.in/rights/chhattisgarh-coal-mining-hasdeo-arand.

46. The quoted text is in paragraph 46, page 45 of the judgment.

47. For a similar view, see Kumar, *Defending the Green Realm*, 111. For a detailed discussion of the WWF case, see S. Khanna, "Exclude and Protect: A Re-

port on the WWF Case on Wildlife Conservation in the Supreme Court of India" (New Delhi: SRUTI, 2008).

48. BBC, "India's Ganges and Yamuna Rivers Are 'Not Living Entities,'" *BBC News*, July 7, 2017, https://www.bbc.com/news/world-asia-india-40537701.

49. Usha Ramanathan scoffed at the Supreme Court's acceptance of the idea that Lafarge did not know at the outset that the area to be mined was forested: "Lafarge case, itself, deserves to be maligned, and has been maligned by many." See U. Ramanathan, "Understanding Reforms in Environment, Land and Labour Laws in India" (talk presented at the Madras Institute of Development Studies, Chennai, January 12, 2015), https://chaikadai.wordpress.com/2015/01/18/understanding-reforms-in-environment-land-and-labour-laws-in-india.

50. N. Chauhan, "CBI Raids Premises of Jayanthi Natarajan for Irregularities in Green Clearances during UPA-II," *Times of India*, September 10, 2017, https://timesofindia.indiatimes.com/india/cbi-books-former-environment-minister-jayanthi-natarajan-in-corruption-case/articleshow/60439030.cms.

51. *Narmada Bachao Andolan v. Union of India*, 2000, and *N. D. Jayal v. Union of India*, 2003.

52. S. Gupta, "Environmental Benefits and Cost Savings through Market-Based Instruments: An Application Using State-Level Data from India", (Centre for Development Economics, Delhi School of Economics, Working Paper No. 111, 2002), table 9, p. 33.

53. In a cap-and-trade method each firm is permitted to pollute to a certain extent but can sell that right to another firm. M. Greenstone, S. Harish, R. Pande, and A. Sudarshan, "The Solvable Problem of Air Pollution in India" (paper prepared for the India Policy Forum, New Delhi, July 2017), xvii. http://www.ncaer.org/Events/IPF-2017/IPF-2017-Paper-Greenstone-Harish-Pande-Sudarshan-Conf-version.pdf.

54. A study conducted in Gujarat found that 29% of audits falsely reported compliance, probably due to collusion between the plant and the environmental lab doing the testing. Greenstone et al., "Solvable Problem," xxii.

55. P. Bhuchar and D. Kumar, "Green Terror: Outdated Environmental Laws and Inflexible Ministers Strangle Indian Economy," *India Today*, October 15, 2012, https://www.indiatoday.in/magazine/cover-story/story/20121015-green-terror-jairam-jayanthi-regime-green-projects-vs-pmo-760070-1999-11-30.

56. Bhuchar and Kumar, "Green Terror."

Chapter Six

1. S. Patnaik, "Recalling Arvind Panagariya's Unsuccessful Labours," *The Wire*, August 6, 2017, https://thewire.in/economy/arvind-panagariya-labour-law-reforms.

2. S. Arnimesh, "'Can't Allow Jungle Raj'—RSS Wing Says UP, MP, Labour Law Changes Bigger Pandemic Than Covid," *The Print*, May 9, 2020, https://theprint.in/india/cant-allow-jungle-raj-rss-wing-says-up-mp-labour-law-changes-bigger-pandemic-than-covid/417710/.

3. R. Ahuja, "Labor Relations in Early Colonial Madras, c. 1750–1800," *Modern Asian Studies* 36, no. 4 (2002): 793–826.

4. T. Roy and A. Swamy, *Law and the Economy in Colonial India* (Chicago: University of Chicago Press, 2016), 107.

5. O. P. Aggarwala, and S. K. Aiyar. *The Constitution of India* (Delhi: Metropolitan Book, 1950), 44.

6. For example, an arbitrary fine may be imposed to keep the worker indebted. See K. Basu, *Analytical Development Economics: The Less Developed Economy Revisited* (Cambridge: MIT Press, 2003), 236.

7. For a more detailed description, see the text of the Bonded Labour (Abolition) Act, February 9, 1976, sec. 2, "Definitions," https://labour.gov.in/sites/default/files/TheBondedLabourSystem(Abolition)Act1976.pdf.

8. Bonded Labour (Abolition) Act,, sec. 11.

9. India, Ministry of Labour and Employment, "Rehabilitation of Bonded Labour Scheme-2016," Press Information Bureau, December 5, 2016, http://pib.nic.in/newsite/PrintRelease.aspx?relid=154895.

10. See R. K. Tiwari's excellent *Human Rights and the Law: Bonded Labour in India* (Delhi: Cambridge University Press, 2010), 137.

11. See P. Bardhan, "Labor-Tying in a Poor Agrarian Economy: A Theoretical and Empirical Analysis," *Quarterly Journal of Economics* 98, no. 3 (1983): 501–14.

12. Tiwari, *Human Rights and the Law*, 52.

13. Tiwari, 61.

14. India, Planning Commission, *A Report on Bonded Labour Rehabilitation Scheme under Centrally Sponsored Bonded Labour System (Abolition) Act, 1976 in the States of Madhya Pradesh, Orissa, Rajasthan, Tamil Nadu and Uttar Pradesh* (New Delhi: Planning Commission, 2010), 2.

15. A recent "Global Slavery Index" estimated that in 2016 there were 8 million people in various forms of unfreedom in India. "India: Global Slavery Index," https://www.globalslaveryindex.org/2018/findings/country-studies/india/.

16. Bandhua Mukti Morcha roughly means Bonded Laborers' Freedom Front.

17. This account is taken from A. Shourie, *Courts and Their Judgments* (Delhi: Rupa, 2001).

18. Under Article 32 of the Constitution, the Supreme Court can be approached to act if a fundamental right is violated.

19. The reader will recall that in 1976 the Constitution had been amended to declare India a socialist republic.

20. See paragraph 20 of the decision.

21. For further discussion of the Public Interest Litigation in the context of bonded labor, see M. Dasgupta, "Public Interest Litigation for Labour: How the Indian Supreme Court Protects the Rights of India's Most Disadvantaged Workers," *Contemporary South Asia* 16, no. 2 (2008): 159–70.

22. Paragraph 34 of the decision.

23. Tiwari, *Human Rights and the Law*, 102.

24. Tiwari, x.

25. Shourie, *Courts and Their Judgments*, 52.

26. Pyare Lal and Ors. v. New Delhi Municipal Corporation, AIR 1968SC133, para 13.

27. Paragraph 33 of the decision.

28. For a lucid discussion of this case see Z. Mody, *Ten Judgments that Changed India* (New Delhi: Shobha De Books, 2013).

29. Paragraph 46 of the decision.

30. Specifically, Article 19 (1) g.

31. R. Jha, "Strengthening India's Urban Informal Economy: The Case of Street Vending," Observer Research Foundation, Issue Briefs and Special Reports, July 25, 2018, https://www.orfonline.org/research/strengthening-urban-indias-informal-economy-the-case-of-street-vending/.

32. National Association of Street Vendors of India, "Historic Street Vendors Law Comes into Force on May Day," National Association of Street Vendors of India, http://nasvinet.org/newsite/historic-street-vendors-law-comes-into-force-on-may-day/.

33. P. Narang and Y. Goyal, "Street Vendors Act 2014: State Compliance Index 2017," Centre for Civil Society (New Delhi: Mehra Impressions, 2017).

34. J. Drèze, "Famine Prevention in India," in *The Political Economy of Hunger*, vol. 2, ed. J. Drèze and A. Sen (Oxford: Clarendon, 1990), 13–122.

35. A. Sen, *Development as Freedom* (New York: Alfred Knopf, 1999).

36. J. Echeverri-Gent, *The State and the Poor: Public Policy and Political Development in India and the United States* (Berkeley: University of California Press, 1993).

37. This has been explained by Jean Drèze, who is widely regarded as one of its architects. See J. Drèze, *Sense and Solidarity: Jholawala Economics for Everyone*. (Ranikhet: Permanent Black, 2017), 146.

38. See P. Mohanty, "Wages Remain below the Minimum Wages, Yearly Hikes Too Little since 2017," *India Today*, April 8, 2019, https://www.indiatoday.in/india/story/mgnrega-wages-remain-below-the-minimum-wages-yearly-hikes-too-little-since-2017-1496629-2019-04-08.

39. J. Ghosh, "India's Rural Employment Programme Is Dying a Death of Funding Cuts," *Guardian*, February 5, 2015, https://www.theguardian.com/global-development/2015/feb/05/india-rural-employment-funding-cuts-mgnrega.

40. J. Bhagwati and A. Panagariya, "Rural Inefficiency Act: Despite Protests about Diluting NREGA, the PM Is Right to Confine It to 200 Poorest Districts," *Times of India*, October 23, 2014.

41. The literature is enormous. For an accessible summary, see S. Mishra, "The Economics of the MGNREGS," *Livemint*, February 7, 2016, https://www.livemint.com/Sundayapp/ueWD2KvNelmsOGEupZND6K/The-economics-of-the-MGNREGS.html.

42. These are approximately the categories in which reforms are being discussed by the government as we write in July 2019.

43. M. K. Varma, "Role of Legislation in Regulating Labor-Management Relations in India," *Labor Law Journal* (1957): 257–71.

44. V. D. Kennedy, "The Conceptual and Legislative Framework of Labor Relations in India," *Industrial and Labor Relations Review* (1958): 487–505.

45. M. D. Morris, "Labor Discipline, Trade Unions, and the State in India," *Journal of Political Economy* 63, no. 3 (1955): 293–308.

46. W. Form and F. C. Pampel, "Social Stratification and the Development of Urban Labor Markets in India," *Social Forces* 57, no. 1 (1978): 119–35.

47. P. Fallon and R. Lucas, "Job Security Regulations and the Dynamic Demand for Industrial Labour in India and Zimbabwe," *Journal of Development Economics* 40, no. 2 (1993): 241–75; S. Bhalotra, "The Puzzle of Jobless Growth in Indian Manufacturing," *Oxford Bulletin of Economics and Statistics* 60, no. 1 (1998): 5–32; R. Nagaraj, "Industrial Policy and Performance since 1980: Which Way Now?," *Economic and Political Weekly* 38, no. 35 (2003): 3707–15.

48. Ancillarization is the practice of firms acquiring a growing share of parts and components from other firms. There is no direct measure of this. But economists have used data creatively to show that this has been happening since the 1990s. The explanation is far from straightforward. The desire to reduce core workforce is only one of the possible factors. See K. V. Ramaswamy, "Liberalization, Outsourcing and Industrial Labour Markets in India: Some Preliminary Results," in *Labour Market and Institutions in India: 1990s and Beyond*, ed. S. Uchikawa (New Delhi: Manohar, 2003), 155–77; P. P. Sahu, "Subcontracting in India's Unorganised Manufacturing Sector: A Mode of Adoption or Exploitation?," *Journal of South Asian Development* 5, no.1 (2010): 53–83.

49. For a discussion of cases, see C. Candland, "Labor Institutions and Industrial Restructuring in India" (IRIS-India Working Paper 24, College Park, MD, 1996); E. Noronha, "Liberalisation and Industrial Relations," *Economic and Political Weekly* 31, no. 8 (1996): L14–L20.

50. For figures on the rise in the extent of contracting in the organized sector, see the essays by S. Uchikawa, "Employment in the Manufacturing Organized Sector in India: The Rise of Medium Scale Units," and K. V. Ramaswamy, "Liberalization, Outsourcing and Industrial Labour Markets in India: Some Prelim-

inary Results," in S. Uchikawa, ed., *Labor Market Institutions in India: 1990s and Beyond* (New Delhi: Manohar, 2002), 39–64, 155–78.

51. For an overview see D. Bhattacharjee, "Globalising Economy, Localising Labor," *Economic and Political Weekly* 35, no. 31 (2000): 3758–64.

52. For a discussion of the literature, see Candland, "Labor Institutions."

53. D. K. Das, H. Choudhury, and J. Singh, "Contract Labour (Regulation and Abolition) Act 1970 and Labour Market Flexibility: An Exploratory Assessment of Contract Labour Use in India's Formal Manufacturing" (Working Paper of Indian Council for Research on International Economic Relations, New Delhi, 2015).

54. K. R. Shyam Sundar, "India's Mismanagement of Labour Law Reform Continues with the Modi Government," *The Wire*, May 7, 2018, https://thewire.in/labour/labour-law-reform-narendra-modi-government.

55. "Bharatiya Mazdoor Sangh Urges the Union Government to Incorporate the Objections of Trade Unions on Labour Codes," https://www.organiser.org/Encyc/2019/6/12/BMS-urges-the-Government-to-incorporate-the-objections-of-Trade-Unions-on-Labour-Codes.amp.html.

56. S. Sen, "Gender and Class: Women in Indian Industry, 1890–1990," *Modern Asian Studies* 42, no. 1 (2008): 75–116.

57. D. Bhattacharya, "Amendment to Maternity Benefits Act Is a Case of Good Intentions Backfiring, Ends Up Disincentivizing Hiring of Women," *Firstpost*, June 30, 2018, https://www.firstpost.com/india/amendment-to-maternity-benefits-act-is-a-case-of-good-intentions-backfiring-ends-up-disincentivising-hiring-of-women-4636421.html.

58. This expression is used by Rina Agarwala as well as K. P. Kannan. See R. Agarwala, *Informal Labor, Formal Politics, and Dignified Discontent in India* (Cambridge: Cambridge University Press, 2013); K. P. Kannan, "The Welfare Fund Model of Social Security for Informal Sector Workers: The Kerala Experience," Working Paper 332 (Thiruvananthapuram: Centre for Development Studies, 2002).

59. K. Jain, "Health Insurance in India: The Rashtriya Swasthya Bima Yojana" (WIEGO Policy Brief [Social Protection] 10, September 2012).

60. T. Besley and R. Burgess, "Can Labor Regulation Hinder Economic Performance? Evidence from India," *Quarterly Journal of Economics* 119, no. 1 (2004): 91–134.

61. R. Hasan, D. Mitra, and K. V. Ramaswamy, "Trade Reforms, Labor Regulations, and Labor-Demand Elasticities: Empirical Evidence from India," *Review of Economics and Statistics* 89, no. 3 (2007): 466–81; P. Sanyal and N. Menon, "Labor Disputes and the Economics of Firm Geography: A Study of Domestic Investment in India," *Economic Development and Cultural Change* 54, no. 4 (2005): 825–54.

62. A. Bhattacharjea, "Labour Market Regulation and Industrial Performance in India: A Critical Review of the Empirical Evidence," *Indian Journal of Labour Economics* 49, no. 2 (2006): 211–32.

63. Y. V. D. M. Rogers and N. Menon, "Labor Regulations and Job Quality: Evidence from India," *ILR Review* 66, no.4 (2013): 933–56.

64. S. Fagernas, "Labor Law, Judicial Efficiency, and Informal Employment in India," *Journal of Empirical Legal Studies* 7, no.2 (2010): 282–321.

65. A. Adhvaryu, A. Chari, and S. Sharma, "Firing Costs and Flexibility: Evidence from Firms' Employment Responses to Shocks in India." *Review of Economics and Statistics* 95, no. 3 (2013): 725–40; R. Chaurey, "Labor Regulations and Contract Labor Use: Evidence from Indian Firms." *Journal of Development Economics* 114 (2015): 224–32.

66. S. Jha, "Govt Drops Move to Make Hire and Fire Easier," Rediff, February 10, 2018. https://www.rediff.com/business/report/govt-drops-move-to-make-hire-and-fire-easier/20180210.htm

67. Jha.

68. See the interview with Manish Sabherwal of Team Lease Services in R. Jagannathan, *The Jobs Crisis in India* (New Delhi: Macmillian 2018), 326.

69. For criticism by the Bharatiya Mazdoor Sangh (BMS), see S. Jha, "Labour Law changes in UP, MP: A Bigger Pandemic in the Offing", *Business Standard*, May 8, 2020.

70. See A. Katju, "Changes in Labour Laws Are Unconstitutional," *Indian Express*, May 19, 2020.

71. P. K. Nanda, "ILO Expresses 'Deep Concern' over Labour Law Changes, Including Appeals to PM Narendra Modi," *Livemint*, May 25, 2020, https://www.livemint.com/news/india/ilo-expresses-deep-concern-over-labour-law-changes-appeals-to-pm-narendra-modi-11590394493866.html.

72. We thank Sanjay Anandaram for this observation.

73. R. Nair, "65% Boost for MGNREGA, Relief for Companies from IBC—Final Part of Modi Covid Package," *The Print*, May 17, 2020, https://theprint.in/economy/65-boost-for-mgnrega-relief-for-companies-from-ibc-final-part-of-modi-govt-covid-package/423486/.

Chapter Seven

1. *Report of the Committee on Industrial Sickness and Corporate Restructuring* (Delhi: Ministry of Finance, 1993), 15.

2. *Report of the High-Level Committee on Law Relating to Insolvency and Winding Up of Companies* (Delhi: Ministry of Law, Justice and Company Affairs, 2000), 42.

3. The first Companies Act appeared in 1856; the last major amendment before independence occurred in 1936.

4. See T. Roy and A. Swamy, *Law and the Economy in Colonial India* (Chicago: University of Chicago Press, 2016), chapter 8, for a fuller discussion of managing agency and its problems.

5. R. Rungta, *Rise of Business Corporations in India 1851–1900* (Cambridge: Cambridge University Press, 1970). On the influence of Rungta's reading, U. Varottil, "The Evolution of Corporate Law in Post-Colonial India: From Transplant to Autochthony" (NUS Law Working Paper 2015.001, Singapore, 2015).

6. Varottil, "Evolution of Corporate Law," 18.

7. Varottil.

8. India, Department of Economic Affairs, Ministry of Finance, *Report of the Company Law Committee* (New Delhi: Department of Economic Affairs, 1952), 213.

9. S. Verma and S. J. Gray. "The Development of Company Law in India: The Case of the Companies Act 1956," *Critical Perspectives on Accounting* 20, no. 1 (2009):110–35.

10. "'Evils' of Managing Agency System: Indian Merchants' Chamber Views," *Times of India*, June 26, 1936, 9.

11. A member of Madhya Pradesh legislature, "Managing Agency System," *Times of India*, March 24, 1955, 9. In a statement by the chairman of Industrial Finance Corporation Ram Nath, in the present times the system "lent itself to abuse"; R. Nath, "Managing Agency System," *Times of India*, April 30, 1951, 3.

12. "Limaye Lashes Out at Managing Agents," *Times of India*, November 17, 1967, 12.

13. "Managing Agency System: Decline Noted," *Times of India*, March 13, 1964, 3.

14. Report of the Commission, cited in M. K. Chaudhuri, "MRTP Act to Competition Act: The Way Forward," *Vikalpa* 41, no.2 (2016): 171–74.

15. Equivalent citations: 1971 AIR 2600, 1972 SCR (2) 201.

16. Neg. Micon A/S Alsvoj 21 Dk 8900 v. Nepc India Limited. Equivalent citations: 2004 120 CompCas 784 Mad, 2000 (3) CTC 107.

17. Other citations: 1993 78 CompCas 167 Delhi, 48 (1992) DLT 723, 1993 RLR 63.

18. O. Goswami, India Committee on Industrial Sickness and Corporate Restructuring, India, Ministry of Finance, *Report of the Committee on Industrial Sickness and Corporate Restructuring* (New Delhi: Ministry of Finance, 1993), 4.

19. Cited text from V. S. Raghavan, "Reference to BIFR of Sickness Will Halt Proceedings before the DRT," Indus Law, Inoflex Newsalert, December 2014.

20. India, Business Portal, "Closing or Changing a Business: Regulatory Requirements: Board for Industrial and Financial Reconstruction (BIFR)," https://archive.india.gov.in/business/closing_business/bifr.php, accessed August 19, 2019.

21. K. Van Zwieten, "The Demise of Corporate Insolvency Law in India: The Role of the Courts" (PhD diss., University of Oxford, 2012).

22. Goswami, India Committee on Industrial Sickness and Corporate Restructuring, India, Ministry of Finance, *Report of the Committee*, 1. The committee report represented the most systematic description of the failure of the regulatory body, BIFR, and discussed the ambiguity in law at length partly drawing on previous work on the subject.

23. O. Goswami, "Corporate Governance in India," in *Taking Action against Corruption in Asia and the Pacific*, ed. Asian Development Bank (Manila: Asian Development Bank, 2002).

24. A. Srinivas and S. Rajagopal, "The Companies Bill, 1993: A Review," *National Law School of India Review* 13 (1995): 13–18.

25. R. Shroff, "India's Sweeping Regulatory and Policy Changes: Heralding a New Era in Investor Protection in M&A Transactions?" *Oxford University Commonwealth Law Journal* 14, no.1 (2014): 105–25.

26. For discussion, see A. Bhattacharjea, "Trade, Development and Competition Law: India and Canada Compared," *Trade, Law and Development* 5, no. 1 (2013): 43–67.

27. In 1977 a significant Supreme Court judgment made the point that actions that the MRTP Act defined as necessarily restrictive practices needed to be assessed in the context of their use (*TELCO v. Registrar of Restrictive Trade Agreements*, 1977). In *Union of India v. Hindustan Development Corporation and Others*, 1993, the court made the rule that horizontal agreements and cartelization could not be inferred from there being identical prices and needed the evidence of an agreement. In a series of cases in 2000–2001, the court rejected the commission's interpretation of restrictive practice on the ground that the actions did not seem to bear on competition. For a fuller discussion of these cases, see A. Bhattacharjea, "India's New Competitive Law: A Comparative Assessment," *Journal of Competition Law and Economics* 4, no.3 (2008): 609–38.

28. A. Bhattacharjea, "Of Omissions and Commissions: India's Competition Laws," *Economic and Political Weekly* 45, no. 35 (2010): 31–37.

29. *Ashoka Kumar Thakur v. Union of India*, (2008) 6 SCC 1 (Supreme Court of India), discussed in A. Kabir, "Completion Laws and the Indian Economy," *National Law School of India Review* 23, no. 1 (2011): 1–8.

30. "Transcript of the VIII NLSIR Symposium on Competition Law," *National Law School of India Review* 27, no. 2 (2015): 197–225.

31. C. Shroff and N. K. Uberoi, "India's New Competition Regime Steadily Gaining Ground," *Competition Law International* (2013): 75–90.

32. A. Bhattacharjea, O. De, and G. Gouri, "Competition Law and Competition Policy in India: How the Competition Commission Has Dealt with Anti-competitive Restraints by Government Entities," *Review of Industrial Organization* 54 (2019): 221–50.

33. S. Chatterjee, G. Shaikh, and B. Zaveri, "Watching India's Insolvency Reforms: A New Dataset of Insolvency Cases" (Indira Gandhi Institute of Development Research Working Paper, Mumbai, 2017). Since then, more cases have come to the tribunal, including that of Jet Airways in 2019, and their resolution will no doubt set an important precedence.

34. N. Kang and N. Nayar, "The Evolution of Corporate Bankruptcy Law in India," *Money and Finance* (2003/2004): 37–58.

35. T. Gormley, N. Gupta, and A. Jha, "Quiet Life No More? Corporate Bankruptcy and Bank Competition," *Journal of Financial and Quantitative Analysis* 53, no. 2 (2018): 581–611.

36. Goswami, "Corporate Governance in India."

37. R. Kali and J. Sarkar, "Diversification and Tunneling: Evidence from Indian Business Groups," *Journal of Comparative Economics* 39, no. 3 (2011): 349–67. Data related to 2004.

38. A. Galani and N. Rehn, "Related Party Transactions: Empowering Boards and Minority Shareholders to Prevent Abuses," *National Law School of India Review* 22, no. 2 (2010): 29–58.

39. U. Varottil, "India's Corporate Governance Voluntary Guidelines 2009: Rhetoric or Reality," *National Law School of India Review* 22 (2010): 1–28.

40. Depository receipts are certificates issued by a bank to represent a foreign company's traded shares. The shares are held by the bank. Instead of the shares, the depository receipts trade in the market.

41. Illegal foreign money held by entities known to the issuer bank or issuer of securities is invested in these securities and brought back to India. See PTI, "Sebi Widens Probe into GDR Misuse for Routing Black Money," *Livemint*, April 3, 2017, https://economictimes.indiatimes.com/markets/stocks/news/sebi-widens-probe-into-gdr-misuse-for-routing-black-money/articleshow/57993527.cms.

42. A. Agarwal, "Corporate Governance: Changing Trends in Interpreting Fiduciary Duty," *Vikalpa* 39, no.3 (2014): 1–12.

43. S. Bhatia, "The Securities Scam: A Legal Perspective," *National Law School of India Review* (1993): 41–45.

44. N. Tiwari, "Resolution of NPA in India: The Role of Asset Reconstruction Companies," *Pratt's Journal of Bankruptcy Law* (2011): 552–80.

45. A. Roy, "The Fall of Saradha Group Revives Old Ghosts of Ponzi

Schemes Going Bust," *Economic Times*, April 24, 2013, https://economictimes.indiatimes.com/the-fall-of-saradha-group-revives-old-ghosts-of-ponzi-schemes-going-bust/articleshow/19702901.cms.

Chapter Eight

1. V. Shiva, "The Neem Tree—Case History of Biopiracy," Third World Network, n.d., https://twn.my/title/pir-ch.htm.

2. R. B. Kumar and P. Rajib, "Characteristics of Merging Firms in India: An Empirical Examination," *Vikalpa* 32, no.1 (2007): 27–44.

3. T. Roy, "Transfer of Economic Power in Corporate Calcutta 1950–1970," *Business History Review* 91, no. 1 (2017): 3–29.

4. On data, see V. S. Kaveri, *Financial Analysis of Company Mergers in India* (Bombay: Himalaya, 1986).

5. On the policy shift and aggregate effect, see P. L. Beena, *Mergers and Acquisitions: India under Globalization* (New Delhi: Routledge, 2014). For several examples, see D. Mehta and S. Samanta, "Mergers and Acquisitions: Nature and Significance," *Vikalpa* 22, no. 4 (1997): 31–38.

6. P. Bhalla, "Mergers & Acquisitions in India: A Sectoral Analysis," *International Journal of Business and Economic Development* 2, no. 2 (2014): 119–34.

7. C. Das Gupta, "Globalisation, Corporate Legal Liability and Big Business Houses in India," *Cambridge Journal of Economics* 34, no. 5 (2010): 895–913.

8. PwC, "Mergers and Acquisitions: The Evolving Indian Landscape," PricewaterhouseCoopers, 2017, https://www.pwc.in/assets/pdfs/trs/mergers-and-acquisitions-tax/mergers-and-acquisitions-the-evolving-indian-landscape.pdf.

9. B. Saraswathy, *The Globalisation of Indian Business: Cross Border Mergers and Acquisitions in Indian Manufacturing* (Abingdon: Routledge, 2018).

10. Securities and Exchange Board of India, "(Substantial Acquisition of Shares and Takeovers) Regulations 2011," SEBI, last updated September 11, 2018. https://www.sebi.gov.in/legal/regulations/oct-2018/securities-and-exchange-board-of-india-substantial-acquisition-of-shares-and-takeovers-regulations-2011-last-amended-on-september-11-2018-_40714.html; J. Banaji, "Thwarting the Market for Corporate Control: Takeover Regulation in India," http://eprints.soas.ac.uk/10920/1/QEH_banaji.pdf.

11. In 2019, Jet Airways stopped working, and its lenders referred the company to the National Company Law Tribunal for bankruptcy proceedings. An offer to take over was expected from Etihad, but it did not come.

12. R. Sethi, S. Dhir, D. Agarwal, "Defining Control: A Study of the Jet-Etihad Case," *National Law School of India Review* 27 (2015): 185–96.

13. Shaun. J. Mathew, "Hostile Takeovers in India: New Prospects, Chal-

lenges, and Regulatory Opportunities," *Columbia Business Law Review* 3 (2007): 800–843.

14. The Drug Price Control Order enabled a system for a quasi-government body to decide which drugs should be called "essential" and thus potentially subject to price regulation. The Essential Commodities Act of 1955 supplied the legal framework for doing this. The order, however, also contains clauses asking for fuller disclosure of contents on packages, among others.

15. In one view the industry had fulfilled its historic mission to deliver innovation, and therefore the special regime should have continued. In another view the industry had failed to deliver on innovation, but this was due to a lack of appropriate environment and sufficient state investment. N. N. Mehrotra, "Patents Act and Technological Self-Reliance: The Indian Pharmaceutical Industry," *Economic and Political Weekly* 24, no. 19 (1989): 1059–64; A. K. Bagchi, P. Banerjee and U. K. Bhattacharya, "Indian Patents Act and Its Relation to Technological Development in India: A Preliminary Investigation," *Economic and Political Weekly* 19, no. 7 (1984): 287–304.

16. S. S. Mondal and V. Pingali, "Competition and Intellectual Property Policies in the Indian Pharmaceutical Sector," *Vikalpa* 42, no. 2 (2017): 61–79.

17. J. Liu, "Compulsory Licensing and Anti-Evergreening: Interpreting the TRIPS Flexibilities in Sections 84 and 3(d) of the Indian Patents Act," *Harvard International Law Journal* 56, no. 1 (2015): 207–15.

18. S. Mani, "Dimensions of India's Intellectual Property Right System. How Many Patents Are Commercially Exploited in India?" (Trivandrum: Centre for Development Studies, 2018).

19. "Transcript of the VIII NLSIR Symposium on Competition Law," *National Law School of India Review* 27 (2015): 197–225.

20. V. K. Unni, "Harnessing IP Awareness for Global Business Dominance: A Tale of Two Indian Companies," *Vikalpa* 33, no. 2 (2008): 74–77.

21. P. P. Naolekar, "Judicial Activism and Patent Law," *National Law School of India Review* (2006): 119–30.

22. S. C. Srivastava, "Geographical Indications and Legal Framework in India," *Economic and Political Weekly* 38, no. 38 (2003): 4022–33.

23. See also K. Vadehra and S. Vadehra, "Solving the India Patent Puzzle," Managing Intellectual Property, 2015/2016, 44–47.

24. G. Linded and G. Somaya, cited in R. Basant, "Intellectual Property and Innovation: Changing Perspectives in the Indian IT Industry," *Vikalpa* 29, no. 4 (2004): 69–82.

25. Basant, "Intellectual Property and Innovation."

26. M. Jayakumar and A. H. Vardhan, "Software Patents in the Indian Framework: An Economic of Problems and Prospects," *National Law School of India Review* 20, no. 2 (2008): 220–28.

27. A. Agarwal, "Growth of IPRs in India: Slow but Steady," *Vikalpa* 33,

no. 2 (2008): 79–81; and S. Mani, S. Chaudhuri, V. K. Unni, C. Pray, and L. Nagarajan, "TRIPS Compliance of National Patent Regimes and Domestic Innovative Activity: The Indian Experience," in *TRIPS Compliance, National Patent Regimes and Innovation*, ed. S. Mani and R. R. Nelson (Cheltenham: Edward Elgar, 2013), 57–112.

28. The attraction of an offshore base was tax treaties between India and the offshore country, which allowed capital gains to be taxed in the latter. Capital gains tax rates were lower in the offshore base. There have been several cases before the quasi-tribunal Authority for Advance Rulings (AAR) involving proof of tax residency. There is little academic literature on the operation of the AAR, but the websites of international accounting firms contain discussion of these rules. See, for example, PwC, "India: AAR Rules That Tax Treaty Relief Is Available at Withholding Stage," PricewaterhouseCoopers, February 13, 2018, https://www.pwc.com/gx/en/services/people-organisation/publications/assets/pwc-indian-ruling-that-treaty-relief-is-available-for-withholding.pdf.

29. S. Abhyankar and S. Chattopadhyaya, "Regulatory Overreach on Holding Structures," *Livemint*, October 24, 2017, https://www.livemint.com/Opinion/BDEZ14YHCYy4MyK4ZLYrNO/Regulatory-overreach-on-holding-structures.html.

30. R. Chinchwadkar and V. Shekhar, "Evolution of Private Equity Regulations in Emerging Markets: A Case of India," *Journal of Private Equity* 20, no. 1 (2016): 38–44.

31. R. Metters and R. Verma, "History of Offshoring Knowledge Services," *Journal of Operations Management* 26, no. 2 (2008): 141–47.

32. Director of Income Tax v. Morgan Stanley Co. Inc., 2007, Supreme Court. Cited and discussed in R. Raghavan, "Permanent Establishment Issues in Indian Outsourcing Transactions," *National Law School of India Review* 24, no. 1 (2012): 10–21.

33. S. Parsheera, A. Shah, and A. Bose, "Competition Issues in India's Online Economy" (National Institute of Public Finance and Policy Working Paper, New Delhi, 2017).

34. J. Armour, J. B. Jacobs, C. J. Milhaupt, "The Evolution of Hostile Takeover Regimes in Developed and Emerging Markets: An Analytical Framework," *Harvard International Law Journal* 52, no. 1 (2011): 219–85.

35. Between 2007 and 2017, Vodafone disputed a tax the Government of India had imposed on a transaction conducted in 2007. After the Supreme Court ruled in Vodafone's favor in 2102, the government passed a law that tax demands would apply retroactively, making the transaction taxable. Foreign investors argued that firms make decisions on the basis of laws prevailing at the time. The controversy raised the issue of state credibility. "Retro Tax Ghost Returns to Haunt Vodaphone," *Business Standard*, February 17, 2016, http://www.business

-standard.com/article/companies/retro-tax-ghost-returns-to-haunt-vodafone-116021600376_1.html.

Chapter Nine

1. Chapter 8 dealt with intellectual property, where jurisprudence builds with reference to global practice rather than the British-Indian tradition.

2. *Sooramani Dasse v. Dena Bando Malick* (1857) 6 MIA 523 (553) recognized this contradiction between wills and the right of the joint family, though the question, whether or not the scriptures recognized an equivalent of testamentary rights, continued to be discussed. See B.B. Mitra, *Indian Succession Act*, 14th ed. (New Delhi: Eastern Law House, 2009), 7, 20–21.

3. *Pious obligation* means the moral duty of the sons to discharge their fathers' debts. The *spiritual benefit principle* refers to rituals sons can perform to confer spiritual benefits to the departed person.

4. To quote H. V. Pataskar, a framer of the Constitution, "to retain the Mitakshara Joint Family and at the same time put a daughter on the same footing as a son with respect to the right by birth, right of survivorship and the right to claim partition at any time, will be to provide for a joint family unknown to the law and unworkable in practice." Cited in Law Commission of India, *Property Rights of Women: Proposed Reforms under the Hindu Law* (New Delhi: Government Press, 2000), 19.

5. See discussion in B. Agarwal, "Gender and Legal Rights in Agricultural Land in India," *Economic and Political Weekly* 30, no. 12 (1995): A39–A56.

6. J. Sen, "Matrimonial Property Rights: Is India Ready for a Law," *Journal of Indian Law and Society* (2009): 129–51.

7. Law Commission of India, *Property Rights of Women*. An excellent analysis of the protests can be found in Agarwal, "Gender and Legal Rights." For a detailed exploration and interpretation of the bill, see E. Newbigin, *The Hindu Family and the Emergence of Modern India: Law, Citizenship and Community* (Cambridge: Cambridge University Press, 2013).

8. Agarwal, "Gender and Legal Rights."

9. M. Kishwar, "Codified Hindu Law: Myth or Reality," *Economic and Political Weekly* 29, no. 33 (1994): 2145–54.

10. *Nalini Rajan v. State*, A.I.R. 1977 Pat. 171, judgment of Patna High Court: "although a daughter can be a member of the Hindu Undivided Family she cannot be given the status of a coparcener in a coparcenary, even after the commencement of the Constitution of India." Cited by S. Singhal, "Women as Coparceners: Ramifications of the Amended Section 6 of the Hindu Succession Act, 1956," *National Law School of India Review* (2007): 50–67.

11. K. Deininger, A. Goyal, and H. Nagarajan, "Women's Inheritance Rights and Intergenerational Transmission of Resources in India," *Journal of Human Resources* 48, no. 1 (2013): 114–41.

12. S. Bhalotra, R. Brulé, and S. Roy, "Women's Inheritance Rights Reform and the Preference for Sons in India," *Journal of Development Economics* 146 (September 2020), art. 102275, https://www.sciencedirect.com/science/article/abs/pii/S0304387818300294?via%3Dihub.

13. S. Anderson, and G. Genicot, "Suicide and Property Rights in India," *Journal of Development Economics* 114 (2015): 64–78.

14. A. A. A. Fyzee, "Recent Developments in Muhammadan Law in India, 1900–1960," *International and Comparative Law Quarterly* 46 (1964): 46–50.

15. For a detailed discussion of the context and aftermath of these two cases, see R. Chitkara, "Pulling the Wool: The Indirect Reform of Religious Family Laws in India," *International Journal of Jurisprudence of the Family* 43 (2015): 43–65.

16. Although personal law as such is not the subject of this book, it may be appropriate to note that Muslim personal law was again in the news in 2016–2017. A Supreme Court judgment, and an act that followed it, made the practice of "triple-talaq," or instant divorce, unconstitutional. The practice has been outlawed in many, perhaps most, Muslim-majority countries. However, in India the public debate around the process was quite fierce in a reminder of the 1980s. On one side was the claim that the reform was an attack on Muslim identity (even though Muslim women led the campaign) and on the other the claim that the reform was a step toward gender justice and empowerment.

17. This merely required the man to say *talaq* (divorce) three times.

18. S. A. Chibber, "Charting a New Path toward Gender Equality in India: From Religious Personal Laws to a Uniform Civil Code," *Indiana Law Journal* 83 (2008): 695–717.

19. N. B. Mody, "The Press in India: The Shah Bano Judgment and Its Aftermath," *Asian Survey* 27, no. 8 (1987): 935–53.

20. N. S. Niaz and Z. Soman, "Muslim Women's Views on Muslim Personal Law," *Economic and Political Weekly* 50, no. 51 (2015): 83–86.

21. S. Dutta, "From Accommodation to Substantive Equality: Muslim Personal Law, Secular Law, and the Indian Constitution 1985–2015," *Asian Journal of Law and Society* 4, no. 2 (2017): 191–227.

22. M. Galanter on "the unwillingness of the courts to interfere with the enforcement of caste rules regulating relations with other castes" in "Law and Caste in Modern India," *Asian Survey* 3, no. 11 (1963): 544–59.

23. A high-profile case involving a large real estate company and the so-called Panchami lands is *V.G.P. Prem Nagar v the State of Tamil Nadu and Others*, Madras High Court, April 5, 2010; WA Nos. 1446 to 1448 of 2008.

24. Among the important acts are the Scheduled Castes and Scheduled

Tribes (Prevention of Atrocities) Act 1989 and the older Untouchability Offence Act 1955, later amended and renamed the Protection of Civil Liberties Act. Several provisions of the Constitution forbid caste-based discrimination. Assessments of these acts suggest that informal discrimination persisted partly because of poor enforcement of these laws. See also G. Agarwal and C. Gonsalves, *Dalits and the Law* (New Delhi: Human Rights Network, 2005).

25. S. S. Jodhka, *Caste in Contemporary India*, 2nd ed. (Abington: Routledge, 2017); A. Rao, *The Caste Question: Dalits and the Politics of Modern India* (Berkeley: University of California Press, 2009); A. Deshpande, *The Grammar of Caste: Economic Discrimination in Contemporary India* (New Delhi: Oxford University Press, 2011); M. Sharma, *Caste and Nature: Dalits and Indian Environmental Politics* (Delhi: Oxford University Press, 2018).

26. S. S. Jodhka, "Caste and Untouchability in Rural Punjab," *Economic and Political Weekly* 37, no. 19 (2002): 1813–23.

27. V. Hnatkovska, A. Lahiri, and S. Paul, "Castes and Labor Mobility," *American Economic Journal: Applied Economics* 4, no. 2 (2012): 274–307.

28. D. Kapur, C. B. Prasad, L. Pritchett, and D. S. Babu, "Rethinking Inequality: Dalits in Uttar Pradesh in the Market Reform Era," *Economic and Political Weekly* 45, no. 35 (2010): 39–49.

29. A. Deshpande, and R. Ramachandran, "Traditional Hierarchies and Affirmative Action in a Globalizing Economy: Evidence from India," *World Development* 118 (2019): 63–78.

30. L. Iyer, T. Khanna, and A. Varshney, "Caste and Entrepreneurship in India," *Economic and Political Weekly* 48, no. 6 (2013): 52–60.

31. S. Tofaris, "Trust Law Goes East: The Transplantation of Trust Law in India and Beyond," *Journal of Legal History* 36, no. 3 (2015): 299–332.

32. The trustee in an English trust or endowment has more legal powers than the head of a waqf.

33. S. S. A. Jafri, "Sunni Auqaf and Waqf Board of Uttar Pradesh: In Need of Rejuvenation," *Economic and Political Weekly* 32, no. 25 (1997): 1450–51.

34. "Muslim Outfits Allege Takeover of Prime Wakf Land," *Times of India*, May 10, 2007, 9.

35. L. Vevaina, "She's Come Undone: Parsi Women's Property and Propriety under the Law," *Political and Legal Anthropology Review* 41, no. 1 (2018): 44–59.

36. Goolrukh Gupta v. The Valsad Parsi Anjuman Trust, 2012.

Chapter Ten

1. M. K. Gandhi, *Hind Swaraj or Indian Home Rule* (1909; repr., Ahmedabad: Navjivan, 1938), sec. 05.

2. D. Thengadi, *The Third Way*, rev. ed. (Bangalore: Sahitya Sindhu Prakashana, 1998), 78.

3. Sanjeev Sanyal, quoted by S. Mundy, "Why India's Bankruptcy Law Is Reshaping Big Business," *Financial Times*, May 27, 2018.

4. H. Sengupta, "An Obscure Book Holds the Key to the RSS View of the Economy," *Fortune India*, October 6, 2018, https://www.fortuneindia.com/polemicist/an-obscure-book-holds-the-key-to-the-rss-view-of-the-economy/102555.

5. D. Thengadi, *Why Bharatiya Mazdoor Sangh*, 2nd ed. (Calcutta: Mahamaya Press, 1981), 47.

6. Thengadi, 81.

7. P. K. Nanda, "BMS Slams Govt Bid to Merge Labour Laws," *Livemint*, November 23, 2018, https://www.livemint.com/Politics/PD0AOZPPTPAZmYHwqptuQP/BMS-slams-govt-bid-to-merge-labour-laws.html.

8. "RSS Arm Swadeshi Jagran Manch Opposes Walmart," *Deccan Chronicle*, August 28, 2019.

Bibliography

Abhyankar, S., and S. Chattopadhyaya. "Regulatory Overreach on Holding Structures." *Livemint*, October 24, 2017. https://www.livemint.com/Opinion/BDEZ14YHCYy4MyK4ZLYrNO/Regulatory-overreach-on-holding-structures.html.

Abraham, C. M., and S. Abraham. "The Bhopal Case and the Development of Environmental Law in India." *International and Comparative Law Quarterly* 40, no. 2 (1991): 334–65.

Abraham, C. M., and A. Rosencranz. "An Evaluation of Pollution Legislation in India." *Columbia Journal of Environmental Law* 11, no. 1 (1986): 101–18.

Adhvaryu, A., A. Chari, and S. Sharma. "Firing Costs and Flexibility: Evidence from Firms' Employment Responses to Shocks in India." *Review of Economics and Statistics* 95, no. 3 (2013): 725–40.

Agarwal, A. "Corporate Governance: Changing Trends in Interpreting Fiduciary Duty." *Vikalpa* 39, no. 3 (2014): 1–12.

Agarwal, A. "Growth of IPRs in India: Slow but Steady." *Vikalpa* 33, no. 2 (2008): 79–81.

Agarwal, B. "Gender and Legal Rights in Agricultural Land in India." *Economic and Political Weekly* 30, no. 12 (1995): A39–A56.

Agarwal, G., and C. Gonsalves, *Dalits and the Law*. New Delhi: Human Rights Network, 2005.

Agarwala, R. *Informal Labor, Formal Politics, and Dignified Discontent in India*. Cambridge: Cambridge University Press, 2013.

Aggarwala, O. P., and S. K. Aiyar. *The Constitution of India*. Delhi: Metropolitan Book, 1950.

Agrawal, R. "Van Panchayats in Uttarakhand." *Economic and Political Weekly* 34, no. 39 (1999): 2779–81

Ahuja, R. "Labor Relations in Early Colonial Madras, c. 1750–1800." *Modern Asian Studies* 36, no.4 (2002): 793–826.

Aiyar, S. "Gujarat Tribals Turn Bamboo Plantation Owners." *Times of India*,

Swaminomics (blog), January 24, 2016. https://timesofindia.indiatimes.com/blogs/Swaminomics/gujarat-tribals-turn-bamboo-plantation-owners/.

Aiyar, S. "Twenty-Five Years of Indian Economic Reform." Cato Institute, Policy Analysis 803, October 26, 2016. https://www.cato.org/publications/policy-analysis/twenty-five-years-indian-economic-reform.

Allen, R. *Enclosure and the Yeoman: The Agricultural Development of the South Midlands 1450–1850*. New York: Oxford University Press, 1992.

Amirapu, A. "Justice Delayed Is Growth Denied: The Effect of Slow Courts on Relationships Specific Industries in India." Working Paper 1706, School of Economics Discussion Papers, University of Essex, 2017.

Ananth, V. "The Evolution of the Land Acquisition Act." *Livemint*, March 9, 2015. https://www.livemint.com/Politics/T2tN2OWzJIy9SuFgsGsmHN/The-evolution-of-the-Land-Acquisition-Act-from-1824-to-2015.html.

Ananth, V. K. *The Indian Constitution and Social Revolution: The Right to Property since Independence*. New Delhi: Sage, 2015.

Anderson, S., and G. Genicot. "Suicide and Property Rights in India." *Journal of Development Economics* 114 (2015): 64–78.

Andrews, E. W. *Labor Law and Practice in India*. Washington, DC: US Government Printing Office, 1967.

ANI News. "Jaitley Defends Clauses of Proposed Land Bill, Part-1." YouTube video, 3:15. Posted February 26, 2015. https://www.youtube.com/watch?v=wxmWdrJUQB0.

Appu, P. S. *Land Reforms in India: A Survey of Policy, Legislation, and Implementation*. New Delhi: Vikas, 1996.

Armour, J., J. B. Jacobs, C. J. Milhaupt. "The Evolution of Hostile Takeover Regimes in Developed and Emerging Markets: An Analytical Framework." *Harvard International Law Journal* 52, no.1 (2011): 219–85.

Arnimesh, S. "'Can't Allow Jungle Raj'—RSS Wing Says UP, MP, Labour Law Changes Bigger Pandemic than Covid." *The Print*, May 9, 2020. https://theprint.in/india/cant-allow-jungle-raj-rss-wing-says-up-mp-labour-law-changes-bigger-pandemic-than-covid/417710/.

Ashar, S. "Maharashtra: Norms for Non-agricultural Use of Farmland Relaxed." *Indian Express*, January 11, 2017. https://indianexpress.com/article/india/maharashtra-norms-for-non-agricultural-use-of-farmland-relaxed/.

Ashar, S. "State Closer to Unlocking Vacant Plots Exempted under Urban Land Ceiling Act." *Indian Express*, November 5, 2017. https://indianexpress.com/article/cities/mumbai/state-closer-to-unlocking-vacant-plots-exempted-under-urban-land-ceiling-act-4924263/.

Ashar, S. "Top Business Families to Benefit, Govt to Free Up Exempted Vacant Lands." *Indian Express*, August 21, 2018. https://indianexpress.com/article/cities/mumbai/top-business-families-to-benefit-govt-to-free-up-exempted-vacant-lands-5318294/.

Asset Yogi. "Urban Land (Ceiling and Regulation) Act 1976 / Repeal Act 1999—Hindi." YouTube video, 13:04. Posted May 19, 2018. https://www.youtube.com/watch?v=9oLer1aej9s.

Atkinson, F. J. "A Statistical Review of Income and Wealth in British India," *Journal of the Royal Statistical Society* 65, no. 3 (1902): 209–83.

Austin, G. *The Indian Constitution: Cornerstone of a Nation.* 2nd ed. New Delhi: Oxford University Press, 1999.

Ayyagari, M., T. Beck, and M. Hoseini, "Finance, Law, and Poverty: Evidence from India." *Journal of Corporate Finance* 60 (2020), art. 101515.

"A Bad Idea: Niti Aayog Rightly Rejects Farm Loan Waivers." *Times of India*, December 20, 2018. https://timesofindia.indiatimes.com/blogs/toi-editorials/a-bad-idea-niti-aayog-rightly-rejects-farm-loan-waivers/.

Bagchi, A. Review of *Law and the Economy in Colonial India*, by T. Roy and A. V. Swamy. *Business History Review* 91, no. 2 (2017): 424–28.

Bagchi, A. K., P. Banerjee, and U. K. Bhattacharya. "Indian Patents Act and Its Relation to Technological Development in India: A Preliminary Investigation." *Economic and Political Weekly* 19, no. 7 (1984): 287–304.

Bahuguna, V. K. "MoEF Order on Removal of Encroachments on Forests." Email, August 18, 2002. http://wgbis.ces.iisc.ernet.in/biodiversity/Environ_sys/doc2001-02/ecomoe220928.html.

Balakrishnan, B. "Resistance to FDI a Hangover of the Past." *The Hindu*, BusinessLine, December 1, 2011. https://www.thehindubusinessline.com/opinion/columns/bhaskar-balakrishnan/resistance-to-fdi-a-hangover-of-the-past/article20371402.ece1..

Banaji, J. "Thwarting the Market for Corporate Control: Takeover Regulation in India." http://eprints.soas.ac.uk/10920/1/QEH_banaji.pdf.

Bandopadhyay, D. "Unfinished Tasks." *Economic and Political Weekly* 38, no. 27 (2003): 2841–42.

Banerjee, A., P. Bardhan, K. Basu, M. Datta-Chaudhuri, M. Ghatak, A. S. Guha, M. Majumdar, D. Mookherjee, and D. Ray. "Beyond Nandigram: Industrialisation in West Bengal." *Economic and Political Weekly* 42, no. 17 (2007): 1487–89.

Banerjee, A., P. Bardhan, E. Duflo, E. Field, D. Karlan, A. Khwaja, D. Mookherjee, R. Pande, and R. Rajan. "Microcredit Is Not the Enemy." *Financial Times*, December 13, 2010.

Banerjee, A., E. Breza, E. Duflo, and C. Kinnan. "Can Microfinance Unlock a Poverty Trap for Some Entrepreneurs?" National Bureau of Economic Research Working Paper 26346, October 2019. https://www.nber.org/papers/w26346.

Banerjee, A., E. Duflo, R. Glennerster, and C. Kinnon. "The Miracle of Microfinance? Evidence from a Randomized Evaluation." *American Economic Journal, Applied Economics* 7, no. 1 (2015): 22–53.

Banerjee, A., P. J. Gertler, and M. Ghatak. "Empowerment and Efficiency: Tenancy Reform in West Bengal." *Journal of Political Economy* 110 (2002): 239–80.

Banerjee, S. "Utilising District Mineral Foundation Funds to Fight the COVID-19 Crisis in India: Current and Future Opportunities." Brookings Institution India Center, April 6, 2020. https://www.brookings.edu/blog/up-front/2020/04/06/utilising-district-mineral-foundation-funds-to-fight-the-covid-19-crisis-in-india-current-and-future-opportunities/.

Bardhan, P. "Labor-Tying in a Poor Agrarian Economy: A Theoretical and Empirical Analysis." *Quarterly Journal of Economics* 98, no. 3 (1983): 501–14.

Bardhan, P. "Nature of Opposition to Economic Reforms in India." *Economic and Political Weekly* 40, no. 48 (2005): 4995–98.

Bardhan, P., and D. Mookherjee. "Subsidized Farm Input Programs and Agricultural Performance: A Farm Level Analysis of West Bengal's Green Revolution, 1982–1995." *American Economic Journal: Applied Economics* 3 (2011): 186–214.

Basant, R. "Intellectual Property and Innovation: Changing Perspectives in the Indian IT Industry." *Vikalpa* 29, no.4 (2004): 69–82.

Basu, K. *Analytical Development Economics: The Less Developed Economy Revisited*. Cambridge: MIT Press, 2003.

Basu, K. *Republic of Beliefs: A New Approach to Law and Economics*. Princeton, NJ: Princeton University Press, 2018.

Baviskar, A. "Displacement and the Bhilala Tribals of the Narmada Valley." In *The Dam and the Nation: Displacement and Resettlement in the Narmada Valley*, edited by J. Drèze, M. Samson, and S. Singh, 103–35. New Delhi: Oxford University Press, 1997.

Baxi, U. "Judiciary as a Resource for Indian Democracy." 2010. http://www.india-seminar.com/2010/615/615_upendra_baxi.htm.

Baxi, U. "Taking Suffering Seriously: Social Action Litigation in the Indian Supreme Court." *Third World Legal Studies* 4 (1985): 107–32.

BBC. "India's Ganges and Yamuna Rivers Are 'Not Living Entities.'" *BBC News*, July 7, 2017. https://www.bbc.com/news/world-asia-india-40537701.

BBC. "India Wins Landmark Patent Battle." *BBC News*. March 9, 2005. http://news.bbc.co.uk/2/hi/science/nature/4333627.stm..

Beena, P. L. *Mergers and Acquisitions: India under Globalization*. New Delhi: Routledge, 2014.

Bell, C. "Interactions between Institutional and Informal Credit Agencies in India." *World Bank Economic Review* 4, no. 3 (1990): 297–327.

Bera, S. "Crop Insurance Flaws Fuel Farm Distress." *Livemint*, November 19, 2019, https://www.livemint.com/news/world/crop-insurance-flaws-fuel-farm-distress-11574185759756.html.

Bera, S. "8 States. Rupees 1.2 Trillion. It's Raining Farm Loan Waivers, but Are Farmers Really Gaining?" *Livemint*, December 21, 2018. https://www

.livemint.com/Politics/zL8mErALC6vw96u5wcKlaP/8-states-19-trillion-Its-raining-farm-loan-waivers.html.

Besley, T., and R. Burgess. "Can Labor Regulation Hinder Economic Performance? Evidence from India." *Quarterly Journal of Economics* 119, no. 1 (2004): 91–134.

Besley, T., and R. Burgess. "Land Reform, Poverty Reduction, and Growth: Evidence from India." *Quarterly Journal of Economics* 115, no. 2 (2000): 389–430.

Besley, T., J. Leight, R. Pande, and V. Rao. "Long-Run Impacts of Land Regulation: Evidence from Tenancy Reform in India." *Journal of Development Economics* 118 (2016): 72–87.

Bhagwati, J., and A. Panagariya. "Rural Inefficiency Act: Despite Protests about Diluting NREGA, the PM Is Right to Confine It to 200 Poorest Districts." *Times of India*, October 23, 2014. https://timesofindia.indiatimes.com/blogs/toi-edit-page/rural-inefficiency-act-despite-protests-about-diluting-nrega-the-pm-is-right-to-confine-it-to-200-poorest-districts/.

Bhalla, P. "Mergers & Acquisitions in India: A Sectoral Analysis." *International Journal of Business and Economic Development* 2, no. 2 (2014): 119–34.

Bhalotra, S. "The Puzzle of Jobless Growth in Indian Manufacturing." *Oxford Bulletin of Economics and Statistics* 60, no. 1 (1998): 5–32.

Bhalotra, S., R. Brulé, and S. Roy, "Women's Inheritance Rights Reform and the Preference for Sons in India." *Journal of Development Economics* 146 (September 2020), art. 102275. https://www.sciencedirect.com/science/article/abs/pii/S0304387818300294?via%3Dihub.

Bhalotra, S., A. Chakravarty, D. Mookherjee, and F. Pino, "Property Rights and Gender Bias: Evidence from Land Reform in West Bengal." *American Economic Journal: Applied Economics* 11, no. 2 (2019): 205–37.

Bhamidipati, N. "PIL Power: How the Public Changed the Law." *Quint*, March 25, 2015. https://www.thequint.com/news/india/pil-power-how-the-public-changed-the-law.

Bharadwaj, A. "Did You Know Gujarat and Rajasthan Passed Land Acquisition Bills? *Newslaundry*, April 29, 2016. https://www.newslaundry.com/2016/04/29/did-you-know-gujarat-rajasthan-passed-land-acquisition-bills.

Bhatia, S. "The Securities Scam: A Legal Perspective." *National Law School of India Review* 5, no. 1 (1993): 41–45.

Bhattacharjea, A. "India's New Competitive Law: A Comparative Assessment." *Journal of Competition Law and Economics* 4, no. 3 (2008): 609–38.

Bhattacharjea, A. "Labour Market Regulation and Industrial Performance in India: A Critical Review of the Empirical Evidence." *Indian Journal of Labour Economics* 49, no.2 (2006): 211–32.

Bhattacharjea, A. "Of Omissions and Commissions: India's Competition Laws." *Economic and Political Weekly* 45, no. 35 (2010): 31–37.

Bhattacharjea, A. "Trade, Development and Competition Law: India and Canada Compared." *Trade, Law and Development* 5, no. 1 (2013): 43–67.

Bhattacharjea, A., O. De, and G. Gouri, "Competition Law and Competition Policy in India: How the Competition Commission Has Dealt with Anticompetitive Restraints by Government Entities," *Review of Industrial Organization* 54 (2019): 221–50.

Bhattacharjee, D. "Globalising Economy, Localising Labor." *Economic and Political Weekly* 35, no. 31 (2000): 3758–64.

Bhattacharya, D. "Amendment to Maternity Benefits Act Is a Case of Good Intentions Backfiring, Ends Up Disincentivizing Hiring of Women." *Firstpost*, June 30, 2018. https://www.firstpost.com/india/amendment-to-maternity-benefits-act-is-a-case-of-good-intentions-backfiring-ends-up-disincentivising-hiring-of-women-4636421.html.

Bhattacharya, N. "Lenders and Debtors: Punjab Countryside 1880–1940." *Studies in History* 1 (1985): 305–42.

Bhuchar, P., and D. Kumar, "Green Terror: Outdated Environmental Laws and Inflexible Ministers Strangle Indian Economy." *India Today*, October 15, 2012. https://www.indiatoday.in/magazine/cover-story/story/20121015-green-terror-jairam-jayanthi-regime-green-projects-vs-pmo-760070-1999-11-30.

Bhende, P. J. "Credit Markets in the Semi-Arid Tropics of Rural South India." ICRISAT, Economics Program Project Report 56, Patancheru, Andhra Pradesh, 1983.

Bhuskute, R. V. "Overview of Land Reforms in Maharashtra." In *Land Reforms in India: Performance and Challenges in Gujarat and Maharashtra*, edited by G. Shah and D. C. Sah, 39–94. New Delhi: Sage, 2002.

Bihar High Court. *Report on the Administration of Civil Justice in the State of Bihar during the Year 1960*. Patna, Bihar: Superintendent Secretariat Press, 1961.

Binswanger-Mkhize, H. P. "Is There Too Much Hype about Index-Based Agricultural Insurance?" *Journal of Development Studies* 48, no. 2 (2012): 187–200.

Biswas, B. "Will MMDR Amendment Act, 2015 Change the Mining Situation in India?" *AlCircle* (blog), May 5, 2015. https://blog.alcircle.com/2015/05/05/will-mmdr-amendment-act-2015-change-mining-situation-india/.

Boehm, J., and E. Oberfield. "(Un)ease of Doing Business: How Congested Courts Hinder Firm Productivity." *VoxDev*, February 7, 2019. https://voxdev.org/topic/institutions-political-economy/unease-doing-business-how-congested-courts-hinder-firm-productivity.

Bogard, W. *The Bhopal Tragedy: Language, Logic and Politics in the Production of a Hazard*. San Francisco: Westview Press, 1989.

Bombay (India: State). *Gazetteer of Bombay State: Poona District*. Bombay: Government Central Press, 1954.

Breza, E., and C. Kinnan. "Measuring the Equilibrium Impacts of Credit: Evidence from the Indian Micro Finance Crisis." *VoxDev*, June 22, 2018. https://voxdev.org/topic/finance/measuring-equilibrium-impacts-credit-evidence-indian-microfinance-crisis.

Burgess, R., and R. Pande. "Do Rural Banks Matter? Evidence from the Indian Social Banking Experiment." *American Economic Review* 95 (2005): 780–95.

Candland, C. "Labor Institutions and Industrial Restructuring in India." IRIS-India Working Paper 24, College Park, MD, 1996.

Catanach, I. *Rural Credit in Western India 1875–1930: Rural Credit and the Co-operative Movement in the Bombay Presidency*. Berkeley: University of California Press, 1970.

Centre for Science and Environment. "Understanding EIA." Centre for Science and Environment. https://www.cseindia.org/understanding-eia-383.

Chandran, R. "Millions of Cases Stuck in Indian Courts Show Need for 'Urgent' Land Reform-Advocacy." Reuters, August 8, 2016. https://www.reuters.com/article/us-india-landrights-court/millions-of-cases-stuck-in-indian-courts-show-need-for-urgent-land-reform-advocacy-idUSKCN10J1GJ.

Chakravorty, S. *The Price of Land: Acquisition, Conflict, Consequence*. New Delhi: Oxford University Press, 2013.

Chatterjee, S., G. Shaikh, and B. Zaveri. "Watching India's Insolvency Reforms: A New Dataset of Insolvency Cases." Indira Gandhi Institute of Development Research Working Paper, Mumbai, 2017.

Chattopadhyay, S. "Notes: Operation Barga." *Social Scientist* 8, no. 87 (1979): 41–48.

Chaudhary, L., and A. V. Swamy. "Microfinance and Predatory Lending: The Same Old Story?" Ideas for India, October 19, 2012. https://www.ideasforindia.in/topics/money-finance/microfinance-and-predatory-lending-the-same-old-story.html.

Chaudhary, L., and A. V. Swamy. "Protecting the Borrower: An Experiment in Colonial India." *Explorations in Economic History* 65 (2017): 36–64.

Chaudhuri, M. K. "MRTP Act to Competition Act: The Way Forward." *Vikalpa* 41, no. 2 (2016): 171–74.

Chauhan, N. "CBI Raids Premises of Jayanthi Natarajan for Irregularities in Green Clearances during UPA-II." *Times of India*, September 10, 2017. https://timesofindia.indiatimes.com/india/cbi-books-former-environment-minister-jayanthi-natarajan-in-corruption-case/articleshow/60439030.cms.

Chaurey, R. "Labor Regulations and Contract Labor Use: Evidence from Indian Firms." *Journal of Development Economics* 114 (2015): 224–32.

Chemin, M. "Does Court Speed Shape Economic Activity? Evidence from a Court Reform in India." *Journal of Law and Economics* 28, no. 3 (2012): 460–85.

Chemin, M. "Do Judiciaries Matter for Development? Evidence from India." *Journal of Comparative Economics* 37, no. 3 (2009): 230–50.

Chibber, S. A. "Charting a New Path toward Gender Equality in India: From Religious Personal Laws to a Uniform Civil Code." *Indiana Law Journal* 83 (2008): 695–717.

Chikermane, G. "70 Policies: Monopolies and Restrictive Trade Practices Act, 1969." Observer Research Foundation, India Matters,. August 6, 2018. https://www.orfonline.org/expert-speak/43035-70-policies-monopolies-and-restrictive-trade-practices-act-1969/.

Chinchwadkarand, R., and V. Shekhar. "Evolution of Private Equity Regulations in Emerging Markets: A Case of India." *Journal of Private Equity* 20, no. 1 (2016): 38–44.

"Chipko Movement Turns 45, Google Celebrates with a Doodle." *Times of India*, Panache, March 26, 2018. https://economictimes.indiatimes.com/magazines/panache/chipko-movement-turns-45-google-celebrates-with-a-doodle/videoshow/63463018.cms.

Chitkara, R. "Pulling the Wool: The Indirect Reform of Religious Family Laws in India." *International Journal of Jurisprudence of the Family* 43 (2015): 43–65.

Choubey, K. N. "The State, Tribals, and the Law." *Social Change* 46, no. 3 (2016): 355–70.

Choudhary, P. K. "Land Reforms in Bihar: Need for a Fresh Appraisal." In *Land Reforms in India: Bihar—Institutional Constraints*, edited by B. N. Yugandhar and K. G. Iyer, 24–33. New Delhi: Sage, 1993.

Choudhry, R. N. *Law of Forests in India*. 1999. Reprint, New Delhi: Orient, 2002.

Chowdhury, I. R., and P. R. Chowdhury. "Holdout and Eminent Domain in Land Acquisition." *Indian Economic Review* 51, no. 1/2 (2016): 1–19.

Cole, S. "Fixing Market Failures or Fixing Elections? Agricultural Credit in India." *American Economic Journal: Applied Economics* 1, no. 1 (2009): 219–50.

Conning, J. H., and J. A. Robinson. "Property Rights and the Political Organization of Agriculture." *Journal of Development Economics* 82, no. 2 (2007): 416–47.

Dandekar, V. M., and G. J. Khudanpur. *Working of the Bombay Tenancy Act, 1948: Report of Investigation*. Poona: Sangam Press, 1957.

Danyal, K. Y. "Land Acquisition in India- Past and Present." http://docs.manupatra.in/newsline/articles/Upload/FF6D173D-E5C-4954-A73A-9D77708DD9B6.pdf. Accessed on August 11, 2019 (no longer posted).

Das, D. K., H. Choudhury, and J. Singh. "Contract Labour (Regulation and Abolition) Act 1970 and Labour Market Flexibility: An Exploratory Assessment of Contract Labour Use in India's Formal Manufacturing." Working

Paper of Indian Council for Research on International Economic Relations, New Delhi, 2015.

Das, M., B. L. Mishra, D. Samanta, and B. Mishra. *Land Governance Assessment Framework for Bihar: Final Report.* Patna, Bihar: Chandrgupt Institute of Management, 2014.

Das Gupta, C. "Globalisation, Corporate Legal Liability and Big Business Houses in India." *Cambridge Journal of Economics* 34, no. 5 (2010): 895–913.

Dasgupta, B. "Sharecropping in West Bengal: From Independence to Operation Barga." *Economic and Political Weekly* 19, no. 26 (1984): A85–A96.

Dasgupta, M. "Public Interest Litigation for Labour: How the Indian Supreme Court Protects the Rights of India's Most Disadvantaged Workers." *Contemporary South Asia* 16, no. 2 (2008): 159–70.

Dattatri, S. "The Kudremukh Saga: A Triumph for Conservation." Conservation India, March 26, 2010. http://www.conservationindia.org/case-studies/the-kudremukh-saga-a-triumph-for-conservation-2.

Dattatri, S. "Silent Valley: A People's Movement That Saved a Forest." Conservation India, September 25, 2015. http://www.conservationindia.org/case-studies/silent-valley-a-peoples-movement-that-saved-a-forest.

Debroy, B. "Legislation on Forests in India Have a Colonial and Complicated Legacy: Bibek Debroy." *Financial Express*, January 11, 2018. https://www.financialexpress.com/opinion/legislation-on-forests-in-india-have-a-colonial-and-complicated-legacy-bibek-debroy/1010169/.

Deininger, K., and A. Goyal. *Going Digital: Credit Effects of Land Registry Computerization in India (English).* Agricultural and Rural Development (ARD) Case Study. Washington, DC: World Bank, 2012.

Deininger, K., A. Goyal, and H. Nagarajan. "Women's Inheritance Rights and Intergenerational Transmission of Resources in India." *Journal of Human Resources* 48, no. 1 (2013): 114–41.

Deininger, K., S. Jin, and H. K. Nagarajan. "Efficiency and Equity Impacts of Rural Land Rental Restrictions: Evidence from India." *European Economic Review* 52, no. 5 (2008): 892–918.

Deininger, K., and Y. Liu. "Economic and Social Impacts of an Innovative Self-Help Group Model in India." *World Development* 43 (2013): 149–63.

Desai, R. "India's Data Localization Remains a Key Challenge for Foreign Companies." *Forbes India*, April 30, 2019. https://www.forbes.com/sites/ronakdesai/2019/04/30/indias-data-localization-remains-a-key-challenge-for-foreign-companies/#5f37ecdbe0a3.

Deshpande, A. *The Grammar of Caste: Economic Discrimination in Contemporary India.* New Delhi: Oxford University Press, 2011.

Deshpande, A., and R. Ramachandran. "Traditional Hierarchies and Affirmative Action in a Globalizing Economy: Evidence from India." *World Development* 118 (2019): 63–78.

Dhavan, R. "Evicting 10 Million Tribals." *The Hindu*, September 20, 2002. https://www.thehindu.com/todays-paper/tp-national/tp-tamilnadu/evicting-10-million-tribals/article27870371.ece.

Divan, S., and A. Rosencranz. *Environmental Law and Policy in India: Cases, Materials, and Statutes*, 2nd ed. Delhi: Oxford University Press, 2001.

D'Monte, D. "Storm over Silent Valley." *India International Centre Quarterly* 9, no. 3/4 (1982): 288–97.

Down to Earth. "The Tendu Leaf." June 28, 2015. https://www.downtoearth.org.in/coverage/the-tendu-leaf-12528.

Drèze, J. "Famine Prevention in India." In *The Political Economy of Hunger*, vol. 2, edited by J. Drèze and A. Sen, 13–122. Oxford: Clarendon, 1990.

Drèze, J. *Sense and Solidarity: Jholawala Economics for Everyone*. Ranikhet: Permanent Black, 2017.

Drèze, J., M. Samson, and S. Singh, eds. *The Dam and the Nation: Displacement and Resettlement in the Narmada Valley*. Delhi: Oxford University Press, 1997.

D'Souza, P. "Decentralization and Local Government: The 'Second Wind' of Democracy in India." In *India's Living Constitution: Ideas, Practices, Controversies*, edited by Z. Hasan, E. Sridharan, and R. Sudarshan, 370–404. London: Anthem, 2005.

Dutta, S. "From Accommodation to Substantive Equality: Muslim Personal Law, Secular Law, and the Indian Constitution 1985–2015." *Asian Journal of Law and Society* 4, no. 2 (2017): 191–227.

Echeverri-Gent, J. *The State and the Poor: Public Policy and Political Development in India and the United States*. Berkeley: University Of California Press, 1993.

Economic Times Bureau. "RBI Removes 26% Interest Cap on MFI Loans." *Economic Times*, February 8, 2014. https://economictimes.indiatimes.com/news/economy/finance/rbi-removes-26-interest-rate-cap-on-mfi-loans/articleshow/30004542.cms?from=mdr.

"Evils of Managing Agency System: Indian Merchants' Chamber Views." *Times of India*, June 26, 1936.

Fagernas, S. "Labor Law, Judicial Efficiency, and Informal Employment in India." *Journal of Empirical Legal Studies* 7, no. 2 (2010): 282–321.

Fallon, P., and R. Lucas. "Job Security Regulations and the Dynamic Demand for Industrial Labour in India and Zimbabwe." *Journal of Development Economics* 40, no. 2 (1993): 241–75.

Fernandes, W. "Liberalisation and Development-Induced Displacement." *Social Change* 36, no.1 (2000): 109–23.

Financial Express Online. "This Portal by Yogi Adityanath Government Will Tighten the Noose around Land Mafia in Uttar Pradesh: Here Is How." *Financial Express*, June 24, 2017. https://www.financialexpress.com/india-news/

this-portal-by-yogi-adityanath-government-will-tighten-the-noose-around-land-mafia-in-uttar-pradesh-here-is-how/733857/.

Forest Research Institute. *One Hundred Years of Indian Forestry*. Vol. 2. Simla: Government of India Press, 1961.

Form, W., and F. C. Pampel. "Social Stratification and the Development of Urban Labor Markets in India." *Social Forces* 57, no. 1 (1978): 119–35.

Fyzee, A. A. A. "Recent Developments in Muhammadan Law in India, 1900–1960." *International and Comparative Law Quarterly* 46 (1964): 46–50.

Gadgil, M., and R. Guha. *This Fissured Land: An Ecological History of India*. New Delhi: Oxford University Press, 1992.

Galani, A., and N. Rehn. "Related Party Transactions: Empowering Boards and Minority Shareholders to Prevent Abuses." *National Law School of India Review* 22, no. 2 (2010): 29–58.

Galanter, M. "Law and Caste in Modern India." *Asian Survey* 3, no. 11 (1963): 544–59.

Gandhi, M. K. *Hind Swaraj or Indian Home Rule*. 1909. Reprint, Ahmedabad: Navjivan, 1938.

Gandhi, R. "Rural Cooperatives-Repositioning." Keynote speech at the National Conference of Cooperative Banks, Lucknow, February 9, 2016. https://www.bis.org/review/r160217a.pdf.

Geary, D. "The Decline of Bodh Gaya Math and Afterlife of Zamindari." *South Asian History and Culture* 4, no. 3 (2000): 366–83.

Ghatak, M., and P. Ghosh. "The Land Acquisition Bill: A Critique and a Proposal." *Economic and Political Weekly* 46, no. 41 (2011): 65–72.

Ghatak, M., and S. Roy. "Land Reform and Agricultural Productivity in India: A Review of the Evidence." *Oxford Review of Economic Policy* 23, no. 2 (2007): 251–69.

Ghatak, S. *Rural Money Markets in India*. Delhi: Macmillan, 1976.

Ghosh, J. "India's Rural Employment Programme Is Dying a Death of Funding Cuts." *Guardian*, February 5, 2015. https://www.theguardian.com/global-development/2015/feb/05/india-rural-employment-funding-cuts-mgnrega.

Ghosh, S. "Corporate Investment and Political Federalism: Does Judicial Efficiency Matter?" *Indian Economic Review* 35, no. 1/2 (2018): 263–85.

Ghosh, S. "The Environment." In *Regulation in India: Design, Capacity, Performance*, edited by D. Kapur and M. Khosla, 203–27. London: Bloomsbury, 2019.

Gine, X., and M. Kanz. "The Economic Effects of a Borrower Bailout: Evidence from an Emerging Market." *Review of Financial Studies* 31, no. 5 (2018): 1752–83.

Global Slavery Index. "Global Slavery Index: India." Global Slavery Index. https://www.globalslaveryindex.org/2018/findings/country-studies/india/.

Gokhale, K. "A Global Surge in Tiny Loans Spurs Credit Bubble in a Slum."

Wall Street Journal, August 13, 2009. http://online.wsj.com/article/SB125012112518027581.html.

Gonsalves, C. "Judicial Failure in Land Acquisition for Corporations." *Economic and Political Weekly* 45, no. 32 (2010): 37–42.

Gopakumar, K. C. "Provision in Law against Moneylenders Rarely Enforced." *The Hindu*, updated May 23, 2016. https://www.thehindu.com/news/national/kerala/provision-in-law-against-moneylenders-rarely-enforced/article6024791.ece.

Gormley, T., N. Gupta, and A. Jha. "Quiet Life No More? Corporate Bankruptcy and Bank Competition." *Journal of Financial and Quantitative Analysis* 53, no. 2 (2018): 581–611.

Goswami, B., and M. P. Bezbaruah. "Incidence, Forms and Determinants of Tenancy in the Agrarian Set-up of the Assam Plains." *Economic and Political Weekly* 62, no. 2 (2013): 60–68.

Goswami, O. "Corporate Governance in India." In *Taking Action against Corruption in Asia and the Pacific*, edited by Asian Development Bank, 85–106. Manila: Asian Development Bank, 2002.

Goswami, O., and India, Ministry of Finance. *Report of the Committee on Industrial Sickness and Corporate Restructuring*. New Delhi: Ministry of Finance, 1993.

Government of Gujarat. "Right to Fair Compensation and Transparency in Land Acquisition, Rehabilitation and Resettlement (Gujarat Amendment) Act, 2016 (Gujarat Act No. 12) of 2016," August 8, Bare Acts Live, 2016, http://www.bareactslive.com/Guj/guj373.htm.

Government of Maharashtra. *Maharashtra State Gazetteers: Kolhapur District*. Bombay: Directorate of Government Printing, 1960. https://gazetteers.maharashtra.gov.in/cultural.maharashtra.gov.in/english/gazetteer/KOLHAPUR/home.html.

Greenstone, M., and R. Hanna. "Environmental Regulations, Air and Water Pollution, and Infant Mortality in India." *American Economic Review* 104, no. 10 (2014): 3038–72.

Greenstone, M., S. Harish, R. Pande, and A. Sudarshan. "The Solvable Problem of Air Pollution in India." Paper prepared for the India Policy Forum, New Delhi, July 2017. http://www.ncaer.org/Events/IPF-2017/IPF-2017-Paper-Greenstone-Harish-Pande-Sudarshan-Conf-version.pdf.

Grove, R. *Green Imperialism: Colonial Expansion, Tropical Island Edens and the Origins of Environmentalism, 1600–1800*. Cambridge: Cambridge University, 1995.

Guha, R. "Forestry in British and Post-British India: A Historical Analysis." *Economic and Political Weekly* 18, no. 44 (1983): 1882–96.

Guha, R. "Forestry in British and Post-British India: A Historical Analysis." *Economic and Political Weekly* 18, no. 45/46 (1983): 1940–47.

Guha, R. *India after Gandhi: A History of the World's Largest Democracy*. New York: Harper Perennial, 2008.

Guha, R. "Savaging the Civilized: Verrier Elwin and the Tribal Question in Late Colonial India." Special issue, *Economic and Political Weekly* 31, no. 35–37 (1996): 2375–89

Guha, R. *The Unquiet Woods*. 1989. Reprint, New Delhi: Oxford University Press, 2001.

Gulzar, S. N. Haas, and B. Pasquale, "Does Political Affirmative Action Work and for Whom? Theory and Evidence on India's Scheduled Areas." *American Political Science Review* 114, no. 4 (2020): 1230–46.

Gupta, C. D. "Globalisation, Corporate Legal Liability and Big Business Houses in India." *Cambridge Journal of Economics* 34, no. 5 (2010): 895–913.

Gupta, D., and B. Paul. "Chhattisgarh's 'No-Go Area' for Coal Mining Faces the Prospect of Being Opened Up." *The Wire*, October 5, 2018. https://thewire.in/rights/chhattisgarh-coal-mining-hasdeo-arand.

Gupta, S. "Environmental Benefits and Cost Savings through Market-Based Instruments: An Application Using State-Level Data from India." Centre For Development Economics, Delhi School of Economics, Working Paper 111, 2002.

Gupta, S. "Environmental Policy and Governance in a Federal Framework: Perspectives from India". In *Environmental Policies in Asia: Perspectives from Seven Asian Countries*, edited by J. Huang and S. Gupta, 15–42. New Jersey: World Scientific, 2014.

Hasan, R., D. Mitra, and K. V. Ramaswamy. "Trade Reforms, Labor Regulations, and Labor-Demand Elasticities: Empirical Evidence from India." *Review of Economics and Statistics* 89, no. 3 (2007): 466–81.

Hart, H. C., and R. J. Herring. "Political Conditions for Land Reform: Kerala and Maharashtra." In *Land Tenure and Peasant in South Asia*, edited by R. E. Frykenberg, 233–93. New Delhi: Orient Longman, 1977.

Henningham, S. "Bureaucracy and Control in India's Great Landed Estates: The Raj Darbhanga of Bihar, 1879 to 1850." *Modern Asian Studies* 17, no. 1 (1983): 35–55.

Herring, R. J. "Abolition of Landlordism in Kerala: A Redistribution of Privilege." *Economic and Political Weekly* 15, no. 26 (1980): A59–A69.

Herring, R. J. *Land to the Tiller: The Political Economy of Agrarian Reform in South Asia*. New Haven, CT: Yale University Press, 1983.

"History." National Green Tribunal. http://www.greentribunal.gov.in/history.aspx. Accessed December 26, 2018 (no longer posted).

Hnatkovska, V., A. Lahiri, and S. Paul. "Castes and Labor Mobility." *American Economic Journal: Applied Economics* 4, no. 2 (2012): 274–307.

Hoda, A., and P. Terway. "Credit Policy for Agriculture in India: An Evaluation." Indian Council for Research on International Economic Relations, Working Paper 302, June 2015.

India, Business Portal. "Closing or Changing a Business: Regulatory Requirements: Board for Industrial and Financial Reconstruction (BIFR)." https://archive.india.gov.in/business/closing_business/bifr.php Accessed August 19, 2019 (no longer posted).

India, Congress Agrarian Reforms Committee. *Report*. 2nd ed. New Delhi: All India Congress Committee, 1951.

India, Department of Cooperation. "Karnataka Money Lenders and Pawn Brokers Act 1961 and Rules 1965." Sahakara Sindhu, Department of Cooperation, Government of Karnataka. http://sahakara.kar.gov.in/faqML&PB.html.

India, Department of Economic Affairs, Ministry of Finance. *Report of the Company Law Committee*. New Delhi: Department of Economic Affairs, 1952.

India, Department of Revenue and Agriculture. *Selection of Papers on Agricultural Indebtedness and the Restriction of the Power to Alienate Interests in Land*. Vol. 3. Simla: Government Central Print Office, 1898.

India, Land Reforms Implementation Committee. *Implementation of Land Reforms: A Review by the Land Reforms Implementation Committee of the National Development Council*. New Delhi: Planning Commission, 1966.

India, Ministry of Labour and Employment. "Rehabilitation of Bonded Labour Scheme-2016." Press Information Bureau, December 5, 2016. http://pib.nic.in/newsite/PrintRelease.aspx?relid=154895. Accessed June 27, 2019 (no longer posted).

India, Ministry of Rural Development. "Draft National Land Reforms Policy." July, 2013.

India, Ministry of Tribal Affairs. "The Provisions of the Panchayats (Extension to Scheduled Areas) Act, 1996, No. 40 of 1996," December 24, 1996. tribal.nic.in/actRules/PESA.pdf.

India, Ministry of Tribal Affairs. *Report of the High-Level Committee on Socio-economic, Health, and Educational Status of Tribal Communities of India*. New Delhi: Ministry of Tribal Affairs, 2014.

India, National Crime Records Bureau. *Accidental Deaths and Suicides in India*. New Delhi: Ministry of Home Affairs: 2015.

India, Planning Commission. *The New India: Progress through Democracy*. New York: Macmillan, 1958.

India, Planning Commission. *Report of the Task Force on Agrarian Relations*. New Delhi: Planning Commission, 1973.

India, Planning Commission. *A Report on Bonded Labour Rehabilitation Scheme under Centrally Sponsored Bonded Labour System (Abolition) Act, 1976 in the States of Madhya Pradesh, Orissa, Rajasthan, Tamil Nadu and Uttar Pradesh*. New Delhi: Planning Commission 2010.

India, Press Information Bureau. "Land Acquisition for Steel Plants." March 18,

2013. http://pib.gov.in/newsite/PrintRelease.aspx?relid=93899. Accessed August 16, 2019 (no longer posted).

India Environment Portal. "Judgement of the National Green Tribunal Regarding Ganga River Pollution." India Environmental Portal, July 13, 2017. http://www.indiaenvironmentportal.org.in/content/445260/judgement-of-the-national-green-tribunal-regarding-ganga-river-pollution-13072017/.

Indian National Congress, Agrarian Reforms Committee. *Report of the Congress Agrarian Reforms Committee*, 2nd ed. New Delhi: All-India Congress Committee, 1951.

Indo-Asian News Service. "UP: Azam Khan Declared Land Mafia by Yogi Adityanath Government." *India Today*, July 19, 2019. https://www.indiatoday.in/india/story/up-azam-khan-declared-land-mafia-by-yogi-adityanath-government-1571131-2019-07-19.

InforMEA. *Samatha vs State Of A.P. And Ors*, July 11, 1997. InforMEA. https://www.informea.org/en/court-decision/samatha-vs-state-ap-and-ors.

"Insolvency and Bankruptcy Code, 2016." India Brand Equity Foundation, Brand India, May 2016. https://www.ibef.org/research/india-study/insolvency-and-bankruptcy-code.

Islam, M. M. "The Punjab Land Alienation Act and the Professional Moneylenders." *Modern Asian Studies* 29, no. 2 (1995): 271–91.

Iyer, G. "Evaluation of Land Ceiling Measures in Bihar." In *Land Reforms in India: Bihar—Institutional Constraints*, edited by B. N. Yugandhar and K. Gopal Iyer, 87–118. New Delhi: Sage, 1993.

Iyer, L., T. Khanna, and A. Varshney. "Caste and Entrepreneurship in India." *Economic and Political Weekly* 48, no. 6 (2013): 52–60.

Jacob, K. T. *Tiller Gets the Land in Kerala*. New Delhi: Communist Party of India, 1970.

Jafri, S. S. A. "Sunni Auqaf and Waqf Board of Uttar Pradesh: In Need of Rejuvenation." *Economic and Political Weekly* 32, no. 25 (1997): 1450–51.

Jagannathan, R. "Forest Rights Act Needs to Go: Tribals Aren't Part of a Tiger Reserve." *Firstpost*, September 12, 2014. https://www.firstpost.com/india/the-forest-rights-act-needs-to-go-tribals-arent-part-of-a-tiger-reserve-1707317.

Jagannathan, R. *The Jobs Crisis in India*. New Delhi: Macmillian 2018.

Jagannathan, R. "UPA Land Act Is Creating 20,000 Rural Crorepatis Every Year and Making Infrastructure Unviable." *Swarajya*. January 17, 2018. https://swarajyamag.com/ideas/upa-land-act-is-creating-20000-rural-crorepatis-a-year-and-making-infrastructure-less-viable.

Jain, K. "Health Insurance in India: The Rashtriya Swasthya Bima Yojana." WIEGO Policy Brief (Social Protection) 10, September 2012.

Jamrisko, M. "The World's Dirtiest Air Is in India." *Bloomberg*, Business, March 4, 2019. https://www.bloomberg.com/news/articles/2019-03-05/the-world-s-dirtiest-air-is-in-india-where-pollution-costs-lives.

Januzzi, F. T. *Agrarian Crisis in India: The Case of Bihar.* Austin: University of Texas Press, 1974.

Jayakumar, M., and A. H. Vardhan. "Software Patents in the Indian Framework: An Economic of Problems and Prospects." *National Law School of India Review* 20, no. 2 (2008): 220–28.

Jha, R. "Strengthening India's Urban Informal Economy: The Case of Street Vending." Observer Research Foundation, Issue Briefs and Special Reports, July 25, 2018. https://www.orfonline.org/research/strengthening-urban-indias-informal-economy-the-case-of-street-vending/.

Jha, S. "Govt Drops Move to Make Hire and Fire Easier." Rediff, February 10, 2018. https://www.rediff.com/business/report/govt-drops-move-to-make-hire-and-fire-easier/20180210.htm.

Jha, S. "Labour Law Changes in UP, MP: A Bigger Pandemic in the Offing." *Business Standard*, May 8, 2020.

Jodhka, S. S. *Caste in Contemporary India*, 2nd ed. Abington: Routledge, 2017.

Jodhka, S. S. "Caste and Untouchability in Rural Punjab." *Economic and Political Weekly* 37, no. 19 (2002): 1813–23.

Johnson, J. "Lunch with the Great Leveler." *Financial Times*, July 21, 2006.

Joshi, P. C. *Land Reforms in India: Trends and Perspectives.* Bombay: Allied, 1975.

Joshi, S. "Ganga Pollution Cases: Impact on Infant Mortality." Ideas for India, February 26, 2016. https://www.ideasforindia.in/topics/environment/ganga-pollution-cases-impact-on-infant-mortality.html.

Kabir, A. "Completion Laws and the Indian Economy." *National Law School of India Review* 23, no. 1 (2011): 1–8.

Kali, R., and J. Sarkar. "Diversification and Tunneling: Evidence from Indian Business Groups." *Journal of Comparative Economics* 39, no. 3 (2011): 349–67.

Kang, N., and N. Nayar. "The Evolution of Corporate Bankruptcy Law in India." *Money and Finance* (2003/2004): 37–58.

Kannan, K. P. "The Welfare Fund Model of Social Security for Informal Sector Workers: The Kerala Experience." Working Paper 332. Thiruvananthapuram: Centre for Development Studies, 2002.

Kapur, D., C. B. Prasad, L. Pritchett, and D. S. Babu. "Rethinking Inequality: Dalits in Uttar Pradesh in the Market Reform Era." *Economic and Political Weekly* 45, no. 35 (2010): 39–49.

Karat, B. "A Glass Half Empty for Adivasis." *The Hindu*, May 1, 2015. https://www.thehindu.com/opinion/op-ed/a-glass-half-empty-for-adivasis/article7162260.ece.

Karthik, M., and A. Kodiveri, "The Great Indian Land Grab Being Carried Out in the Name of Compulsory Afforestation." *The Wire*, January 30,

2018. https://thewire.in/environment/great-indian-land-grab-carried-name-compensatory-afforestation.

Katju, A. "Changes in Labour Laws Are Unconstitutional." *Indian Express*, May 19, 2020.

Kaveri, V. S. *Financial Analysis of Company Mergers in Mergers*. Bombay: Himalaya, 1986.

Kennedy, V. D. "The Conceptual and Legislative Framework of Labor Relations in India." *Industrial and Labor Relations Review* (1958): 487–505.

Khanna, S. "Boundaries of Forest Land: The Godavarman Case and Beyond." In *Democratizing Forest Governance in India*, edited by S. Lele and A. Menon, 225–60. New Delhi: Oxford University Press, 2014.

Khanna, S. "Exclude and Protect: A Report on the WWF Case on Wildlife Conservation in the Supreme Court of India." New Delhi: SRUTI, 2008.

Khasnabis, R. "Operation Barga: A Further Note." *Economic and Political Weekly* 17, no. 36 (1982): 1468–72.

Kishwar, M. "Codified Hindu Law: Myth or Reality." *Economic and Political Weekly* 29, no. 33 (1994): 2145–54.

Kochar, A. "The Distributive Consequences of Social Banking: A Microempirical Analysis of the Indian Experience." *Economic Development and Cultural Change* 59 (2011): 251–80.

Kotwal, A., K. P. Krishnan, T. N. Ninan, and I. Patnaik. "141 Panel Discussion: The Way Forward for the Indian Economy." Ideas for India, January 29, 2019. https://www.ideasforindia.in/topics/miscellany/the-way-forward-for-the-indian-economy.html.

Kranton, R., and A. V. Swamy. "The Hazards of Piecemeal Reform: British Civil Courts and the Credit Market in Colonial India." *Journal of Development Economics* 58, no. 1 (1999): 1–24.

Krishnan, E. "Private Speculations and the Public Interest: N.C. Kelkar's Land Acquisition Bill." *Social-Legal Review* 78 (2012): 78–105.

Kumar, D. *Defending the Green Realm: The Forest Conservation Act of India in Theory and Practice*. Bangalore: Institute of Social and Economic Change, 2015.

Kumar, H., and R. Somanathan. "The Right to Shelter: An Evaluation of the Land Transfer Program to Mahadalits." IGC project report, May 2016.

Kumar, P. S. "Law against Lenders Rarely Enforced." *Hans India*, August 22, 2017. https://www.thehansindia.com/posts/index/Hans/2017-08-22/Law-against-lenders-rarely-enforced/320732.

Kumar, R. B., and P. Rajib. "Characteristics of Merging Firms in India: An Empirical Examination." *Vikalpa* 32, no.1 (2007): 27–44.

Kumar, V. "Hollowness of Relief Laws." *Cochin University Law Review* (1997): 100–111.

Kundapura, V. "Crackdown on Moneylenders: 40 Arrested in Kolar, Chickballapur. *The Hindu*, July 17, 2015

Kurzman, D. *A Killing Wind: Inside Union Carbide and the Bhopal Catastrophe*. New York: McGraw-Hill, 1987.

Law Commission of India. *Property Rights of Women: Proposed Reforms under the Hindu Law*. New Delhi: Government Press, 2000.

Leelakrishnan, P. "Law and Sustainable Development in India." *Journal of Energy and Natural Resources Law* 9, no. 3 (1991): 193–206.

Lele, S., and A. Menon, eds. *Democratizing Forest Governance in India*. New Delhi: Oxford University Press, 2014.

Lele, S., and V. Saberwal. "Locating Local Elites in Negotiating Access to Forests: Havik Brahmins and the Colonial State 1860–1920." *Studies in History*, n.s., 20, 2 (2004): 273–303.

Levien, M. *Dispossession without Development: Land Grabs in Neoliberal India*. New Delhi: Oxford University Press, 2018.

Lewis, B., N. Agrawal, C. Gadi, D. Goyal, J. Kulkarni, A. Tawakley, S. Viswanathan, et al. *India: The Growth Imperative*. Report, McKinsey Global Institute, October 1, 2001. http://www.mckinsey.com/insights/india/growth_imperative_for_india.

Lilienfeld-Toal, U., D. Mookherjee, and S. Visaria. "The Distributive Impact of Reforms in Credit Enforcement: Evidence from Indian Debt Recovery Tribunals." *Econometrica* 80, no. 2 (2012): 497–558.

"Limaye Lashes Out at Managing Agents." *Times of India*, November 17, 1967.

Lindsay, J., K. Deininger, and T. Hilhorst. "Compulsory Land Acquisition in Developing Countries: Shifting Paradigm or Entrenched Legacy?." In *Eminent Domain: A Comparative Perspective*, edited by I. Kim, H. Lee, and I. Somin, 118–55. Cambridge: Cambridge University Press, 2017.

Liu, J. "Compulsory Licensing and Anti-Evergreening: Interpreting the TRIPS Flexibilities in Sections 84 and 3(d) of the Indian Patents Act." *Harvard International Law Journal* 56, no.1 (2015): 207–15.

Maharashtra Forest Department. "Brief Review and Statistical Analysis of Forest Offence Cases during Last Quarter-Century (25 Years)." N.d. https://mahaforest.gov.in/report_file/1424264710Report%20-%20Analysis%20of%20Forest%20Offence%20Cases.pdf.

Maharashtra Forest Department. *A Statistical Outline*. Nagpur: Office of the Principal Conservator, 2016.

"Managing Agency System." *Times of India*, March 24, 1955.

"Managing Agency System: Decline Noted." *Times of India*, March 13, 1964.

Mandke, A. "Land Acquisition for 'Companies': Part II or Part VII?" *PL WebJour* 15 (2004). http://www.ebc-india.com/lawyer/articles/850.htm.

Mani, S. "Dimensions of India's Intellectual Property Right System: How Many

Patents Are Commercially Exploited in India?" Working Paper of Centre for Development Studies. Trivandrum: Centre for Development Studies, 2018.

Mani, S., S. Chaudhuri, V. K. Unni, C. Pray, and L. Nagarajan. "TRIPS Compliance of National Patent Regimes and Domestic Innovative Activity: The Indian Experience." In *TRIPS Compliance, National Patent Regimes and Innovation*, edited by S. Mani and R. R. Nelson, 57–112. Cheltenham: Edward Elgar, 2013.

Mann, H. "Review of the General Report of the Committee of Direction: All India Rural Credit Survey." *Indian Economic Review* 3, no. 4 (1957): 76–80.

Mathew, S. J. "Hostile Takeovers in India: New Prospects, Challenges, and Regulatory Opportunities." *Columbia Business Law Review* 3 (2007): 800–843.

Mehrotra, N. N. "Patents Act and Technological Self-Reliance: The Indian Pharmaceutical Industry." *Economic and Political Weekly* 24, no. 19 (1989): 1059–64.

Mehta, D., and S. Samanta. "Mergers and Acquisitions: Nature and Significance." *Vikalpa* 22, no. 4 (1997): 31–38.

Mehta, M. C. *In the Public Interest: Landmark Judgements and Orders of the Supreme Court of India on Environmental and Human Rights*. New Delhi: Prakriti, 2009.

Menon, M., and Uzramma. *A Frayed History: The Journey of Cotton in India*. Delhi: Oxford University Press, 2018.

Menon, S. "Microfinance Industry Is out of an Unprecedent[ed] Crisis, Thanks to Regulations, Diligent Borrowers." *Economic Times*. April 19, 2016. https://economictimes.indiatimes.com/industry/banking/finance/microfinance-industry-is-out-of-an-unprecedent-crisis-thanks-to-regulations-diligent-borrowers/articleshow/51886097.cms.

Merillat, H. C. L. *Land and the Constitution in India*. New York: Columbia University Press, 1970.

Metters, R., and R. Verma, "History of Offshoring Knowledge Services." *Journal of Operations Management* 26, no. 2 (2008): 141–47.

Ministry of Tribal Affairs, Government of India. *Forest Rights Act, 2006: Act, Rules, and Guidelines*. 2014. https://tribal.nic.in/FRA/data/FRARulesBook.pdf.

Mishra, P., and R. Suhag. "Land Records and Titles in India." PRS India, September 2017. http://www.prsindia.org/policy/discussion-papers/land-records-and-titles-india.

Mishra, S. "The Economics of the MGNREGS." *Livemint*, February 7, 2016. https://www.livemint.com/Sundayapp/ueWD2KvNelmsOGEupZND6K/The-economics-of-the-MGNREGS.html.

Mitra, A. "Chipko: An Unfinished Mission." *Down to Earth*, June 7, 2015. https://www.downtoearth.org.in/coverage/chipko-an-unfinished-mission-30883.

Mitra, B. B. *Indian Succession Act*, 14th ed., New Delhi: Eastern Law House, 2009.

Mody, N. B. "The Press in India: The Shah Bano Judgment and Its Aftermath." *Asian Survey* 27, no. 8 (1987): 935–53.

Mody, Z. *Ten Judgments That Changed India*. New Delhi: Shobha De Books, 2013.

Mohanty, P. "Wages Remain below the Minimum Wages, Yearly Hikes Too Little since 2017." *India Today*, April 8, 2019. https://www.indiatoday.in/india/story/mgnrega-wages-remain-below-the-minimum-wages-yearly-hikes-too-little-since-2017-1496629-2019-04-08.

Mondal, S. S., and V. Pingali. "Competition and Intellectual Property Policies in the Indian Pharmaceutical Sector." *Vikalpa* 42, no. 2 (2017): 61–79.

Morris, M. D. "Labor Discipline, Trade Unions, and the State in India." *Journal of Political Economy* 63, no. 3 (1955): 293–308.

Mundy, S. "Why India's Bankruptcy Law Is Reshaping Big Business." *Financial Times*, May 27, 2018.

"Muslim Outfits Allege Takeover of Prime Wakf Land." *Times of India*, May 10, 2007.

MyLaw. "Justice Must Be for the Common Man." YouTube video, 8:02. August 2, 2011. https://www.youtube.com/watch?v=OrXO8CAi98E.

Nagaraj, R. "Industrial Policy and Performance since 1980: Which Way Now?" *Economic and Political Weekly* 38, no. 35 (2003): 3707–15.

Naidu, N. *Report of the Economist for Enquiry into Rural Indebtedness*. Madras: Government of Madras Press, 1946.

Nair, K. N., and V. Menon. "Lease Farming in Kerala: Findings from Micro Level Studies." *Economic and Political Weekly* 41, no. 26 (2006): 2732–38.

Nair, R. "65% Boost for MGNREGA, Relief for Companies from IBC—Final Part of Modi Covid Package." *The Print*, May 17, 2020. https://theprint.in/economy/65-boost-for-mgnrega-relief-for-companies-from-ibc-final-part-of-modi-govt-covid-package/423486/.

Nanda, P. K. "BMS Slams Govt Bid to Merge Labour Laws." *Livemint*, November 23, 2018. https://www.livemint.com/Politics/PD0AOZPPTPAZmYHwqptuQP/BMS-slams-govt-bid-to-merge-labour-laws.html.

Nanda, P. K. "ILO Expresses 'Deep Concern' over Labour Law Changes, Appeals to PM Narendra Modi." *Livemint*, May 25, 2020. https://www.livemint.com/news/india/ilo-expresses-deep-concern-over-labour-law-changes-appeals-to-pm-narendra-modi-11590394493866.html.

"The Nandigram Story till Now." *Livemint*, March 19, 2007. https://www.livemint.com/Politics/I1CAfbH2Und58UkVckctVP/The-Nandigram-story-till-now.html.

Naolekar, P. P. "Judicial Activism and Patent Law." *National Law School of India Review* 18, no. 1 (2006): 119–30.

Narain, U., and A. Krupnick. "The Impact of Delhi's CNG Program on Air Quality." RFF Discussion Paper 07–06, 2007. https://papers.ssrn.com/sol3/papers.cfm?abstract_id=969727.

Narang, P., and Y. Goyal. "Street Vendors Act 2014: State Compliance Index 2017." Centre for Civil Society. New Delhi: Mehra Impressions, 2017.

Nath, M. "Do Institutional Transplants Succeed? Regulating Raiffeisen Cooperatives in South India, 1930–60." *Business History Review* (forthcoming).

Nath, R. "Managing Agency System." *Times of India*, April 30, 1951.

National Association of Street Vendors of India. "Historic Street Vendors Law Comes into Force on May Day." National Association of Street Vendors of India. N.d. http://nasvinet.org/newsite/historic-street-vendors-law-comes-into-force-on-may-day/.

Nayak, G. "For-Profit MFIs Worse Than Money Lenders." *Economic Times*. November 23, 2010. https://economictimes.indiatimes.com/opinion/interviews/for-profit-mfis-worse-than-money-lenders/articleshow/6973551.cms.

Newbigin, E. *The Hindu Family and the Emergence of Modern India: Law, Citizenship and Community*. Cambridge: Cambridge University Press, 2013.

"New Land Acquisition Act Will Weaken Maoist Ideology: Ramesh." *The Hindu*, October 2, 2013. https://www.thehindu.com/todays-paper/tp-national/new-land-acquisition-act-will-weaken-maoist-ideology-ramesh/article5191902.ece.

Niaz, N. S., and Z. Soman. "Muslim Women's Views on Muslim Personal Law." *Economic and Political Weekly* 50, no. 51 (2015): 83–86.

Noronha, E. "Liberalisation and Industrial Relations." *Economic and Political Weekly* 31, no. 8 (1996): L14–L20.

Oak, M., and A. V. Swamy. "Only Twice as Much: A Rule for Regulating Lenders." *Economic Development and Cultural Change* 58, no. 4 (2010): 775–803.

Pal, M. "Rehabilitation of the 'Project Affected': Eminent Domain and Just Compensation." In *Law and Economics*, vol. 2, *Practice*, edited by S. Gangopadhyay and V. Santhakumar, 1–18. New Delhi: Sage, 2013.

Panagariya, A. *India: The Emerging Giant*. New York: Oxford University Press, 2010.

Pananchikal, J. "Why the Aravalli Forest Range Is the Most Degraded Zone in India." *Outdoor Journal*, September 20, 2018. https://www.outdoorjournal.com/featured/environment/aravalli-forest-range-degraded-zone-india/.

Papola, T. S., and J. Pais. "Debate on Labour Market Reforms in India: A Case of Misplaced Focus." *Indian Journal of Labour Economics* 50, no. 2 (2007): 183–200.

Pargal, S., and M. Mani, "Citizen Activism, Environmental Regulation, and the Location of Industrial Plants: Evidence from India." *Economic Development and Cultural Change* 48, no. 4 (2000): 829–46.

Parsheera, S., A. Shah, and A. Bose. "Competition Issues in India's Online

Economy." National Institute of Public Finance and Policy Working Paper, New Delhi, 2017.

Pathak, A. *Contested Domains: The State, Peasants, and Forests in Contemporary India*. New Delhi: Sage in association with Book Review Literary Trust, 1994.

Pathak, A. *Law, Strategies, Ideologies: Legislating Forests in Colonial India*. New Delhi: Oxford University Press, 2019.

Patil, S. G. *Report of the High-Powered Committee on Cooperatives*. New Delhi: Ministry of Agriculture, 2009.

Patnaik, S. "Recalling Arvind Panagariya's Unsuccessful Labours." *The Wire*, August 6, 2017. https://thewire.in/economy/arvind-panagariya-labour-law-reforms.

Paulini, T. *Agrarian Movements and Reforms in India: The Case of Kerala*. Saarbrucken: Breitenbach, 1979.

Pradhan, N. C. "Persistence of Informal Credit in Rural India: Evidence from All India Debt and Investment Survey and Beyond." RBI Working Paper Series, 2013.

PTI. "Land Acquisition a Difficult Task in India: Panagariya." *Times of India*, August 1, 2015. https://timesofindia.indiatimes.com/india/Land-acquisition-a-difficult-task-in-India-Panagariya/articleshow/48308944.cms.

PTI. "Land Act Bit Draconian, Frame Own Laws: Arvind Panagariya to States." *Economic Times*, September 10, 2015. https://economictimes.indiatimes.com/news/economy/policy/land-act-bit-draconian-frame-own-laws-arvind-panagariya-to-states/articleshow/48901548.cms.

PTI. "Naxalism Biggest Threat to Internal Security: Manmohan." *The Hindu*, updated November 11, 2016. https://www.thehindu.com/news/national/Naxalism-biggest-threat-to-internal-security-Manmohan/article16302952.ece.

PTI. "President Ram Nath Kovind Likely to Nod for Karnataka Land Reform Amendment Bill in Day or Two." *Financial Express*, October 10, 2017. https://www.financialexpress.com/india-news/president-ram-nath-kovind-likely-to-nod-for-karnataka-land-reform-amendment-bill-in-day-or-two/889084/.

PTI. "Sebi Widens Probe into GDR Misuse for Routing Black Money." *Economic Times*, April 3, 2017. https://economictimes.indiatimes.com/markets/stocks/news/sebi-widens-probe-into-gdr-misuse-for-routing-black-money/articleshow/57993527.cms.

PTI. "Supreme Court Shocked over Disappearance of 31 Hills in Aravalli Area of Rajashan." Indian Express, October 23, 2018. https://indianexpress.com/article/india/supreme-court-shocked-over-disappearance-of-31-hills-in-aravalli-area-of-rajasthan-5414912/.

Punjab, Board of Economic Inquiry. *Agricultural Statistics of the (British) Punjab*. Lahore: Board of Economic Inquiry, n.d.

PwC. "India: AAR Rules That Tax Treaty Relief Is Available at Withholding Stage." PricewaterhouseCoopers, February 13, 2018. https://www.pwc.com/gx/en/services/people-organisation/publications/assets/pwc-indian-ruling-that-treaty-relief-is-available-for-withholding.pdf.

PwC. "Mergers and Acquisitions: The Evolving Indian Landscape." PricewaterhouseCoopers, 2018. https://www.pwc.in/assets/pdfs/trs/mergers-and-acquisitions-tax/mergers-and-acquisitions-the-evolving-indian-landscape.pdf.

Qureshi, A. I. *The Future of the Cooperative Movement in India*. Madras: Oxford University Press, 1947.

Raghavan, R. "Permanent Establishment Issues in Indian Outsourcing Transactions." *National Law School of India Review* 24, no. 1 (2012): 10–21.

Raghavan, V. S. "Reference to BIFR of Sickness Will Halt Proceedings before the DRT." Induslaw, Infolex Newsalert, December 2014. https://induslaw.com/publications/pdf/alerts-2014/SICA-Info-alert-new.pdf.

Raianu, M. "A Mass of Anomalies: Land, Law, and Sovereignty in an Indian Company Town." *Comparative Studies in Society and History* 60, no. 2 (2018): 367–89.

Rajagopalan, S. "India Needs to Trust Its Farmers and Set Them Free." *Livemint*, updated March 20, 2018. https://www.livemint.com/Opinion/Ur1gpECTWdd3VnbpuuUD9O/India-needs-to-trust-its-farmers-and-set-them-free.html.

Rajagopalan, S. "Our Founders and the Right to Property." *Pragati*, July 24, 2017. https://www.thinkpragati.com/opinion/1849/founding-fathers-right-property/.

Ramanathan, U. "Understanding Reforms in Environment, Land and Labour Laws in India." Talk presented at the Madras Institute of Development Studies, Chennai, January 12, 2015. https://chaikadai.wordpress.com/2015/01/18/understanding-reforms-in-environment-land-and-labour-laws-in-india.

Ramanathan, U. "A Word on Eminent Domain." In *Displaced by Development: Confronting Marginalisation and Gender Injustice*, edited by L. Mehta, 133–45. New Delhi: Sage, 2009.

Ramaswamy, K. V. "Liberalization, Outsourcing and Industrial Labour Markets in India: Some Preliminary Results." In *Labour Market and Institutions in India: 1990s and Beyond*, edited by S. Uchikawa, 155–78. New Delhi: Manohar, 2003.

Ramesh, J. and M. A. Khan. *Legislating for Justice: The Making of the 2013 Land Acquisition Law*. Delhi: Oxford University Press, 2015.

Ram Mohan, M. P., and H. Pabreja. "Public Hearings in Environmental Clearance Process: Review of Judicial Intervention." *Economic and Political Weekly* 51, no. 50 (2016): 68–75.

Ramnath, M. "Impact of Ban on Timber Felling." *Economic and Political Weekly* 37, no. 48 (2002): 4774–76.

Rao, A. *The Caste Question: Dalits and the Politics of Modern India*. Berkeley: University of California Press, 2009.

Ray, Amrita. "Sardar Sarovar Dam LIVE: PM Narendra Modi Inaugurates Narmada Dam on Birthday." NDTV, updated September 17, 2017. https://www.ndtv.com/india-news/sardar-sarovar-dam-live-pm-narendra-modi-to-inaugurate-narmada-dam-on-birthday-1751278.

Reserve Bank of India. *All-India Rural Credit Survey: Report of the Committee of Direction*, vol. 2, *The General Report*. Bombay: Reserve Bank of India, 1954.

Reserve Bank of India. *Report of the Technical Group to Review Legislations in Money Lending*. Mumbai: Reserve Bank of India, 2007. https://www.thehinducentre.com/multimedia/archive/03217/78893_3217517a.pdf.

Reserve Bank of India. *A Review of the Agricultural Credit System in India: Report of Agricultural Credit Review Committee*. Bombay: Reserve Bank of India, 1990.

"Retro Tax Ghost Returns to Haunt Vodaphone." *Business Standard*, February 17, 2016. http://www.business-standard.com/article/companies/retro-tax-ghost-returns-to-haunt-vodafone-116021600376_1.html.

Rodrik, D. "Diagnostics before Prescription." *Journal of Economic Perspectives* 24, no. 3 (2010): 33–44.

Rogers, Y. V. D. M, and N. Menon. "Labor Regulations and Job Quality: Evidence from India." *ILR Review* 66, no. 4 (2013): 933–56.

Roodman, D. "Quick: What's the Grameen Bank's Interest Rate?" Center for Global Development, September 24, 2010. https://www.cgdev.org/blog/quick-whats-grameen-banks-interest-rate.

Rosencranz, A., and S. Lele "Supreme Court and India's Forests." *Economic and Political Weekly* 43, no. 5 (2008): 11–14.

Roy, A. "The Fall of Saradha Group Revives Old Ghosts of Ponzi Schemes Going Bust." *Economic Times*, April 24, 2013. https://economictimes.indiatimes.com/the-fall-of-saradha-group-revives-old-ghosts-of-ponzi-schemes-going-bust/articleshow/19702901.cms.

Roy, T. "Transfer of Economic Power in Corporate Calcutta 1950–1970." *Business History Review* 91, no. 1 (2017): 3–29.

Roy, T. "Why Was British India a Limited State?" In *Fiscal Capacity and the Colonial State in Asia and Africa, c. 1850–1960*, edited by A. Booth and E. Frankema, 77–109. Cambridge: Cambridge University Press, 2020.

Roy, T., and A. Swamy. *Law and the Economy in Colonial India*. Chicago: University of Chicago Press, 2016.

"RSS Arm Swadeshi Jagran Manch Opposes Walmart." *Deccan Chronicle*, August 28, 2019.

Rudolph, L. I., and S. H. Rudolph, *In Pursuit of Lakshmi: The Political Economy of the Indian State*. Chicago: University of Chicago Press, 1987.

Rungta, R. *Rise of Business Corporations in India 1851–1900*, Cambridge: Cambridge University Press, 1970.

Saberwal, V., and S. Lele. "Locating Local Elites in Negotiating Access to Forests: Havik Brahmins and the Colonial State 1860–1920." *Studies in History*, n.s., 20, no. 2, (2004): 273–303

Sahu, P. P. "Subcontracting in India's Unorganised Manufacturing Sector: A Mode of Adoption or Exploitation?" *Journal of South Asian Development* 5, no. 1 (2010): 53–83.

Sanjiva Row, T. *The Land Acquisition Act, 1894: Act 1 of 1894, With Case-Law Thereon*. Madras: M. E. Press, 1907.

Sanyal, P., and N. Menon. "Labor Disputes and the Economics of Firm Geography: A Study of Domestic Investment in India." *Economic Development and Cultural Change* 54, no. 4 (2005): 825–54.

Sarap, K. "Transactions in Rural Credit Markets in Western Orissa, India." *Journal of Peasant Studies*, 15, no. 1 (1987): 83–107.

Saraswathy, B. *The Globalisation of Indian Business: Cross Border Mergers and Acquisitions in Indian Manufacturing*. Abingdon: Routledge, 2018.

Saravanan, V. *Environmental History and Tribals in Modern India*. Singapore: Springer Singapore, 2018.

Sarin, M. "Undoing Historical Injustice: Reclaiming Citizenship Rights and Democratic Forest Governance through the Forest Rights Act." In *Democratizing Forest Governance*, edited by S. Lele and A. Menon, 100–146. Delhi: Oxford University Press, 2014.

Sarkar, A. "Development and Displacement: Land Acquisition in West Bengal." *Economic and Political Weekly* 42, no. 16 (2007): 1435–42.

Sarkar, S. "Land Acquisition for the Railways in Bengal, 1850–62: Probing a Contemporary Problem." *Studies in History* 26, no. 2 (2010): 103–42.

Sastry, S. H. M. "Karnataka Opens Up Land Purchase for All," *Deccan Herald*, June 11, 2020. https://www.deccanherald.com/state/top-karnataka-stories/karnataka-opens-up-agricultural-land-purchase-for-all-848465.

Sawant, S. D. "Comparative Analysis of Tenancy Statistics: Implications for Concealed Tenancy." *Artha Vijnana* 23, no. 1 (1991): 12–23.

Saxena, N. C., S. Parasuraman, P. Kant, and A. Baviskar. *Report of the Four Member Committee for Investigation into the Proposal Submitted by the Orissa Mining Company for Bauxite Mining in Niyamgiri*. New Delhi: Ministry of Environment and Forests, Government of India, 2010.

Saxena, N. C., and J. Ravi. "Realising Potential of Panchayati Raj in India." Working Paper id:202, eSocialSciences, 2005. http://www.esocialsciences.org/Download/repecDownload.aspx?fname=Document1109200540.1757013.pdf&fcategory=Articles&AId=202&fref=repec.

Securities and Exchange Board of India. "(Substantial Acquisition of Shares and Takeovers) Regulations 2011." SEBI, last updated September 11, 2018. https://www.sebi.gov.in/legal/regulations/oct-2018/securities-and-exchange-board-of-india-substantial-acquisition-of-shares-and-takeovers-regulations-2011-last-amended-on-september-11-2018-_40714.html.

Seetharaman, G. "The Biggest Lessons for India from the PMC Bank Fiasco." *Economic Times*, October 13, 2019. https://economictimes.indiatimes.com/industry/banking/finance/banking/the-biggest-lessons-for-india-from-the-pmc-bank-fiasco/articleshow/71557920.cms.

Seetharaman, G. "How Community Rights under the Forest Rights Act Could Transform the Lives of Millions of Forest Dwellers." *Economic Times*, August 9, 2015. https://economictimes.indiatimes.com/news/economy/policy/how-community-rights-under-the-forest-rights-act-could-transform-the-lives-of-millions-of-forest-dwellers/articleshow/48405279.cms.

Seetharaman, G. "The Story of One of the Biggest Land Conflicts: No Mine Now, but Is It All Fine in Niyamgiri?" *Economic Times*, updated April 18, 2018. https://economictimes.indiatimes.com/industry/indl-goods/svs/metals-mining/theres-no-mine-but-isP-it-all-fine-on-niyam-hills/articleshow/63763978.cms?from=mdr.

Sethi, R., S. Dhir, and D. Agarwal. "Defining Control: A Study of the Jet-Etihad Case." *National Law School of India Review* 27, no. 2 (2015): 185–96.

Sen, A. *Development as Freedom*. New York: Alfred Knopf, 1999.

Sen, J. "Matrimonial Property Rights: Is India Ready for a Law." *Journal of Indian Law and Society* (2009): 129–51.

Sen, S. "Gender and Class: Women in Indian Industry, 1890–1990." *Modern Asian Studies* 42, no. 1 (2008): 75–116.

Sengupta, H. "An Obscure Book Holds the Key to the RSS View of the Economy." *Fortune India*, October 6, 2018. https://www.fortuneindia.com/polemicist/an-obscure-book-holds-the-key-to-the-rss-view-of-the-economy/102555.

Shah, G. "Caste and Land Reforms in Gujarat." In *Land Reforms in India: Performance and Challenges in Gujarat and Maharashtra*, edited by G. Shah and D. C. Sah, 127–44. New Delhi: Sage, 2002.

Shah, M., R. Rao, and P. S. Vijay Shankar. "Rural Credit in 20th Century India: An Overview of History and Perspectives." *Economic and Political Weekly* 42, no. 15 (2007): 1351–64.

Sharma, M. *Caste and Nature: Dalits and Indian Environmental Politics*. Delhi: Oxford University Press, 2018.

Shiva, V. "The Neem Tree—Case History of Biopiracy." Third World Network, n.d. https://twn.my/title/pir-ch.htm.

Shourie, A. *Courts and Their Judgments*. Delhi: Rupa, 2001.

Shrivastava, A., and A. Kothari. *Churning the Earth: The Making of Global India*. New Delhi: Penguin, 2012.

Shroff, C., and N. K. Uberoi. "India's New Competition Regime Steadily Gaining Ground." *Competition Law International* (2013): 75–90.

Shroff, R. "India's Sweeping Regulatory and Policy Changes: Heralding a New Era in Investor Protection in M&A Transactions?" *Oxford University Commonwealth Law Journal* 14, no. 1 (2014): 105–25.

Shyam Sundar, K. R. "India's Mismanagement of Labour Law Reform Continues with the Modi Government." *The Wire*, May 7, 2018. https://thewire.in/labour/labour-law-reform-narendra-modi-government.

Singh, A. K. "Determination of Farzi Transfers and Transactions in Gaya District." In *Land Reforms in India: Bihar—Institutional Constraints*, edited by B. N. Yugandhar and K. Gopal Iyer, 119–28. New Delhi: Sage, 1993.

Singh, J. "Separation of Powers and the Erosion of the 'Right to Property' in India." *Constitutional Political Economy* 17, no. 4 (2006): 303–24.

Singh, S. "On Repealing the Urban Land Ceiling Act." *Economic and Political Weekly* 41, no. 8 (February/March 2006): 698–99.

Singhal, S. "Women as Coparceners: Ramifications of the Amended Section 6 of the Hindu Succession Act, 1956." *National Law School of India Review* 19, no. 1 (2007): 50–67.

Sinha, A. "Legal Loopholes: To Landlords' Rescue." *Economic and Political Weekly* 13, no. 42 (1978): 1758–60.

Sivaramkrishnan, K. "Colonialism and Forestry in India: Imagining the Past in Present Politics." *Comparative Studies in History and Society* 37, no. 1 (1995): 3–40.

Srinivas, A., and S. Rajagopal. "The Companies Bill, 1993: A Review." *National Law School of India Review* 7, no. 1 (1995): 13–18.

Srinivas, L. "Land and Politics in India: Working of the Urban Land Ceiling Act, 1976." *Economic and Political Weekly* 26, no. 43 (1991): 2482–84.

Srinivasan, R. *State of Rural Finance in India: An Assessment.* New Delhi, Oxford University Press, 2016.

Srivastava, S. C. "Geographical Indications and Legal Framework in India." *Economic and Political Weekly* 38, no. 38 (2003): 4022–33.

Sud, N. "From Land to the Tiller to Land Liberalisation: The Political Economy of Gujarat's Shifting Land Policy." *Modern Asian Studies* 41, no. 3 (2007): 603–37.

Sud, N. "The State in the Era of India's Sub-National Regions: Liberalization and Land in Gujarat." *Geoforum* 51 (2014): 233–42.

Sundar, N. "Law, Policies, and Practices in Jharkhand." *Economic and Political Weekly* 40, no. 41 (2005): 4459–62.

Swaminathan, Madhura. "Segmentation, Collateral Undervaluation, and the Rate of Interest in Agrarian Credit Markets: Some Evidence from Two Villages in South India." *Cambridge Journal of Economics* 15, no. 2 (1991): 161–78.

Tatpati, M., A. Kothari, and R. Mishra, *The Niyamgiri Story: Challenging the Idea of Growth without Limits?* Pune: Kalpaviriksh, 2016.

Thengadi, D. *The Third Way*. Rev. ed. Bangalore: Sahitya Sindhu Prakashana, 1998.

Thengadi, D. *Why Bharatiya Mazdoor Sangh*. 2nd ed. Calcutta: Mahamaya Press, 1981.

Thorner, D. *The Agrarian Prospect in India: Five Lectures on Land Reform Delivered in 1955 at the Delhi School of Economics*. Delhi: Allied, 1976.

Thorner, D. *Agricultural Cooperatives in India: A Field Report*. New Delhi: Asia Publishing House, 1964.

Tofaris, S. "Trust Law Goes East: The Transplantation of Trust Law in India and Beyond." *Journal of Legal History* 36, no. 3 (2015): 299–332.

Tiwari, N. "Resolution of NPA in India: The Role of Asset Reconstruction Companies." *Pratt's Journal of Bankruptcy Law* 7, no. 6 (2011): 552–80.

Tiwari, R. K. *Human Rights and the Law: Bonded Labour in India*. Delhi: Cambridge University Press, 2010.

Tiwary, D. "In 80 Per Cent Farmer-Suicides Due to Debt, Loans Taken from Banks, Not Moneylenders." *Indian Express*, January 7, 2017. https://indianexpress.com/article/india/farmer-suicides-due-to-debt-in-80-per-cent-cases-loans-taken-from-banks-not-moneylenders-4463986/.

TNN. "CM: Will Look into Grievances of Bhakra Dam Oustees." *Times of India*, January 4, 2018. https://timesofindia.indiatimes.com/city/shimla/cm-will-look-into-grievances-of-bhakra-dam-oustees/articleshow/62362448.cms.

TNN. "50 Years on, Bhakra Dam Oustees Wait for Rehabilitation." *Times of India*, India News, October 22, 2013. https://timesofindia.indiatimes.com/india/50-years-on-Bhakra-Dam-oustees-wait-for-rehabilitation/articleshow/24504585.cms.

"Transcript of the VIII NLSIR Symposium on Competition Law." *National Law School of India Review* 27, no. 2 (2015): 197–225.

Tripathi, B. "Liberalising Land Leasing Necessary for Growth, Says Tajamul Haque." *Business-Standard*, updated March 31, 2018. https://www.business-standard.com/article/economy-policy/liberalising-land-leasing-necessary-for-growth-says-tajamul-haque-118033100560_1.html.

Tucker, R. P. *A Forest History of India*. New Delhi: Sage, 2012.

Uchikawa, S. "Employment in the Manufacturing Organized Sector in India: The Rise of Medium Scale Units." In *Labor Market Institutions in India: 1990s and Beyond*, edited by S. Uchikawa, 39–64. New Delhi: Manohar, 2002.

"Understanding EIA." Centre for Science and Environment. https://www.cseindia.org/understanding-eia-383.

United Nations. *Report of the United Nations Conference on the Human Envi-*

ronment. Stockholm, June 5–16, 1972. http://www.un-documents.net/aconf48-14r1.pdf.

Unni, V. K. "Harnessing IP Awareness for Global Business Dominance: A Tale of Two Indian Companies." *Vikalpa* 33, no. 2 (2008): 74–77.

Vadehra, K., and S. Vadehra. "Solving the India Patent Puzzle." Managing Intellectual Property, 2015/2016, 44–47.

Vanashakti. "Vanashakti's Response to the Campaign for Survival and Dignity." https://forestrightsact.files.wordpress.com/2016/04/vanashakti_response.pdf.

Van Zwieten, K. "The Demise of Corporate Insolvency Law in India: The Role of the Courts." PhD diss., University of Oxford, 2012.

Varma, M. K. "Role of Legislation in Regulating Labor-Management Relations in India." *Labor Law Journal* 8, no. 4 (1957): 257–71.

Varottil, U. "The Evolution of Corporate Law in Post-Colonial India: From Transplant to Autochthony." NUS Law Working Paper 2015.001, Singapore, 2015.

Varottil, U. "India's Corporate Governance Voluntary Guidelines 2009: Rhetoric or Reality." *National Law School of India Review* 22, no. 2 (2010): 1–28.

Verma, S., and S. J. Gray. "The Development of Company Law in India: The Case of the Companies Act 1956." *Critical Perspectives on Accounting* 20, no. 1 (2009): 110–35.

Vevaina, L. "She's Come Undone: Parsi Women's Property and Propriety under the Law." *Political and Legal Anthropology Review* 41, no. 1 (2018): 44–59.

Visaria, S. "Legal Reform and Loan Repayment: The Microeconomic Impact of Debt Recovery Tribunals in India." *American Economic Journal: Applied Economics* 1, no. 3 (2009): 59–81.

Visvanathan, S. "Chronicle of a Struggle Retold." *The Hindu*, updated March 29, 2016. https://www.thehindu.com/opinion/lead/chronicle-of-a-struggle-retold/article7504666.ece.

Wadhwa, D. C. *Agrarian Legislation in India (1793–1966)*. Poona: Gokhale Institute of Politics and Economics, 1973.

Wadhwa, D. C. "Guaranteeing Title to Land: A Preliminary Study", *Economic and Political Weekly* 24, no. 41 (1989): 2323–2334.

Wadhwa, D.C. *Guaranteeing Title to Land: The Only Sensible Solution*. Poona: Gokhale Institute of Politics and Economics, 2002.

Wahi, N. "The Fundamental Right to Property in the Indian Constitution." In *The Oxford Handbook of the Indian Constitution*, edited by S. Choudhry, M. Khosla, and P. B. Mehta, 943–63. Oxford: Oxford University Press, 2017.

Washbrook, D. "Law, State and Agrarian Society in Colonial India." *Modern Asian Studies* 15, no. 3 (1981): 649–721.

Weber, T. *Hugging the Trees: The Story of the Chipko Movement*. New Delhi: Penguin India, 1989.

"Women Allege Coercive Loan Recovery by Microfinance Firms." *The Hindu*, updated January 6, 2017. https://www.thehindu.com/news/national/karnataka/Women-allege-coercive-loan-recovery-by-microfinance-firms/article17000680.ece.

World Bank. *Ease of Doing Business in India*. 2015. https://www.doingbusiness.org/en/data/exploreeconomies/india.

Yadu, C. R., and C. K. Vijayasuryan. "Triple Exclusion of Dalits in Land Ownership in Kerala." *Social Change* 46, no. 3 (2016): 393–408.

Index

Page numbers in italics refer to figures and tables